HOUSE OF COMMONS

The
Falklands Campaign

*A Digest of Debates
in the House of Commons
2 April to June 1982*

HER MAJESTY'S STATIONERY OFFICE

© *Crown copyright 1982*
First published 1982

ISBN 0 11 701059 6

Introduction

This book is only a digest of the six debates and countless questions and statements that occupied the attention of the House of Commons from 2 April to 15 June 1982. It largely follows Hansard style, although some linking additions have had to be made. Inevitably, however, much has been attenuated or even omitted. My guiding principle has been Hansardian impartiality and accuracy modified only by the need for concision. Those who criticise its incompleteness must turn to the Official Report for a verbatim record. The purpose has been to provide in one volume a record of the exchanges in the House of Commons. Omissions have been indicated and italics show added words.

I have been concerned only with the campaign and the events immediately leading to it. The editing has been a matter for my personal judgment and I must take full responsibility for my decisions, many of them made with the benefit of hindsight.

I am deeply grateful to Mr. Speaker Thomas for his permission to produce this volume.

K. S. MORGAN
Editor, Official Report
House of Commons

July 1982

CORRECTION SLIP

HOUSE OF COMMONS

The Falklands Campaign

A Digest of Debates in the House of Commons 2 April
to 15 June 1982

Correction;

Page 165, paragraph 4, line 17:

<u>Before</u>   "We have no complaint ...."

<u>Insert</u>   Mr Julian Critchley (Aldershot)

LONDON: HER MAJESTY'S STATIONERY OFFICE

Report One

2 APRIL 1982

The House of Commons heard the first official news of the developing
Falkland Islands crisis on Friday 2 April 1982 in a statement from Mr.
Humphrey Atkins, senior Foreign Office spokesman in the Commons.

The Lord Privy Seal (Mr. Humphrey Atkins): With permission, Mr.
Deputy Speaker, I shall make a statement on the situation in the Falkland
Islands.

Over the past 24 hours the situation has become increasingly grave.
There is now a real expectation that an Argentine attack against the
Falkland Islands will take place very soon. It was for this reason that we
sought an emergency meeting of the Security Council yesterday and
associated ourselves immediately with a request from the President of the
Security Council that both Britain and Argentina should exercise restraint
and refrain from the use or threat of force, and continue the search for a
diplomatic solution. There was no Argentine response to this; nor has the
Argentine President responded to the many appeals that have been made
to him to draw back from the use of force.

We are taking appropriate military and diplomatic measures to sustain
our rights under international law and in accordance with the provisions
of the United Nations charter. The House will not expect me to give details
at this stage of the military steps we have taken to respond to the worsening
situation. In the meantime, we continue to hope that the Argentine
Government, even at this late stage, will reconsider their rejection of the
diplomatic channel as a means for settling the differences between our two
countries.

Mr. John Silkin (Deptford): The Labour Party pledges full support for
the right of the people of the Falkland Islands to stay British, as they wish,
and we believe that it is our duty to defend that right. We pledge our full
support to the men of the Royal Navy and the Royal Marines. We believe
that the Government were right to inform the Security Council that there
was a threat to peace. Nevertheless, there are some questions that we must
ask.

First, did the Government misjudge the situation? Is it not a fact that
whenever the tinpot Fascist junta that rules Argentina is in deep trouble
at home it threatens the Falkland Islands, and were not the signs there to
be seen some time ago? Secondly, did not the Secretary of State for Defence
contribute, to some extent, to the possibility of an invasion by his talk of
scrapping HMS "Endurance" and a large proportion of our surface fleet,
thus perhaps giving the false impression that Britain might be willing,

1

though she will not, to abdicate her responsibilities in the area? Are we confident that we can protect the islanders?

Thirdly, did the British Government consult other members of the Security Council before advising the Secretary-General of the threat to peace and have we any support inside the Security Council? Finally—and perhaps this is more a matter for the Leader of the House—the situation is incredibly fluid. Will the Lord Privy Seal be able to make further statements to the House during the day should that be necessary?

Mr. Atkins: I thank the right hon. Gentleman for his expression of support, not only for the Government but for the people of the Falkland Islands, who, as he rightly said, are determined to remain British.

[The Government did not misjudge the situation.] It has become increasingly evident over the past few days that the Argentine had assembled a fleet . . . in the vicinity. . . .

[We have responded appropriately and taking the matter to the United Nations was the proper course.] . . . If the Argentines had wanted to wait until "Endurance" was not there—which she is—they would not be acting now as they are.

We consulted our friends before taking the matter to the Security Council, and we have support there.

Dr. David Owen (Plymouth, Devonport): . . . We fully support the Government in every measure that they see fit to take to defend the Falkland Islands and the interests of the islanders . . . every hon. Member recognises the Lord Privy Seal's difficulties in questions of military and naval deployment. We all hope that contingency measures were taken some weeks ago to ensure that naval forces are in the area and are capable of intervening if necessary.

Is the Security Council to be called . . . later today? What action do we intend to take in the Security Council if an invasion takes place? *[Are we right to believe that the Lord Privy Seal is not aware]* of any invasion and that the report on the tapes that Argentinians have landed in Port Stanley is incorrect?

I fully associate myself with the remarks of the right hon. Member for Deptford (Mr. Silkin) about the need for the House to be kept informed. *[Are we to debate the issue later today?]*

Mr. Atkins: . . . We were in touch with the governor half an hour ago and he said that no landing had taken place at that time.

There are no immediate plans for another session of the Security Council, but it will be called together if the situation becomes worse. I undertake . . . to keep the House fully informed. . . .

We shall sustain and defend the Falkland Islands to the best of our ability. . . .

No invasion has taken place. The Government of Argentina have been called on by the Security Council to desist from the use or threat of force. It is our hope that they will heed the appeals made to them from all over the world. . . .

I do not think that it is possible to say exactly how this situation was planned to develop by the Argentine Government. But the problem that we are discussing today has nothing to do with the presence of 12 scrap merchants. The House is anxious about the possibility of an invasion of Port Stanley. . . .

The threat to the Falkland Islands has existed for at least 15 years from a country which is a great deal closer to them than we are. Successive Governments have taken what they believed to be the appropriate steps to defend the Falkland Islands. We shall to do the same. . . .

The governor has been kept fully in touch by the Government with all the developments. It is now about three-quarters of an hour ago that we were in touch with him. No troops had landed at that time. . . .

There is no doubt under international law who has sovereignty over the Falkland Islands. As the House knows, everyone living on the Falkland Islands, with virtually no exception, wishes that position to be maintained. . . .

I repeat that we were in touch with the governor direct only about 50 minutes ago.

Later—
The Lord President of the Council and Leader of the House of Commons (Mr. Francis Pym): . . . There is no confirmation of any change in the position in relation to the Falkland Islands since the statement of my right hon. Friend the Lord Privy Seal this morning.

[The House will be recalled during the week-end, if that is necessary, and we are still in touch with the governor, as far as I am aware.]

Report Two

SATURDAY 3 APRIL 1982

Parliament was recalled on a Saturday for the first time in more than 20 years on 3 April for an emergency debate. The day began with a personal statement.

11.5 am

The Lord Privy Seal (Mr. Humphrey Atkins): Following my statement to the House at 11 o'clock yesterday, I said . . . that we had been in touch with the governor of the Falkland Islands half an hour before I made my statement. That was inaccurate. We had in fact been in touch two hours earlier, at 8.30 am our time. No invasion had then taken place, and when I made my statement I had no knowledge of any change in the situation.

I very much regret that I inadvertently misled the House, and I am grateful to you, Mr. Speaker, for allowing me this opportunity to set the record straight and to apologise to the House.

[The House divided on a proposal to sit until 5 pm instead of 2 pm, as announced. The proposal was defeated by 204 votes to 115.]

The Prime Minister (Mrs. Margaret Thatcher): The House meets this Saturday to respond to a situation of great gravity. We are here because, for the first time for many years, British sovereign territory has been invaded by a foreign power. After several days of rising tension in our relations with Argentina, that country's armed forces attacked the Falkland Islands yesterday and established military control of the islands.

Yesterday was a day of rumour and counter-rumour. Throughout the day we had no communication from the Government of the Falklands. Indeed, the last message that we received was at 21.55 hours on Thursday night, 1 April. Yesterday morning at 8.33 we sent a telegram which was acknowledged. At 8.45 am all communications ceased. I shall refer to that again in a moment. By late afternoon yesterday it became clear than an Argentine invasion had taken place and that the lawful British Government of the islands had been usurped.

I am sure that the whole House will join me in condemning totally this unprovoked aggression by the Government of Argentina against British territory. [HON. MEMBERS: "Hear, hear".] It has not a shred of justification and not a scrap of legality.

It was not until 8.30 this morning, our time, when I was able to speak to the governor, who had arrived in Uruguay, that I learnt precisely what had happened. He told me that the Argentines had landed at approximately 6 am Falkland's time, 10 am our time. One party attacked the capital from the landward side and another from the seaward side. The governor then sent a signal to us which we did not receive.

4

Communications had ceased at 8.45 am our time. It is common for atmospheric conditions to make communications with Port Stanley difficult. Indeed, we had been out of contact for a period the previous night.

The governor reported that the marines, in the defence of Government House, were superb. He said that they acted in the best traditions of the Royal Marines. They inflicted casualties, but those defending Government House suffered none. He had kept the local people informed of what was happening through a small local transmitter which he had in Government House. He is relieved that the islanders heeded his advice to stay indoors. Fortunately, as far as he is aware, there were no civilian casualties. When he left the Falklands, he said that the people were in tears. They do not want to be Argentine. He said that the islanders are still tremendously loyal. I must say that I have every confidence in the governor and the action that he took.

I must tell the House that the Falkland Islands and their dependencies remain British territory. No aggression and no invasion can alter that simple fact. It is the Government's objective to see that the islands are freed from occupation and are returned to British administration at the earliest possible moment.

Argentina has, of course, long disputed British sovereignty over the islands. We have absolutely no doubt about our sovereignty, which has been continuous since 1833. Nor have we any doubt about the unequivocal wishes of the Falkland Islanders, who are British in stock and tradition, and they wish to remain British in allegiance. We cannot allow the democratic rights of the islanders to be denied by the territorial ambitions of Argentina. . . .

There had, of course, been previous incidents affecting sovereignty before the one in South Georgia, to which I shall refer in a moment. In December 1976 the Argentines illegally set up a scientific station on one of the dependencies within the Falklands group—Southern Thule. The Labour Government attempted to solve the matter through diplomatic exchanges, but without success. The Argentines remained there and are still there. . . .

In the meantime, we had been in touch with the Argentine Government about the [South Georgia] incident. They claimed to have had no prior knowledge of the landing and assured us that there were no Argentine military personnel in the party. For our part we made it clear that, while we had no wish to interfere in the operation of a normal commercial contract, we could not accept the illegal presence of these people on British territory.

We asked the Argentine Government either to arrange for the departure of the remaining men or to ensure that they obtained the necessary permission to be there. Because we recognised the potentially serious nature of the situation, HMS "Endurance" was ordered to the area. We told the Argentine Government that, if they failed to regularise the position of the party on South Georgia or to arrange for their departure, HMS "Endurance" would take them off, without using force, and return them to Argentina.

This was, however, to be the last resort. We were determined that this apparently minor problem of 10 people on South Georgia in pursuit of a commercial contract should not be allowed to escalate and we made it plain to the Argentine Government that we wanted to achieve a peaceful

5

resolution of the problem by diplomatic means. To help in this, HMS "Endurance" was ordered not to approach the Argentine party at Leith but to go to Grytviken.

But it soon became clear that the Argentine Government had little interest in trying to solve the problem. On 25 March another Argentine navy ship arrived at Leith to deliver supplies to the 10 men ashore. Our ambassador in Buenos Aires sought an early response from the Argentine Government to our previous requests that they should arrange for the men's departure. This request was refused. Last Sunday, 28 March, the Argentine Foreign Minister sent a message to my right hon. and noble Friend the Foreign Secretary refusing outright to regularise the men's position. Instead it restated Argentina's claim to sovereignty over the Falkland Islands and their dependencies.

My right hon. and noble Friend the Foreign and Commonwealth Secretary then sent a message to the United States Secretary of State asking him to intervene and to urge restraint.

By the beginning of this week it was clear that our efforts to solve the South Georgia dispute through the usual diplomatic channels were getting nowhere. Therefore, on Wednesday 31 March my right hon. and noble Friend the Foreign Secretary proposed to the Argentine Foreign Minister that we should dispatch a special emissary to Buenos Aires.

Later that day we received information which led us to believe that a large number of Argentine ships, including an aircraft carrier, destroyers, landing craft, troop carriers and submarines, were heading for Port Stanley. I contacted President Reagan that evening and asked him to intervene with the Argentine President directly. We promised, in the meantime, to take no action to escalate the dispute for fear of precipitating— [Interruption]—the very event that our efforts were directed to avoid. May I remind Opposition Members—[Interruption]—what happened when, during the lifetime of their Government . . . Southern Thule was occupied. It was occupied in 1976. The House was not even informed by the then Government until 1978. . . .

Mr. Edward Rowlands (Merthyr Tydfil): The right hon. Lady is talking about a piece of rock in the most southerly part of the dependencies, which is totally uninhabited and which smells of large accumulations of penguin and other bird droppings. There is a vast difference—a whole world of difference—between the 1,800 people now imprisoned by Argentine invaders and that argument. The right hon. Lady should have the grace to accept that.

The Prime Minister: We are talking about the sovereignty of British territory—[Interruption]—which was infringed in 1976. The House was not even informed of it until 1978. We are talking about a further incident in South Georgia which—as I have indicated—seemed to be a minor incident at the time. There is only a British Antarctic scientific survey there and there was a commercial contract to remove a whaling station. I suggest to the hon. Gentleman that had I come to the House at that time and said that we had a problem on South Georgia with 10 people who had landed with a contract to remove a whaling station, and had I gone on to say that we should send HMS "Invincible", I should have been accused of war mongering and sabre rattling.

6

Information about the Argentine fleet did not arrive until Wednesday. Argentina is, of course, very close to the Falklands—a point that the hon. Member for Merthyr Tydfil cannot and must not ignore—and its navy can sail there very quickly. On Thursday, the Argentine Foreign Minister rejected the idea of an emissary and told our ambassador that the diplomatic channel, as a means of solving this dispute, was closed. President Reagan had a very long telephone conversation, of some 50 minutes, with the Argentine President, but his strong representations fell on deaf ears. I am grateful to him and to Secretary Haig for their strenuous and persistent efforts on our behalf.

On Thursday, the United Nations Secretary-General, Mr. Perez de Cuellar, summoned both British and Argentine permanent representatives to urge both countries to refrain from the use or threat of force in the South Atlantic. Later that evening we sought an emergency meeting of the Security Council. We accepted the appeal of its President for restraint. The Argentines said nothing. On Friday, as the House knows, the Argentines invaded the Falklands and I have given a precise account of everything we knew, or did not know, about that situation. There were also reports that yesterday the Argentines also attacked South Georgia, where HMS "Endurance" had left a detachment of 22 Royal Marines. Our information is that on 2 April an Argentine naval transport vessel informed the base commander at Grytviken that an important message would be passed to him after 11 o'clock today our time. It is assumed that this message will ask the base commander to surrender.

Before indicating some of the measures that the Government have taken in response to the Argentinian invasion, I should like to make three points. First, even if ships had been instructed to sail the day that the Argentines landed on South Georgia to clear the whaling station, the ships could not possibly have got to Port Stanley before the invasion. *[Interruption.]* Opposition Members may not like it, but that is a fact.

Secondly, there have been several occasions in the past when an invasion has been threatened. The only way of being certain to prevent an invasion would have been to keep a very large fleet close to the Falklands, when we are some 8,000 miles away from base. No Government have ever been able to do that, and the cost would be enormous.

Mr. Eric Ogden (Liverpool, West Derby): Will the right hon. Lady say what has happened to HMS "Endurance"?

The Prime Minister: HMS "Endurance" is in the area. It is not for me to say precisely where, and the hon. Gentleman would not wish me to do so.

Thirdly, aircraft unable to land on the Falklands, because of the frequently changing weather, would have had little fuel left and, ironically, their only hope of landing safely would have been to divert to Argentina. Indeed, all of the air and most sea supplies for the Falklands come from Argentina, which is but 400 miles away compared with our 8,000 miles.

That is the background against which we have to make decisions and to consider what action we can best take. I cannot tell the House precisely what dispositions have been made—some ships are already at sea, others were put on immediate alert on Thursday evening.

The Government have now decided that a large task force will sail as

7

soon as all preparations are complete. HMS "Invincible" will be in the lead and will leave port on Monday. . . .

We are now reviewing all aspects of the relationship between Argentina and the United Kingdom. The Argentine chargé d'affaires and his staff were yesterday instructed to leave within four days.

As an appropriate precautionary and, I hope, temporary measure, the Government have taken action to freeze Argentine financial assets held in this country. . . .

Mr. Michael Foot (Ebbw Vale): . . . I first wish to set on record as clearly as I possibly can what we believe to be the international rights and wrongs of this matter, because I believe that one of the purposes of the House being assembled on this occasion is to make that clear not only to the people in our country but to people throughout the world.

The rights and the circumstances of the people in the Falkland Islands must be uppermost in our minds. There is no question in the Falkland Islands of any colonial dependence or anything of the sort. It is a question of people who wish to be associated with this country and who have built their whole lives on the basis of association with this country. We have a moral duty, a political duty and every other kind of duty to ensure that that is sustained.

The people of the Falkland Islands have the absolute right to look to us at this moment of their desperate plight, just as they have looked to us over the past 150 years. They are faced with an act of naked, unqualified aggression, carried out in the most shameful and disreputable circumstances. Any guarantee from this invading force is utterly worthless—as worthless as any of the guarantees that are given by this same Argentine junta to its own people.

We can hardly forget that thousands of innocent people fighting for their political rights in Argentine are in prison and have been tortured and debased. We cannot forget that fact when our friends and fellow citizens in the Falkland Islands are suffering as they are at this moment.

On the merits of the matter, we hope that the question is understood throughout the world. In that respect I believe that the Government were right to take the matter to the United Nations. It would have been delinquency if they had not, because that is the forum in which we have agreed that such matters of international right and international claim should be stated.

Whatever else the Government have done—I shall come to that in a moment—or not done, I believe that it was essential for them to take our case to the United Nations and to present it with all the force and power of advocacy at the command of this country. The decision and the vote in the United Nations will take place in an hour or two's time. I must say to people there that we in this country, as a whole, irrespective of our party affiliations, will examine the votes most carefully.

I was interested to hear how strongly the President of France spoke out earlier this morning. I hope that every other country in the world will speak in a similar way.

If, at the United Nations this afternoon, no such declaration were made—I know that it would be only a declaration at first, but there might be the possibility of action there later—not merely would it be a gross injury to the rights of the people of the Falkland Islands, not merely would it be an injury to the people of this country, who have a right to have their claims upheld in the United Nations, but it would be a serious injury to the United Nations itself. It would enhance the dangers that similar, unprovoked aggressions could occur in other parts of the world.

That is one of the reasons why we are determined to ensure that we examine this matter in full and uphold the rights of our country throughout the world, and the claim of our country to be a defender of people's freedom throughout the world, particularly those who look to us for special protection, as do the people in the Falkland Islands. . . .

What has happened to British diplomacy? The explanations given by the right hon. Lady, when she managed to rise above some of her own party arguments—they were not quite the exclusive part of her speech—were not very full and not very clear. They will need to be made a good deal more ample in the days to come. . . .

The right hon. Lady, the Secretary of State for Defence and the whole Government will have to give a very full account of what happened, how their diplomacy was conducted and why we did not have the information to which we are entitled when expenditure takes place on such a scale. Above all, more important than the question of what happened to British diplomacy or to British intelligence is what happened to our power to act. The right hon. Lady seemed to dismiss that question. It cannot be dismissed. Of course this country has the power to act—short, often, of taking military measures. Indeed, we have always been told, as I understand it, that the purpose of having some military power is to deter. The right to deter and the capacity to deter were both required in this situation.

The previous Government had to deal with the same kind of dictatorial regime in the Argentine, the same kind of threat to the people of the Falkland Islands, and the same kinds of problems as those with which the Government have had to wrestle over the past weeks and months. . . .

No one can say for certain that the pacific and honourable solution of this problem that was reached in 1977 was due to the combination of diplomatic and military activity. These things cannot be proved. There is, however, every likelihood that that was the case. In any event, the fact that it worked on the previous occasion was surely all the more reason for the Government's seeking to make it work on this occasion, especially when, according to the Secretary of State for Foreign and Commonwealth Affairs—I refer again to the diplomatic exchanges—it had been going on for some time. According to the diplomatic exchanges, the Argentine Government were still awaiting an answer from the Secretary of State on some of the matters involved. . . .

I have not the slightest doubt that, at some stage, an inquiry . . . without any inhibitions and restraints, that can probe the matter fully will have to be undertaken. . . .

We are paramountly concerned . . . about what we can do to protect those who rightly and naturally look to us for protection. So far, they have been betrayed. The responsibility for the betrayal rests with the Government. The Government must now prove by deeds—they will never be able to do it by words—that they are not responsible for the betrayal and cannot be faced with that charge. That is the charge, I believe, that lies against them. Even though the position and the circumstances of the people who live in the Falkland Islands are uppermost in our minds—it would be outrageous if that were not the case—there is the longer-term interest to ensure that foul and brutal aggression does not succeed in our world. If it does, there will be a danger not merely to the Falkland Islands, but to people all over this dangerous planet.

Mr. Edward du Cann (Taunton): There are times, Mr. Speaker, in the affairs of our nation when the House should speak with a single, united voice. This is just such a time. The Leader of the Opposition spoke for us all. He did this nation a service when, in clear and unmistakable terms, he condemned what he called this brutal aggression and when he affirmed the rights of the Falkland Islanders to decide their own destiny. I warmly applaud that part of his speech. I resent and reject his charge of betrayal.

I have a single simple point to make and I can make it shortly. It is right that the House should also, at this moment of crisis for our nation and for the Government, pledge full support to my right hon. Friend the Prime Minister and her colleagues in their heavy and awesome responsibility. As the Leader of the Opposition said, we must do what is necessary and what is right. However, let us see that what we do is well done.

Undoubtedly, there will be questions to be asked. There will also be questions to be answered. I agree with the Leader of the Opposition that there will be a need for a full account of this affair. . . .

It is astounding that, for all our defence expenditure, which in absolute and proportional terms is huge, and for all our capacity for diplomatic activity and intelligence, we appear to have been so woefully ill prepared. It is extraordinary that conventional forces were not deployed on standby against an occupation. . . .

Let us declare and resolve that our duty now is to repossess our possessions and to rescue our own people. Our right to the Falkland Islands is undoubted. Our sovereignty is unimpeachable. British interest in that part of the world . . . is substantial. . . .

If one tolerates a single act of aggression, one connives at them all. In the United Kingdom we must accept reality. For all our alliances and for all the social politenesses which the diplomats so often mistake for trust, in the end in life it is self-reliance and only self-reliance that counts. Suez, when I first came into the House 25 and more years ago, surely taught us that not every ally is staunch when the call comes. We have one duty only, which we owe to ourselves——the duty to rescue our people and to uphold our rights. Let that be the unanimous and clear resolve of the House this day.

Let us hear no more about logistics—how difficult it is to travel long distances. I do not remember the Duke of Wellington whining about Torres Vedras. [HON. MEMBERS: "Hear, hear."] We have nothing to lose now except our honour. I am clear that that is safe in the hands of my right hon. Friend.

Mr. J. Enoch Powell (Down, South): . . . I agree with the right hon. Member for Taunton (Mr. du Cann) that the House today is not primarily concerned with inquests—there will be a time for inquests and more abundant material for them—but with what is now to be done. Those who take part in this debate ought to declare clearly what they believe ought now to be done. . . .

When the sovereign territory of a country is invaded without warning, without provocation and without excuse, there is nothing which requires

10

us to wait upon the decisions or upon the condition or upon the deliberations or upon the resolutions of the United Nations before we take the appropriate steps which ought to follow. . . .

There is only one reaction which is fit to meet unprovoked aggression upon one's own sovereign territory; that is direct and unqualified and immediate willingness—not merely willingness, but willingness expressed by action—to use force. The Government have set in train measures which will enable them to do that; but there must be nothing which casts doubt upon their will and their intention to do it.

The Prime Minister, shortly after she came into office, received a soubriquet as the "Iron Lady". It arose in the context of remarks which she made about defence against the Soviet Union and its allies; but there was no reason to suppose that the right hon. Lady did not welcome and, indeed, take pride in that description. In the next week or two this House, the nation and the right hon. Lady herself will learn of what metal she is made.

Sir Nigel Fisher (Surbiton): Hitherto, Britain's policy for the Falkland Islands has been genuinely bipartisan. Neither side of the House has ever made any attempt in the long drawn out negotiations with the Argentine to make party political capital. We have all been united in our support of the Falkland Islands, *[but the Government cannot have expected a bipartisan reaction from the Opposition.]* Indeed, Ministers will not escape criticism from Conservative as well as from Opposition Members.

Wherever the blame may lie, no one can deny that the islanders have been let down and that Britain has been humiliated. What can now be done? One's natural instinct is to get the invaders out, but it is much easier said than done. Logistically it would be very difficult and it would take a considerable time—I understand about two weeks—but far more serious would be the consequence for the islanders themselves.

A full-scale battle for the Falkland Islands would mean that the islanders, including women and children, would be caught in the crossfire and many of them killed. We could avoid that by leaving the Argentine land forces in possession and confining our retaliation to a battle at sea. But then what? We could not keep our warships in the area indefinitely, with no base from which to supply them. . . .

As a first step, all available sanctions against the Argentine should, of course, be taken. For example, I understand that the people of the Argentine are great football enthusiasts. The very least we should do is to ensure the exclusion of the Argentine from the World Cup. . . .

The Government can be excused only if our intelligence was very bad and if we genuinely did not know that an invasion was a possibility. That would be some sort of excuse, but not a very good one. Either way, we have been humiliated. Ministers have much to answer for today to the House, to the country and to the loyal people of the Falkland Islands.

Dr. David Owen (Plymouth, Devonport): The Government have the right to ask both sides of the House for the fullest support in their resolve to return the Falkland Islands and the freedom of the islanders to British sovereignty. They will get that support and they deserve it in every action that they take in the Security Council and elsewhere. However, the

11

Government must restore the confidence of the country and the House in their ability to carry out that mission.

I agree with the Leader of the Opposition that this is not the time to have an examination. There will come a time when an inquiry will be necessary and we must examine in great detail all that has happened or not happened during the past six weeks. However, it is necessary to examine a central question: why was no preparatory action taken a month ago? . . .

There was ample warning that the position was deteriorating. We knew of the horror of the military junta in the Argentine and we knew of its actions. Only a few days ago, 3,000 political prisoners were taken, only to be released amid the euphoria of the invasion of the Falkland Islands. We knew that the military were jockeying for position in the navy, the army and the air force. We have known that for many years. It was for that reason four years ago, when a similar position developed, that naval forces were sent. . . .

We all know that there will be great difficulties in a resisted offensive against the Falkland Islands. There are massive forces on the islands, but nothing said in the House should exclude any possibility of repossessing them. I believe that they will be repossessed by a combination of firm diplomacy backed by the use of the Navy. . . .

The Prime Minister misjudged the atmosphere of the House most seriously. It is now necessary for the message to come from the House that we are grossly dissatisfied with the conduct of the Government during the past month. We shall sustain them despite that, because we recognise that our service men's lives might be put at risk. . . .

[The absence of a decision to send forces a month ago has meant humiliation.] The House must now resolve to sustain the Government in restoring the position.

Mr. Julian Amery (Brighton, Pavilion): The third naval power in the world, and the second in NATO, has suffered a humiliating defeat. It is always painful in a state of war to criticise a Government, particularly a Government of one's own friends, but the purpose of recrimination at a time like this is to prevent the repetition of error. . . .

After the withdrawal from Simonstown, we no longer had a fleet almost permanently in the South Atlantic, but no attempt was made to carry out the main recommendation of the Shackleton committee to enlarge the airfield so that, when weather conditions allowed, we could have reinforced the Falkland Islands with a big enough garrison in a time of crisis. . . .

My right hon. Friend the Prime Minister has done her best to serve as an air-raid shelter for her colleagues directly responsible, and that she has done with her customary loyalty. However, we should recognise that we have suffered the inevitable consequences of the combination of unpreparedness and feeble counsels.

We have lost a battle, but have not lost the war. It is an old saying that Britain always wins the last battle. It will not be an easy task.

Mr. Edward Rowlands (Merthyr Tydfil): I wish to put some basic and serious questions to the Government, but first I want to say that our thoughts and prayers at this time must be with the islanders. . . .

Having been involved in a handful of crises and incidents during four and a half years of negotiations with the Falkland Islands and with the Argentine Government, I can say that I try to follow these affairs closely.

In view of the bipartisan spirit that generally prevails when we handle these issues, I deeply regret saying that I have failed to understand completely the Government's handling of the crisis over the past six to eight weeks. I profoundly reject the suggestion made by the Prime Minister, the Foreign Secretary and the Secretary of State for Defence that we could not have foreseen what was happening. . . .

Secondly, I have great difficulty in understanding how the intelligence failed. Our intelligence in Argentina was extremely good. That is why we took action in 1977. We found out that certain attitudes and approaches were being formed. I cannot believe that the quality of our intelligence has changed. . . .

What should the House say to the Government? First, it should remind the Government that successive Governments and successive Parliaments have upheld the principle that the wishes, interests, rights, security and safety of the Falkland Islanders are paramount. Secondly, we should charge both the Secretary of State for Defence and the Foreign Secretary to proceed as speedily as possible to restore to the Falkland Islanders their rights, safety and security as urgently as possible. However, if they cannot, and if it turns out that as a result of their massive misjudgment over the past few days they have failed the islanders and Parliament, they should go. The islanders have already paid a high price for the initial set of blunders. They have lost their freedom for the first time for 150 years. The guilty men should not go scot free if we do not retrieve the islands as quickly as possible.

Mr. Patrick Cormack (Staffordshire, South-West): My right hon. Friend the Prime Minister should go forth from this debate strengthened, reassured and grateful. She has heard from both sides of the House a unanimous sentiment and a united voice.

I have never been more impressed by the eloquence and oratory of the Leader of the Opposition than I was today. For once he truly spoke for Britain, and so, too, did the right hon. Member for Plymouth, Devonport (Dr. Owen). They were constructive, statesmanlike, sensible speeches. I hope that my right hon. Friend the Prime Minister realises that she will have the fortification that a previous Conservative Prime Minister at a time of grave international crisis did not have. If she feels that it is necessary, and if it becomes necessary, to use force, it will be used with the united and unanimous backing of the House of Commons, every Member of which looks upon the 1,850 Falkland Islanders as he or she looks upon his or her constituents. In a sense, that is what they are, and we must do something to protect and preserve them.

But what a blunder, what a monumental folly, that the Falkland Islanders should be incarcerated in an Argentine gaol. That is what it amounts to. It is always better to anticipate than to react. It is always easier to anticipate than to react. The great blunder—we shall all want detailed explanations—was that the Government failed to anticipate, and they will now have the greatest difficulty in knowing how to react. . . .

It will require greater courage to bombard or sink Argentine ships than to have landed 2,000 marines two weeks ago, which could have been done. Someone has blundered. I do not know who and I do not know how, but I have my suspicions, and they are directed inevitably—and regretfully—at both the Secretary of State for Defence and the Foreign Secretary. . . .

Mr. Arthur Bottomley (Middlesbrough): . . . May I ask the Prime Minister whether she has already assured our friends, and the Commonwealth, in particular, that so long as the Falkland Islands and their inhabitants wish to remain in the Commonwealth, Britain will see that they do so?

Mr. Raymond Whitney (Wycombe): I should like to offer a few words which I know will not be popular in the House, but they are based on three years' work in Argentina, trying to avoid the eventuality that now confronts us. . . .

Between 1970 and 1972 we negotiated a communications agreement which seemed to offer the promise of a long-term resolution of the dispute and to be very much in the interests of the Falkland Islanders and absolutely in tune with their wishes. I am referring to the opening up of links with the Argentine in terms of travel, medical cover, educational and postal facilities and holidays. All those things now seem trivial and irrelevant, but in those days they seemed to offer hope of a gradual resolution of the crisis that has gone on for so long. That effort was made against the background of a large British community in Argentina, which was also trying to help the people of the Falkland Islands out of the dreadful situation. However, we now face the situation that all of us were trying hard to avoid. . . .

The easy way would be to respond thoughtlessly. I should like to outline to the Government the real problems that we shall face when we move in. Are we ready as a nation, and shall we continue to be ready, to accept the military implications of what is involved in a landing on the islands? If we are, well and good, but are we ready to maintain that effort not for a week, not for a month, but for years? Or, if we speak of a blockade, are we ready to accept the implications of that for the Falkland Islanders now under the Argentine military occupation, or, I may say, for the large British community in Argentina? Are we ready to accept those considerations? It may be that we are, but I hope that we shall consider them carefully. . . .

[Are we] ready to maintain at 8,000 miles' distance the scale of military operation involved 200 or 300 miles from the Argentine mainland? . . .

If we show that we are ready to overcome these immense problems, and at the same time pursue our diplomatic efforts, it is not a question of defeatism—it is a question of realism and the avoidance of another humiliation for our country.

Mr. Russell Johnston (Inverness): . . . I shall say nothing at this stage about the Government's lack of preparedness, as that ground has been well covered. . . . It is not just a matter of our apparent inability to sustain an effective intelligence-gathering operation. What about the Americans—our allies? Surely the Americans have an effective intelligence-gathering operation in the Argentine. Surely, too, they should be in a position to tell us what is happening. If they do not do so, that is a matter of real concern within the alliance.

I am a member of the Falkland Islands Association. I also have several constituents who have lived in the Falkland Islands and have families there. One knows of the islanders' loyalty and also of the sustained low profile adopted by successive British Governments in relation to the Falkland Islands. We have looked weak in the Falkland Islands for a very long time.

The Foreign Office has not been the friend of the Falkland Islands. . . .
I support the Government in sending the task force announced by the
Prime Minister. Clearly, it must be of sufficient size to operate a
blockade. . . .

Even more serious, however, are the consequences of allowing this type
of unprovoked aggression to pass without response. The Government have
an enormously difficult task, but some of it is of their own making. They
must now face up to it, and in doing so they will have our support. . . .

Sir John Eden (Bournemouth, West): . . . Like many hon. Members,
I have long suspected that elements within the Foreign Office have been
wanting to be rid of what they have regarded as a tiresome problem. The
one factor that has so far prevented that from happening has been the
resolution of Ministers that it should not be so, but there has been a basic
weakness within the Administration, and that has undermined our negotiating position and has deprived us of the possibility of having an alternative
fall-back plan.

I hope that we shall never again hear about the dangerous doctrine that
we cannot deploy force while talks are under way. Whatever the pressures
against decisive action, which will undoubtedly be mounted in the international arena over the next few days and weeks, I hope that my right hon.
Friend, who has now taken direct charge of these matters, will ensure that
the Government's commitment is carried through to the earliest possible
fulfilment, for the credibility of the Government and the honour of the
country demand nothing less.

Mr. Donald Stewart (Western Isles): . . . I, too, have constituents who
have worked in the Falkland Islands. In fact, some of their families are
there now. For many years, I have also been a member of the Falkland
Islands committee. . . .

I was interested in the comments of the right hon. Member for
Bournemouth West (Sir J. Eden) about the Foreign Office, because one
wonders on which side it has operated. That was illustrated by the Prime
Minister's use of the phrase "discussing a dispute". There was no dispute.
A totally unfounded claim was made by the Argentine over the sovereignty
of the Falkland Islands. By regarding the matter as a dispute, we started
from a position of weakness.

It is clear that there has been a lack of intelligence, information and
preparedness, but . . . this is not the time to go into that. The fact remains
that for many years successive Governments have given the people of the
Falkland Islands an assurance that their interests would be protected. They
are entitled to the right to self-determination, and they have said quite
clearly that they have no wish to be taken under the wing of the
Argentine. . . .

I hope that this matter can be resolved without force, but if force is
necessary, so be it.

Sir Peter Emery (Honiton): . . . Two things must be certain—that any
military action taken by Britain must be 99·9 per cent. certain of being
victorious. We must risk nothing that could bring about defeat . . . *[in the]*
period before the task force arrives, we should announce to the world that
we expect, and we will take positive action to ensure, that every diplomatic,

trade and economic pressure is brought to bear upon the Argentines in order that they should withdraw before action becomes necessary.

The use of the United Nations in this manner is the proper and accepted use of that body. If that action of withdrawal has not been taken within the 10 or 14 days stipulated by the Government, a state of war should exist between Argentina and Britain. . . .

Mr. Douglas Jay (Battersea, North): . . . In spite of all that we have heard today, I find it inexplicable that the Government made no preparations and, apparently, did not know what was going on throughout the whole of last month. . . .

The whole story will inevitably lead some people to think that the Foreign Office is a bit too much saturated with the spirit of appeasement. I hope that, apart from anything else, the Foreign Office will now examine its conscience, if it has one.

Secondly, I trust that this event will put an end to the policy of unilateral disarmament of the Royal Navy, which the Government have been carrying on. Unilateral disarmament always invites aggression, and unilateral disarmament of the Navy has invited aggression in this case. . . .

Thirdly, I do not believe that diplomacy is enough in this situation. . . . Diplomacy can succeed only if it is visibly supported by effective action. . . . The rights of the people of the Falkland Islands are at stake. It does not matter how the British forces originally got there 150 years ago. What matters now is that these people wish to remain British, and that is the right of self-determination. . . . As the whole history of this century has shown, if one gives way to this sort of desperate, illegal action, things will not get better, but will get worse. Therefore, if the Government act effectively they will have the support of the House and the country. But if they do not, they will be unreservedly condemned.

Sir Bernard Braine (Essex, South-East): . . . We are dealing here not with a democratic country that has some claim to the Falkland Islands—with which the matter could be thrashed out in a civilised way—but with a Fascist, corrupt and cruel regime. . . .

The very thought that our people, 1,800 people of British blood and bone, could be left in the hands of such criminals is enough to make any normal Englishman's blood—and the blood of Scotsmen and Welshmen—boil, too.

This is not a day for judgments to be made. True, it is a sad day, but not one for judgment yet. The Prime Minister was frank and open with the House. At present, none of us expects the Government to reveal the dispositions of our forces and any decisions that they may have taken. We do not expect that, but we do expect results. Unless firm and effective action is taken within a reasonable period of time to remove the invaders and to restore the islands to British sovereignty, the effect on the Government's standing will be dire. They will not be able to rely on my support. . . .

The time for weasel words has ended. I expect action from the Government; and I hope that we shall get it. However, let there be no misunderstanding. Unless the Falkland Islands are quickly restored to lawful British sovereignty, and unless their people are freed from the

16

dreadful shadow under which they have lived for a decade or more, the effect on the Government will be dire.

Mr. George Foulkes (South Ayrshire): I find it difficult to understand why the British Government were not aware of something of which the people of the Argentine seemed to be aware. . . .

I should like to know—I hope that we shall have an answer today from the Secretary of State—what our embassy was telling us about what was happening in Argentina. I should like to know what was the Foreign Office's interpretation of what the embassy was saying. . . .

I have some worries about how we can take effective action. It ought and needs to be said that, if we are to take effective action, we must examine the consequences. Inevitably, thousands of Argentines will be killed. We may not wish to weep any tears over them, but thousands of British troops will be killed as well. We must face those consequences. Inevitably, there will be recriminations against British people in the Argentine. If we know anything about the Argentine Government, we must know that.

What is more, can anyone with military knowledge tell me how we can retake the Falkland Islands without loss of life to the men, women and children whom we are saying that we are interested in protecting?. . .

My gut reaction is to use force. Our country has been humiliated. Every hon. Member must have a gut reaction to use force, but we must also be sure that we shall not kill thousands of people in the use of that force. I am in favour of the firmest possible diplomatic action and sanctions against the Argentine. I am in favour of asking the United States and all our allies to unite against the Argentine. However, I am against the military action for which so many have asked because I dread the consequences that will befall the people of our country and the people of the Falkland Islands.

Mr. John Silkin (Deptford): . . . Today, I agree, is not a day of judgment—we cannot have recriminations—but it is a day of questions. It is on those questions and on the answers to those questions that this House must make its judgment. . . .

Our thoughts are with our fellow citizens in the Falkland Islands. I share the concern expressed by many right hon. and hon. Members that what has taken place is the aggression of a Fascist dictatorship and a Fascist junta whose latest leader, General Galtieri, is probably the worst of the bunch of its leaders—a man who wears upon his chest the medals that he won in repressing his own people. When he says to us that he will respect the rights and property and, above all, the lives and freedom of our people, we have a right to wonder whether that is true in view of what he does to his own people. . . .

Let us ensure that our dear fellow citizens in the Falkland Islands are kept in touch with us as much as possible. Let us extend our broadcasts. I do not know the technicalities that are involved. But let them hear our voice. Let them know they are not deserted. Let them know that we are thinking of them. That must be the first consideration. We must give them what advice we can in what are difficult times for them. They may be tempted to do things that it may not be prudent for them to do and that may interfere with our own plans. We must keep in touch with them whatever happens.

The Opposition agree absolutely with the Government that all the diplomatic measures necessary in the United Nations Security Council must be taken. We must press ahead with those diplomatic considerations as rapidly as possible. . . .

We are being asked to support the Prime Minister, the Secretary of State for Foreign and Commonwealth Affairs and the Secretary of State for Defence in what may or may not be a dangerous and difficult operation when all the indications are that heretofore they have blundered and bungled over the defence of the Falkland Islands. Had they acted speedily, with effect and force, and . . . with foresight, this whole danger might never have occurred. It is right, before we give the Government any trust whatever, that we should ask and receive answers to three vital sets of questions.

Is it not a fact that all—no, not all, but large-scale—signals were being received by the Argentine junta that we did not perhaps mind so much, wrongly, I know, what might become of the Falkland Islands? It is within the recollection of the House that, in December 1980, the then Minister of State, Foreign and Commonwealth Office met a very cold reception in the House over the manner in which he had been speaking to people in the Falkland Islands. He had been saying to them "We are talking over with the Argentines the question of giving them your land and leasing it back. What do you think of that?" The House gave a very clear view. What, however, was the view taken in Buenos Aires? Was this not perhaps a signal to Buenos Aires that the will of the British Government and the British people was weakening? . . . I have heard twice that the talks at the end of February this year between the present Minister of State and his Argentine opposite number were cordial and positive. Cordial and positive for whom? What sort of effect did that have on the Argentines? . . .

What was the substance of those talks, which were so cordial and positive that they have ended up with an Argentine invasion of British territory in the Falkland Islands?

On 29 March, Monday last, at a time when the Prime Minister assured us . . . that the British Government were becoming well aware of Argentine intentions and beginning to counter them, the hon. Member for Ashford (Mr. Speed) intervened in the speech of the Secretary of State for Defence and asked:

"Will my right hon. Friend answer this riddle, which is worrying many people: how can we apparently afford £8,000 million to meet a threat in 13 years' time, which may possibly be true, when we cannot afford £3 million to keep HMS 'Endurance' on patrol to meet a threat that is facing us today?"

The answer to the riddle came from the Secretary of State for Defence. He said:

"I do not intend to get involved in a debate about the Falkland Islands now."

This was last Monday. He continued:

"These issues are too important to be diverted into a discussion on HMS 'Endurance'."—[*Official Report,* 29 March 1982; Vol. 21, c. 27.]

Whatever the Secretary of State's personal position, these signals were being heard loud and clear in Buenos Aires. The Argentines felt that Her Majesty's Government were no longer in a position or had the will to protect their fellow citizens in the Falkland Islands. . . .

18

There is a second question that the right hon. Gentleman must answer. In December last year, when this present bargain basement Mussolini, Galtieri, seized power in the Argentine, he never made any pretence about what he intended to do. Not a day went by when he did not talk about recovering the Falkland Islands. He was the kind of man—we ought to have known it—who meant it.

Again, as the right hon. Gentleman said on 25 February and at the beginning of March, we were getting clearer and clearer indications that such an invasion was imminent. Where was the Foreign Office and where was the Foreign Secretary when all this was happening? Why did the Foreign Office not alert the Secretary of State for Defence? If it did not alert him, why did he not alert himself? It is extraordinary that we are spending £14·5 billion a year on defence, yet apparently were not ready, when the Argentine fleet set sail, although we had five or six weeks' notice of its intentions, to defend our people in the Falkland Islands.

Therefore, we have a right to ask a third question of the Secretary of State for Defence. Were we not totally unprepared by him for what was to come? Should we not have been prepared and should we not, in defence terms, have been ready to meet the attack? Why was it so long before we began to answer the threats that were being made—so long that even now we are apparently still assembling a task force? . . .

Why were we not prepared for what has happened? Why did the Secretary of State for Defence, as recently as last Monday, find himself in the position of saying that this was a tiny matter and a matter of no importance compared with the vital matters of Britain's defence, as he saw it, in 13 years' time? . . .

So the Secretary of State for Defence, the Secretary of State for Foreign and Commonwealth Affairs and the Prime Minister herself have something to answer for. This is a collective decision of the three most guilty people in the Government. I acquit most of the others. They probably did not know what was going on. They probably believed that we were capable of defending the Falkland Islands and that the British people who live in those islands could sleep easily at night because they would be protected, as they had been under the previous Labour Government and, to be fair, under Administrations before that. So it is those three Ministers who are on trial today. It is not the moment for judgment, it is not the moment for recriminations, but it is the moment when those questions must be put and answered. . . .

The Secretary of State for Defence (Mr. John Nott): I wish to join the right hon. Member for Deptford (Mr. Silkin) in saying that today all our thoughts are with the British people of the Falkland Islands. I know that the whole House agrees with him on that.

Two main criticisms of the Government have emerged in the debate, certainly in my area of responsibility. . . .

The first main criticism is that in some way the changes that we have made to our naval programme and our other defence arrangements have diminished our capability to respond to such a crisis. The second criticism is that the specific events that developed 14 days ago in South Georgia have caught us unprepared militarily.

The pledge of the right hon. Member for Deptford yesterday that we could count on the support of the official Opposition was welcome. Of course, there is much criticism of the Government on both sides of the House, but I hope that we can unite behind our Armed Forces and that they will have the full backing of the House in the difficult circumstances that we face. It is clear that the whole House accepts that the guarantee of political integrity granted to the Falkland Islands by successive Governments has been breached by an act of flagrant territorial aggression in the face of a determined diplomatic effort to solve the problem peacefully—without any sabre-rattling by the British Government. Our attempt to achieve a peaceful resolution of a long-standing dispute stretching back for many years under Governments of both parties might have been expected to appeal to the Leader of the Opposition. He welcomed our peaceful attempts to resolve the dispute. We shall all remember that, speaking for the whole House, he said that we would not wish to see foul, brutal aggression succeed anywhere in the world. My right hon. Friend the Member for Taunton (Mr. du Cann) and the whole House applauded him for that remark, which we shall remember. . . .

The other major criticism that has been echoed on both sides of the House is that we should have reacted earlier with the despatch, either covertly or overtly, of some surface ships. There are two questions on that issue. First, should we have despatched earlier than we did a Naval task force? [Hon. Members: "Yes."] Secondly, should we have deployed covertly some frigates, as the right hon. Member for Cardiff, South-East (Mr. Callaghan) did in 1977? With the wisdom of hindsight, the despatch of a large surface task force sufficient to deter or destroy the Argentine navy might have given pause to the Argentines. [Interruption.] Perhaps the House will allow me to argue the point through. As the incident at South Georgia began just 14 days ago, such a task force would not have reached the Falkland Islands in order to perform its task. It is impossible, as the right hon. Gentleman said, to know what psychological impact such a force might have had on Argentine intentions, but certainly in deterrence terms, had it been successful, that large task force would have had to remain perhaps indefinitely in Falkland waters, in detriment to its other tasks. But, as my right hon. Friend the Prime Minister said in opening this debate, we were throughout seeking a peaceful solution through the United Nations and by other means. . . . Such an act, at a moment when we might have been going to the United Nations, would have seemed highly provocative. . . .

The other option would have been the deployment of a small force insufficient to resist the Argentine Navy, as was done in 1977. . . .

Presumably to deter, the presence of the force must have been known. If so, to have sent it, then it would have had precisely the same objections to a peaceful solution. [Interruption.] If this were a covert deployment, which I believe that it was, it could not have deterred if its presence was not known; and even if the size of the force had been revealed, it could have provided nothing more than a tripwire of exactly the same kind provided by HMS "Endurance" and provided by the Royal Marine garrison on Port Stanley.

Mr. Foot: The right hon. Gentleman is trying to say that there was some difference of opinion, but it was clearly stated by my right hon. Friend when the fact became known without fuss and publicity, and it had a success. That is the difference. What happened in 1977 was a success. This is a terrible failure.

Mr. Nott: I do not think that one is able to draw that conclusion.

Dr. Owen: If the right hon. Gentleman as Secretary of State for Defence has not understood the value to a Foreign Secretary of being able to negotiate in a position of some military influence and strength, he should not be Secretary of State for Defence.

Mr. Nott: Of course I understand that. However, . . . there can be no evidence that the position of the frigates in the South Atlantic at that time brought about the settlement of that dispute.

Several hon. Members have spoken of the problems that we now face. I do not seek to hide from Parliament the formidable difficulties with a crisis 8,000 miles away. However, the United Kingdom has the ability to mount a major naval task force and to sustain it for a period at that distance. The charge that the Royal Navy cannot do this is flagrantly and patently untrue. We have that capability, as will certainly be evident, and it amounts to a formidable force which no other nation in the world possesses with the exception of the Soviet Union and the United States. . . .

The Government do not pretend that the situation is anything but extremely grave. The resolution of this problem will undoubtedly be all the more difficult since the occupation. We intend to solve the problem and we shall try to solve it continuingly by diplomatic means, but if that fails, and it will probably do so, we shall have no choice but to press forward with our plans, retaining secrecy where necessary and flexibility to act as circumstances demand.

The military problems are formidable, but they are certainly not insoluble because of the professionalism, the preparedness and the quality of our defences, which for our nation's size are unique in the free world. . . .

Report Three

5 APRIL 1982

On Monday 5 April the House was told of the freezing of Argentine financial assets and of the requisitioning and chartering of ships, including the "Canberra".

The Secretary of State for Trade (Mr. John Biffen): It was announced on 3 April that the Government had frozen all Argentine financial assets held in this country, that ECGD would not provide new export credit cover for Argentina, and that exports of military equipment and arms to Argentina had been prohibited. Other economic measures are being urgently examined, and we are consulting our European Community and other allies. British citizens are advised not to travel to Argentina, and British companies to withdraw their non-essential British staff. British firms must decide what action they should take in relation to existing commitments in the light of the present circumstances, the measures which have so far been announced, and the terms of their own individual arrangements with Argentine firms. They are advised not to enter into new commitments.

Meanwhile, right hon. and hon. Members will recall that the Prime Minister told the House on 3 April of the Government's intention to despatch a substantial naval task force to the Falkland Islands. I should like to take this opportunity to announce to the House that Her Majesty assented to an Order in Council enabling the Government to requisition any vessels that may be needed, under the long-standing contingency plans available to meet national emergencies of this kind. The P & O liner "Canberra", whose captain is an officer in the Royal Naval Reserve, is being transferred to naval control this afternoon. Other ships will be requisitioned and chartered as necessary. . . .

No general ban currently exists on exporting to the Argentine. . . .

There is a ban on the export of arms and supplies from this country, and undoubtedly we shall do our utmost and shall expect our allies to assist us in that prohibition. . . .

We are in consultation with our European Community partners with a view to co-ordinating as far as possible and making economic response to the present situation. . . .

It is true that any interruption of trade which derives from a conflict such as this results in losses to a very large number of companies and people. This has always been true historically, and no doubt it will be equally true on this occasion. The same convention will apply on this occasion as applied within the lifetime of previous Parliaments.

As for our taking economic action, of course, this is a matter under careful review. . . .

Mr. Kenneth Warren (Hastings): . . . Will my right hon. Friend make urgent representations to the Heads of Government of France, Italy and the United States, whose ground support in Argentina not only made the invasion possible technically for the navy and air force of the Argentine but would also make it possible for the Argentine to sustain a counter-attack against our own Forces?

Mr. Biffen: I am certain that any helpful economic response in this dispute can best proceed if we are supported fully by our nearest allies in the European Community.

Mr. Eric Deakins (Waltham Forest): Is the Secretary of State confident that our trading relationships with other Latin American States will not be disrupted by them as a result of the continuance of this dispute?

Mr. Biffen: No one can be confident in replying to such a question, but I hope very much that the dispute can be localised and that the mutual good interests that lie between this country and other Latin American States can be sustained.

Report Four

6 APRIL 1982

On Tuesday 6 April there came the first questions to the Prime Minister on the issue following the Argentine invasion.

Mr. Bob Cryer: . . . *[Has the Prime Minister]* noted that even President Reagan has called for a peaceful solution to the Falkland Islands crisis, without bloodshed? Does she not accept that, as she is responsible in the final analysis for the conduct of her Government, she should consider an early resignation and allow someone else to meet President Reagan on his visit?

The Prime Minister: We shall welcome President Reagan as the President of our senior NATO ally, the most powerful defender of liberty in the West and throughout the world. I understand that President Reagan, like most of us, would wish a peaceful solution to the crisis in the Falkland Islands. We shall be happy if anyone is able to secure the withdrawal of the Argentines from the Falkland Islands, the restoration of British sovereignty and the respecting of the wishes of the people to live under sovereignty without a drop of blood being shed. If anyone can do that, we shall warmly welcome his co-operation. With regard to resignation—No. Now is the time for strength and resolution.

Mr. John Browne: Does my right hon. Friend accept, with regard to her action over the Falkland Islands issue, that she has the overwhelming support of the House and the nation? Can she confirm whether our mission is to destroy the Argentine invasion fleet? If my right hon. Friend cannot confirm that, would she say whether she believes it either possible or desirable in the long-term security interests of the Falkland Islands, and to protect the exposed southern flank of NATO, that a NATO base should be established in the Falkland Islands?

The Prime Minister: Our mission is to restore British sovereignty to the islands and to give the people what they want—the right to live under British rule and to owe allegiance to the British Crown. That is our task. I do not think that the idea of a NATO base in the Falkland Islands would be well received, because the islands are far out of the NATO area.

Mr. Foot: Has the right hon. Lady been able to study this morning the reports in many newspapers such as *The Daily Telegraph* and *The Times* that the information about the attack was known in London 10 days before the invasion? Is the right hon. Lady aware that this is claimed to be on unimpeachable sources and that, if that was true, it would have been possible for action of interception to have been taken? Will the right hon. Lady say whether that information is correct and, if it was received, what action was taken by the Government?

The Prime Minister: . . . As I told the House on Saturday, even had we known at the time of 19 March, when there was the landing at South Georgia at Leith—which is a long time before the 11 days to which the right hon. Gentleman was referring—we could not have got ships of the fleet there in time. . . . The first time we had precise information was on Wednesday. If the right hon. Gentleman looks at his copy of *The Times* he will see that there is a phrase to the effect that they knew there were ships but did not know their intent. *[Interruption.]* I am telling the right hon. Gentleman with the greatest possible accuracy, as information came to me.

The first information that I had was on Wednesday of last week, when we took action. Previously, we had been very worried about the situation in South Georgia, where HMS "Endurance" had been, and it was suggested that she take off the Argentines by force. We had understood that there were ships on the way for that and when we understood that we also took certain dispositions.

Report Five

7 APRIL 1982

With the resignation of Lord Carrington, Mr. Francis Pym became Foreign Secretary and opened the second debate, on 7 April. The debate concluded with the announcement of a maritime exclusion zone.

The Secretary of State for Foreign and Commonwealth Affairs (Mr. Francis Pym): I come to the House to open this debate less than two days after becoming Foreign and Commonwealth Secretary. . . .

The circumstances of my predecessor's departure were most unfortunate and I come to my new post at a critical time in the history of the Falkland Islands. I shall bring to this task all the determination that I can command, and I approach it in a spirit of realism and, I hope, of calm—determination, because we intend to show Argentina and the whole world that Britain is resolved to succeed in this crisis; realism, because I shall proceed in full recognition of the major difficulties that lie ahead; and calm, because we must give the most careful consideration to the practical options open to us and reach the right decisions as we advance towards our objectives. . . .

We intend to see that the Falkland Islands are freed from occupation and returned to British administration at the earliest possible moment. To do that, we must look forward in confidence, and not backwards in anger.

The whole House and the country are struck by the appalling nature of the aggressive action the Argentine regime has committed. As recently as the end of February, as the House is aware, we had held talks with Argentina about the Falkland Islands. The Argentine Government were fully aware of Britain's position: that is to say, total firmness on the right of the islanders to determine their own future; but, subject to that, willingness—indeed, desire—to deal with the Falkland Islands problem by means of fair negotiation. . . .

Harassed by political unrest at home, and beset by mounting economic difficulties, the regime turned desperately to a cynical attempt to arouse jingoism among its people. The Falkland Islanders have thus become the victims of the unprincipled opportunism of a morally bankrupt regime. Our purpose is to restore their rights.

Since the debate on Saturday, there have been a number of developments, and I should bring the House up to date. The governor of the Falkland Islands and the Marines from Port Stanley have been evacuated to this country. I am sure that the whole House will wish to join me in paying tribute to them.

The governor, Mr. Hunt, conducted himself with courage and dignity amid the danger and confusion. . . . The Royal Marines . . . gave the invaders a sharp taste of what even a very small detachment from the British Armed Services can do when attacked by overwhelming force.

On Saturday, the Argentines occupied South Georgia. The small detachment of Royal Marines on that island put up a gallant and spirited resistance, but of course they could not stand up against overwhelming strength.

The Argentines have also been consolidating their presence in the Falkland Islands themselves. We believe that they may now have a sizeable occupation force. While we have no reports of direct maltreatment of the islanders, it is quite obvious that the occupation force has no intention of treating them other than as a conquered population. Tight restrictions have been placed on their activities. It is essential, at the very least, that the Argentine authorities respect their international obligations to the civilian population.

The House is aware that we have despatched a large task force towards the South Atlantic. We are confident that it will be fully adequate for any action that may be required in exercise of our undoubted right of self-defence under the United Nations charter. While no formal state of war exists between this country and Argentina, we are fully entitled to take whatever measures may be necessary in the exercise of this right. This task force is an essential part of the means for attaining our objectives. It gives the strength from which to urge a settlement, and in the end it may only be strength that the regime in Argentina will understand.

There will be time before the task force reaches the area to do everything possible to solve the problem without further fighting. We would much prefer a peaceful settlement. We will do all we can to get one, and we shall welcome and support all serious efforts to that end. The House and the country should be in no doubt about that. But if our efforts fail, the Argentine regime will know what to expect: Britain does not appease dictators.

This is a tense and difficult period. We are using the interval immediately ahead for maximum diplomatic activity. The need is for all the world to bring pressure on Argentina to withdraw her armed forces from the islands. Britain herself has already taken various measures. We have broken diplomatic relations with Argentina. The British ambassador in Buenos Aires and most of his staff are being withdrawn. We have informed Argentina that its consulates in Liverpool and Hong Kong must now be closed. I might add here that we have increased our broadcasts in Spanish to Argentina and in English to the Falkland Islands.

A small British interests section will continue to work in the Swiss embassy. . . . We have been advising the many British subjects living in Argentina to depart, unless they have special reasons for remaining. We have frozen all Argentine financial assets in this country. We have stopped new credit cover for exports to Argentina. We have banned the exports of arms to Argentina, and, as the House was informed yesterday, we have imposed an embargo on the import of all goods from Argentina from midnight last night. . . .

The Security Council of the United Nations promptly and decisively endorsed the British view of the invasion of the islands. It adopted—the very day after the invasion—a resolution put forward by Britain. That resolution demands an immediate cessation of hostilities and an immediate withdrawal of all Argentine forces, and it calls on the Governments of Argentina and the United Kingdom to seek a diplomatic solution to their differences and to respect the United Nations charter. Britain immediately accepted the injunction to seek a diplomatic solution and observe the charter.

But Argentina displayed her contempt for world opinion by coldly declaring that she would not comply with the resolution. The resolution is mandatory. It represents the expression of world opinion. It is binding in international law. I hope that the Argentine regime will be brought by the pressure of world opinion to fulfil its legal obligations.

The whole world has an interest in the fulfilment of this resolution. There are many such territories across the world which are vulnerable to aggression from more powerful neighbours. The preservation of peace depends on the exercise of responsibility and restraint. It depends on the strong not taking the law into their own hands and imposing their rule on the weak. It depends on the international community supporting the principle of self-determination and punishing those who wilfully and forcibly violate that principle. It is the Falkland Islanders who today are being deprived of their right to live in accordance with their wishes. If the world does not oblige Argentina to restore their rights, tomorrow it will be someone else's turn to suffer aggression and occupation. The world will become an even more dangerous place. . . .

Active discussion is now under way about measures by the European Community against Argentina. We have also been in close contact with the members of the Commonwealth, many of whom have responded with support, which bears witness to the strength and value of our Commonwealth links. All this diplomatic activity will continue.

The case for other countries to follow Britain in taking economic measures is very strong. The Argentine economy depends greatly on export earnings and on raising finance to pay for imports and cover the external deficit. The scope for measures by our friends is extensive. About 40 per cent. of Argentina's exports go to our major partners, including the members of the Community. Argentina frequently tries to raise funds in the leading financial centres of the Western world.

We are asking our friends to do everything they can to help us. They may not be able to take exactly the same measures as Britain herself . . . but the supply of arms and military equipment to Argentina must be stopped in present circumstances, and I hope that our friends and partners will encourage their banks to make no new loans to Argentina. I hope, too, that they will follow us in terminating official export credits. Above all, we are asking our friends and friendly countries to take measures against imports from Argentina. I ask also that they should announce what they are doing. This will impress Argentina and encourage others to follow suit.

We are confident of the support of the world community and in particular of our friends. With this support, we hope to make it clear to Argentina that withdrawal from the Falkland Islands and a negotiated settlement constitute the only legal and acceptable approach in the dispute and the only one which is in Argentina's own interests.

The first responses to our approaches to friendly countries have been encouraging. Many countries across the world have condemned Argentina's aggression. Our friends in Europe and the United States were among the very first. New Zealand has severed diplomatic relations with Argentina. Canada has placed an immediate ban on military supplies. Canada and Australia have withdrawn their ambassadors from Buenos Aires. The Netherlands, France, Belgium and Germany have taken action on arms sales. We hope that this list will soon grow much longer both in terms of action taken and the number of countries involved. . . .

It is intolerable that the peaceful people of the Falkland Islands, who are British by choice and by inheritance, should be the victims of unprovoked invasion by a powerful and covetous neighbour. It will be far from easy to reverse this situation. The difficulties speak for themselves. We shall spare no effort to reach a peaceful solution. The Falkland Islanders have reacted with courage and dignity to their rape of the islands. I assure them now that Britain will stand by them. We have always said that their wishes are paramount. We shall do all in our power to show that their confidence in us is justified. . . .

What we in Britain must now do, with the support and backing of all freedom-loving countries right across the world, is to see to it that Argentina's illegal and intolerable defiance of the international community and of the rule of law is not allowed to stand.

Mr. Denis Healey (Leeds, East): I think that I should start by congratulating the right hon. Member for Cambridgeshire (Mr. Pym) on his new post and on the vigour of his speech. . . . He must guide our nation through the most dangerous crisis that it has faced for a quarter of a century—one for which not only Lord Carrington, his predecessor, who has resigned, but the Prime Minister, who remains in office, carry overwhelming responsibility. . . .

I shall not concentrate unduly on the inexplicable errors of action and judgment that led to the Government betraying their duties to the Falkland Islanders—except in so far as they are relevant to the future—but in view of the Prime Minister's performance yesterday I must draw the attention of the House to a sequence of events that raise questions which still demand an answer.

In January . . . the American Government were given positive intelligence of the Argentine Government's intention to launch an assault on the Falkland Islands. At the same time, the leading Argentine paper, *La Prensa*, said that the Argentine Government would threaten military action against the Falklands in the near future.

At the end of February the then Minister of State met the Argentine Deputy Foreign Minister to agree a framework for negotiations, but the agreement was never published in the Argentine. On the contrary, a day or two later statements were made by Argentine officials and by the Argentine press threatening unilateral action.

On 3 March . . . the then Minister of State told the House that [that statement] had created grave concern in the Government, but no action was taken by the Government to follow up their concern.

On 3 March the then Minister of State knew that at that very time a large NATO naval force, consisting of 30 ships, including a British submarine, a frigate and Nimrod maritime patrol aircraft, was embarking on an exercise, which was to last until 18 March, in the Gulf of Mexico—not to deter aggression by the Argentine against the Falklands, but to frighten Cuba and Nicaragua, with neither of whom we had any dispute. . . .

On 23 March the hon. Member for Shoreham (Mr. Luce), who was then a Minister of State, Foreign and Commonwealth Office, made a statement to the House on the Argentine landings in South Georgia, but failed to disclose in his opening statement that the invaders had raised the Argentine flag and had arrived there in a naval vessel. That had to be brought out in subsequent questioning. There is now conclusive evidence that on 29 March—the Prime Minister almost admitted this yesterday—the Government received detailed intelligence of the assembly of a large Argentine naval force. But that very day the Secretary of State for Defence pooh-poohed a question . . . drawing attention to the danger. . . .

The next day, on 30 March, the only concession that the Government would make to the deep and widespread concern on both sides of the House was that they would keep HMS "Endurance" in the area as long as necessary. Three days later, when the Argentine forces landed on the Falkland Islands, the Government knew nothing about it until hours after the rest of the British people had heard of it.

I learnt from journalists that the governor had no independent means of communication with the Government in London, although scores of amateur radio enthusiasts were sending messages every day. When the invasion was known to be imminent, no steps were taken to crater the runway on the islands, and I am told that no explosives were available for that purpose. . . . I believe that Her Majesty's Government's conduct over three months, if not longer, was seen by the Argentine Government as an open invitation to invasion. . . .

We know that if the Argentine Government had waited until 1984 half of the frigates and destroyers in the task force would have been sold to foreigners or would be in the scrapyards. HMS "Invincible" would already have been serving in the Australian Fleet and HMS "Hermes" would have been in the junkyard.

If the British Government had behaved in that way on a vital British interest 200 years ago, the Prime Minister would have been impeached. The right hon. Lady has chosen to stay, but from this moment she has no moral or political rights whatever to ask the Opposition to give her a blank cheque. No responsible Opposition in this situation could surrender their freedom of thought and action to a Prime Minister who had demonstrated such a monumental lack of judgment. However, we have a duty to the nation and we shall fulfil it, as my right hon. Friend the Leader of the Opposition did on Saturday when he spoke for Britain as a whole and was praised for so doing by nearly everyone on the Government Back Benches. . . .

Some people have sought to see a precedent for the despatch of this force in what happened at Suez a quarter of a century ago. The argument in Suez was about property rights—that in the Falkland Islands is about human rights. At Suez a British Government violated the United Nations charter. In the Falkland Islands crisis the Argentine Government have violated the United Nations charter and the British position has won overwhelming endorsement from the Security Council. Suez offers no precedent here.

Others say, as was said in 1938, that the Falkland Islands is a far-away country that is indefensible and that we must accept the geographical and strategic realities. However, I hope that the whole House supports the right of the Falkland Islanders to self-determination and to live in peace under a Government of their own choosing, as they have been able to do for the past 150 years.

The right of self-determination is a fundamental human right that we are responsible for restoring. . . .

I agree with the Foreign Secretary that the United Nations now has a duty to take action to prove that dictators cannot get away with the product of their aggression. If the United Nations is unable to take such action, the whole framework of world order would be under threat. . . .

Britain has a major responsibility to help the United Nations. She has the right to do so under article 51 of the United Nations Charter. However, I remind the House that the resolution to which the right hon. Gentleman referred commits Britain to seeking a diplomatic settlement of the crisis. That commitment was drafted by the British Government in presenting the resolution to the Security Council.

We all know from bitter experience that it is impossible to negotiate with a military dictatorship except against a background of strength. A dictator will not concede in negotiation what he can keep by force. Therefore, the Opposition support the despatch of the task force to the area, but I must warn the House of the appallingly difficult and dangerous situation to which the Government have exposed the nation. The wrong use of that task force could lead to the unnecessary loss of life among our soldiers, sailors and marines in the task force and to appalling economic and political consequences. The Government must now tread a narrow path between two dangers. The first danger is surrender in a diplomatic settlement that sells the Falkland Islanders down the river and is totally inconsistent with the objectives that the right hon. Lady set herself on Saturday—to see the islands freed from occupation and returned to British administration.

I understand that the Government are not insisting on British sovereignty as a result of the settlement that might be reached. I say that because the Prime Minister added on Saturday that if there is to be a change of sovereignty it must be with the consent of the islanders and with the approval of the House. The Prime Minister will know that under her own Administration the Foreign Office raised with the Argentine Government a couple of years ago the possibility of a transfer of sovereignty with a lease-back over 25 years.

First, there is the danger of a settlement that is inconsistent with our responsibilities to the Falkland Islanders. The other danger is that of a large-scale military conflict with Argentina in circumstances that cost us the support of the United Nations and world opinion. Even if we won such a conflict, in those circumstances we would be thought to have acted inconsistently with the Security Council resolution and the situation of the islanders following our victory would be intolerable. They would be threatened permanently by a new invasion and, as we were told on Saturday, Britain could not conceivably give permanent protection against such an invasion.

Perhaps the most dangerous enterprise of all—

Mr. Robert Mellish (Bermondsey): . . . I understand the importance of avoiding what could be a major conflict in which thousands of lives could be lost. Let us suppose that the Fleet sails to the Falkland Islands and diplomatic overtures have been made. The United Nations, and all that it represents, might ask to be part of the Fleet and that request might be refused. That will mean that, in spite of diplomatic efforts, the Fleet will be off the Falkland Islands. Is my right hon. Friend saying that in those circumstances the Fleet should turn round and go home?

Mr. Healey: I am coming to deal with that question.

Sir Bernard Braine (Essex, South-East): Answer.

Mr. Healey: I am coming to deal with the question and I shall do so in my own way and in my own time.

Mr. Robert Atkins (Preston, North): Answer now.

Mr. Healey: I wish to put to the House—[HON. MEMBERS: "Answer".]—that perhaps the most dangerous scenario of all would be that of an all-out assault on the Falkland Islands at a time when we were dangerously weak in air power and when the Argentine forces would have had a further two or three weeks to build up their strength and their stores on the islands, and would certainly outnumber the forces that we could mount against them. For that type of sea-borne assault a superiority of 3:1 or 5:1 is normally reckoned to be required. . . .

Worst of all, an opposed landing would inflict intolerable casualties on the Falkland Islanders, whom it is our duty to protect. They are not asking for the peace of the cemetery. Somehow—I am coming to answer the question of my right hon. Friend the Member for Bermondsey (Mr. Mellish)—between the extremes we must seek and find a diplomatic solution that the Falkland Islanders can accept and that is consistent with the commitment that we have made to the Security Council.

The main purpose of our naval task force—I believe that the Government see it in this way—is to give us the strength with which to negotiate. I make the following point as someone who was Secretary of Defence for six years and someone who for most of the last world war was involved in combined operations in various parts of the Mediterranean. Too many people without experience of war see the choice as being between Armageddon and surrender. I hope that the principle of the economy of force will always be the key to the British use of armed forces in a situation that requires a diplomatic settlement. . . .

We cannot guarantee that we shall not be involved either by the accident of war or through attacks by the Argentine forces in a much larger-scale conflict than I would wish. However, that prospect must lead the United States Administration to use all its influence for a peaceful solution. The evidence that has been published so far is that the United States is now engaged in continuous activity to try to find a way of getting under way the process of reaching a diplomatic settlement. . . .

I hope that we shall also involve the United Nations at the first opportunity. . . .

I hope that we shall involve it in an active search for a solution, which has not so far happened. It is possible that, while negotiations proceed, the United Nations might provide an administrator for the islands and perhaps a peacekeeping force after the withdrawal of the Argentine forces. I note that the Government propose secession of sovereignty with lease-back over 25 years, and there have been proposals for a condominium. . . .

Any solution that is reached between Britain and Argentina with help from the United Nations must be acceptable to the Falkland Islanders. They may take a different view of what is acceptable to them after the experience of the past two weeks, and even more so after the experience of the coming months. . . .

Our central concern, interest and responsibility at present—I think that the Foreign Secretary was emphasising this—must be the Falkland Islanders themselves, their rights and what they will accept. We must not allow any other consideration to impede the search for a solution that is acceptable to them. . . .

The Government must recognise that their record on this issue has not only faced our nation with difficult and dangerous choices, which I have attempted to put to the House, but has damaged their authority not just in Britain but throughout the world, as can be seen from the behaviour of the financial markets in the past few days.

The problems have also put the Opposition in the difficult and unenviable position of supporting the nation's interest even when that interest is represented abroad by a Cabinet that has lost its authority at home. Nevertheless, we shall support the Government's efforts to solve this crisis so long as we are satisfied that their activities are inspired by the desire for a diplomatic solution consistent with the wishes of the Falkland Islanders and the principles of the United Nations, and that their actions are well calculated to fulfil those principles. That is where our confidence has been badly shaken over recent weeks. . . .

Last Saturday hon. Members in all parts of the House spoke to a united nation. We must continue to fulfil that honourable role as long as the present crisis persists. The Opposition will put the unity of the nation first. I call on the Government to do the same. . . .

Mr. John Peyton (Yeovil): . . . Last Saturday's debate was a very sad occasion for all of us. It has not been made any the less sad since then by the departure of Lord Carrington from the Foreign Office. I am sure that today we are all bound together, as we were on Saturday, by feelings of sorrow, shame and anger.

We feel sorrow for the people of the Falkland Islands, the framework of whose lives has been smashed; shame for ourselves that undertakings or assurances given, perhaps unwisely, by successive Governments to defend the islands to the best of our abilities, should, in the event, have meant so little; and anger at a piece of gross international misconduct.

Sorrow, shame and anger may not be good counsellors now. They can easily drive us to take as little account of the unpalatable circumstances that now confront us as we apparently did of the growing and mounting dangers. I do not believe that it is either cowardice or defeatism to take note now of this formidable combination of difficulties that confront us.

First, there is the plain fact of geography—the difference between the 400 miles that separate the islands from their nearest neighbour—the Argentine—and the 8,000 miles that separate us from the islands. . . .

One wonders what form of defence will ever be effective against a near neighbour. The 100 Royal Marines were not enough, but it is inconceivable in our country's present circumstances that we could mount and establish such a huge naval base as would render at all times the defence of the Falkland Islands beyond all doubt. . . . We have to face the fact that the Falkland Islands will inevitably depend for much of their sustenance on their nearest neighbour—the Argentine—for supplies, education services and medical requirements.

We also have to face the fact that we are confronted by an entirely odious regime. One wonders what confidence it will ever be possible to place either in that regime or in any successor. . . . Whatever may happen, it is hard to believe that from this tragic episode there will not be a legacy of bitterness and mistrust which it will be extremely hard for the islanders to live with. . . .

As time passes, it is likely under such circumstances that the support, sympathy and understanding of friends will be eroded. It already appears from reports in the newspapers that the United States, the President and the Secretary of State have shifted somewhat to a neutral position. They have put themselves halfway between right and wrong.

What defence arrangements will be made by those who have raped the islands? It seems that they will have an unlimited opportunity to prepare for defence. Undoubtedly, the islanders will have a special role in that defence as hostages. There are those who are not our friends who will undoubtedly use the opportunity to fish in troubled waters. . . .

Those considerations are likely to appear with increasing starkness in the coming weeks. So, too, will the advantages that are always enjoyed by bullies and thugs as opposed to the inhibition under which those who care for peace and justice always labour.

The Government have acted with, I believe, the support of Parliament and the nation. Believing that both their honour and the nation's is involved, they have committed themselves to the recovery of the islands. . . .

We must also bear in mind that British forces are on their way to we know not what. It is clear that they must be assured of our support. . . . The Government must ally caution and wisdom to their courage and be prepared to move slowly. I am certain, too, that the Government will need to watch with care the sympathy and support of their friends, which in foul weather cannot be taken for granted.

Mr. James Callaghan (Cardiff, South-East): . . . It is correct to point out the difficulties with which the Royal Navy has been charged in the mission that the Government have given it. It is correct to ask questions about it. But there must be a spirit in which the House approaches the matter that makes it clear that the position of those living in the Falkland Islands must be protected and restored. Moreover, aggression that has been condemned by the United Nations must be repelled and set on one side. . . .

Since the House met last Saturday—I regret that I was not present—the Fleet has sailed. That will alter the nature and temper of today's debate. The Navy has been given the task of restoring and re-establishing British administration——

Sir Bernard Braine: Sovereignty.

Mr. Callaghan: —or is it sovereignty? Which is it? The Foreign Secretary used the word "administration". To my recollection, the Prime Minister also said "administration" last Saturday. We should have an answer immediately, because it would clear up much misapprehension. I was half intending to interrupt the Foreign Secretary to ask whether there was a significant difference in the meanings of the two words. Will he tell us now whether by "administration" he means "sovereignty"?

Mr. Pym: I was quoting my right hon. Friend the Prime Minister. She used the word "administration"—advisedly, I believe. . . . The intention is to restore the rights of the people of the Falkland Islands. The words that we phrased, we believe, describe that accurately.

Mr. Callaghan: The Prime Minister had no difficulty in muttering the word "sovereignty" when I put the question. She could put the matter beyond dispute if she will now make it clear that that is what she means.

The Prime Minister (Mrs. Margaret Thatcher): . . . I regard the Falkland Islands as being still British and us as still having sovereignty. . . . An invasion, an unprovoked aggression, has not altered and does not alter the fact and the law of British sovereignty over those islands.

Mr. Callaghan: I am much obliged to the right hon. Lady, but I am not sure that she has cleared the matter up. British sovereignty, as she said in her speech on Saturday, has been clear and sustained by everyone for 150 years. But there is a difference between sovereignty and administration. It is not possible, as I understand it, to equate those words.

For example, if the islands were handed back under some form of leasing arrangement—I understand that that has been discussed by the Foreign Office—and then leased back to Britain for our administration, would that solution satisfy the Prime Minister? . . .

The Prime Minister: It is the Falkland Islanders' wishes that are paramount. In every negotiation—if the right hon. Gentleman calls it that, and I have called it that—that we had, we had some of the Falkland Islands Council with us. They were with us in New York. It is their wishes that must be paramount.

Mr. Callaghan: I do not press the Prime Minister further this afternoon. I do not regard her answers as satisfactory. I shall come later to ways in which I believe that these issues must be solved and worked out. We have embarked on a most difficult and dangerous exercise which carries very great risk. . . .

The world has shown a remarkable and, to me, rather surprising understanding of Britain's position. With resolution 502 at the United Nations, New Zealand, Australia, Canada, France and the European Commission all supported us in the position that we have taken. So far, so good. But when I hear Government spokesmen use the words "we are ahead on points", I must say that I feel a little squeamish. This is not a game of tennis. We are engaged on a most serious operation. . . .

The Prime Minister's defence is that she did not know and could not possibly know and, until Argentina had taken the decision to invade, she could not possibly take action, but that is not the real question. The real question is this. Was the available evidence of such a character that she should prudently have taken precautions at an earlier date? My answer to that question must be "Yes". . . .

That is my first charge against the Government and particularly against the Prime Minister on this matter. Today our Fleet is sailing towards hostilities that could have been prevented. That is my case. I shall not spend time on the fact that we are sending an aircraft carrier that has already been sold to meet cash limits from a port that is to be closed and with 500 sailors holding redundancy notices in their pockets. I find that humiliating, too, and I hope that other hon. Members feel the same.

This, if it ever came to it, would be the unnecessary war—a war that need not have taken place and which yet, I trust, will not take place. In my view, the seeds of the present invasion were sown when our will to protect the people of the Falkland Islands seemed to be weakened in the eyes of the Argentines by the announcement on 25 June 1981 that HMS "Endurance" was to be withdrawn. . . .

The Government were warned time after time about this. . . .

I cannot conceive of a more naive invitation to a military dictator to invade than to say that there are other, higher claims on our defence budget. When I consider the cost that the present expedition will eventually bring home in bills, I can only say that we have wasted a great deal of funds and resources by not taking precautions at the time when we should have done. . . .

I urge the Prime Minister to do what has been done on earlier occasions—not only to establish a group of Ministers inside the Cabinet who will have to take full responsibility for handling these matters, but to ensure that a Minister, not distracted by day-to-day affairs, as other Ministers will be, can take charge and co-ordinate this interlocking and difficult task that we must face.

We have given ourselves a self-imposed ultimatum of a fortnight. It is a fortnight before the Fleet arrives at the Falkland Islands. It will not get there, turn round and come back if there has been no settlement. . . .

It is absolutely vital that the Navy should understand what are its orders and that we should know exactly what objective it is fulfilling. . . .

The Government must give us and the Fleet a clear lead on those issues and on the limitation of the Fleet's orders. The Navy must be empowered to use the minimum force. My right hon. Friend was correct to say that if we cannot achieve our objective in any other way, the Fleet must be empowered to use minimum force to do two things. The first is to ensure that the islanders' wishes to live in freedom are met and the second is to ensure that aggression does not pay. . . .

The United Nations' resolution demands an immediate withdrawal of all Argentine forces from the Falkland Islands. That is the initial condition that must be met if the United States is to start putting forward conditions that we are asked to accept. . . .

One of the issues for a co-ordinating Minister in conjunction with whatever group of Ministers is made responsible for these matters is to decide quickly whether Britain intends to declare a war zone. I dare say that even now enterprising newspapers are chartering aircraft to fly over the Fleet so that journalists can see what is happening when it reaches the South Atlantic. I am sure that Soviet submarines will be poking their noses in—possibly submarines from other fleets, too—perhaps from friendly nations. If we want to avoid third party incidents, one of the earliest decisions that the Government must reach is whether to declare a war zone. . . .

It is our responsibility to put jingoism on one side . . . we are talking about a peaceful and inoffensive community of British subjects which has been occupied by a repressive and Fascist regime. Those people have been threatened with 60 days' imprisonment without trial if they show disrespect. . . . Britain must do its best to secure peace with honour. Despite our heavy criticisms of the Prime Minister and the Government, we shall support that end.

Mr. David Steel (Roxburgh, Selkirk and Peebles): Since the humiliation of the takeover of the Falkland Islands and our debate on Saturday, the Foreign Secretary and two other experienced Ministers in the Foreign Office have resigned. It is right that we on the Liberal Bench should place on record our appreciation of the distinguished services rendered to this country by Lord Carrington, particularly during his period in office as Foreign and Commonwealth Secretary. . . .

There is no doubt that we and our allies in the United States spend quite a lot of money—rightly so—on intelligence. I cannot believe that intelligence information was not available over the days immediately before the naval attack by the Argentine. Clearly, a political misjudgment of the most serious type was made.

During the debate on Saturday the Prime Minister said that if she had sent an aircraft carrier to the islands she would have been accused of being bellicose. That is a fair point. But, as I remember, no one suggested sending an aircraft carrier. The right course would have been to send one or two of the fast hunter-killer submarines to the islands, and to make it clear to the Argentine Government through the normal private channels that any intrusion on the territorial waters of the Falkland Islands would be firmly dealt with by those submarines. . . .

We have witnessed a deliberate policy of priority decisions, particularly in forward spending, which have involved the resignation of the Minister responsible for the Navy and a change in the Secretary of State for Defence. Further, as a result of those decisions, of the two aircraft carriers leading the expedition to the Falkland Islands one is already under sale to the Australians and the other is due to be scrapped. When this immediate episode is over, I do not think that the House can do other than return to the question of defence priorities and the defence budget.

I wish to say something that I hope the House will accept in the right spirit. The Prime Minister has chosen not to consult other party leaders on the expedition. The country, therefore, is not on a war footing. We who have to maintain a responsible position in the House leading other political parties have no choice but to support our Service men, in the expectation that the Government do have a strategy and know precisely what they intend to do.

I wish to make it clear that in giving that support we register it with the aim of safeguarding the lives and freedom of the 1,800 citizens on the Falkland Islands. That must be the objective. The objective must not be to conduct a necessarily bloody battle over the recovery of imperial territory, much of which might be destroyed in the process, and still less should it be to save the Government's reputation. Its clear purpose must be to display the unacceptability of this invasion from the Argentine and to secure by diplomatic means conditions in which the Falklanders can make a free choice about their future. . . .

It is not enough just to get the approval of the United Nations for the resolution adopted by the Security Council. We should explore the possibility of the United Nations' role as a means of getting the Argentine off the hook of our sovereignty argument. The Government would be right to explore the possibility, as we are one of the five Powers involved, of a role for the United Nations Trusteeship Council.

Our objective must be to safeguard the interests of the 1,800 citizens principally concerned. When the settlement is made, we shall have to make compensation to those islanders who wish to leave the islands. We may also have to consider compensation for those who are prepared to stay on, in view of the suffering that they have endured. I repeat that what matters is our responsibility to those people, and not to any isolated territory.

Mr. Richard Luce (Shoreham): As the House knows, last Monday it was with much regret that I resigned from the Government. I approach this debate with the greatest of humility. Last Friday, as the House knows to its pain, Argentine military aggression took place on British sovereign territory in the Falkland Islands. This was, as we all feel, a humiliating experience and a grave affront to the people of the Falkland Islands above all, and to the people of the United Kingdom. That action was totally and utterly unacceptable to all of us.

In these circumstances, I believe that it matters not whether the invasion took place 80 or 8,000 miles away. It matters not whether it is 18,000 or 1,800 or 18 million British subjects who have been invaded. Whatever the circumstances, it remains a great affront to the islanders and to our nation. In these circumstances, at a time of great national difficulty, I felt that it was vital that the Government should have the full confidence and support of the country. To that end I thought that it was right for a new Minister to take my place. . . .

At this difficult and challenging time we must look to the future. The islanders will be foremost in our minds. Their wishes are paramount. Above all, we need a sense of national unity to face these tasks. . . .

As for the past, of course there has been much agonising criticism. I must tell the House in all humility that in the past few days I have thought carefully about the events of the past few weeks. I can only say that, irrespective of whatever judgments will be made by the country—and the country is entitled to make them—I do not see that in the circumstances of the time my right hon. Friends and I would have made any different decisions. I say that in all honesty. But with the benefit of hindsight—I have noticed that in the past few days a number of hon. Members have been enjoying the benefit of hindsight—we were wrong, and that is now a fact of history. . . .

For the future, we must keep our sights on the objective. With the support of all other parties in the House as well as of the country, we must see two things done—first, the withdrawal of the Argentine forces and, secondly, the restoration of the right of the islanders to choose their own way of life and allegiance. To that end all diplomatic means must be used, including working closely—as my right hon. Friend is doing—with all our allies and friends. . . .

I have total faith in the competence and courage of our Services. They will serve our country faithfully in the weeks and months to come.

I give my right hon. Friend the Prime Minister and her ministerial colleagues all my support. I believe that they will show the wisdom and determination that is required. I wish them god-speed.

Mr. Ioan Evans (Aberdare): . . . Did the Prime Minister know that there would be an invasion of the Falkland Islands? If she did, she is guilty of a dereliction of duty as Prime Minister. If she did not, she is incompetent and should not be Prime Minister. . . .

Only a week ago, during our debate on Trident, the hon. Member for Ashford (Mr. Speed), the former Navy Minister who was sacked because he said that the Government were doing away with our Navy defences, argued that the Government were now putting all their eggs in a nuclear basket. They are spending £8 billion to £10 billion on a Trident force, but to do so they have had to cut our naval defences.

The Falkland Islands issue has exposed the Government's defence policy. We have the nuclear capacity, but the Argentine does not. Are the Government prepared to use nuclear weapons against the Argentine? Are they prepared to have a Hiroshima in Buenos Aires? It shows how fantastic the Government's policy is that they are prepared to cut conventional forces in order to concentrate on nuclear weapons. . . .

The two ships that have invaded the shores of the Falkland Islands are British-made and were sold by the Government to the Argentine. We have two ships that the Government have said are to be scrapped, and another that was sold to the Australians but which has been brought back into service. Those are the ships that will fight in what may yet be a major conflict. . . .

The Leader of the Opposition and other Labour Party spokesmen have put our position clearly. We condemn without qualification the action of the Argentine military Fascist Government in taking over the Falkland Islands by force. I hope that the Government will not in future sell arms to the Argentine or train Argentine sailors, as they have in recent weeks, to fight against British forces . . .

The 1,800 inhabitants of the Falkland Islands and the 17,000 or 18,000 British citizens in Argentina have been put in a position that could have been avoided had the Government taken proper action.

We should support the efforts being made to restore the position by diplomatic means and we should especially welcome the support of the United Nations Security Council. . . .

If the Prime Minister is to carry the people of Britain with her—which she is not doing at the moment—she must tell the House what is happening. We are in this plight because of her blunders, and if she wishes to have the assistance of the Opposition parties to extract her from the war that is the consequence of her actions and inaction, she must tell us fully what she intends to do.

Sir Hugh Fraser (Stafford and Stone): I congratulate my right hon. Friend on his admirable speech on assumption of the great office of Secretary of State for Foreign and Commonwealth Affairs. I also wish to congratulate the Ministry of Defence on the swift mobilisation of a remarkable armada.

I must call to mind the immense gravity of the problem that faces Britain and the House. Already this century there have been two major battles around the Falkland Islands. The House must face the fact that now the world is in danger of a third. . . .

I do not want to attribute blame in the short term to either Front Bench, but I see why the people of the Falklands should feel themselves betrayed. Neither the defence committee of the Labour Government nor, I believe, the defence committee of this Government faced up to the danger should something happen to the Falkland Islands 8,000 miles away. That is, I fear, the grim fact that the House should face. . . .

I have many friends in the Falklands. I have been a devout supporter of the remarkable, independent people of those islands. I have many friends in the Argentine. Once the British Fleet has brought to bear the sanctions that have never previously been behind British policy in the Falklands, we must have a policy in the South Atlantic that can be sustained and that can last. The idea of freeing the Falklands only to have to re-invade them every five years is a policy not worth pursuing. This is where realism must be brought into play. . . .

The history of this country, the liberation and help that we have given to the Argentine and the manner in which we have built up Argentine resources, the friends we have there and the British population mean that, far from being enemies, we should be natural allies. Let us talk, as the Prime Minister and others have said, from strength, as we can talk today but as we have been unable to talk in the past 25 years in the region. Let there emerge a policy in the South Atlantic that will hold and that will not be destroyed by the whim of any dictator.

Mr. Robert Mellish (Bermondsey): . . . I tried hard to understand the point of view of the right hon. Member for Stafford and Stone (Sir H. Fraser), but he did not answer for me the fundamental question of working out a policy in the South Atlantic—a policy in which the Government know where they are going in this vast area that we are supposed to cover. What happens now? That is the important question. . . .

The Prime Minister's political nous will tell the right hon. Lady that this is not the last time that there will be an inquest on the Falkland Islands and all that has led up to the situation. Papers will be demanded. There will be need for further searching inquiries.

We are confronted by an enormous challenge not only to Britain but to our so-called allies. They are on test as much as us. . . .

One cannot say that the United Nations and all that it stands for and represents is not on our side. . . . The Security Council has voted overwhelmingly to back Britain. . . . I put this question to the Americans and to NATO. What is the purpose of the NATO pact if it does not help at a time like this? The British Fleet should not be on its own. There should be other ships with it.

We should be saying to the Argentine Fascists "This is not simply Britain talking but 10 nations. Now get out before you are attacked by the whole world". In that event, the Argentines would want to get out. However, I am a realist and that may not happen. I understand that we are going through all the diplomatic manoeuvres possible. However, even if the Fleet is composed only of British ships, we may ultimately have no alternative but to go in. That is a terrible thing to say because there could be the most appalling loss of British life. Let it be recorded that some of us will hold our so-called allies just as responsible as anybody else for the deaths of some of our lads. There is no point in having NATO, the Common Market and the United Nations if they will not stand up to be counted when we are in great distress. That is what the issue is all about.

Dr. David Owen (Plymouth, Devonport): I congratulate the Foreign

Secretary on his speech and wish him well in the onerous task that lies ahead of him. . . .

The Foreign Secretary's speech was notable for his emphasis on withdrawal and a negotiated settlement, and for its stress on his wish to see a peaceful settlement and on his readiness to reinforce diplomacy with strength. As has been said, diplomacy without arms is like music without instruments. In this world, it is a fact of life that one cannot negotiate if one has no reserves and no strength and if one has no basic readiness to assert one's will.

On Saturday, I committed my right hon. and hon. Friends to support the Government's decision that the Royal Navy should set sail for the Southern Atlantic. I see no reason to qualify that support in any way today. It is of paramount importance that the House should demonstrate to the world that there is no weakening or wobbling and that the decisions and judgments that were reached collectively on Saturday remain as firm and resolute today.

Mr. Tam Dalyell (West Lothian): For how long would the right hon. Gentleman commit significant forces to the Antarctic? Would he commit them for as long as the lifetime of the youngest among us?

Dr. Owen: Of course not. The hon. Gentleman is sensible enough to know that the dispute will ultimately be solved by negotiation. The question is how to negotiate and on what basis. . . .

At this juncture, it is dangerous to be drawn too far into the United Kingdom's negotiating position. However, it is vital that the Government should know that the House's support for our armed Service men is not totally without conditions. . . .

The Prime Minister must recognise that it is in the interests of the whole country that we do not continue with a post mortem on what went on during the past few weeks and months. However, we are entitled to expect a clear-cut pledge from the Prime Minister about the form of the investigation of these events. An inquiry should be set up that can look at the telegrams, the intelligence reports and at all the documents in the Government's hands. . . .

The right hon. Member for Bristol, South-East (Mr. Benn) . . . is a powerful figure and probably speaks for many people in Britain. Therefore, he deserves to be taken seriously. When a former Privy Councillor, who has served in four successive Administrations, makes the speeches and takes the action that he has during the past few days, it is right that he should be answerable for it. The papers tell us that he has urged that the Labour Party should dissociate itself from what he would call "Mrs. Thatcher's military adventure" . . . because it would endanger the people of the Falklands, whose safety and security should be Britain's first concern. . . .

The right hon. Member for Bristol, South-East, as Secretary of State for Energy, was present when the decision was taken to buttress our negotiating position by deploying a force of sufficient strength to convince the Argentines that military action by them would meet resistance. The right hon. Gentleman was as much a party to that decision as was anyone else. It did not necessarily involve a force of sufficient size to ensure the defeat of a determined attack with reinforcements. It could not have done so. It also did not imply that a decision had been taken to fight.

However, it was a decision to negotiate from a position of strength and it is about time that the right hon. Member for Bristol, South-East faced up to some of the decisions that he took in Government and stopped parading himself around the country as a symbol of conscience and of everything that he did not represent when he was in Government.

It is time that some of the right hon. Gentleman's comments were made in the House and not in Salisbury, Wiltshire. Our Fleet is sailing to the Southern Atlantic and it is time that the right hon Gentleman was challenged to justify why he could support that decision in 1977 but is unable to support negotiations now—and we are talking only of negotiations and a recognition of the need to negotiate from a position of strength. . . .

The Government are right to take action, but they must take account of the mandatory decision of the Security Council, which commits the House and the Government to use every diplomatic means to achieve a settlement. . . .

The United States has a heavy responsibility. I say to the United States, as a friend, that it cannot just be even-handed in the issue. It has to be clear in its condemnation of naked aggression. We are dealing not with aggression between two countries, but with aggression from one country—Argentina. The United States has an important role as a mediator. It must obtain withdrawal and a negotiated settlement, but we shall then have to be ready to listen to the United States about what form of settlement is possible and we shall also have to listen to the views of the Falkland Islanders. . . .

I believe that the islanders may be more realistic than many hon. Members about the possibilities of a negotiated settlement. Do not let us be more militaristic, more stubborn or more zealous in the protection of the interests of the Falkland Islanders than the islanders themselves would be.

Sir Anthony Kershaw (Stroud): . . . I share the view expressed by many hon. Members that an essential ingredient in the solution to the problem is that the Argentines must leave the Falkland Islands—preferably through negotiation; if not, they should be made to do so by force.

We have the legal sovereignty of the islands. That has never been sacrificed, and my right hon. Friend the Prime Minister was right to insist on the return of administration as well. I hope that nothing said by any hon. Member has called into question our sovereignty over the islands. . . .

It would be unrealistic to suppose that we could maintain a garrison of sufficient size to defend the islands against a serious attack. If we had maintained such a garrison to ward off an attack, a terribly high price would have been paid over the years. It would have been very expensive and we might have left other areas less well defended. We would also have faced the hostility of the Hispanic nations of the world, who are important to us and cling together more than some hon. Members may realise. Lastly, I am sure that we should have been condemned by many of the Third world countries for maintaining that posture. . . .

What shall we do now to rectify the situation? After the lesson that we have had, we cannot go back to the status quo ante. Even if we destroyed the Argentine navy—I hope that it will not come to that—that would only postpone for a short time the military situation and it would raise terrible questions of morality for the rest of our future. Thus, the alternative of a large permanent defence force seems out of the question.

If one does not have a large permanent defence force or try to sit on one's bayonets for the rest of time, one must negotiate. There has to be some form of sharing the responsibilities or the sovereignty in that part of the world. . . .

Whatever is decided, there must be cast-iron guarantees in which the United Nations join to make sure that such a situation does not happen again when the Armed Forces leave.

The negotiations can be conducted in the sphere of the United Nations. We are already doing that, with success. The negotiations can also be helped by the United States, which has a great influence in that part of the world. . . .

Finally, our European colleagues could bring some influence to bear. The right hon. Member for Bermondsey (Mr. Mellish) suggested that they should be associated in a warlike fashion with our expedition. That is perhaps too much to hope, but by diplomatic expressions, by using their economy to take measures against the Argentine economy, they could give us important help during the coming weeks and months. To hurry along the negotiations, I believe that the threat of force is justifiable. . . .

If we do not defend the Falkland Islands, some may believe that we will not defend other territories and interests. Would we be led, step by step, down a road of appeasement, which some of us have seen before? Would we defend ourselves in NATO? Would we even defend ourselves in this island? If such questions were asked and were not answered clearly, sooner or later the choice would be offered to us again and again until finally our option would be world war or defeat and humiliation.

Mr. Tony Benn (Bristol, South-East): The major change that has occurred since the debate on Saturday is that a battle fleet is now under way towards the South Atlantic. We should make it quite clear that the Prime Minister herself has full responsibility for giving orders that that fleet should sail. Some hon. Members have said that when our sailors are moving across the oceans towards a possible enemy we must unite around them. Let us be clear: they did not choose to sail to the Falklands; the Prime Minister has sent them. It would be absolutely improper for those who have sent them then to ask us to unite around those they have sent when the decision rests here. That is what parliamentary accountability is about.

The second point that I want to make is that now that a battle fleet has been sent with instructions, to which I shall come to in a moment, events cease to be under the control of the Prime Minister. Having followed what was said by the Secretary of State for Defence, it seems that the Argentine Government are now in a position where they can take the initiative against the battle fleet. So this may well be the last occasion on which Parliament meets to discuss the matter before our troops are fired on. . . .

The House is united in saying that an act of aggression in international law has taken place. No one disputes that. No one has defended the junta or the Government of the Argentine, or has argued anything other than that we are faced with an aggressive fait accompli. The real question is quite different: What do we do now? . . .

There is all the difference in the world between saying that we are going to recover the sovereignty of the Falkland Islands under the British flag—which is what I thought the Prime Minister was hinting at—and saying that all that we want is an administration under anybody's sovereignty, where the Falkland Islands can be safe. The Prime Minister must be clear on that. . . .

Is the Prime Minister saying that the task force is there to restore sovereignty under the British flag to the position as it was before Friday? . . .

What orders have been given to the Fleet? No one expects the operational orders to be revealed . . . .

If the instructions are that we do not exclude an attack upon the mainland to recover the full sovereignty of the island, then, in effect, we are waiting for the Fleet to engage this country in major war. . . .

Will the Prime Minister give a categorical assurance that there are no nuclear weapons of any kind in the task force that we have sent to the Falkland Islands? Not for one moment do I imagine that the Prime Minister has in mind the use of such weapons, but were a ship that carried such weapons to be sunk, that would be a major question too. . . .

The risks of this exercise far exceed the gains and, indeed, contradict the legitimate objectives of the Government.

If the islanders are first blockaded and then bombarded, and then a landing is made, there may then be no islanders to consult. Therefore, to speak of this as a great military operation, with photographs in the newspapers of marines landing at the training camp on the South Coast, is to describe—in anticipation—the death sentence on those who live in the Falkland Islands and whose welfare must be our prime concern.

To commit Service men in the Falkland Islands at this time of the year—it is winter there—in territory they do not know, against a fleet that is armed with British weapons, the spares for which were supplied recently . . . [is wrong]. . . .

I wonder also whether it is conceivable—because no one has fought a naval battle of this character with the sort of weapons now available—that some military defeat might be inflicted upon us. If the Prime Minister knew about these events only last week, could the chiefs of staff really have favoured or advised the filling of the ships for a task force within four days and then sending them off like some armada in medieval times?

I tell the Prime Minister that this is an ill-thought-out enterprise and will not achieve the purposes to which it is put. By acting in that way, she has lost the support that was carefully garnered for the Security Council resolution. . . .

The United Nations has been urging negotiations for ages. The Falkland Islanders were reluctant to have them, because they knew that the United Nations would want some settlement involving sovereignty. . . .

I tell the Prime Minister that President Reagan will not only be neutral; he will be bitterly hostile to any act of war against the Argentine, because American power rests on the rotten military dictatorships of Latin America. . . .

The Prime Minister must have an astonishing view of her power if she thinks that she can bring 1,800 hostages out of the Falkland Islands with the British Fleet, operating 8,000 miles from home, when Carter had the humiliation of seeing the inauguration of his successor before the Ayatollah Khomeini would release the hostages. . . .

What was done by my right hon. Friend the Member for Cardiff, South-East (Mr. Callaghan), the previous Prime Minister, was correct. He tried to have some sort of show, to indicate that negotiation would bring about a solution. But to say that to do what he did, without fuss and bother, is the same as launching a battle fleet with the orders that this fleet has been given is completely to misunderstand what the whole thing is about. . . .

I give three objectives to the Government. First, the safety of the islanders should be our prime concern. If we get it wrong, as I said, there will be no one to consult. That must mean seeking a local administration that will protect the islanders from the tyranny of their new, occupying pro-consul. Alternatively, there must be resettlement, but do not threaten them with landing craft. Their little wooden houses would quickly be destroyed by either the invader or our assault troops.

Secondly, a United Nations peace-keeping force must be established in the Falkland Islands. . . .

If that proposal includes a United Nations mandate, the question of sovereignty could be merged into the United Nations, and the world will support Britain against Argentina. It will not support us with the Prime Minister's strategy of threatened war, bluff, or both.

Thirdly . . . Now is the time to come forward with concrete diplomatic proposals. . . . Now is the time for the Prime Minister to say that we would be prepared to cede sovereignty to a condominium or to the United Nations. Sovereignty is not what we want: it is the welfare of the people. . . .

None of those legitimate and constructive proposals requires the task force. The task force involves enormous risks. I say as a neutral observer that it will cost this country a far greater humiliation than we have already suffered, and if history repeats itself, it will cost the Prime Minister her position. The attempt will fail. What would win world support and help the Falkland Islanders would be a decision not to send the task force. My advice, for what it is worth, is that the task force should be withdrawn.

Mr. Geoffrey Rippon (Hexham): . . . If we accept what the Prime Minister and the Secretary of State said, it is clear that we are saying that the islands must be freed from occupation—to repeat the phrase used by the Prime Minister on Saturday—before we can or will negotiate. In that sense, there must be a restoration of British sovereignty. Thereafter, negotiations of the kind that have been discussed for some time can take place . . . *[that]* can only mean that if a withdrawal is not negotiated we must use force to whatever extent is necessary to secure our objective. That follows clearly from what my right hon. Friend the Secretary of State for Defence said on television last Sunday . . . that the Government are prepared, without hesitation, to order the sinking of Argentine ships if necessary, or to storm the Falkland Islands. . . .

We must make it clear that if the invaders do not withdraw they must not assume that there would be no attack on the Argentine mainland. That is, of course, different from saying that that is our intention, but it must not be assumed by the Argentine Government that they can just sit there.

The best, if not the only, hope of securing withdrawal by negotiation is through strength. That is not just through strength of force, but strength of will. The best and perhaps only hope of avoiding bloodshed is to make it plain beyond any shadow of doubt that we stand rock firm behind the Prime Minister in a declaration that these islands remain British territory and that no aggression or invasion can alter that fact.

We have perhaps had our bluff called once by Argentina. We must not let that happen again. . . .

If we are to ensure the success of our policy and our objective, it is . . . of the utmost importance to mobilise our own public opinion and world opinion to support and sustain us. That requires unity at home. . . .

We have at present the support of the mandatory resolution of the United Nations Security Council, which demands the withdrawal of the invading forces. That opens up possibilities of sanctions and other action. The resolution by its very nature acknowledges British sovereignty—so far so good. However, the recent performances of the United Nations . . . have not been exhilarating when it has come to following up the words with the necessary action. . . .

We should emphasise the implications for us and for the 21 other signatories of the Antarctic treaty of 1959. If we can inspire world opinion and get confidence in the justice of our cause, the Prime Minister will be proved right when she said . . . that we must go calmly and quietly to success. That means, as she said, using all our professionalism, all our flair, every bit of native cunning and all our equipment.

It will be fine if we achieve withdrawal and the restoration of administrative sovereignty. At that stage we shall negotiate, but we must have the political will to succeed in our present activities. As an old Malay proverb has it:

"Where there's a will, there are 1,000 ruses. Where there is not, there are 1,000 excuses."

There must be no excuses this time, because they will not be readily accepted.

Mr. George Cunningham (Islington, South and Finsbury): . . . I suggest to the House that the mood on Saturday, when the House was virtually united, could be summed up as one of gung ho. That ought to give way to the more serious discussion of the merits and the methods that are open to us which is taking place today.

That should not be seen as undermining our forces in the Atlantic. It is doing them no service not to contemplate the difficulties that will be faced physically not by us but by them. . . .

It is desirable to look backwards in the interests of learning some lessons that need to be immediately applied not actually to the Falklands' case but elsewhere. The failure is best illustrated by this fact—the battle fleet is on its way down the Atlantic and the Argentines are surprised. That is the very essence of the failure of diplomacy. The object always should be that the person to whom you may do something knows that you may do it. . . .

I do not think that anyone can envisage the scenario through to the end. It must involve the possibility of sinking Argentine ships and going ashore with troops. There was no point in sending the battle fleet unless that was in our minds to do, and it should be in our minds to do that if necessary, subject, however, to one thing.

As has been said by others, we have never claimed the Falkland Islands as bits of territory. We have claimed them because of the wishes of the people. At least in the last 50 years our claim has been that we could not give in to the Argentine because the people of the Falkland Islands did not want us to do so. If they had wanted us to do so, that would have been a different situation and we would have behaved differently. . . .

I should like to see the United States take the initiative of proposing that there should be an international commission headed by itself and associated with it, let us say, Australia and Sweden—not Switzerland because Switzerland is acting for our interests in Argentina. An international commission would go to the Falkland Islands to which the United Nations would require—persuade—the Argentine to give the commission access.

The commission would have two functions in the Falkland Islands. The first would be to satisfy itself that the people of the Falkland Islands were being well treated. The second would be to talk to the people of the Falkland Islands—after all it is only about 1,000 families—in order to ascertain what their current attitudes were about their future. The commission would report back to Britain, as the power with legal responsibility, and to the United Nations. . . .

We cannot go on behaving in various ways without knowing the attitude of people of the Falkland Islands in the situation in which they now find themselves. I hope that if the United States were prepared to take such an initiative we would be prepared to encourage it to do so, and go along with it.

Mr. Michael Mates (Petersfield): . . . Of course we have suffered indignity and humiliation. Of course we are angry and shocked that the country should have been taken completely by surprise when we might have been warned and better prepared. However, let us remember that, when incidents such as this occur and undemocratic regimes take illegal action contrary to international law and use the violence with which they sustain their internal dictatorships against others, it is always the aggrieved party that comes off worst to start with. Recent history is littered with examples too familiar to need rehearsing at length. . . .

Armchair strategists and those with wisdom of hindsight proliferate daily in an atmosphere such as this. . . .

Several hon. Members . . . have been advertising the panacea of the nuclear-powered submarine as providing the instant solution to a problem that might have arisen . . . The strongest card that we have in our hands at the moment is our international standing. Because we have behaved in a correct fashion in the United Nations and because we have been seen to be totally in the right, the Argentines have been seen to be totally in the wrong over what has happened. . . .

On Friday morning had we, in the fog of war, caused the first casualties, if 1,000 Argentines had been killed and if their aircraft carrier had been sunk, I wonder what our friends' attitude to us would have been and what the international voices would have said. Some people may say that they do not care. That is the sort of remark that we would have lived to regret through the difficult days and weeks ahead. . . .

There is no escaping the logistic difficulties of mounting this operation. . . . The Ministry of Defence and the Services have done a magnificent job in getting the show on the road on the morning tide on Monday. . . .

Another argument which does not bear examination is that the changes in the posture of the Fleet proposed in the defence White Paper are somehow responsible for the fact that we do not have a fleet in the South Atlantic. We have not had a fleet in the South Atlantic that we have been able to sustain for 20 years. . . .

If we believe that we have problems, my goodness, the Argentines must think that they have problems. First, I do not believe that they expected the swift and certain response that the Prime Minister and the Cabinet have given. Secondly, I do not believe that they thought that we would send the might of our Fleet down there to sort them out. We may have to sustain some losses. Let us not gloss over that. But they cannot afford to sustain any losses. Their navy is limited. Their ships are irreplaceable anywhere else and they have an uncomfortable relationship with their neighbours. Therefore, there is enormous pressure upon them now for a diplomatic solution. That is why I believe that, despite all the peril that we are in, there is ground for some cautious optimism. . . .

The Government will fail at their peril to match the resolution in all parts of the House for firm action. I do not believe that they have any intention of doing that. The best approach for the House is to give the Government the maximum support and the minimum interference. We should let the Government get on with the job with all the facts that they have at their disposal and leave the inquest until afterwards.

Dr. John Gilbert (Dudley, East): The first and most emphatic message that ought to go out from the House is that Britain has absolutely no quarrel with the Argentine people. We have many friends in Argentina and other parts of Latin America. . . .

I take absolutely no pleasure in saying that I support the use of force. There is something profoundly unattractive in the sight and sound of middle-aged men baying for brave young men to put their lives in peril—a peril that none of us is ever likely to face again. We should think carefully about our posture before we speak too loudly about these matters. . . .

So far as I am aware, none of the British planes involved in the task force is nuclear-capable. Nor, so far as I am aware, do any of our torpedoes have nuclear warheads. Nor, so far as I am aware, do any of the missiles—either surface to surface or surface to air—on our ships or aircraft have nuclear warheads. . . .

I find it inconceivable that the Government could not have had clear political intelligence before Christmas of what was about to happen. General Galtieri has never made the least secret . . . that his principal preoccupation was to regain sovereignty of the Falkland Islands for his country. . . .

I wish to turn to a point made by the right hon. Member for Plymouth, Devonport (Dr. Owen). With respect to the instance of 1977—I have some slight knowledge of this also—he said that the force that was then despatched was done wholly privily. The force was assembled—it was a puny force by comparison with what we are sending to the Atlantic today—and we allowed its existence to be known. That is a crucial difference between my recollection and that of the right hon. Gentleman. . . . We also sent a clear message that, so long as no Argentine warships came within 50 miles of the Falkland Islands, no Argentine warship was in danger of attack or being sunk by one of our warships. We know the result. No Argentine warship came within 50 miles of the Falkland Islands. It worked. . . . If it had not worked, I would have pursued the same policy as have the Government. I would have assembled a task force and sent it down to the Falkland Islands and made it clear beyond any doubt that we were prepared to use force. . . .

The situation in the Falkland Islands . . . gives no safe guide for future naval strategy. Whatever happens there, whoever wins or loses, I believe

48

that there will never again be the need for a permanent military or naval presence down there. There will be a conclusion to the matter one way or the other in the next few weeks.

I emphasise again the good fortune of the Secretary of State for Defence. Not only is he lucky that this has happened now, while he still has HMS "Invincible". He is also very lucky that the Argentines have not yet taken delivery of all their new Super-Etendard planes. Only 10 days ago, I and my colleagues in the Defence Committee visited the Dassault factory just outside Bordeaux where planes had already been painted in Argentine colours. So let nobody think that the Argentine armed forces are not brave and skilful or do not have very good kit and they will shortly have even better kit. . . .

The waters between the Falkland Islands and the entrance to Buenos Aires are very shallow for the use of nuclear-powered submarines . . . there would be a great danger from the risk of mining of those waters. . . . Furthermore, on the land side, the enemy already has substantial quantities of armour ashore. . . .

We must make it clear that we have no quarrel with the Argentine people. We must give unstinting support to our Service men. In the last resort, we must make it clear that we are prepared to use force. If we are not—I address my remarks to some of my hon. Friends—there is no hope whatever of General Galtieri coming to the negotiating table.

The Prime Minister's only hope lies with President Reagan and the pressure that he can bring to bear on the Argentine Government. The biggest danger for the Prime Minister will be if the Argentines stall, make pacific noises and string the dispute out, thereby giving her no excuse immediately to use force. But there must be no use of force just to save the face of the Government or the Prime Minister. We must offer—not accept an offer—to take a United Nations force in. We must offer a condominium.

One cannot witness the prospect of brave young men taking up arms against one another with anything but great sadness. There are already thousands of anguished mothers, wives and families, not only British mothers, wives and families but Argentine mothers, wives and families. We must all hope that that anguish is not heightened by the shedding of blood, but if it is, the House and the country will take a dreadful revenge on those who are responsible.

Mr. Maurice Macmillan (Farnham): . . . With one or two exceptions, all hon. Members agree that the Falkland Islands must be liberated and that this act of wanton aggression against Britain must be successfully resisted by every means. We all agree that, if it can be achieved by political and diplomatic activity, so much the better. Almost all of us are agreed that force must be used if necessary, and only if necessary. . . .

If force becomes necessary, we must be prepared to inflict casualties and risk suffering casualties ourselves. There is no way out of that—it is not agreeable but it is inevitable. We must face that possibility now. . . .

If there were serious doubts about the will of Her Majesty's Government and the willingness of the House to support the Government in the use of force when all else had failed, those doubts would make any peaceful solution even less likely, and the task of those of our friends who are trying to help us through political and diplomatic means to reach such a solution that much the harder. I would go as far as to say that those doubts would damage the whole concept of Western security now and in the future.

Now we must do what we can short of force, and we must hope that those who are working on our behalf will do what they can in the United Nations and elsewhere. . . . But our friends must know that willingness to accept their good offices and to consider negotiations in the future does not mean a willingness to accept a proposition now or in the near future that is tantamount to a sell-out.

I hope that we are more willing to go further once the Argentines withdraw than we are even prepared to consider before the withdrawal. The Argentines must realise—and it is only honourable that we should make it clear—that to get any sort of settlement that is helpful to them in the future they must be prepared now to withdraw or face the use of force.

After all, in the longer term, there is a great deal of common interest between the United Kingdom and the Argentine. If there is oil in the area, have the Argentines the capital, the know-how or the technique to develop it? No, but they have the need to share in the prosperity that it could bring. This country must be always prepared to negotiate rather than use force. That is both our strength and our weakness. It is our strength because of the reassurance it gives to countries such as the Argentine and others who have become justly nervous of the over-quick use of force. But willingness to talk and negotiate can be a weakness because it may be taken as a lack of will. It may, however unjustly, have been so taken in this dispute. We have shown, wrongly and mistakenly perhaps, attitudes which could be taken as a lack of will. It is all the more necessary to show resolution now.

Therefore, I hope that the Goverment will not flinch even from a minimum demonstration of force, even before all the other methods are totally exhausted, if they believe that that would mean giving up the need to use greater force at a later stage. Surely our objective must be to achieve what we want with the minimum use of force whenever it may have to be used. . . .

It is important, now and in the future, that neither our friends nor our enemies should have cause to doubt our will. Most of us hate the idea of using force, but nothing is more likely to make the Government's final choice be between using extreme force or facing defeat than the present showing of any weakness or reluctance to go as far as is ultimately necessary.

Mr. Frank Allaun (Salford, East): This Government have got us in a mess by failing to act as the Government in 1977 did; by ignoring the warning signals; and by not acting in time. For that incompetence those at the top must bear the blame, and they are the Prime Minister and the Secretary of State for Defence. It was they who encouraged the Fascist generals of the Argentine by selling them arms. It may well be that British lads will lose their lives as a result of arms sold to the Argentine by this Government and British arms manufacturers.

The House may not generally be aware that this afternoon on television there was a film of the last Argentine pilots trained in Britain going home. That means that our lads may be killed by those pilots, and that is a scandal beyond words.

The Government are now faced with two choices. The first is a fight between the two navies. This is supposed to be a means of defending the

Falklanders. On the contrary, many of those 1,800 Falklanders will be wiped out in the cross fire. . . .

A total of 17,000 British people living in Argentine will be at obvious risk. . . .

One homing torpedo could sink HMS "Invincible" at a cost of 1,000 lives. That is how this military engagement may result. One does not need to be a military expert to realise the difficulties of fighting a war 8,000 miles away from home. I can see a disastrous outcome to this military adventure, and I want in no way to be associated with it.

Even if the task force won after all the blood had been spilt, what of the future? Will our forces stay there indefinitely? How else shall we protect the 1,800 islanders? . . .

I ask for an assurance—this is not an extravagant demand—that no nuclear or chemical weapons are being carried by that defence force. . . .

The alternative is to negotiate, and to offer to resettle those Falkland Islanders who wish it in Britain or New Zealand. If offered the choice, rather than be caught in the cross fire, and rather than cause the loss of thousands of other lives, I believe that they would prefer to come to Britain. That is a serious alternative. There are 600 familes on the islands. If we offered each £30,000 compensation, which is not a small sum, that would cost £18 million, which is chicken feed compared with the loss in blood and money that might well follow. . . .

Mr. Antony Buck (Colchester): The speech of the hon. Member for Salford, East (Mr. Allaun) was disgraceful. He was suggesting that the Falkland Islanders should be put up for sale or barter. They have a right to live there, which we have guaranteed. We shall do our damnedest to ensure that their rights are preserved. . . .

This is not a time for inter-party rivalry. British subjects have been taken by force and their lands usurped. It is a matter that no British Government can possible regard with anything but horror. This Parliament, with its traditions—valued by so many Members on both sides of the House—of legality and freedom, would not be worthy of its great history if it did not back what the Government are doing in order to restore the rule of law. This has been a monstrous act of illegality, which the dictatorship cannot be allowed to get away with. . . .

First, will the Government keep the nation in general and hon. Members fully informed about the progress of events? . . . Is there any possibility of some hon. Members, besides the many journalists who are rightly there, visiting the task force to show our total support and commitment to the Armed Forces? I know that there would be considerable logistic difficulties about that.

What steps are being taken to ensure, probably through the Privy Council, that the Opposition are kept in the picture? This is a great national crisis. There are many fervent patriots in the Labour Party. I do not agree that we have a monopoly on patriotism or concern about such matters in the Conservative Party. . . .

I hope that the Secretary of State can tell us something of the pressures that will be put on the Argentines while the force is gathering. All of us wish to avoid the use of force in the Falkland Islands if possible . . . one realises that there are financial pressures that could bring down a shaky regime with the help of our allies and the power of the City. The Argentines must be made to come to their senses. . . .

I do not believe that any great glory save for our Armed Forces will come out of this, but we must ensure the restoration of the rule of law. Conservative Members will support my right hon. Friend and her colleagues in all steady, firm and sensible approaches to the matter and in the use of force, if necessary, in the last resort.

Mr. S. C. Silkin (Dulwich): There will be no lack of support on the Opposition Benches for upholding the rule of law, if necessary by force. If hon. Members have detected, as I have, a certain difference between the tone of the debate today and the tone on Saturday, it is not in any sense due to a feeling of weakness having crept in. On Saturday, in the immediate aftermath of an act of vicious aggression and duplicity by a brutal dictator, perhaps we were more inclined to stress our virility than to consider the realities of the matter. Today, speakers on both sides of the House have taken a much more realistic and necessarily, therefore, much more cautious line. It is right that we should do so. . . .

In saying all that, I emphasise again that there is no lack of will to use force if necessary. . . . I am shocked and disappointed when I hear the Prime Minister or other senior Ministers say that negotiation is impossible until these islands have been evacuated and restored to our control. If there is any possibility of negotiation that will produce a satisfactory result, backed up, of course, by the force that we have set in motion through sending a Fleet towards the South Atlantic and backed up by the knowledge of the Argentine that the force, if necessary, will be able to inflict casualties upon its ships and its men, we should lose no opportunity of negotiating, through Mr. Reagan or any other person or body willing to intercede.

The fears that are expressed about what can happen are not all on our side. They are fears that must certainly be in the hearts and minds of Argentines. I do not want to assume that negotiation will not necessarily be a fruitless exercise. It is, however, necessary to ask a few questions about the direction in which we are going. . . .

[Are we] contemplating a land invasion, an invasion from the sea, of the Falkland Islands themselves? I hope, I am bound to say, that we are not. I do not want to obtain the liberation of the Falkland Islanders through their liquidation. That seems to me the last possible option of any. . . . Our Fleet might blockade the Falkland Islands rather than the coast of the Argentine. . . . For how long would we be able to sustain such a blockade 8,000 miles from our bases and within 400 miles of the coast of Argentina? . . .

[Are we] seriously contemplating a naval attack upon the Argentine Fleet? If that is contemplated, are we satisfied that, in the place where the naval engagement might occur, we would have the necessary air cover to protect our ships against the Argentine air fleets? . . .

We are concerned to rescue our fellow British subjects from the domination of a cruel dictator. Secondly, as a nation that subscribes to international law, we are the representative of the international community in upholding the international rule of law. . . . It must surely be a test of the strength of the NATO alliance whether our allies are prepared to give us their help and support. . . .

It is a supreme test of the political reality of the Community and the political reality that made many of us pro-Marketeers whether we are to have the help and material support from our partners in the Community that we have a right to expect. . . . I believe and hope that we shall get that support. I believe and hope that with it we shall be able eventually to reach a settlement of this problem, not necessarily by victory in battle, but by sufficient concession to what we are seeking to enable us to have peace with honour.

Mr. Keith Speed (Ashford): . . . It is inconceivable that our friends in the EEC or in NATO can be neutral on this matter. In most parts of the House—with one or two notable exceptions—there is a general feeling that we should now support our forces. We hope that there will be the minimum number of casualties, whether they involve Argentines, Falkland Islanders or British troops and sailors. Ultimately, a solution will have to be reached by diplomacy. We shall have to regain our sovereignty. I certainly do not flinch from that word.

If force has to be used in one operation or another, we should not flinch from it. It would be wrong and we should fail the task force sailing down the Atlantic if there were any hint that the vast majority of hon. Members were not prepared, in extremis, to use that force and to stand behind it.

Our first priority must be the 1,800 people on the Falkland Islands with whom we have such a close affinity. They wish to live in freedom under British law. However, I should not wish the debate to pass before we have considered several other aspects of the Falkland Islands. . . . There are strong indications that there is considerable wealth both in and under the seas. . . .

Both world wars have shown the strategic importance of the Falkland Islands. . . . Given the instability of the Argentine Government, it is not impossible that, if events move in a certain way and we do not regain our sovereignty and control over the Falkland Islands, they could become naval bases for a power that is by no means friendly towards us. Indeed, the Falkland Islands could become Soviet naval bases. That should concern our friends and allies in NATO. . . .

A great deal will depend on events during the next fortnight, on the diplomatic moves made by our various friends and on internal pressures within the Argentine. During the past few days I have been persuaded that to provide for the minimum loss of life and the maximum pressure there should probably be a blockade, in the fullest sense of the word, of the Falkland Islands. That might put some worthwhile cards in the hands of our diplomats, because they do not have too many now.

There should be a blockade by sea, a blockade of airborne supplies to the islands and an electronic warfare blockade. If we can make those islands, and particularly the occupying forces, incommunicado with the outside world, we may bring pressure to bear. That has the added advantage that Argentines who try to run the blockade will be seen as the aggressors. However, we must face the fact that we may then be forced to take military action against Argentine surface ships, submarines or aircraft. Again, we cannot flinch from that harsh decision. . . .

We do not want the Soviets, or anyone else, becoming involved in an incident that is at present limited between the Argentine and us and that might then flare up into something else. . . .

I am not one of those who believe that we should rely entirely on guarantees. Some naval presence—certainly a thicker and more substantial tripwire than HMS "Endurance" and 80 or 40 Royal Marines—is required. That need not be too expensive. We are talking about three destroyers and the occasional visit of a nuclear submarine. By definition, one would never know when that submarine was in those waters. We should have to have an oiler to provide the essential logistic support. Such a force would cost about £20 million to £25 million per year. . . .

The operation in the Falkland Islands—particularly if there is a block-ade—will not be solved in weeks. It will take much longer than that. In fairness to our NATO force levels and capabilites, we should use the standby squadron for the purpose for which it is designed. . . . The Falkland Islands issue has demonstrated—if nothing else—that maritime power is still essential if Britian intends to discharge its obligations to itself as well as to the Alliance. . . .

I make no apology for repeating the words that I quoted in my first speech after resigning as Navy Minister. They are the words of Admiral Gorshkov, the Soviet commander-in-chief, and they encapsulate the Falkland Islands problem and the action of my right hon. Friend the Secretary of State for Defence in sending a force to the islands. Admiral Gorshkov said:

> "In many cases a show of naval strength without taking armed action may achieve political ends merely by exerting pressures through its latent power or by threatening to take military action."

Could there be a clearer or simpler definition of what the Argentines have done, what we used to do, what we must do now and what we must have the capability to do in future?

Mr. Frank Hooley (Sheffield, Heeley): In the past 15 years I have argued in the House and outside that it was unwise for the United Kingdom to hold on to colonial possessions that we had acquired, usually by force, throughout the eighteenth and nineteenth centuries, that could only be dangerous and embarrassing to us and were of no national advantage. . . .

It is supremely ironic that the Government, who claim to be so concerned about the interests of the Falkland Islanders, have devalued their nationality, made them second-class British citizens and denied them the right to come back to the United Kingdom if they wish.

The second consideration is the security of the people involved. That is a responsibility which we retain for as long as we govern those territories. I have in mind particularly Hong Kong, Gibraltar and the Falkland Islands. It is dishonest and dishonourable to accept an obligation for security which we cannot discharge.

The Falkland Islands fracas, crisis, disaster—call it what one will—has demonstrated that with our present economic and military powers we are not able to discharge our security obligation, certainly not for the Falkland Islands. . . .

We have been wrong and misguided to give the impression to the Falkland Islanders and others that we were prepared to uphold obligations when we could not do so. . . . We have been wrong to give the Falkland Islanders the impression over the past 10 or 15 years that there was an absolute commitment, whatever their desires, which it has become impos-sible for us to discharge. . . .

[The Security Council resolution] demanded an immediate cessation of

hostilities, an immediate withdrawal of all Argentine forces from the Falkland Islands and called on

"the Governments of Argentina and the United Kingdom to seek a diplomatic solution to their differences and to respect fully the purposes and principles of the Charter of the United Nations."

The Government put that resolution to the Security Council. It was not dictated by anyone else. However, there is nothing in that resolution which talks about sending a battle fleet to the South Atlantic. There is nothing in that resolution to justify or encourage this country to go to war. . . .

I find it odd, to put it mildly, that in presenting that resolution to the Security Council, and in using all their diplomatic skill to get it passed, the Government should simultaneously scrabble together a massive naval force, the only purpose of which can be to wage war.

A wide range of possibilities is open to this Government, through the machinery of the United Nations. . . .

We should build a worldwide coalition to apply . . . sanctions to the Argentine to compel or induce it to relinquish its hold on the Falkland Islands. . . .

If we pursued a policy of war and became involved in hostilities—even assuming that we sank the Argentine ships and dominated the islands by force—I believe that a vast coalition in the world would be against us. . . . However, as of now, we are four square within the law within the United Nations, and we have its support, backing and judgment. . . .

We should be wiser to pursue and exploit that judgment and pursue some of the ideas put forward by other hon. Members about a United Nations peacekeeping force, United Nations trusteeship, United Nations mediation, or United States mediation, if necessary. Those are the methods that we should pursue. The despatch of a major naval armada with all the unforeseeable consequences that arise from it will not promote the interests of the Falkland Islanders, nor will it promote the interests of this country. . . . I am concerned about the right to life of the people who are living in the Falkland Islands. I am concerned about their genuine rights—not the vanity and the national pride of some Government or Prime Minister. That is why I argue in these terms. . . .

I have no desire to see Argentine people killing British people and the British people killing Argentine people over the possession of a few windswept islands in the South Atlantic. The machinery of international co-operation is there. We have the judgment of the international community in our favour. We should exploit and use that and not resort to the unilateral use of armed force.

Mr. Churchill (Stretford): . . . The record of the United Nations—and before it, of its predecessor, the League of Nations—in bringing to heel Fascist dictators is not an encouraging one. It is for this reason that the House today is, in my view, massively endorsing the action undertaken by the Government thus far. . . .

Today, with the Fleet on the high seas, sailing towards the South Atlantic, is neither the time for recriminations nor for indulging in party political points. . . .

Let there be no weasel words uttered today in this House that would give any comfort to the Argentine dictator or make our men's task more hazardous than it is already. . . .

The objective of our policy is clear. First and foremost, it is to liberate the Falkland Islanders from Fascist dictatorship; and, secondly, to restore British sovereignty and administration to the Falkland Islands and their dependencies. What we do beyond then is open to negotiation, and I think we would certainly be willing to be very generous in such arrangements for the dependencies if this episode were to be peacefully resolved.

The failure to achieve these objectives would have repercussions far beyond the fate of the Falkland Islanders and the Falkland Islands themselves. Britain's standing and credibility in the world, in the eyes of both her adversaries and her allies, will be judged by the resolution and determination with which we meet this challenge. . . .

The people of Argentina should know that we who traditionally regard them as our friends have no wish to sink their proud—over proud—navy, let alone to kill thousands of the finest of their young men. Nor should they be in any doubt as to our resolve as a nation to restore British sovereignty and rule to the Falkland Islands and liberate our people who live there.

Effectively that means that the Argentine has only a short time to withdraw its forces of occupation from the Falkland Islands, and that our friends in the United States, and other countries that are friendly to both sides, have only a short time span in which to secure that withdrawal.

I take issue with the right hon. and learned Member for Dulwich (Mr. Silkin), the former Attorney-General, who suggested that we should negotiate first and secure the withdrawal of the invasion forces later. That would be unacceptable, and the Government should guard most strongly against any solution that left Argentine military forces in occupation of the islands pending the outcome of peace talks.

Now that the Argentine has achieved all its objectives by force of arms it will be doing everything in its power to see the matter resolved peacefully. It will do everything short of military withdrawal to achieve a peacefully negotiated settlement. I trust that it will be made clear today that Argentina can expect no allies in this House for such a solution. . . .

The Royal Navy remains the third most powerful naval force in the world, but man for man and ship for ship it is the finest navy in the world. That will be recognised by everyone who has seen the Navy at sea. What other navy, friend or foe, could within four days have completed the transformation from peace to war and have half of its strength at sea, on its way and ready for action with a full complement of war stocks, equipment and spare parts? . . .

There must be no doubt in Buenos Aires and in Washington about the determination of the British Parliament and nation to free our people from Fascist rule. Let the word go out from this House today that the nation stands united behind the Government, and above all behind the Forces of the Crown, in that resolve. We wish all those who sail with the Fleet god-speed, a victorious outcome and a safe return.

Mr. Michael English (Nottingham, West): I am sure that every hon. Member realises, although no one seems yet to have mentioned it, that no debate of this character could take place in Argentina. That is because there is no elected legislature in Argentina. It is a country that is ruled by rebel generals. . . .

It is almost inconceivable to us that there can be circumstances in which crooks rule. I think that that is the fault that the Government fell into.

56

They fell into the problem of being honest, decent English gentlemen . . .
We should remember that we are not dealing with law-abiding people. It
is a pity that we are not. . . .

There is a reasonable Argentine case. . . . A settlement was once reached
between Spain and the United Kingdom whereby the East Falklands, which
happens to be where Port Stanley is, were Spanish and the West Falklands
were ours.

There is a Spanish claim and there was a Spanish claim and there is
therefore an Argentine claim. However, Argentina illustrates its bad faith
by claiming far more. It wants all of the South Atlantic. It wants the
Chilean South Atlantic, the Argentine South Atlantic, the British South
Atlantic and a chunk of Antarctica as well, the latter being 10 per cent.
of the earth's surface. . . .

We are not defending the Falkland Islands and we are not, odly
enough—even though, like every other hon. Member, I hope there are no
casualties among them—defending 1,800 Falkland Islanders. That is not
what we are defending. That is why—I hate to say it to my right hon. and
hon. Friends—if some of them are killed, that is not necessarily the most
important thing.

The most important thing is that what we are defending is the rule of
law in the world.

The lives of the Falkland Islanders are already at stake because they are
under the rule of a military dictator. It is as simple as that. As honest
democratic citizens of what I believe to be a civilised world, can we disagree
with the genuine representatives of that world, poor and not always efficient
though they may be in the Security Council of the United Nations? Can
we not stand up and defend democracy? A couple of years ago we gave
the Falkland Islanders the right to elect the majority of their legislative
council, a right which millions of people in Argentina do not now possess.
May we not say what we are defending? May we not say that we are
defending democracy and law? We are defending civilisation against
barbarians as our ancestors did centuries ago elsewhere. . . .

Mr. Michael Ancram (Edinburgh, South): . . . If a solution can be
achieved through diplomacy, everyone in the House would welcome it. . . .

It is only now that I have become convinced that we would be justified
. . . in using that force and if necessary sacrificing lives. The reasons for
coming to that view are simple. Some of them, such as sovereignty, have
been mentioned. . . .

The people of the Falkland Islands are not foreign to us. They are of
us. . . .

Their land has been taken over by military force. They are prisoners in
their own houses and their property and land have been raped. I ask
myself: if that was my family, would I stand back from using whatever
means were necessary to try to protect them? I came to the conclusion that
I would not. Those people are our family. We should take that view.

The second reason was a different one. . . . Deterrence depends upon
the state of mind of the potential aggressor. The potential aggressor must
believe sufficiently that if he makes an aggressive move against this country
there will be retaliation. To that extent, deterrence is indivisible. If we are
faced with aggression in a small set of islands at the far side of the world
and we are not prepared to retaliate with the necessary force, the credibility

of our deterrent is questioned from top to bottom by our lack of confidence in ourselves. . . .

Our fervent hope must be that, before the task force arrives, Argentina will see sense and realise that its position is untenable in every respect—morally, legally and strategically. Every effort must be made to persuade it to face that reality. If it does not, we cannot afford to falter in our determination, however painful may be the consequences. We must openly face the fact that there will be pain and loss if that decision has to be taken.

The alternative is to back down and turn neatly away, not just from those in the Falkland Islands who look at us through a welter of semantic but empty declarations, but from here on out. That is not what is expected of the House, the Government or the country.

We have a duty to give to those who follow us that legacy of self-respect and integrity which is today being challenged. I trust that the Government will have the wisdom and courage to defend it.

Mr. David Ennals (Norwich, North): My claim to a few minutes of the time of the House is that when I was Minister of State at the Foreign Office under my right hon. Friend the Member for Cardiff, South-East (Mr. Callaghan), who was then Foreign Secretary, I had special responsibility for the Falkland Islands and our relationship with Argentina.

Inevitably, therefore, I felt close to the 1,800 individuals on the Falkland Islands—quiet people wanting to do no other than live on the islands on which they and their parents before them had lived—who trusted in us. They trusted that we would stand by them and that what has happened would not happen. . . .

Of course it was right in 1977, when the writing was on the wall, to send the forces that we did to act as a deterrent. It is no use seeking diplomacy if one has no forces behind one. . . . That is why I believe that there must be some show of force at this stage. Otherwise, I fear that the prospect of negotiations is very slight indeed. . . .

I am glad that the United Nations came down strongly, by a majority of 10 to one, against this act of aggression by a militaristic and brutal dictatorship—the kind of dictatorship with which the Conservatives seem to have been very friendly in the past few years, selling them arms and equipment which I fear will now be used against our own men who are setting off perhaps to do battle.

Are those forces setting off to do battle? If so, what kind of battle will it be? What will be the instructions? Perhaps the object is to establish a blockade between the Argentine and the Falkland Islands. If so, how long are we prepared for that blockade to remain? If our ships are shot at, naturally we shall shoot back at Argentine ships. If Argentine ships come closer than the line that we determine, we shall shoot at them, anyhow. But when all this has happened, if it happens, what will happen to the 1,800 Falkland Islanders? . . .

If we tell the Argentines that unless they withdraw we shall launch an invasion of the Falkland Islands and throw them off by battle, how many Falkland Islanders will be left at the end of that kind of battle? . . .

The Government must think coolly. It is almost unbelievable that they embarked upon this major operation without consulting the Leader of the Opposition. That was almost as unbelievable as failing to read any of the signs that should have been obvious to the Foreign Office, the Ministry of Defence and the Prime Minister about what was likely to happen. The Government cannot expect us to give them a blank cheque unless they take us into their confidence. . . .

Mr. Kenneth Warren (Hastings): On Monday morning I saw the Fleet sailing proudly down the Solent, the ships lined with young men who, in serving their country, will probably experience the fear which none of us of an earlier generation would wish on any young men of today—the fear and experience of battle. The House is with them in heart, and we wish them well. We are confident that they can carry out the duties for which they have volunteered and that they will carry them out in the best fashion and the traditions of the forces in which they serve. . . .

The sadness of seeing that departure gave me a sense of how much we need to find the diplomatic solution that has evaded us for decades. Now we are seeking to find a solution not in decades but in days. In our determination to find an alternative to the war that is swarming over those young men, we look towards the United States. I wish to ask our new Foreign Secretary—whom I wish well—how clear he is about the part that the United States thinks it is to play in the broking process.

I am concerned that the United States should make a clear declaration that it is only promoting and participating in the diplomatic solution because it wants an unqualified return of the Falkland Islands to British Government control. I am wary of the Mr. Nice-Guy process that one sees so often from the United States, particularly in its ventures in South America, where for sincere, clear and well-known reasons it inevitably puts its own interests first. I hope that the British and United States Governments will clear up this nagging fear which I sense I am not alone in feeling. . . .

I am concerned about the new wave of gobbledegook that is becoming part of *Hansard* vocabulary—words such as "lease back" and "condominium". I do not know exactly what they mean, and I very much doubt whether many other hon. Members know what they mean. It is not only a question of definition, but how we in this House and other people will interpret those words. . . .

I hope that the Foreign Secretary will make it absolutely clear that in any diplomatic negotiations British sovereignty is unaffected by the invasion, as it is unaffected in legal terms, and that British sovereignty itself is not up for discussion. I should like an assurance—the Falkland Islanders may find this of help—that no nationality problems could beset them in terms of their relationship with this country. . . .

I hope that the Government will carefully examine the routes by which data is available to ensure that in no way is raw data held up from arriving on the desks of Ministers who have the responsibility of promoting the interests of the task force as well as the interests of the diplomatic solution.

It would be helpful if it could be made known that we have the kind of data that our task force requires to carry out its task in the South Atlantic. It would also be helpful to know that good communications are available and that they are not in doubt. As part of our deterrent process, we should make it clear to the Argentine navy and air force that the task force commander not only has the right but the freedom to destroy Argentine military forces as he requires and when he desires it.

At some later date we must examine how, after successive Governments have spent so much money on armaments, we appear to have ended up with inadequate defence.

Mr. Eric Ogden (Liverpool, West Derby): . . . My purpose is to speak for the British people of the British Falkland Islands. . . . I ask the House, the Government and the British people to regain and restore to the Falkland Islanders their rightful freedom, security, sovereignty and British administration. I ask them to commit every resource at our command, every asset at our disposal, every endeavour and device of peace or war, without reserve or qualification and with courage, thought, quiet determination and conviction to restore to the people of the Falkland Islands what they have lost through no fault of their own.

The first duty of every Member and every Government is the defence of the realm; to maintain and secure the freedom of British citizens in every part of British sovereign territory. . . . That is what the hon. Member for Uxbridge (Mr. Shersby) and I said to the people of the Falkland Islands when we had the privilege to visit them as an official Commonwealth Parliamentary Association delegation, with the full support of the British Government last September. . . . On 31 September 1981 the free Falkland Islanders elected, by free adult suffrage, the members of their Legislative Council. Every elected member of that council, which is less than six months old, had campaigned on the strong principle, platform and conviction of the continuing British sovereignty and security of the islands and the rejection of any sort of leaseback, sell-out bribery by Argentina. That is their latest declaration and one we should not forget. . . .

As they are good neighbours to each other, so they would be good neighbours to the other people of the South Atlantic. Neither they nor we have any quarrel with the people of the Argentine, only that Government. No Minister, new or old, of this Government, past or future, should have any doubt that these people are British. We should not expect that they will accept anything less for themselves than we would accept for any British citizen of the Isle of Wight, Anglesey, the Western Isles, Orkney, Jersey, or Alderney, the Isle of Man, or for any part of the British territories and islands of the United Kingdom. . . .

Someone might perhaps have to ask sometime what happened to the contingency plans that were supposed to be available to enable a British communication base to exist, perhaps for only two days out in camp. That would nevertheless have been important. . . .

There has to be some contact between the occupying forces and the civilian population. The Falkland Islanders are brave people but we want no dead hereos among them. Life of some kind has to go on. Peat has to be dug and gathered, food obtained, services maintained, schools, medical and social services conducted. Farming and the feeding of sheep and cattle have to continue. Will the Foreign Secretary advise the islanders in Stanley and in Camp and authorise them to choose from among their numbers spokesmen to conduct minimum negotiations with the military authorities for the maintenance of basic human needs? This will probably mean in Stanley that the Legislative Council members will choose someone from among their numbers as an official spokesman for the islanders in the town areas. . . .

If the aggressors are persuaded that we shall defend only the Isle of Wight and not the Falkland Islands, there will be death and destruction.

With the proper use of the resources available, there is a way in which we can prevent a war. However, we can do so only if the junta is convinced that we are determined to use every means to free the islanders. The Foreign Secretary must have the right to negotiate to remove the occupying power from the islands. However, future negotiations about the long-term security of the islands should not be undertaken when the Falkland Islanders are occupied by a foreign power, or immediately afterwards, when they are still in a state of shock.

I smell the smoke of appeasement. I smell a sell-out. These are words that have to be used. Part of the difficulty may be that two different sets of advice are being given to Ministers. The Prime Minister says that we shall keep our word, restore faith and regain our sovereignty over the Falkland Islands. However, someone else says that the Falkland Islanders might not be as anxious to insist on something that they insisted on before they were invaded and that the Fleet is going there only to restore British administration. If that is so, by the time the Fleet has reached the Falkland Islands, the Argentine Government will have offered a 25-year package deal of administration and of a lease-back in return for sovereignty. I sense a new Pym/Haig pact that will have too much in common with that of Hoare and Laval. That is not the way forward. . . .

The motto of the Falkland Islands is "Desire the right." If the Government follow that, we shall be on safe ground and the Falkland Islanders will be safe in trusting us. If we do any less we shall have betrayed them a second time. We desire the right.

Mr. Nigel Spearing (Newham, South): . . . The present situation has arisen out of our inability as a country to come to terms with the new world and our post-imperial phase and our inability to make with dependencies a proper settlement that is recognised not only by the old and new Commonwealth, but by many nations throughout the world, particularly Third world countries and members of the United Nations. . . .

If we are to recruit world support for our position, as the Foreign Secretary says is necessary, it is vital to take account of the discussions at the United Nations. . . .

The Security Council resolution does not give carte blanche for our Fleet. It calls for negotiations, but most hon. Members would accept that successful negotiations may require some back-up.

The question that disturbs the House and the country is the extent to which the back-up is regarded as the first or only option and the extent to which it is one of the necessary reserves in the background. The only reason why the Fleet is on its way is that there has been some misunderstanding and miscalculation in Government. We all know that.

The Fleet is really that of HMS Government, whose purpose is not only to right the wrongs over the Falkland Islands but to retrieve the reputation of the Government. The claimed and actual objectives are a dangerous and explosive mixture.

Part of the problem has been solved by some of the resignations, but in the past few days the Prime Minister has emphasised a solution by the use of the Fleet alone. Indeed, she said at one time that negotiation had failed. I do not believe that she would still take that view, because many hon. Members on both sides have pointed out that we shall have to choose at some time between what is negotiated at the United Nations and going on into the unknown, with all the risks and consequences associated with that.

The Prime Minister seems to have forgotten that, although force may be necessary, it should not necessarily be the first priority. . . .

Mr. David Crouch (Canterbury): I had a green card sent in at the beginning of this debate for two of my constituents, who wanted to hear this debate. They had travelled 8,000 miles from the Falkland Islands, and they were the last two to leave before the Argentines landed. They are sheep farmers, and I hope that they are listening now. . . .

I have no doubt that our commanders will . . . devise their plans to liberate the islands and their people without harming them in the process. However, it will not be easy. We must hope that the Argentines will respond to the strong diplomatic activity and be influenced by the firm resolve of the Government to recapture the islands, by force if necessary. Now is the time for us to show resolve and to encourage our sailors, marines and other troops. Now is the time for us to show resolve and to encourage all the efforts by our country, by the United States and other countries in the diplomatic activity which must equally produce the result that we want.

We do not want to lose face in these matters, but nor must we lose our heads. When we have achieved our aims and liberated the islands, as I am confident we shall, by all these means—and I hope by peaceful means—what will the islanders think then? Will they want to stay and get on with their sheep farming? Will they have the same enthusiasm, and the confidence that Britain, 8,000 miles away, will safeguard them from another attack?

I believe that when the Argentine has suffered a major reverse and withdrawal, or has been driven out of the islands, it would not be credible for it to attempt to defy us or world opinion a second time, but shall we have to keep a protective naval force there in future, and a rather more effective military presence than a detachment of Royal Marines?

We have embarked on a major military operation to regain our territory and to save 1,800 British subjects. We are right to do so. We would be wrong not to. A great principle in the defence of freedom is at stake. But I cannot help thinking of the sad and angry people. . . .

The Falkland Islanders, too, will have had their minds concentrated by what has happened to them. We may find that they want to call it a day and come home. We cannot know this now, but at least we have to give it a thought. . . .

Mr. Tam Dalyell (West Lothian): . . . *[How long can we]* sustain a force in the Antarctic? It is one thing to put a force into the Antarctic; it is quite another matter to get it out. . . .

Secondly, what is the position of the British Antarctic survey? Although some of the headquarters' staff have left the Falkland Islands, the survey is dependent on South Georgia, and it is certainly dependent on the good will of the Argentine. . . .

My third question concerns the resignation of the Foreign Secretary, Lord Carrington. I am puzzled about it. There has been a great deal of schadenfreude and possibly humbug about it. Ever since I was the late Dick Crossman's Parliamentary Private Secretary, I have known Peter Carrington, and by nature he is not the kind of man who flinches from a hard task. I refuse to believe that he resigned simply because of the formidable task in front of the Government. Those who know him will realise that he did not leave because the task was hard. Either he was let down or deceived by colleagues, and possibly doublecrossed, or he simply did not believe in Government policy. . . .

What advice was given to the Government by the Chiefs of Staff? I take it on my responsibility—every hon. Member is responsible for his statements—to say that some Chiefs of Staff advised that the task force was not a feasible operation. The House is entitled to know what the Chiefs of Staff said to the Covernment on this issue. Some of us believe that the Fleet should turn round and come back to Portsmouth and Rosyth as soon as possible.

Mr. Alan Clark (Portsmouth, Sutton): . . . The people we are talking about are . . . our own family. They are our own family with an absolute right to their homesteads and their land. . . . These people inhabit an area of tremendous riches and potential for future generations of our own people. Is it not extraordinary, and fortunate, that the moral and material imperatives co-exist? What possible reason can there be, either moral or material, for abandoning them?

Many of my hon. Friends will have seen the scenes on television when the Fleet set sail, with sailors standing on the deck in lines, each individual bluejacket joined by an invisible cord to his family on the quayside who were waving him god-speed. Surely I cannot have been alone among my hon. Friends in recognising that they showed a simple faith and pride in our country, which they showed naturally and spontaneously. That is something that in the last resort I entered politics to protect. When they cheered I believe that they did so in the knowledge—it was surer than ours in this place because it came from their hearts—that everything was at stake. . . .

I believe that this is the last chance, the very last chance, for us to redeem much of our history over the past 25 years, of which we may be ashamed and from which we may have averted our gaze.

Mr. David Lambie (Central Ayrshire): Throughout the debate right hon. and hon. Members on both sides of the House have said that we cannot let down the people of the Falkland Islands. Those who have said that have forgotten that we have let them down. The Falkland Islanders were British subjects in a British colony who had a right to the protection of British forces. They did not get that protection because of the Government's actions. . . .

I visited the Falkland Islands . . . in the latter part of 1978 . . . to try to get the islanders to agree to a proposal made by the then Labour Government that representatives of the Falkland Islands should take part in negotiations between the Argentine and British Governments. The Falkland Islanders have always refused to take part in such negotiations. . . .

During our journey we visited the British embassy at Buenos Aires. From the ambassador down—perhaps this is why Lord Carrington resigned—the people in the British embassy were pro-Argentina and anti-Falkland Islands. . . .

I am one of the Opposition Members who believe that it was the wrong decision to send a task force to the South Atlantic. I accept the case put by my right hon. and hon. Friends that that force was going down to the South Atlantic to show the flag and to make a show of strength to get the Argentine Government to a negotiating table to get a negotiated settlement. I have to accept that.

However, . . . I realised that the task force was going not merely to show our strength, but to take part in a naval battle to defeat the Argentine navy, to invade the Falkland Islands and, if necessary, to invade the mainland of the Argentine. In that case I am not sure that we are following the correct line.

If we are to have the support of the United Nations, we have to cease the show of strength in the South Atlantic and we must use the power that we have to get the United Nations and all our friends in the United Nations to come in on our side. . . .

The Falkland Islanders themselves would never allow a debate to take place on the future of the Falkland Islands in the United Nations because they recognised that the former colonies, which constitute the majority of the members of the United Nations, would always come down against Britain as a colonial power. Therefore, if we go to the United Nations, and especially if we do so after having taken part in a battle with the Argentines, we shall not get world support, and we shall be out on a limb. . . .

In view of the special relationship that the Prime Minister has with the United States and with President Reagan, why has not President Reagan adopted the same policy against the Argentine as he adopted against the Russians on Afghanistan? . . .

The Prime Minister must take full responsibility for the present situation. I say this to anyone who has never been to the Falkland Islands. It is impossible in winter in the area of the "Roaring Forties" to carry out an invasion of the Falkland Islands without massacring the 1,800 Falkland Islanders who live there. The attack can take place only at Port Stanley. The rest of the Falkland Islands is desolate and is composed of marshland and bog. Heavy equipment could not travel in those areas. The only area in the Falkland Islands that has roads that can be used by heavy equipment is Port Stanley, where 900 of the 1,800 people live. . . .

If the Americans intervened in this dispute, there would be only one result: the Argentine forces would withdraw from the Falkland Islands and there would be a return to normality so that we would be given the opportunity to reconsider the situation.

Mr. John Silkin (Deptford): . . . We have heard a great deal about the jingoist mood in the House last Saturday. I do not believe that it was a jingoist mood. What I did get was a gigantic sense of outrage that a small, democratic group of people, Britons every one of them, had been overrun by a Fascist dictatorship. The Foreign Secretary called it a brutal dictatorship today. We shall not quarrel about the words. It is the same thing. The House was ashamed that we had allowed that invasion to take place. We had a sense of deep horror that it had taken place at all. That was the mood of the House. It was a sombre mood, not a jingoist mood.

If today the mood has changed somewhat, perhaps it is right that it should. It is not as emotional as it was on Saturday. It is now much more introspective. That is right, too. We are doing our best to try to work out a solution. Nevertheless, that sense of outrage is still with us. If President Galtieri and his bunch of hangmen think that the differences of approach to the matter by hon. Members represents approval or acquiescence in what he has done, let the message go from the House that that is not so. President Galtieri does not know what a free parliament means.

Let us examine what should be the objectives of the Opposition now. They should not coincide with everything that the Government believe. There is every reason why we should divide, except on the fundamental basis that I have just outlined. First, we go with the Government on the matter of the United Nations resolution. . . . the Security Council resolution was drafted by an official of the British Government. . . . That resolution demands the immediate withdrawal of all Argentine forces from the Falkland Islands. I hope and trust that that will be the view of every hon. Member. . . .

The second point of that resolution, passed by the Security Council by 10 votes to one, with five abstentions, calls on:

"The Governments of Argentina and the United Kingdom to seek a diplomatic solution to their differences and to respect fully the purposes and principles of the Charter of the United Nations."

There should be no difference of opinion on that. . . .

The second objective for the Opposition is to support, respect, sympathise with, comfort and do everything else that we can for our fellow British citizens of the Falkland Islands. That means looking after their best interests as they would wish. That has emerged strongly both in this debate and last Saturday. That desire is common to all hon. Members.

The Opposition believe fundamentally and passionately—this will be agreed by everyone—that we should support our forces. I come, however, to a matter where some differences may arise. It is a well-known, historic and right basis that if an Opposition does not trust the political leaders of the forces, it has a national duty to say so. That has nothing to do with our support for the forces. That remains. . . . Let us be under no illusion. We do not have to give our trust to those who allowed the house to burn down, and we certainly do not have to applaud their being made chief of the fire brigade. . . .

Is it a fact—the Secretary of State must know—that 10 days before the invasion the Argentine Government agent in London asked for 01 priority spares for military equipment? Is it true that the right hon. Gentleman was advised against providing them? Who overruled that advice? The right hon. Gentleman must answer, and we expect that answer tonight. . . .

What are the objectives of the expedition? We have a right to know. . . .

How many ships—and what is their state of readiness—of the standby squadron are coming out of reserve to cover the hole made in the NATO services? We have heard a great deal about the need for readiness in NATO. We are entitled, therefore, to ask the right hon. Gentleman for details on the availability of standby squadron ships. . . . It is right that we should talk about fulfilling the wishes of the islanders, but what are those wishes and what means will be used in order to see what those wishes are and how they may be fulfilled? Successive Governments have said that the wishes of the islanders should be paramount. It has been repeated today. . . . Is it the Government's policy that the freehold of the Falkland Islands must be returned to the islanders or is it the Government's policy that it would be sufficient if the leasehold were to be given to the islanders and the freehold retained by Argentina? . . .

Labour Party policy is to get rid of Trident and to have a strong conventional force. Government policy is now in tatters. Let us imagine what that policy would be had the Falkland Islands dispute taken place a year from now, after the White Paper had begun to take effect. By then, the dockyard at Gibraltar would be closed, Chatham would be deserted, Pompey would be run down, "Invincible" would have sold to Australia and "Hermes" would be on the way to the scrapheap. That is precisely what would have happened. As we know, 500 sailors with redundancy notices in their pockets are at present travelling on ships that have either been sold or are due for the scrapheap, to return to dockyards that are to be closed down. That is the reality of the Government's defence White Paper. Will they change it? . . .

The future of the Falkland Islands is shared and worried about by all of us. We sympathise with the islanders and we shall do our best to help them. In that, we can be united. I hope that the fact that we remain a free Parliament and that we shall not have any truck with the Fascist dictatorship in Argentina will unite us. But we can never tolerate the incompetence, the bungling and the blundering of a Government that did for the Falkland Islands in the first place.

The Secretary of State for Defence (Mr. John Nott): On Friday 2 April, Argentina seized the Falkland Islands by force of arms, in flagrant disregard of international law and, subsequently, of resolution 502 of the Security Council. Her Majesty's Government have made it absolutely clear that we do not, and will not, accept this position. The Falkland Islands are sovereign British territory. The Falkland Islanders wish to remain under British administration.

We are now deploying to the South Atlantic a powerful task group and other naval units capable of a range of operations. Should it become necessary, we shall use force to achieve our objective. We hope that it will not come to that. We hope that diplomacy will succeed. Nevertheless, the Argentines were the first to use force of arms in order to establish their present control of the Falklands. The islands are now subject to an illegal and alien military rule. That is a position which must not endure for one day longer than is necessary.

Our first naval action will therefore be intended to deny the Argentine forces on the Falklands the means of reinforcement and re-supply from the mainland. To this end, I must tell the House that through appropriate channels the following notice is being promulgated to all shipping forthwith:

"From 0400 Greenwich Mean Time on Monday 12 April 1982, a maritime exclusion zone will be established around the Falkland Islands. The outer limit of this zone is a circle of 200 nautical mile radius from latitude 51 degrees 40 minutes South, 59 degrees 30 minutes West, which is approximately the centre of the Falkland Islands. From the time indicated, any Argentine warships and Argentine naval auxiliaries found within this zone will be treated as hostile and are liable to be attacked by British forces. This measure is without prejudice to the right of the United Kingdom to take whatever additional measures may be needed in exercise of its right of self-defence, under article 51 of the United Nations Charter." . . .

Let me make it clear to the House that the illegal occupation of the Falkland Islands and their dependencies by the Argentine armed forces in no way affects the fact of British sovereignty over all these territories.

Sovereignty cannot be taken away by force. It is the administration which has been usurped, and it is the administration which we shall be making every effort to restore. . . .

I would only say that we have always made clear our wish to resolve the dispute with Argentina. That has been the wish of previous Governments, too. We have made continuous and constructive efforts to achieve that goal. . . . *[But what matters]* is what the islanders want. It is their rights that have been taken away by naked aggression. It is their rights that we shall restore.

The House will no doubt wish to hold an inquest on what went wrong. . . . I believe, however, that the time for an inquest will arise when we have returned the Falkland Islands to British administration and not while our task force is at sea. . . .

At Question Time yesterday, my right hon. Friend the Prime Minister made it clear that it was not until 31 March that we received information that a large number of Argentine ships were heading for Port Stanley. On 1 April, further evidence made clear that the Argentine force was preparing for the assault of the Falkland Islands. I believe, in fact, given the considerable knowledge that we possessed over the previous weeks and months, that others, had they been in our position, would have drawn the same conclusions as ourselves. But clearly we were wrong. We are not disputing that.

My right hon. and noble Friend Lord Carrington, whose tremendous services to the nation we shall all miss deeply, in speaking on this subject publicly last Monday, accepted that we had misread the signs. . . .

If, however, I may be permitted to hazard a personal opinion—I emphasise that it is a personal opinion and the interpretation of the evidence that we received—I do not in fact believe that a firm intention had been made to invade the Falkland Islands until the last week in March. I would like, in this connection, emphatically to deny the report contained in some newspapers yesterday that intelligence reports had been received in this country several weeks ago indicating that an Argentine invasion on the Falklands had already been agreed. . . .

To have assembled a task force of the present size and to have despatched it ready to fight a battle 8,000 miles from home should be convincing proof of our preparedness. We were in fact able to assemble such a task force—in such a short time—only because our plans were prepared, both in terms of our fighting units and of their essential logistic support. . . . At the Royal dockyards and naval stores depots and establishments there was a splendid response from the civilians of the Ministry of Defence who worked long hours, often throughout the night, to get the Fleet to sea. We are immensely grateful to them. I would also like to express my thanks to the shipping industry for its co-operation and support.

There is one other acknowledgement that I must make. It goes to the Royal Marine contingents that defended the Falkland Islands and South Georgia. The 75-strong detachment put up a splendid fight against overwhelming odds. The initial assault on Government House by a large company of troops was repulsed. On being thrown back, the Argentines showed no stomach to press their attack until the arrival of the marine battalion, some 600 strong and equipped with armoured personnel carriers armed with cannon, one hour later. The Royal Marines succeeded in bringing this convoy to a halt by knocking out the leading vehicle. They were still defending the residence several hours later when the governor, in his capacity as commander-in-chief, decided that it would be wrong to continue in view of the risk of bloodshed and injury to the immediate population living nearby.

With similar gallantry, the Royal Marine contingent of 22 men in South Georgia inflicted many casualties, including several killed. They damaged an Argentine corvette and destroyed a large Argentine helicopter. . . .

The Commander-in-Chief Fleet, Admiral Sir John Fieldhouse, is in overall command of all forces allocated to the operation. This he exercises from his operational headquarters at Northwood where he controls all communications and has access to all available intelligence. Similar arrangements would apply for any operations both out of area and in the Atlantic.

Operational command of our surface ships and embarked forces is vested in Rear-Admiral Woodward, the Flag Officer First Flotilla. He is an officer of very wide experience, including sea commands. Brigadier Thompson, the officer commanding 3 Commando Brigade, will command the landing force. I mention that only to show that I am satisfied that this normal and well-tried command and control structure for maritime and amphibious operations works well and I see no reason to depart from it at this time. . . .

The force is capable of taking on any maritime threat, be it airborne, surface or sub-surface, and it contains a sizeable amphibious lift capability in the assault ship HMS "Fearless" and the five landing ships. Arrangements are in hand to supplement the force as necessary, either for reinforcement or replacement . . . there are no ships in the stand-by squadron. . . .

I urge the House to say nothing in public that gives comfort or assistance to Argentina. Great caution and restraint are needed over the coming weeks in what is broadcast on radio and television or published in the press. A military operation is under way and lives are at stake. I know that the press and media will take that fully into account in their reporting. . . .

When one stops a dictator, there are always risks and, as my right hon. Friend the Prime Minister said the other day, there are greater risks in not stopping a dictator—a lesson which this nation has learnt before.

There are also those who doubt our military capability to mount or sustain the level of operations that may conceivably be needed in the last resort. In this connection, I shall answer some of the remarks made about the naval programme and the defence changes that I have made. In particular, I shall respond to what the leader of the Liberal Party said. Our defence programme is shaped round the response to the Soviet threat. That remains our overriding defence priority. In terms of the sea-air battle, the plans give emphasis to our submarine and maritime air effort, and it is right that they should. Indeed, the lesson that this incident, too, makes very clear is that we are right to increase the number of our force of SSNs—our hunter-killer submarines. In my view, I have endorsed the full plans which we inherited. . . .

In the future, we shall still be spending more on the conventional Navy, even when expenditure on modernising the strategic deterrent is at its peak, than was spent on the conventional Navy when the Labour Party was in office. I have not sought to make a particularly partisan speech, but we cannot be criticised for cutting back the conventional Navy when it is far larger today than it was when we took office, and so it will be in the late 1980s. . . .

68

It has been suggested that the Argentines were encouraged to invade the Falkland Islands by the news of last year's decision to withdraw HMS "Endurance" from service. With the wisdom of hindsight, I accept that it could have provided the wrong signal to the Argentines, but, as I think most hon. Members would agree, for all the useful work that she has carried out over the years, HMS "Endurance" does not pose an appreciable military capability and would not in herself have constituted a deterrent to an invasion. Indeed, if "Endurance" had been seen by the Argentines as a deterrent they would surely have waited until she had left the area. . . .

Under the terms of the United Nations charter . . . we are fully entitled to take whatever measures may be necessary—I announced one to-night—including the use of force in the last resort, to secure the withdrawal of Argentine forces from the Falklands Islands in the exercise of our inherent right of self-defence under article 51. . . .

We are determined to resist aggression and return full rights to the British people of the Falkland Islands. The British people are to be protected wherever they may choose to live, even 8,000 miles away from the Houses of Parliament, and if we have to fight to restore to the people of the Falkland Islands their right to self-determination, we shall do so. If these dictators can get away with this today, as has been said already, it will be someone else's turn tomorrow.

I agree with the sentiments expressed repeatedly throughout the debate—that, however firm our resolve, it is still a time for cool heads, for realism and for calm. The deployment of a formidable task force does not mean that the Government have abandoned diplomacy in seeking to recover the Falkland Islands from Argentine military occupation. Yesterday's communiqué, for example, by the European Commission is another indication of the growing international revulsion at Argentine's actions. But if diplomatic efforts fail, and the economic measures outlined by my right hon. Friend the Foreign Secretary . . . a forceful solution will be necessary.

We have no wish to shed blood, but we shall not acquiesce in an act of unprovoked aggression—undertaken, presumably, in the false belief that we lacked the courage and the will to respond. Let the world be under no illusion. These people are British and we mean to defend them. We are in earnest, and no one should doubt our resolve.

Report Six

8 APRIL 1982

On Thursday 8 April, the Prime Minister again answered questions.

The Prime Minister: . . . The Falkland Islands . . . remain British territory—no invasion can alter that simple fact. It is the Government's objective to see that the islanders are freed from occupation at the earliest possible moment.

Our partners in the EEC have been, and are being, extremely helpful in respect of our problems in the Falkland Islands. Both President Mitterrand and Chancellor Schmidt have been in touch with me personally and are taking action to support us. . . .

Throughout the Western world and beyond there is a realisation that if this dictator succeeds in unprovoked aggression, other dictators will succeed elsewhere. We are fighting a battle against that type of aggression, and once again it is Britain that is fighting it. . . .

Mr. William Hamilton: Does the Prime Minister agree with the statement made by the Secretary of State for Defence yesterday that the Falkland Islands exercise will go ahead regardless of cost? Has she any idea of what that cost will be—£100 million, £500 million, £1,000 million? How will it be paid for, and how does it come within the cash limits of the Ministry of Defence?

The Prime Minister: I wish to make it perfectly clear to the hon. Gentleman that when this information first came to me—I said when it did—I took a decision immediately and said that the future of freedom and the reputation of Britain were at stake. We cannot therefore look at it on the basis of precisely how much it will cost. That is what the Contingency Reserve is for. I understand that my right hon. and learned Friend the Chancellor of the Exchequer has said that, should we need to raise more money, that money will be raised in orthodox ways, and that it will not be done in an inflationary way.

Mr. Neil Thorne: A report has just been received to the effect that the Argentine reserve forces are being called up. Will my right hon. Friend find time today to consider whether it will be necessary to make an announcement soon about our own reserves, particularly in view of the importance of providing effective cover in Europe, and particularly in Northern Ireland?

The Prime Minister: If we thought it necessary to do so, we should of course consider it, but I do not believe that it is necessary at the moment. . . .

Dr. David Owen: In the light of the debate yesterday and the clear wish of all right hon. and hon. Members to unite and avoid endless post mortems, will the Prime Minister institute discussions between the parties about the form of an inquiry which will have to take place? The House should be given an assurance about that matter at the earliest possible moment so that we may look at the whole conduct of the affair up to the invasion of the Falkland Islands.

The Prime Minister: . . . We are considering exactly what form that review or inquiry should take and what its timing should be. I am quite happy to consult on that matter. What I want to make clear is that we think that some form of review of inquiry is advisable under the circumstances, and we shall consult later.

Mr. J. Grimond asked the Prime Minister if she will order an inquiry into the conduct of the Foreign and Commonwealth Office in recent years and the sufficiency of the advice and information supplied to Ministers.

The Prime Minister: I do not think that so wide an inquiry would be appropriate. I believe, however, that there should be a review of the way in which the Government Departments concerned discharged their responsibilities in the period leading up to the Argentine invasion of the Falkland Islands. I am considering the form which this review might take, and I will make a statement to the House in due course. . . .

The Government have given repeated assurances that no agreement affecting the status of the Falkland Islands will be concluded without the consent of the Islanders and of Parliament. . . .

We have made no request for mediation. As part of our wide international representations, we have approached the Holy See asking their support in the international condemnation of the Argentine invasion. . . .

Five ships have been requisitioned so far, the "Canberra", "Elk" and "Salvageman", "Irishman" and the "Yorkshireman"; further requisitions are likely. Compensation would be assessed and paid under sections 4 and 5 of the Compensation (Defence) Act 1939, and the provisions about tribunals in sections 7 and 8 of that Act would also apply if necessary.

[Written answers to questions were given by Mr. Wiggin, Mr. Pattie, Mr. Onslow and Mr. Pym.]

The Under-Secretary of State for the Armed Forces (Mr. Jerry Wiggin): . . . It can be stated that no members of the Argentine armed forces are currently receiving training with HM Forces. . . .

In addition to the six Argentine officers at the Argentine Embassy, and one Argentine naval officer attached to the Inter-Governmental Maritime Consultative Organisation, there were three Argentine naval officers, and one associated civilian, acting as technical representatives at Westlands Helicopters, Yeovil, in connection with the contract for the purchase of Lynx helicopters, and one lieutenant at the Admiralty surface weapons establishment in connection with the earlier work-up of type 42 frigates for Argentina. . . .

After trials in the United Kingdom the Argentine navy ships ARA "Hercules" and ARA "Santisima Trinidad" carried out sea training at

Portland in June 1976 and November 1981 respectively. Both ships also conducted demonstration trials of missiles at Aberporth.

Mr. Michael Grylls asked the Secretary of State for Defence if, in the light of recent developments, he will reconsider his proposals to sell HMS "Invincible" to the Australian Navy.

The Under-Secretary of State for Defence Procurement (Mr. Geoffrey Pattie): No. . . . HMS "Illustrious" is on sea trials and HMS "Ark Royal" is now building. Until HMS "Ark Royal" enters service HMS "Hermes" will run on.

Mr. Pym: In 1947 and subsequently the British Government offered to submit the dispute over the Dependencies to the International Court of Justice. In 1955 the Government approached the Court unilaterally. Argentina has refused to submit to the Court's jurisdiction on this issue.

The Minister of State, Foreign and Commonwealth Office (Mr. Cranley Onslow): As a geographical fact, there is of course already a median line between Argentina and the Falkland Islands. But no agreement has been reached between the United Kingdom and Argentine Governments on the delimitation of the zones within which each enjoys the economic rights of a coastal state in that area. In the absence of an agreed boundary, neither party, in Her Majesty's Government's view, would be entitled to exercise coastal State rights beyond the median line. . . .

Under the terms of the Continental Shelf Convention of 1958 and the applicable rules of international law, the United Kingdom has exclusive jurisdiction over the exploration and exploitation of the continental shelf areas adjacent to the Falkland Islands. Certain powers to license exploration and exploitation are conferred on the governor of the Falkland Islands under the Falkland Islands (Continental Shelf) Order in Council 1950 and the Falkland Islands Mining (Mineral Oil) Regulations of 1964.

Mr. Pym: At the time of the Argentine invasion of South Georgia there were 13 British Antarctic survey personnel at Grytviken, four at Bird Island, four at the Lyell Glacier hut, two at Schlieper Bay and three together with two wild life television film producers at St. Andrew's Bay. The position of those at Grytviken is not yet clear. Those at other places, according to our latest information, are safe and well. Further information is being sought urgently in order to arrange for the safe return of all concerned. . . .

There has been no evidence of intervention by the Argentine Government at any of the British Antarctic survey stations in the Antarctic Treaty area. All stations are continuing to pursue their normal scientific research programmes. There are 13 men at Signy, 13 at Faraday, 13 at Rothera and 19 at Halley.

Report Seven

14 APRIL 1982

On Wednesday 14 April the House was recalled from the Easter Recess for an emergency debate—debate number three.

The Prime Minister (Mrs. Margaret Thatcher): It is right at this time of grave concern over the Falkland Islands and their people, that Parliament should be recalled so that the Government may report and the House may discuss the latest developments.

Our objective, endorsed by all sides of the House in recent debates, is that the people of the Falkland Islands shall be free to determine their own way of life and their own future. The wishes of the islanders must be paramount. But they cannot be freely expressed, let alone implemented, while the present illegal Argentine occupation continues.

That is why our immediate goal in recent days has been to secure the withdrawal of all Argentine forces in accordance with resolution 502 of the United Nations Security Council and to secure the restoration of British administration. Our strategy has been based on a combination of diplomatic, military and economic pressures and I should like to deal with each of these in turn.

First of all, we seek a peaceful solution by diplomatic effort. This, too, is in accordance with the Security Council resolution. In this approach we have been helped by the widespread disapproval of the use of force which the Argentine aggression has aroused across the world, and also by the tireless efforts of Secretary of State Haig, who has now paid two visits to this country and one to Buenos Aires. . . .

We made clear to Mr. Haig that withdrawal of the invaders' troops must come first; that the sovereignty of the islands is not affected by the act of invasion; and that when it comes to future negotiations what matters most is what the Falkland Islanders themselves wish.

On his second visit on Easter Monday and yesterday, Mr. Haig put forward certain ideas as a basis for discussion—ideas concerning the withdrawal of troops and its supervision, and an interim period during which negotiations on the future of the islands would be conducted. Our talks were long and detailed, as the House would expect. Some things we could not consider because they flouted our basic principles. Others we had to examine carefully and suggest alternatives. The talks were constructive and some progress was made. At the end of Monday, Mr. Haig was prepared to return to Buenos Aires in pursuit of a peaceful solution.

Late that night, however, Argentina put forward to him other proposals which we could not possibly have accepted, but yesterday the position appeared to have eased. Further ideas are now being considered and Secretary Haig has returned to Washington before proceeding, he hopes shortly, to Buenos Aires. That meeting, in our view, will be crucial.

These discussions are complex, changing and difficult, the more so because they are taking place between a military junta and a democratic Government of a free people—one which is not prepared to compromise that democracy and that liberty which the British Falkland Islanders regard as their birthright.

We seek, and shall continue to seek, a diplomatic solution, and the House will realise that it would jeopardise that aim were I to give further details at this stage. Indeed, Secretary Haig has been scrupulous in his adherence to confidentiality in pursuit of the larger objective. We shall continue genuinely to negotiate through the good offices of Mr. Haig, to whose skill and perseverance I pay warm tribute.

Diplomatic efforts are more likely to succeed if they are backed by military strength. At 5 am London time on Monday 12 April, the maritime exclusion zone of 200 miles around the Falkland Islands came into effect. From that time any Argentine warships and Argentine naval auxiliaries found within this zone are treated as hostile and are liable to be attacked by British forces.

We see this measure as the first step towards achieving the withdrawal of Argentine forces. It appears to have exerted influence on Argentina, whose navy has been concentrated outside the zone. If the zone is challenged, we shall take that as the clearest evidence that the search for a peaceful solution has been abandoned. We shall then take the necessary action. Let no one doubt that.

The naval task force is proceeding with all speed towards the South Atlantic. It is a formidable force, comprising two aircraft carriers, five guided missile destroyers, seven frigates, an assault ship with five landing ships, together with supporting vessels. The composition of the force and the speed with which it was assembled and put to sea clearly demonstrate our determination.

Morale on board the ships in the task force is very high. The ships and aircraft are carrying out exercises on passage, and by the time the force arrives off the Falklands it will be at a very high state of fighting efficiency.

A number of civilian ships have now been chartered or requisitioned. These include the "Canberra" for use as a troop ship, and the "Uganda", which will be available as a hospital ship. Recourse to the merchant marine is traditional in time of naval emergency and its response has been wholehearted on this occasion as in the past.

Men and equipment continue to be flown out to Ascension Island to meet up with the task force. These additional elements will enhance the fighting capability of the force and the range of operations which can be undertaken. Nimrod maritime patrol aircraft are now patrolling the South Atlantic in support of our fleet.

Sustaining a substantial force 8,000 miles from the United Kingdom is a considerable undertaking. As the Ministry of Defence announced this morning, additional measures are now in hand to provide extra capability for the force over an extended period. In particular, the second assault ship, HMS "Intrepid", is being recommissioned for operational service. She will significantly add to the amphibious capability of the task force now entering the South Atlantic, which already contains her sister ship, HMS "Fearless".

Arrangements are in hand to adapt a large cargo ship for the sea lift of additional Harriers. This will nearly double the size of the Harrier force in the South Atlantic. All these aircraft have a formidable air combat and ground attack capability.

Our diplomacy is backed by strength, and we have the resolve to use that strength if necessary.

The third aspect of our pressure against Argentina has been economic. We have been urging our friends and allies to take action parallel to our own, and we have achieved a heartening degree of success. The most significant measure has been the decision of our nine partners in the European Community to join us not just in an arms embargo but also in stopping all imports from Argentina.

This is a very important step, unprecedented in its scope and the rapidity of the decision. Last year about a quarter of all Argentina's exports went to the European Community. The effect on Argentina's economy of this measure will therefore be considerable, and cannot be without influence on her leaders in the present crisis. I should like warmly to thank our European partners for rallying to our support. It was an effective demonstration of Community solidarity.

The decision cannot have been easy for our partners, given the commercial interests at stake, but they were the first to realise that if aggression were allowed to succeed in the Falkland Islands, it would be encouraged the world over.

Other friends, too, have been quick to help, and I should like to thank Australia, New Zealand and Canada for their sturdy and swift action. They have decided to ban imports from Argentina, to stop export credits and to halt all sales of military equipment. New Zealand has also banned exports to Argentina. We are grateful also to many other countries in the Commonwealth which have supported us by condemning the Argentine invasion.

What have the Argentines been able to produce to balance this solidarity in support of our cause? Some Latin American countries have, of course, repeated their support for the Argentine claim to sovereignty. We always knew they would. But only one of them has supported the Argentine invasion, and nearly all have made clear their distaste and disapproval that Argentina should have resorted to aggression.

Almost the only country whose position has been shifting towards Argentina is the Soviet Union. We can only guess at the cynical calculations which lie behind this move. But Soviet support for Argentina is hardly likely to shake the world's confidence in the justice of our cause and it will not alter our determination to achieve our objectives.

One of our first concerns has been and remains the safety of the British subjects who have been caught up in the consequences of the crisis. They include, apart from the Falkland Islanders themselves, the marines and the British Antarctic survey scientists on South Georgia and the British community in Argentina. In spite of all our efforts, we have not been able to secure reliable information about the 22 marines who were on South Georgia and the 13 British Antarctic survey personnel who are believed to have been evacuated from Grytviken at the same time.

According to Argentine reports these people are on a ship heading for the mainland. There are also reports that the six marines and the one member of the crew of "Endurance" who were captured on the Falkland Islands are now in Argentina.

Finally, there are 13 members of the British Antarctic survey team and two other British subjects who remain on South Georgia. The survey team's most recent contacts, on 12 April, with their headquarters in this country indicate that they are safe and well.

On 5 April, we asked the Swiss Government, as the protecting power, to pursue all these cases urgently with the Argentine Government. We trust that their efforts will soon produce the information which we and their families so anxiously seek.

On the same day we also sought the assistance of the International Red Cross with regard to the position of the population in the Falkland Islands. So far the Argentine Government have not responded to its request to visit the islands.

Last night, a party of 35 people from the islands, including the Chief Secretary, arrived in Montevideo and a report from the Chief Secretary on conditions in the islands is expected at any moment.

Recently the Government received a message from the British Community Council in Argentina urging a peaceful solution to the present conflict and asking that due consideration be given to the strong British presence in Argentina and the size of the British community there. We have replied, recognising the contribution which the British community has made to the development of Argentina—but making it plain that we have a duty to respond to the unprovoked aggression against the Falkland Islands and insisting that Argentina should comply with the mandatory resolution of the Security Council calling upon it to withdraw its troops.

Mr. Tam Dalyell (West Lothian): . . . Does the right hon. Lady not remember what happened to "Prince of Wales" and "Repulse"? Does she not know that there are at least 68 Skyhawks as well as the Mirages and R5-30s in the Argentine air force? That is a formidable force, if the task force is to go near the Falkland Islands. . . .

The Prime Minister: I have indicated to the hon. Member for West Lothian (Mr. Dalyell) and to the House that we have taken steps to double the provision of the Harriers. We believe that that will provide the air cover that the hon. Gentleman and the House seek. I trust that he and the House will express confidence in our naval, marine and air forces. That is what they are at least entitled to have from the House.

We are also being urged in some quarters to avoid armed confrontation at all costs, and to seek conciliation. Of course, we too want a peaceful solution, but it was not Britain who broke the peace. If the argument of no force at any price were to be adopted at this stage, it would serve only to perpetuate the occupation of those very territories which have themselves been seized by force.

In any negotiations over the coming days we shall be guided by the following principles. We shall continue to insist on Argentine withdrawal from the Falkland Islands and dependencies. We shall remain ready to exercise our right to resort to force in self-defence under article 51 of the United Nations charter until the occupying forces leave the islands. Our naval task force sails on towards its destination. We remain fully confident of its ability to take whatever measures may be necessary. Meanwhile, its very existence and its progress towards the Falkland Islands reinforce the efforts we are making for a diplomatic solution.

That solution must safeguard the principle that the wishes of the islanders shall remain paramount. There is no reason to believe that they would prefer any alternative to the resumption of the administration which they enjoyed before Argentina committed aggression. It may be that their recent experiences will have caused their views on the future to change, but until they have had the chance freely to express their views, the British Government will not assume that the islanders' wishes are different from what they were before.

We have a long and proud history of recognising the right of others to determine their own destiny. Indeed, in that respect, we have an experience unrivalled by any other nation in the world. But that right must be upheld universally, and not least where it is challenged by those who are hardly conspicuous for their own devotion to democracy and liberty.

The eyes of the world are now focused on the Falkland Islands. Others are watching anxiously to see whether brute force or the rule of law will triumph. Wherever naked aggression occurs it must be overcome. The cost now, however high, must be set against the cost we would one day have to pay if this principle went by default. That is why, through diplomatic, economic and, if necessary, through military means, we shall persevere until freedom and democracy are restored to the people of the Falkland Islands.

Mr. Michael Foot (Ebbw Vale): I thank the Prime Minister for responding to our request that Parliament should be recalled today. It was a wise decision and I thank the right hon. Lady for taking it. . . . We shall continue to act and respond in what we conceive to be the best interests of our country. Included high among those interests in this dispute is that the matter should be settled by peaceable means. The right hon. Lady has also declared her interest in that procedure. I believe that that is the overwhelming desire of the British people. The more that is understood throughout the world the better for us all.

Mr. Russell Johnston (Inverness): . . . If the Prime Minister invited the right hon. Member for Ebbw Vale (Mr. Foot) to have . . . discussions . . . would he agree to do so?

Mr. Foot: I would wish to see the circumstances. That has been the position in the House for a long time. That has been the position of Opposition parties in previous circumstances. . . . We shall make our response in the best interests of what we consider to be serving the country and enabling us to achieve the purposes that have been commonly described. . . .

The aggression occurred some time ago but that does not make the aggression any better. It does not mean that we should in any sense forget the origin of the crisis. It was an unprovoked aggression. That is why the problem has arisen and until that is dealt with properly it will remain a major factor in the situation. We certainly do not wish anyone to disguise that fact.

Another pre-eminent aspect is the threat to the United Nations charter and the influence that that charter may have throughout the world. It is that charter that is attacked. It is a resolution of the United Nations that calls upon the Argentine to withdraw its assault. It is that charter, and the United Nations as an institution, which are under threat. That is a matter of major importance in the crisis but it is not only the United Nations charter that is involved.

There is also an Organisation of American States, which has a definition of what aggression is or can be. . . .

There is no part of the world where a recrudescence of international anarchy in the sense of aggression being allowed to be undertaken with impunity would cause such dangerous results as in Central and South America. . . .

I hope that one of the longer-term outcomes of this crisis, once it is satisfactorily settled, is that the British Government, the United States Government and all the Governments concerned will look into the whole question of the supply of arms to these different States to see how the unrestrained, or scarcely restrained, supply of arms to these States has contributed to the crisis.

There is no part of the world where there is a greater danger from unprovoked aggression being allowed to proceed with impunity than in Central and South America. I believe that the Government are right and the British people are right to act on that principle.

It is partly because I subscribe to that principle that I support the despatch of the task force. I support it because I believe that it can have strong diplomatic results. . . .

If there were no task force, I do not believe that there would have been any prospect of negotiations with the junta in the Argentine. If any of my hon. Friends, or anyone else, were to say that this is not the case, I would say that I think they put too great a store on General Galtieri's good nature. I have no great faith in that. I believe that there has to be a combination of pressures. If, at the time of the despatch of the task force or subsequently, there were to have been strong opposition in this country represented by the Labour Party to the despatch of that force, my fear is that one of the consequences would have been to injure at least the world-wide support that we have received. It was of absolutely major importance, in the interests of the peaceable settlement of this dispute, that we should sustain in the highest degree the support that we have received from so many countries. . . .

I acknowledge fully the tribute that the Prime Minister has paid to General Haig. All hon. Members must understand the appalling personal pressures under which he must have been placed by the service that he has done. We must, however, say to General Haig and to his Government that we believe that the case about aggression is clear. We believe that the vote of the United States at the United Nations was clear, as indeed was the vote of many other nations. Those votes, we believe, must be carried into effect. I am not seeking to detract from the efforts that General Haig has made and is still making to secure a settlement. I am not seeking to diminish them. That would be foolish. They are, however, not the only propositions for trying to secure a peaceable settlement. There was the proposal from the Peruvian Government for a "holdfire" or whatever term was used. At any rate, there was a proposal that I presume was made in good faith for trying to ensure more time for solving the matter. Even if the latest proposals from the American Administration do not succeed—I am not hoping that this will happen—it will not be the final failure. We must go on again and again seeking the peaceable method of settling this dispute. The other forms that are not exhausted include the United Nations itself. It has means whereby we can look afresh at the matter.

I was eager at the beginning that this matter should be taken to the United Nations. It was proved to be right that we should have done so. It was right for the way in which the matter was presented. I congratulate the spokesman of this country who put his case there so effectively. It was the case itself, I believe, that enabled him to succeed. But we can go back at some stage—I do not say immediately—to the United Nations. We can prove to the whole world the simple truth that this country is not only determined to protect the rights of its people against aggression but that we seek to deal with these grave matters by the most peaceable means that are available to us. Anyone in the world who puts a different construction on what is happening misconstrues the real nature of what this country wishes to secure from the dispute. . . .

The right hon. Lady has referred to the crucial meeting that might take place when Mr. Haig goes to Buenos Aires. It may well be crucial, but that does not mean final, and I repeat that there are still other possibilities in the search for peace and in the attempt to re-establish the rights that the right hon. Lady fairly described at the beginning of her speech.

I hope that out of this tragic and peculiar affair there may come a fresh vindication of the United Nations charter and a fresh vindication of the idea that no nation should resort to force or seek to establish its way through aggression against other nations. We can all live in a safer world if that principle is established. We can all live in a safer world if we uphold the doctrine that it is better for the people of the world to know that Britain keeps its word. The peace of the world has been assisted by that doctrine in the past, and I believe that it can be assisted by it in the present circumstances. I do not think that we need any further history lessons in that regard.

We can play our best part in the dispute by the firmness with which we oppose the aggression and by the intelligence, the skill and determination with which we pursue peaceful methods of solution. By that combination we can live up to the highest ideals of Britain and make a contribution, not merely to the safety, the security and well-being of the Falkland Islanders, but to that of many other peoples, and in particular many small nations throughout the world. . . .

Dr. David Owen (Plymouth, Devonport): The House has just listened to a speech from the Leader of the official Opposition with which I do not disagree in any particular. I pay tribute to what the right hon. Member for Ebbw Vale (Mr. Foot) has said, because I think that he has spoken for the whole House. He has not sought in his speech in any way to embarrass the Government in their negotiating position. . . .

I believe that two messages will go out from the House as a result of the debate. There will be a reaffirmation—if it needs to be made—that we are resolute in our resistance to any form of armed aggression, and that we are persistent and steady in our pursuit of peace. I believe that it is right that the Government—not yet able to come forward with a proposition for a peaceful and negotiated settlement—should continue with the deployment of the naval and marine forces. No one should weaken our negotiating position by casting doubt as to the length of time or as to our intention to see the issue through. . . .

We have made it very clear on many occasions that our retention of the administration and sovereignty of the Falkland Islands does not relate to the possibility of there being gas or oil in the region. We are not there for a commercial purpose. We are not balancing up whether there is a positive or a negative trade. We are there because the islanders, successively through their Legislative Council, have made it clear that they wish us to be there. That is the issue which I, with the right hon. Member for Ebbw Vale, believe will be upheld within the United Nations. . . .

The United Nations must be the protector of the small countries. There are now—often as a result of British decolonisation—many very small independent States. They are watching with great anxiety what is happening in the Falkland Islands. If the interests of the Falkland Islands were to be ridden over roughshod, it would be extremely damaging to world security.

Mr. Dalyell: If what the right hon. Gentleman says about the United Nations is true, why is it not a United Nations task force but a British task force that is on its way to the Falklands?

Dr. Owen: The day may come when the United Nations will seek the power to enforce peace around the world. As the hon. Gentleman knows, the original charter envisaged a much more active role for the United Nations than it has been able to play. At the time of the formation of the military committee in 1945, it was envisaged that the United Nations would not only be able to despatch peacekeeping forces after the event, but that it would be able to take action prior to an aggression.

I believe that what has happened in recent years—and in particular what is now happening in the Falklands—may result in authority beginning to come back to the United Nations as more and more in an interrelated world it is realised that national Governments are not capable of ensuring international security. But it is at this stage a fact of life that a United Nations peacekeeping force could not be mobilised, and the charter envisages the right of an independent nation to use all peaceful means to defend its interests. It is purely and rightly within the context of the United Nations charter that the British peacekeeping force has been despatched. We are upholding a democratic right in so doing.

The response of our allies and friends has given us great comfort. I pay tribute to the work that has been done by Secretary of State Haig. The United States is in a crucial position. . . . Obviously, it does not wish to be provocative to one side, but it has to be said—I believe that it is well understood by Secretary of State Haig and, I hope, by the entire United States Administration—that the United States cannot be neutral on the question of aggression. One cannot be neutral as between a fire and a fire brigade. . . .

We have learnt lessons in this House from history. No one can draw too many parallels, but one thing that we do know is that weakness in the face of aggression only increases the appetite. . . .

Therefore, we are upholding not some minor issue 7,000 miles away from our shores but a fundamental issue, and we are showing, perhaps above all, the readiness of a major nation to negotiate for peace. I suspect that some compromises will be necessary from every hon. Member before a peaceful solution is achieved. It would be wrong to go to the international community with an image that we are so resolute that we are not prepared to look at any concessions or at any necessary face-saving arrangements. . . .

On the fundamental principles there is no shift in our position. We are with the Government.

Sir Philip Goodhart (Beckenham): . . . It would be wrong . . . to think that British and American interests in this dispute are identical. The Americans have a general interest in seeing that aggression is stopped. . . . Our legal interest is the greater, but paradoxically the strategic interest of the United States in the area is infinitely greater than our own. . . .

When the present crisis has been resolved I do not think that this country should be committed indefinitely to keeping a major naval presence close to the Falkland Islands, but it is now quite plain that the Western Alliance must have some secure naval and air facilities in the South Atlantic. It is plain that NATO as a whole will never agree to an out-of-area presence. Facilities can be provided only by ourselves, with, I would hope, the assistance of the United States and Canada— and, conceivably, eventually, Argentina. After all, we have no quarrel with the Argentine people. . . .

I join in the congratulations given to those who have been responsible for organising the task force. As *The Times* rightly said, it was an astonishing achievement. The more that one knows about the problem of mobilisation, the more astonishing it seems. . . .

The speed with which the Fleet has set sail has had important diplomatic repercussions. As the Leader of the Opposition said, if the task force had not sailed, it is doubtful whether those in Buenos Aires would be willing to talk. If we had been as dilatory as we were at Suez, other Governments would have been given the opportunity to forget that there is only one reason for this crisis, which is that there has been aggression. All concerned in the Royal Navy deserve our congratulations, and the Government deserve our continued support.

Mr. J. Enoch Powell (Down, South): Given the initial failure, which we do not yet fully understand, to anticipate and therefore to frustrate the invasion of the Falkland Islands, it is difficult to fault the military and especially the naval measures which the Government have taken. . . .

It would be deluding ourselves if we imagined that, the islands being . . . invested and a substantial fleet being present in those waters, matters could then continue indefinitely without change. There would come a point at which further action became necessary to repossess the islands. But, at any rate for a matter of days, I do not think that that is the event that we need envisage. There are, however, imminent and present dangers . . . —dangers of a political character—which are with us now. . . .

We are in some danger of resting our position too exclusively upon the existence, the nature and the wishes of the inhabitants of the Falkland Islands. Quite obviously, if the population of the Falkland Islands did not desire to be British, the principle that the Queen wishes no unwilling subjects would long ago have prevailed; but we should create great difficulties for ourselves in other contexts, as well as in this context, if we rested our action purely and exclusively on the notion of restoring tolerable, acceptable conditions and self-determination to our fellow Britons on the Falkland Islands. Logically, this would mean that, had the Falkland Islands perchance been uninhabited, we would not have been justified in resenting and repelling armed aggression against our territory. It would mean, presumably, that if another flag were flown from Rockall, that would be a matter of indifference to us. Coming nearer to the Falkland Islands, it would mean that, since South Georgia is not permanently inhabited and since British Antarctica . . . is inhabited principally by penguins, we would stand idly by when a similar unprovoked and unjustified act of piracy was committed upon those territories.

I do not think that we need be too nice about saying that we defend our territory as well as our people. There is nothing irrational, nothing to be ashamed of, in doing that. Indeed, it is impossible in the last resort to distinguish between the defence of territory and the defence of people. . . .

[The Security Council resolution cannot mean] that one country has only to seize the territory of another country for the nations of the world to say that some middle position must be found between the two parties, that some compromise must be the object of diplomacy, some formula that takes account of the objects and interests of the aggressor as well as of those of the aggressed.

If that were the meaning of the resolution of the Security Council, the charter of the United Nations would not be a charter of peace; it would be a pirates' charter. It would mean that any claim anywhere in the world had only to be pursued by force, and points would immediately be gained and a bargaining position established by the aggressor. . . .

I hope it will be made clear that what we seek is the reversal by peaceful means, by diplomatic and other pressures, if that can be brought about, of the aggression upon our territory, but that we seek no compromise, no diminution of our undoubted rights. By maintaining that position we shall do no harm to all those interests, which the right hon. Gentleman the Leader of the Opposition so eloquently displayed, not only of this country but of the world at large. We should rather injure them if it were thought that aggression in itself could put some new complexion upon our rights and upon our duties.

Dame Judith Hart (Lanark): . . . I have listened with the keenest interest to the Prime Minister and to my right hon. Friend the Leader of the Opposition, than whom, in the whole of his history and in the history of this House, there has been no greater man of peace . . . I should first like to express where I am in no disagreement whatever with anything so far said in the debate by the Prime Minister or by my right hon. Friend.

First, we are all agreed, I think, that there has been an act of intolerable aggression by Argentina against the Falkland Islands; secondly, we are all agreed that the Argentine Government are a particularly brutal and nasty Fascist regime. . . .

Thirdly . . . the interests of the Falkland Islanders must be at the very front of our minds. The Prime Minister talked about their need to have freedom to express their views, and she was absolutely right to say so. Fourthly, we are all agreed that we must all observe the United Nations resolution calling for an immediate withdrawal of all Argentine forces from the territory, for an immediate cessation of hostilities in the region of the Falkland Islands—that is a very significant phrase of which we need to take very careful note—and for Argentina and the United Kingdom to seek a diplomatic solution to their differences. . . .

I think that we are also agreed that no one in this House wants a war. . . . In pursuing one's rights one has a responsibility towards peace that we here in Britain should be able to exercise with the deepest care. . . .

The negotiations undertaken by Secretary of State Haig and the proposals made by members of the United Nations, from Peru and other sources, have not yielded any diplomatic solution that at this moment could prevent a war. More time is needed for the first stage, for clearly there are two stages. The first is the establishment of peaceful negotiation to prevent a war. The second is the negotiation of a longer-term solution that will meet the needs of the Falkland Islanders. As the Prime Minster said, the people of the Falkland Islands must have freedom to express their choice. . . .

The crucial need is therefore for a pause for peace, so that there may be more breathing space for negotiations. That means, in my view, that at this stage we should not retreat but halt the task force and allow time for negotiations. I am well aware that I express a minority view in the House, but that will not prevent me, as it has not prevented a number of hon. Members in years past, from expressing a personal view. I believe that we should now halt the task force and suspend the "shoot first" maxim of the Secretary of State for Defence so that there is time to negotiate a settlement that will prevent war. . . .

The consequences of a shooting war would not serve the interests of our people or of the Falkland Islanders, who should be our prime concern. Nor would they serve the long-term interests of the United Nations in ensuring that, wherever possible, peaceful solutions are found to international disputes and international aggression.

We need a pause for peace—and it should start now.

Mr. Michael Shersby (Uxbridge): . . . I speak today on behalf of many Falkland Islanders whom I had the privilege to meet last September, when, with the hon. Member for Liverpool, West Derby (Mr. Ogden), I spent two weeks in the Falkland Islands meeting a large number of the inhabitants. We were there as a Commonwealth Parliamentary Association delegation visiting the Falkland Island branch. Our job was to talk to the islanders and to ascertain their views about the constitutional dispute with the Argentine, and at the same time to reassure them that this Parliament cared about them and that we would support them if difficulties arose in the future. . . .

The hon. Member for West Derby and I were left in no doubt as to what the people wanted. They wanted to continue their peaceful life as loyal subjects of the Crown. They were deeply concerned about the future and the discussions about Britain and the Argentine that have been taking place for many years and involve the possibility of ceding sovereignty to Argentina and the possibility of a condominium. . . .

Nevertheless, we all hope and pray that armed confrontation can be avoided and that diplomatic solutions can be found. . . .

Had we tried a little harder a little earlier, perhaps with international guarantees from three or four powerful countries, it might have been possible to put at rest the Falkland Islanders' minds and to have achieved a lease-back solution. That would have had the advantage of ensuring that British rule continued along with the British way of life and that our people would have felt safe under the British Crown. For the Argentine, it would have meant that its long-held views, and tremendously strong emotive feeling, that the Falkland Islands are part of its territory, would have been met by the ceding of titular sovereignty. Such an agreement would have offered both the Argentine people and the Falkland Islanders considerable opportunities for economic development, oil exploration, trade and tourism. However, guarantees would have been needed to the effect that under no possible circumstances could an invasion have taken place. That would have meant that HMS "Endurance", and undoubtedly some other tangible evidence of Britain's intention to protect her people, would have had to remain off the Falkland Islands and in the South Atlantic for the foreseeable future. . . .

All hon. Members present today must recognise that the Falkland Islands are 8,500 miles from Britain. The only method of air communication with them is through the South American continent–through Argentina or perhaps Chile. In the long term we must try to restore the relations that have become strained by this tragic situation.

I back the policy of Her Majesty's Government 100 per cent. as it was expressed by my right hon. Friend the Prime Minister this afternoon. Argentina must withdraw from the Falkland Islands. The authority of the United Nations must be seen to run in those islands, as anywhere else in the world. If we do not see British administration restored to the Falkland Islands, the future for our people there and for other territories round the world in a similar position is indeed bleak.

Many of those brave people in the Falkland Islands are sixth generation British subjects. They believe that Britain will do its duty. I know that they will take heart from what they hear from the House this afternoon. It will bring them great comfort in their hour of trial. They will know that we shall never abandon them.

Mr. A. E. P. Duffy (Sheffield, Attercliffe): The whole affair over the last fortnight remains a salutary lesson in the nature of power in the modern world. It is easy to shrink—as I perceive that some hon. Members do—from the logic of our possession of that power and to call for a halt to the exercise of such power. It is much more difficult to close one's mind and eyes, after nearly a fortnight, to the obvious lesson of last Friday week's invasion. In the end, one cannot negotiate successfully from a position of weakness, especially when dealing with the present rulers in Buenos Aires, who are, after all, as my right hon. Friend the Leader of the Opposition reminded us, the scourge of democrats and trade unionists and of the peace of mind of their neighbours.

Another unpalatable lesson for some hon. Members is that the Argentine Government undoubtedly believed that they had achieved a fait accompli. The logic of that situation is that if the Argentines knew that nothing could happen to them, they were hardly likely to entertain the idea of compromise. We can all see now that on the surface in Buenos Aires words may be as resolute as ever. There has certainly been movement behind the scenes. That undoubtedly justifies the sailing of the task force.

Given our responsibilities to the Falkland Islanders, as well as to the United Nations and to the international rule of law—as my right hon. Friend the Leader of the Opposition argued so powerfully a few minutes ago—somehow, some time, the Argentine forces must be induced or forced to leave the Falklands. I say that in those terms because I do not believe that it is just our responsibility. As my right hon. Friend reminded us, it is the responsibility of all those who care for the rule of law and who are aware of the risks that we run in its disregard and of the penalties that we have paid in times gone by.

I believe that the House is united in its belief that diplomacy must be given the first chance. The friends of Britain and the Argentine must exhaust every opportunity of organising negotiations, of giving constructive advice, of cajoling and of warning by turn to propagate the cause of peace. . . .

We are on the soundest moral ground, but we must stay there. The United Nations is a forum for both sides and obviously it must continue to be used in full.

We are fortunate in having the EEC's backing, but I suspect that it wants not only to provide us with support but to act as a restraining force on any over-adventurousness on our part. . . .

We cannot look for a peaceful settlement or expect the Argentines to withdraw—even in the face of force—unless we offer them some inducement. Therefore, the first condition is that we all accept, in our hearts, that there is an Argentine dimension to the Falkland Islands. We must, therefore, give an early indication that we are prepared actively to explore its implications. As soon as circumstances permit, we must urgently seek agreement. Options that have already been mentioned will then be open to us. Any such proposals should involve, as a condition, a commitment to sound out the Falkland Islanders about the future that they would wish. . . .

In this crisis, the Royal Navy must know that it has the fullest support of the House and of the British people. On the Saturday before last that support rang out loud and clear. I hope that it will continue to ring out loud and clear. . . .

I know that the Fleet is worthy of our support. I hope that we shall stay worthy of the Fleet.

Mr. Michael McNair-Wilson (Newbury): . . . We all recognise that force will be the counsel of last resort in solving this crisis, but because at least I hold that view, following the mandatory resolution of the Security Council, which tries to persuade the Argentines to withdraw from the Falkland Islands, it also follows that that mandatory resolution must be backed up by further action from the Security Council. Although I welcome all statements of unilateral sanctions being imposed against Argentina, I cannot help but feel that that is not as impressive or as likely to be persuasive to the Argentine Government as sanctions imposed by the Security Council. To that extent, the concept of mandatory sanctions passed by that body should be the next step in New York. . . .

Those who live on the islands should make their views known and those who have an interest in the islands—whether they be in the United Kingdom, Argentina or, dare I say, the United Nations—should pay due respect to the views expressed. . . .

It follows that if the Argentines really wish a resolution of the Falkland Islands dispute, it is as much in their interests as in ours that the islanders give an answer that can be respected by either party.

I was glad that my right hon. Friend the Prime Minister referred three times in her speech to the right of the islanders to be free to determine their own way of life. . . .

If the Argentines believed that their aggression would present Her Majesty's Government with a fait accompli to which they would not react, clearly they sadly misjudged the reaction of a democratic Government who have responsibilities that they intend to carry out for the sovereign parts of their territory. Perhaps all dictatorships are likely to make such a mistake, so none of us should be surprised. However, the Argentine Government must now recognise their miscalculation. Whether they recognise it from the words used in this House or whether they choose to recognise it from the United Nations Security Council or the EEC, it is there, written for them all to see and hear, from three great bodies with international responsibilities. . . .

Whatever decision we make, it is surely unrealistic to talk about the next steps until the Argentines withdraw and it is unrealistic for the Argentines to believe that might will succeed when nearly all the world is against them.

I continue to support the Government's original recourse to the Security Council and its endorsement that Argentina must withdraw. I see the task force as a follow-through to resolution 502. . . .

None of us wants bloodshed over this intractable problem, but none of us can flinch from that possibility in a crisis of this magnitude. To do so would be to give way to aggression and to renege upon the concept of self-determination which we have all held so important for so long. Lastly, it would be to undermine the United Nations, which in future may be a more important body than it has been in the past.

Miss Betty Boothroyd (West Bromwich, West): . . . The majority of the British people believe and accept that the task force was a correct initial response to the invasion. I believe also that those self-same people do not give that support wholly without conditions. . . . What is now needed is for new initiatives to justify the support of the British people and to justify the support of the actions taken by and the decisions arrived at by the international community. . . .

The Foreign Secretary said that we shall need the support of the world community. We have that support but it is not sufficient to chalk it up on a scoreboard. It is not sufficient merely to obtain the approval of international bodies. We must justify that approval by seeking to implement the United Nations resolution, by exploring the possibilities of a role that the United Nations may be able to adopt as a mediator and in providing a mechanism whereby Argentina can be assisted to move off the hook of the Government's earlier arguments about sovereignty.

I have always believed that if statesmanship means anything it places demands on those who regard themselves as statesmen. It demands that those who aggress sometimes need to be provided with a face-saving formula; they sometimes need to be provided with an opportunity to retreat without loss of face. If we believe in the rule of law, we must develop our actions in concert with the United Nations charter, to which we have been committed for many years.

The Government have demonstrated that they have the military force. They have demonstrated that there is a will to use it. They must now demonstrate their belief in the rule of law and must put that belief into practice. They must be prepared to examine and contemplate a range of solutions and take some initiatives in presenting them. . . .

The offices of the United Nations may have to be involved in seeking a withdrawal of both Argentine and British defence personnel and administrative personnel from the entire area. We may have to examine the possibility of filling the vacuum with a United Nations peacekeeping force, which would administer the islands until such time as a more permanent solution could be found.

We may have to refer the issues to the International Court so that it may state its views of the future of the islands. . . . We cannot turn back the clock. I believe that the islanders are aware of that. They must be aware that we cannot provide a large and permanent military and naval presence in the area and that things will never be the same again in that part of the world. . . .

The islanders may be more realistic about a negotiated settlement and about how they see their future than perhaps some of us give them credit for. Let us not be more aggressive in seeking their protection than the islanders themselves would be. We must be honest with the islanders about what they can expect. The time has not come for appeasement. The Government have shown their potential military and naval strength. However, the time has come to try to implement the solidarity which has been demonstrated to us by world opinion. We should, perhaps, use the United Nations to explore all the possibilities that may bring a solution to the area—not through continued aggression or military might, but through the rule of law to which this country and this House are firmly committed.

Mr. Russell Johnston (Inverness): In our first debate on 3 April, the day after the invasion, much was properly made of the fact that during the past few years we have been giving signs to Argentina of a lack of commitment to the Falkland Islands. . . . The consequent invasion could almost be seen by Argentina as a move which would be greeted with a sigh of relief in this country—admittedly suitably concealed with expressions of indignation, but a sigh of relief nevertheless—rather than the genuine outrage which has been expressed by both sides of the House and by the country as a whole which led to the support for the despatch of our Fleet. . . .

Force has been used against us, but no one wants to see force used in response, as was said by many hon. Members. Equally, if we must use force, it must be the minimum necessary.

I would briefly put on record . . . our gratitude and pleasure at the firm and united response from our European Community partners in immediately instituting economic sanctions at considerable cost to themselves. Critics of the Community should recognise how greatly this strengthens our position. However, I should like the Government to say how rapidly those measures will be implemented. . . .

In conjunction with that, while Mr. Haig's efforts and the way in which he has acted are greatly to be commended, one cannot let pass President Reagan's reference to an even-handed attitude being necessary between two friends of the United States, or the even more unfortunate remarks of Mrs. Fitzgerald, the United States' representative at the United Nations. Many hon. Members have already said that the United States must be informed that one cannot be even-handed between an aggressor and his victim. . . .

Sovereignty is what the Falkland Islanders want. They want the continuing sovereignty of the British crown. They regard that as the best safeguard for their welfare. . . .

In talking of options, whether condominiums, leasebacks, or United Nations trusteeship, we are in logic saying that we cannot sustain the position indefinitely if we are to be faced indefinitely with the hostility of the Argentine and the possibility of further aggression at some unpredictable time or times in the future. If options are to be debated . . . we should not seek to cloak them with verbiage about diplomacy, equable solutions and just compromises, and so on. . . .

I firmly stress that the principle of self-determination must be upheld, and the trust of the Falkland Islanders must not be betrayed by this country. . . .

Our prayers must be with the Falkland Islanders in the dreadful circumstances that they now face.

Mr. Hal Miller (Bromsgrove and Redditch): . . . I have a deep sense of outrage at the violent aggression on a British colony and a burning sense of shame that we were unable to protect, and do our duty by, the inhabitants and the British citizens of that territory.

I am therefore grateful to my former Colonial Service colleague, the hon. Member for Shoreham (Mr. Luce), for his courage in resigning and for the dignified speech that he made to the House on that occasion, on which he deserves sincere congratulations. My hon. Friend and his more senior colleagues will be a great loss to the Administration, but I am sure that his chance will come again to offer distinguished service. . . .

My right hon. Friend the Foreign Secretary . . . has said that the wishes of the islanders will be dominant. Have we the right to be confident of their decision? . . .

What have we done to earn the continued confidence of the Falkland Islanders, and what do we now propose? It is not enough just to restore British administration and to regain our effective sovereignty over the islands. . . .

We cannot go back to the status quo ante. What is being offered to the Falkland Islanders? In considering that, we must recall the signals that we have given in the past.

I am ashamed to say that we have a record of neglect of the islands. We have provided them with inadequate communications. Indeed, the airstrip was adequate only for service from the Argentine. Their oil supplies come from the Argentine. It even appears that at the crucial moment in the invasion the transmitters were inadequate to impart the information. If we were embarked on a high risk policy ever since we gave up maintaining a South Atlantic squadron, at least we should have ensured that there was adequate communication so that we could be constantly aware of what was taking place. . . .

We should not blind ourselves to the strategic importance of the islands. It is highly significant that units of the Soviet Navy are already present in the area.

It is not enough for us to seek to determine the views of the islanders. We must have something to offer them. That is the course that I counsel most earnestly on my right hon. Friend. I urge him constantly to pursue the withdrawal of the Argentines in accordance with United Nations resolution 502.

I do not shrink from force, if necessary, but the restoration of Pax

Britannica by itself is not enough. May we please have some positive plans for the future?

Mr. Peter Hardy (Rother Valley): . . . I hope that at the end of this unhappy chapter there can be an improving quality of life for the people in the Falkland Islands.

At the outset, it is clear that one of two Governments are at risk—either the Government here or that in Buenos Aires. My hon. Friends and I have very little cause to admire the present Administration here, but in the national interest and to avoid further international ignominy one hopes that the Buenos Aires Government collapses rather than ours. It was interesting that recently the Prime Minister recognised the nature of the regime in Buenos Aires. As some of my hon. Friends have pointed out, it is perhaps a pity that she did not do so earlier.

Whether or not the Buenos Aires Administration collapses, it is clear that, while the Government have given a commitment that there will be an inquiry, that inquiry will have to be very searching if it is to satisfy the British people. . . .

South Georgia is as far away from the Argentine as Athens is from the United Kingdom. From the United Kingdom to Warsaw is only two-thirds of the distance from the Argentine coast to South Georgia. Therefore, the Argentine claim to South Georgia is even more questionable than its claim to the Falkland Islands. While the Falkland Islands are much closer to the Argentine than to Britain, they are as far away from the nearest point on the Argentine coast as the Swiss border or, indeed, the Norwegian border is from Westminster. Our friends in Norway have as much entitlement to invade Iceland—indeed, the Irish Republic has much more entitlement to invade the Shetlands—as has any Argentine general to invade the Falkland Islands.

My right hon. Friends are correct to suggest that the Government cannot look idly at this aggressive invasion. We should not enter war lightly. I hope that the orders to fire that will be given by the Prime Minister will not be swiftly given, so that there can be time for negotiation. However, given the importance, investment and interest in the Antarctic throughout the past 100 years—Britain has led the world in Antarctic development—and given the important minerals and oil that may be available in Antarctica, it would be highly undesirable for us to allow 1,800 Falkland Islanders to decide by referendum that territory in South Georgia or the South Sandwich Islands could be lightly given away.

We must consider the question of territory as well as the question of people. One hopes that the future of the islands will be well served by an Administration . . .

The Government have brought about a considerable humiliation for Britain. That has had the unfortunate result of arousing a degree of jingoism in Britain that is hardly appropriate to the twentieth century. But the fact remains that, if the task force does not continue to sail, the Government will have surrendered an opportunity to serve principle and international decency. For that reason, my support continues to go with Her Majesty's Navy.

Mr. John Stokes (Halesowen and Stourbridge): . . . It is of course

89

right that we have been recalled again today and it is right that we should be kept informed by Her Majesty's Government about what is happening. . . .

Our vital role is to express the will of the nation as we understand it and, on this occasion, to give our unstinted backing to my right hon. Friend the Secretary of State for Foreign and Commonwealth Affairs and to the Government. The nation expects us to meet when there is a crisis. People somehow feel better when they know that Parliament is sitting. I was told that the crowds outside the Houses of Parliament on the last special sitting on Saturday were the largest since the abdication crisis of 1936. May we live up to the high regard in which, apparently, the public hold us.

I consider that our main role today is to represent the wishes and feelings of our constituents—which are that the Government should see this matter through to the end. That is the message that I am receiving loud and clear from my constituents, and I believe many other colleagues have had the same experience. That means that the Argentine must remove its troops from the Falkland Islands before we can enter into negotiations. We can then have perfectly sensible and reasonable negotiations.

The nation is quite remarkably united at present. All the previous conflicts that seem to have divided us appear to have faded into the distance. . . . We have now national unity and cohesion in Britain which is something precious and not, I hope, to be lost. That is not to say that the nation yet realises how long and protracted the struggle may be; nor are some people yet ready to accept that if we have to fight it is inevitable that some British blood will be spilt. We may face some very difficult weeks or even months. As we know from our long history, blockade is, in essence, a slow business. . . .

We have many cards in our hands. Our cause is self-evidently just. We are supported by a resolution of the Security Council of the United Nations and we have received remarkably strong support from the EEC. I hope that some of those who are invariably critical—I am sometimes critical—of the EEC will think that this must be its finest hour.

We must never forget that Soviet Russia—not the Argentine, and certainly not the people of the Argentine, with whom we have the friendliest relations—presents the greatest threat to us. The decision to stand and, if necessary, to fight is not just about the Falkland Islands, about their 1,800 inhabitants, or about the possibility of finding oil and gas in the South Antarctic. It is a question of national will. The answer that we give will be noted not only in Gibraltar and in Hong Kong but in West Berlin and wherever the West may be threatened. Soviet Russia, above all, is watching on the sidelines. The successful resolution of this conflict will not be lost on it.

There is little point at this time in worrying in too much detail about what form the eventual negotiations will take. The wishes of the Falklanders are of the highest importance, as will be the desires of the British Government and our people. Meanwhile, the Argentine troops must be removed from the islands—by diplomacy we hope, by total blockade, possibly, and, if not, and finally, by all means of force, difficult and bloody though that may be. . . .

I find that the nation, as a whole, is remarkably calm and resolute and that it trusts the Government to see this matter through to the end. I am sure that they will.

Mr. Alexander W. Lyon (York): . . . I confess that for the last fortnight I have been racked by a real feeling of conscience about what is right and what is wrong in this situation. If I speak in a manner that is out of sympathy with the consensus that has emerged in the House, it is not because I have any disrespect for the judgment or experience of many hon. Members who have spoken in a contrary sense.

If the Fleet gets to the Falkland Islands and by that time the Argentines have withdrawn from the islands and there is a settlement that is acceptable to the Falkland Islanders and to the Argentine, no one will breathe a greater sigh of relief than myself. I am bound to say, however, that in questioning the consensus that has emerged here I find it almost impossible to believe that such a situation awaits our Fleet when we get to the destination. . . .

It may well be the intention of Her Majesty's Ministers at the moment simply to surround the islands in such a way that they cannot be easily provisioned from the sea. All the indications are that the islands are capable of withstanding such a blockade for some considerable time. We know that the airfield is sufficiently intact for the islands to be provisioned by air. In those circumstances, the question that arises, if the Government are serious that they will not negotiate about the future status of the Falkland Islands unless the Argentines withdraw, is whether we are committed to anything short of bloodshed and war. I find that a horrifying prospect. . . .

The idea that we should shed blood over this issue tends to transcend the principles inherent in it. . . .

To assert that the issues of a number of islands, the remainder of our colonies around the world, are to be determined simply by the will of the inhabitants of those islands is a wholly unrealistic principle. To allege that the right of a people to decide whether they want to be an independent country is the same as the right of a small island that cannot be an independent country, because it is not viable as a country, to assert that it should remain part of the British Commonwealth as a colony seems wholly unrealistic in relation to some of the areas that we are discussing.

There are not only the Falkland Islands; there is Gibraltar. If the facts of the situation suggest that the islands are within the economic area of a larger territory which has always regarded them as its own, it is difficult for us, approaching the twenty-first century, to go on asserting that they are British and that they have the right to remain British because their people claim that that should be so. . . .

It is not enough to say, as some of my colleagues have said, that this is a Fascist dictatorship and that therefore we should not give any consideration to its claim upon the Falkland Islands. If that be the case—I recognise that most hon. Members see it differently—I do not find it easy to say that we should shed the blood of Britons or Argentines in seeking a settlement when the reality, in my judgment, is that the Falkland Islands ought to go back to the Argentine. . . .

I feel immense sympathy with the 1,800 inhabitants of the Falkland Islands, who are not Argentines, do not speak Spanish, do not have a Spanish culture and do not want to be part of the Argentine. I would certainly make provision, in any settlement, for them to have the right to come and live in Britain if they wanted to do so, but what I would not say is that they have a right to determine whether we shall, in pursuance of their right to self-determination, expend not only money, ships and aeroplanes but people's lives in order to ensure that the 1,800 islanders are entitled to maintain the way of life that they already have. . . .

I ask what will happen if and when the Chinese occupy Hong Kong. It is, of course, true that the New Territories are on lease and will go back to China at the end of the lease, but the island is British. . . .

I do not believe that we can reoccupy the islands and drive the Argentines back to Argentina—but it is a wholly different thing to presume that from now until the Falkland Islanders change their view of the situation we can police the area in a way that will stop the Argentines going back on to the islands. I do not believe that we have the capacity, in the late twentieth century, to mount such an operation permanently in the South Atlantic. . . .

If we do not come to terms with reality, what we have in prospect is disaster on a massive scale. I do not care whether it brings down a Government. What I care about is whether human beings are to lose their lives, whether they are Argentines or British, just in order that we can preserve a bereft principle so that we can preserve an illusion about the power of the British Empire which in my view is out of tune with what we have and what we are capable of achieving.

Dr. Alan Glyn (Windsor and Maidenhead): We have listened to a speech by the hon. Member for York (Mr. Lyon) in which he admitted that he is in a minority in the House. The feeling in the House has been demonstrated by the Leader of the Opposition, the right hon. Member for Plymouth, Devonport (Dr. Owen) and my right hon. Friend the Prime Minister. They have made it clear that they regard this act of aggression as unwarranted, and something that should be put right. Sovereignty and the rule of law should be restored. If we fail to do that we fail not only in the Falkland Islands but in the world and we shall pay for it in future. . . .

As we all know, this country has many friends in the Argentine but we are compelled by events and by an act of aggression against our territory to act in the way that we have and to follow the path so well laid by the Prime Minister. She has gone to every possible means and spent hours with our American allies in an effort to avoid any warlike action. At the same time, she has had the backing of the EEC and the Security Council. . . .

If we give way to the forces of dictatorship, we pay for it in the long run. . . .

Therefore, our first duty is to clear the island of the invading forces. A great deal of nonsense has been talked about flags. There is only one flag that should be flying over the Falkland Islands—the British flag. There is no place or justification for the Argentine flag. As far as we are concerned it is sovereign territory inhabited by British subjects. . . .

The only time that we can ever obtain the views of the islanders is when the Argentine troops have gone. We must then have some form of referendum to find out the views of the islanders, because their future is of paramount importance, although it may well have been changed by the recent events. . . .

With 9,000 troops on the island, unless they voluntarily withdraw, how long will it take to get rid of the invaders? It will be an immensely difficult task, even if they are subjected to long periods of economic sanctions, both by the EEC and other countries. . . .

We all want to see the matter resolved by a diplomatic solution but if that is not possible we know that we have the superiority to be able to achieve that objective by force. Let us hope that after the objective has been achieved, whatever negotiations take place, we do not give away any sovereignty and we recognise the importance not only of the islands but the area in that vicinity. . . .

For my part I believe that the House has shown that it is firmly behind my right hon. Friend, the Prime Minister, with a few exceptions. I hope and pray that this matter will be brought to a swift conclusion.

Mr. William Hamilton (Fife, Central): Having listened to all three debates on this matter in the course of the last two or three weeks the impression that I have is that the House has a feeling of helplessness in circumstances where no solution that will be satisfactory to us either in the short or the long term is possible. The great danger is that there will be a battle not so much of principle but of survival of one Government or another—the survival of our Prime Minister or the Argentine President. All matters of principle may go out of the window. . . .

Let the Prime Minister be under no illusion as to the support that she gets from the Labour Benches. . . .

It is her ineptitude, more than anything else, that has brought us and the country to this impasse. . . .

If the United States Government took action in conformity with their own Organisation of American States, they could stop the Argentine Government in their tracks within a week. But they will not do it because they have too many vested interests in Argentina and in South and Central America as a whole. So it must be understood clearly that some of us do not trust the United States Government to deliver the goods, even though the Prime Minister has fallen over backwards ever since she took office to defend every action that the Reagan Administration has taken.

That is the first factor that I want to get on the record. The other one concerns the task force, and here I take issue with my right hon. Friend the Member for Lanark (Dame Judith Hart). Now that it is on the ocean, I do not believe that any useful purpose would be served by, as she said, halting it in its tracks. Halting it where? In the middle of the ocean? Sending it back and dismantling it?

Dame Judith Hart: Essentially.

Mr. Hamilton: My right hon. Friend did not make it clear. She simply said "Halt it". That would be a tremendous fillip to the junta in the Argentine—the very thing to which my right hon. Friend objects. Like me, she objects to the junta. To do what she suggests at this moment would been a great fillip to a regime that we want to bring down at the earliest moment.

We are faced with this dilemma. That is why so many Opposition Members are uncomfortable and uncertain about the outcome. Meanwhile, we owe loyalty to those men who are on the ocean not because they volunteered but because that woman, the Prime Minister, said "You will go whether you like it or not". . . .

If that force is used, it fails. I ask hon. Members to imagine the scenario. The guns fire from our ships, the bombs are dropped, the torpedoes are let loose, and we raze those islands to the ground with the result that every one of the 1,800 inhabitants is killed. What happens then? The Prime

Minister has not a clue, and nor has anyone else. But anyone who pretends that that is a solution to the problem must be wrong in his mind. That is why my right hon. Friend the Leader of the Opposition is right to insist that, come what may, however long it takes, there must be a peaceful solution. . . .

We have had bellicose noises from successive Ministers, including the Secretary of State for Defence, saying that we would be quite prepared to sink ships and to blow everyone to Hell—as if that would solve anything. My right hon. Friend the Leader of the Opposition is right to say that we must at all costs get a peaceful solution. If it means losing face, it is better to lose face than to lose lives. . . .

We should not hesitate to say to the Argentine Government that we are prepared if need be to use economic sanctions and to engage in peaceful negotiations over an extended period of time. . . .

A great deal of romantic nonsense has been talked about the rights of 1,800 people to determine how we should use our Armed Forces, no matter what the expenditure, if they say that they want our protection. It will cost us half our Budget, but if they want that protection, we shall give it to them. What nonsense! We should spell out to them that the restoration of the status quo is impossible. They cannot have back what has been taken from them. We must rely on the United Nations to protect them as best they can, but we must make them understand, if they do not understand it already, that our days of empire and our days in the role of international policeman are long since over—and thank goodness for that.

The Prime Minister must understand that the apparent unanimity of the House now is more apparent than real. She will get her desserts in due course.

Mr. Ian Lloyd (Havant and Waterloo): . . . Although the dislike of war and of bloodshed is widely shared on both sides of the House because we are fully aware of the consequences of that kind of action, equally we are fully aware of the consequences of inaction.

The Falkland Islands situation has raised two major issues. The first is the question of intelligence, which I believe to be quite fundamental, both to any past failure there may have been and to any future success which we may have and deserve. The second is the influence on policy and procedure which we should be prepared to concede to circumstances. . . .

[The Argentine response would surely be] to keep our fleet at bay and avoid battle. They will rely on four admirals—Admiral Attrition, Admiral Expense, Admiral Indifference and Admiral Boredom. But if they are brought to battle, as they might well be by skilful commanders, this will be the first battle whose outcome will be decided by computer software written probably over two years ago.

As I see it, there are only four possible outcomes. First, the engagement will be limited, successful and brief—that is obviously the hope of the House. Secondly, the engagement will be limited, inconclusive and long-drawn-out. Thirdly, the engagement, whether successful or not, in the first instance will involve other South American powers. Finally, other major powers will be involved.

Clearly, if diplomatic pressure fails, our primary objective must be to achieve the first of those outcomes. Any of the remainder will not only be costly, dangerous and possibly disastrous: they would also indicate a calamitous failure on the part of the civilised world to recognise that we had not sent an expeditionary force to reimpose British sovereignty, which is a limited if legitimate objective, but to uphold and reassert the rule of law. I believe that to be common ground.

The Argentine has not just offended British pride and seized what it may regard as disputed territory. It has undermined everything that the allied powers fought to establish and protect in both world wars—the rule of law and international order.

The Argentines have also undermined and challenged the whole philosophy underlying the attempts to impose that rule of law in the League of Nations and the United Nations. That is why it is so serious; . . .

First and foremost, therefore, we must not weaken our resolve. . . . The contrivance and execution are well within our grasp and capability, and always have been.

Secondly, we must not modify our objective to the point at which it becomes unrecognisable.

Thirdly, as always, we must leave tactics and operational decisions to those on the spot.

Fourthly, we must do all that we can to bring home to the Argentine people, with the minimum of damage to their economy and livelihood but the maximum damage to their ill-advised Government, that as part of the West they have as much to lose and nothing to gain from salvaging the decrepit pride of decadent oligarchy.

Fifthly, we must make it clear to all that we are defending a general interest—the rule of law, the charter of the United Nations and civilised procedure in the relationship between States in dispute. . . . The Argentines should be asked to choose which side they are on—we do not know—and help to distinguish between the nationalist fervour and the long-term interests of their country.

Therefore, my support for the Prime Minister, which is unequivocal, does not rest on the narrow interest of the nation State, although I believe, as the Security Council has decided, that ours is entirely legitimate in this context. It rests rather on the threat to international order in a world that has paid a staggering price in life and wealth to establish the present precarious and fragile structure of international relations. . . .

It is conceivable that this operation may run into difficulties, but that is no reason why this House should in any sense diminish or restrict its support for the Prime Minister and the Government. It is my earnest wish and hope that the operation will succeed. It deserves to succeed, it has right on its side, and we should support it wholeheartedly.

Mr. Dafydd Wigley (Caernarvon): . . . The speeches of a number of Opposition Members will have made it clear that there is not unanimity on this matter and that there is an understandable worry. There is unanimity in condemnation of the Argentine junta and the way in which it has attacked and occupied the Falkland Islands, but the view falls short of unanimity, outside the House in the counties of these islands, on the question of where our present course will take us. If it leads us into an escalation towards a general war, many people ask at what point we should withdraw from that course. The possibility of Russian submarines around the coast now brings home the point clearly.

I see this matter from a standpoint slightly different from that of many hon. Members in that there have been close links between Wales and the Argentine over the years. There are now 20,000 people of Welsh descent living in the Argentine. I had the opportunity to go there and meet many of them, and I know from discussions 15 or 20 years ago that even among that community, let alone among the community of Spanish descent, there is a strong feeling of the affinity between the Falkland Islands and the Argentine. Whether or not we in this House or in these islands like that, that is the reality. The strength of that feeling can be judged from the number of people who turned out for the demonstrations in Buenos Aires and the way in which a tin-pot dictator who was a month ago on the way to oblivion appears to have been rescued by the sad sortie that he has undertaken. That must be borne in mind.

I have discussed the position with officers of the Welsh Argentine Society, of which I am a member. It is concerned and worried at the possibility of a war in which Welsh people in the forces now going to the Falklands could be confronting their cousins who have been conscripted into the Argentine army. . . .

Problems like this can be resolved without resort to the force of arms. It would be a terrible indictment of the failure of diplomacy if we have to resort to other methods.

The Falkland Islands are a small community 7,000 to 8,000 miles away. They are to a large extent dependent on South America for food, education and health services. That is a day-to-day reality for those 1,800 people when they look beyond the present occupation. It is a small population which could not possibly be self-sufficient in all aspects of life in the modern world. There are many of that community who would like to leave the island if it were possible to do so. . . .

I hope that in any negotiated settlement the Falkland Islanders will be given an opportunity, once the troops have been withdrawn—we appreciate that the troops must be withdrawn before there can be a meaningful settlement—to make their voice heard on their long-term future. . . .

If there is to be a negotiated settlement and the Argentines withdraw their fleet, there may be some dispute about whose flag is to fly on the islands. However, if that is the only question remaining in the short term, the United Nations' flag could fly for a limited period until the other problems have been sorted out. Surely it is not worth risking a war that could escalate by arguing about national flags. Although people want the Argentines out of the Falkland Islands, they do not want bloodshed if it can be avoided. They certainly do not want the situation to escalate into war. . . .

While there is still time I urge the Government to start seeking a de-escalation of the situation and to find a peaceful solution.

Sir Hector Monro (Dumfries): . . . Never, at any time since the last war, has there been a more important period during which the nation should stand together. I welcome the views expressed by the leaders of the Opposition parties. The situation may last for quite a long time—months or more—and we must not falter. This is no time for the faint-hearted. We have heard some of their voices during our recent debates. Of course, we shall have an inquiry later, but until then let us forget our differences and be united. . . .

We all welcome the maximum diplomatic activity towards finding a peaceful solution and our thanks are due to the United States of America for its efforts during the past week. Of course we wish to save lives through diplomacy and it will be far less expensive and perhaps more enduring if we can win through diplomacy. But Argentina has committed an act of war that has been condemned by the Security Council of the United Nations. Argentina has been required to withdraw, but it has taken no notice of that order from the Security Council. I doubt whether there is any way in which the Argentine Government's face can be saved through a compromise that would be acceptable to Britain.

The first condition—my right hon. Friend the Prime Minister has rightly brought it home to the nation time and time again—is that the Argentine invader must leave the Falkland Islands forthwith, flags and all. There must be no "ifs" and no "buts" and no quibbling. The Argentines must leave the islands before we can begin to negotiate. . . .

The message that we all wish to send is that the Government have the full support of the vast majority of the House in their determination to succeed. The sovereignty of the Falkland Islands is ours. We insist that it returns to our administration as soon as possible. Then we shall consider the future in the light of the wishes of the islanders, many of whom are of good Scottish descent. . . .

So good luck to our force. Let us remain a united House until victory is ours.

Mr. Dick Douglas (Dunfermline): . . . I do not think that the House is united behind the Government in their desire and outlook. The Government must spell out much more clearly to the nation their essential aims. . . .

It is said that the United Kingdom must maintain sovereignty over the Falkland Islands and the dependencies, no matter what. However, the Argentine troops are there and it is not right for us to be so inflexible that we refuse to negotiate as long as those troops remain on the islands. They are there and, therefore, there must be some flexibility. . . .

We shall be involved in an enormously costly exercise. The British people might not have known that on 1 or 2 April, but they are beginning to realise that now. More important is the fact that the Argentines know that. In the next few weeks or months we might defeat them, but in the longer run it will be impossible to maintain a force of the magnitude of the task force that will have consequences for the Argentine military regime. That is the reality. I accept that it is not palatable. Being a wee fellow, I never like giving way to a bully, but we have to face facts. . . .

I have great respect for the principle of self-determination. However, the people of the Falklands cannot hold a veto over us in terms of what they want.

That is not a long-term viable position in which we should be engaged, or one that should be maintained until Kingdom come. That should be made clear. I support the Navy and I support the task force, but above all I plead that a clear indication of our longer-term aims should be given to the people of this country. In the mid-term there must be extreme flexibility in negotiations and a resolve to try to solve this crisis by peaceful means through the medium of the United Nations.

Sir Anthony Meyer (Flint, West): I have set myself a hard and disagreeable task that has been made harder and more disagreeable by the wise speeches with which the debate was opened, particularly by the very balanced and judicious speech of my right hon. Friend the Prime Minister.

I shall say two things that will be distasteful to both sides of the House. The first is that I believe that the clamour that the House set up on 3 April for the resignation of Lord Carrington marked one of the lowest points in its history. Lord Carrington's offence was to believe in the absolute necessity to reach some kind of agreement with the Argentines over the Falklands, since to defend them against a hostile neighbour in perpetuity would be prohibitively costly. Events will prove him right. . . .

The second and still more distasteful thing I must do is question some part of the consensus in this House, excluding only the far Left and the hon. Members for West Lothian (Mr. Dalyell) and for South Ayrshire (Mr. Foulkes), about what to do next.

The Government have, rightly, the unanimous support of the House for the two propositions that the Argentines must not be allowed to enjoy undisturbed the fruits of their wanton and unprovoked aggression, and that the people of the Falkland Islands must recover their right of self-determination. They have the overwhelming support of this House for the proposition that it is both right and expedient to despatch the task force to demonstrate the firmness of our resolve and to use that task force, if need be, to enforce a blockade. I am part of that consensus, although not without misgivings caused by the gap that is now left in our defences against our real enemy—the Soviet Union.

There is also overwhelming support on both sides of the House for the proposition that we should seek a peaceful solution to the crisis, but that if diplomacy fails we must be ready to use force to restore British sovereignty or, at any rate, British administration to the islands. I have to tell my right hon. Friends with great sadness, having given many hours of agonising thought to the matter, that I for one on this side—and, perhaps, only for one—am not part of that consensus. . . .

I do not believe that it would be right, I do not believe that it would in the end help us to achieve our objectives, to use force in such a way as to kill people, Service men or civilians, just to ensure that the Union Jack—the Union Jack alone—flies over what would be left of public buildings in the Falklands. . . .

What I cannot accept is that the task force should at any time be given instructions to seek out and destroy Argentine vessels or installations or to attempt an opposed landing in circumstances where substantial casualties are to be expected.

If the Government really intend . . . to carry matters as far as that, I have no doubt that they will have the overwhelming support of this House, certainly of Conservative Members and of the majority of Opposition Members. I must tell them that at that stage they will no longer have mine.

Mr. Douglas Jay (Battersea, North): Despite the Government's blunders that led up to this crisis, today almost for the first time I found myself in almost total agreement with both Front Bench speeches.

Now, as we near the end of the debate, let us be clear about the real issues that are at stake. It is not the Union Jack or national prestige that are primarily at stake, but two crucial principles. The first is the principle of self-determination. . . .

At any rate, the inhabitants of the Falkland Islands have never freely expressed a wish to be governed either wholly or partly by the Argentines, least of all by the present military clique that rules there. . . .

The second fundamental principle . . . is that it is vital to show that unprovoked armed aggression does not pay, if the post-war system of international law and order is to survive. . . .

The case for resistance now is made all the more overwhelming by the right of self-defence that is written into the United Nations charter, by the almost unanimous United Nations resolution and by the support given to Britain by both Commonwealth and European countries. Of course, a diplomatic solution must be sought eventually, and, of course, loss of human life must be avoided if that can be done. But that solution must be one which is consistent with the paramount aim of showing that armed aggression does not succeed.

Therefore, the Government are right in my view to refuse negotiations on the future of the Falkland Islands until the Argentine forces have been withdrawn. There will be plenty of time later to discuss all sorts of possible eventual solutions. We do not do much good, I believe, by discussing them at this moment.

Ministers are also right to refuse any conditions about Argentine administration, Argentine flags or power-sharing during the interim period. If the economic and naval blockade can succeed without any loss of life, that is plainly by far the best alternative. But if there is loss of life, let there be no doubt that the responsibility lies squarely and wholly on the Argentine regime, which first took armed action. . . .

If international law is to be vindicated and a civilised and secure future assured for the Falkland Islanders, we must, together with other UN members, prove indisputably that this armed assault does not pay the aggressors.

Mr. John Browne (Winchester): Although we have been tricked and humiliated we have not yet been beaten. The two main reasons for our being tricked and humiliated and that stimulated the Argentine attack were, first, that the Argentine military junta was insecure internally and in need of an external successful adventure and secondly, externally, that the junta was encouraged by Britain's weakness—or apparent weakness. . . .

The future freedom of all nations is affected by this aggression. The reception of the Prime Minister's speech today shows that she has undoubted support in the House. Her clear statement of the aims, the fact that our sovereignty is not affected by the invasion and the fact that we have a clear resolution to aim for a diplomatic and peaceful settlement but to use force if necessary, is good. It shows that our clear duty as hon. Members is to ensure that the spirit of resolution outlined by the Prime Minister is impressed upon the military dictatorship in Argentina, that it is made entirely clear, and that there is no further room for misunderstanding. . . .

I wonder whether Russia has already had a hand in the operations to date. When I look at Argentina and consider the sophistication of the invasion, my suspicions are aroused. First, there was the very successful transfer of an exercise into an operation; secondly, there was an invasion during a period of radio silence when the Falkland Islands Government were out of contact with the United Kingdom; thirdly, there was the willingness of the Argentines, in that very successful invasion, to accept casualties themselves while not inflicting a single casualty on a British civilian or soldier. There was, indeed, great expertise and great sophistication. There was also the immediate repatriation of prisoners out of the war zone and back to the United Kingdom. . . .

In regard to the wish for the long-term security of the Falkland Islands and in the interests of NATO, I suggest that we should aim for the sovereignty of the United Kingdom over the islands, because I believe that no one will accept any longer the sovereignty of the Argentines. They have thrown away what trust they had.

I think that it is necessary to maintain, in the long term, United Kingdom sovereignty, but that we should accept joint United Kingdom-Argentine administration. We should also establish a NATO naval outpost in the islands. That would have the effect of assuring the long-term security of the Falkland Islands. It would also influence the southern area of the South Atlantic, while at the same time providing a source of earnings to the Falkland Islanders.

I repeat that we have been tricked and humiliated, but we have not been beaten. We must win and I believe that we can win if we remain determined and united. It is the clear duty of all of us in this House to see that we win. We must leave no room for doubt in the mind of anybody—least of all the Argentine junta—that we mean business.

Mr. Denis Healey (Leeds, East): I think that the House will agree that it has been a necessary and a useful debate. Although we have had little new information—and I do not blame the Prime Minister for being unable to give us more at this delicate moment—it has enabled us to establish a broad consensus rather more firmly and precisely than in the earlier debate on the major issues at stake in the Falklands crisis. . . .

Overwhelmingly we agree that we are dealing here with an act of aggression. It was recognised as such by the Security Council. It has been seen as an offence against the United Nations charter. After listening to the arguments again today, I find it more difficult than ever to understand the odd line of reasoning used by the American ambassador to the United Nations, Mrs. Kirkpatrick, that a Government who use force to pursue a territorial claim that they believe to be justified on historical grounds are not committing aggression. . . .

We are also agreed on what the rest of the United Nations Security Council resolution said, when it demanded an Argentine withdrawal and a diplomatic solution to the dispute. We are mostly agreed that we shall not get either the withdrawal or the solution unless the British Government are able to provide the strength against which to negotiate. Therefore, we have supported the despatch of the naval task force. I support today the recent decision by the Prime Minister to increase the air power available to the task force, and an early decision to provide it with something that was peculiarly lacking in early descriptions of the force—a capability to sweep mines in deep waters. . . .

It seems to me that if we are to believe what has appeared in the newspapers over the last few days, the shape of a diplomatic settlement falls into two phases. The first phase is that in which we secure the withdrawal of the Argentines from the Falkland Islands lock, stock and barrel, as the Prime Minister said—and not only the military personnel but the civilian personnel and any drapery that they happen to have with them. On the other hand, it seems to appear from recent news reports that we are very unlikely to secure the withdrawal of the Argentines from the Falklands unless we can arrange for them to be replaced by some authority whose presence does not pre-empt the solution of the second stage of the diplomatic negotiation.

The second stage, which has been discussed a good deal in these debates, is the negotiation for a future status of the Falkland Islands which will offer the islanders greater military security and perhaps more material prosperity than they have enjoyed till now. . . .

I hope that the Government will seriously consider replacing the Argentines during this first phase with some form of United Nations presence, whether it is as an administrator or as a truce team. . . .

In a situation such as this one the United Nations might have many advantages as a temporary presence on the islands, not least to be able to canvass the views of the islanders on possible solutions in the longer term in a position where neither Britain nor the Argentine, the main parties to this dispute, could be accused of exerting undue pressure. . . .

The great majority of us agree—there were one or two notable exceptions during the debate—that the views and interests of the islanders must be paramount. . . . But I was glad that last Sunday the Foreign Secretary echoed my words that we cannot say how the attitude of the islanders may have been affected by recent events. . . .

The negotiations, of course, will be difficult and they must be conducted from a position of strength. But there is still some time left even before our task force is on the spot, fully equipped with the new facilities we have been told about today and yesterday. The only thing I would say is that we do not have infinite time. I do not think that time is necessarily on the side of a diplomatic solution. . . .

I think that there is the risk that impatience or despair might produce a spark which sets off a major conflict. In addition, of course, as time passes, the risk of a conflict involving other countries than Britain and Argentina—other countries in Latin America, perhaps other countries like the Soviet Union—will be liable to increase.

Most of our discussions today have revolved around the principles at stake—the principle of not allowing the aggressor to get away with it and the principle of self-determination. But there is even more than principle at stake. There is the stability of the Western hemisphere, which may depend—in my view, will depend—on early and successful action, in which the United States must take a more active and positive role than it has until now.

The Secretary of State for Foreign and Commonwealth Affairs (Mr. Francis Pym): . . . The debate has shown a very broad measure of agreement and a broad measure of support for the actions that the Government have taken and are taking. It is a very good example of the way in which our democratic procedures in Parliament are a source of strength to our nation. . . .

There has been unity in the resolve that the rule of law must be re-established by the withdrawal of the invaders from the Falklands in accordance with the mandatory resolution of the Security Council, of which the Argentine is in breach. There has been unity in our determination to do all that we can to achieve a solution by peaceful means, provided that such a solution is in accordance with the basic principles that successive

British Governments have upheld—principles which we know to be essential if small countries are not to be at the mercy of their larger neighbours. There has been unity, too, in the sober recognition of our right to use force in self-defence—that is unquestionable—and is the recognition that, if needs be, that right will be exercised.

At the outset, I wish to give the House a first report that I have just received from the Chief Secretary in the Falklands Administration, who arrived last night in Montevideo. He stated that he and other senior officials who left with him had all been deported from the Falklands. Until his departure, the Administration in Port Stanley had succeeded in maintaining essential services for the islands—including medical services, water, electricity, telephones and police—but restrictions had been imposed on the radio-telephone links with outlying farms and the internal air service had been stopped.

According to the Chief Secretary, the conduct of the Argentine forces so far has been correct. The report contains no indication that there is serious hardship among the people of the Falkland Islands, but the deportation of their senior officials is a cause for concern and underlines the need for the involvement of the International Red Cross, which Her Majesty's Government are trying to secure. . . .

This act of aggression—unprovoked, illegal and unforgivable—must be reversed. The House, the country and the world would prefer it to be reversed by peaceful means. In the interests of avoiding bloodshed we are working with all our strength for just such a peaceful solution—a solution consistent with our commitment to the Falkland Islanders. . . .

Nobody can say whether a peaceful solution will prove possible. If it does not, Argentina knows what to expect. Let it not doubt it. . . .

Withdrawal . . . is an absolute prerequisite for any progress of any kind whatever. . . .

Britain's support for the islanders is no empty commitment. Our national response to this crisis has demonstrated that. It was Argentina's great mistake to imagine that there would be a lack of will on Britain's part to defend the Falkland Islands if the need arose. Britain has had a lot of experience of dealing with unprovoked aggression and invaders. That is unfortunate, but we have had it. We understand the vital need not to permit aggression to succeed. It makes no difference to us whether that takes place on our doorstep or 8,000 miles away. Freedom under the law is at stake. . . .

The Argentine reckoned without the response of the international community. It was not in any way prepared for what was going to happen. No doubt it expected the world to deprecate the use of force, but, in its ill-judged enthusiasm and perhaps even in a bit of excitement, it failed to foresee the revulsion and anxiety felt by nations all round the world at seeing an act of aggression by a large country against a small, nearby territory. The Argentine was unprepared for the resolution that was passed by the Security Council and was certainly unprepared for the task force's rapid departure from the United Kingdom. It was certainly unprepared for the response that we received from the international community by way of economic measures. It failed to realise that countries all around the world would see its act as totally repugnant and intolerable and that they would condemn it almost unanimously.

The Argentine also failed to see the strength which that condemnation would give Britain in its efforts to rally support to the cause of repelling aggressors. In other words, the Argentines misjudged the situation from the start. They anticipated what might happen, but they did not get it right. The Argentine must now be dismayed at the solidarity shown to Britain by our major allies. It did not see that the United States of America would be bound to condemn invasion. . . .

Above all, it totally failed to foresee the strong political solidarity that so many years of common endeavour have built up in the European Community. The Community's decision to ban all imports from the Argentine was wholly unexpected in Buenos Aires. Condemnations and diplomatic sanctions it could perhaps have lived with, but to see about one quarter of its export trade wiped out at a stroke was a body blow to its already rather shaky economy. . . .

Many hon. Members have raised the principle of self-determination and the wishes of the islanders. Certainly no one pays more attention to that or gives more weight to it than the Government. However, although we have not set our faces against any idea of change in the future, we cannot accept that some form of change should be imposed on the islanders. Of course, at the moment their views cannot be known. They are bound to be affected by the trauma that they have gone through. I have always taken the view that, as a result of it, they would be likely to wish to be even more British than they were before, if that is possible. But no one knows. . . .

All that I am trying to convey to the House is that the wishes of the islanders are all-important to us. That implies quite clearly that if another form of government is required by the islanders, the Government would not wish to stand in their way and neither would the House. . . .

The priority of the invading Argentines leaving the islands is crucial so that we can get on with the process that will lead to a long-term settlement. . . .

As my right hon. Friend the Prime Minister said earlier, the Argentine navy is concentrated outside the zone. We hope very much that that will continue to be so. We believe that the Argentines, like ourselves, desire above all else a peaceful solution if it can be achieved without prejudice to the principles that are involved. It is vital to us that the Argentine navy stays outside the zone so that no incidents are invited. . . .

As Mr. Haig's admirable efforts continue, we shall see whether reason and responsibility will prevail in Buenos Aires. Should Mr. Haig's diplomacy fail to produce a settlement, it will not be for lack of efforts or of reasonable flexibility on his part or on ours, but on Argentina's. Britain will remain determined to achieve peace if possible but ready for conflict if necessary, because we shall not be deflected from the objectives reaffirmed today by the Prime Minister.

The priority is the withdrawal of the Argentine forces from the Falkland Islands as a first step towards a settlement that accords with the wishes of the islanders. In the name of international law and order, they must go.

Report Eight

19 APRIL 1982

With the return of the House from the interrupted Easter Recess, the Foreign Secretary made a statement on 19 April.

The Secretary of State for Foreign and Commonwealth Affairs (Mr. Francis Pym): . . . Our objectives remain as already stated to the House. However, I should provide an account of developments since the debate last Wednesday.

Mr. Haig is continuing in his efforts to persuade the Argentine Government to agree to the implementation of Security Council resolution No. 502. His mission provides the best hope of achieving that objective.

The position is still delicate and the House will not expect me to reveal details of the negotiations. I know that the House understands that. We remain grateful to Mr. Haig and will continue to co-operate fully with his efforts to secure the implementation of resolution No. 502.

Meanwhile, we are stepping up the military, economic and diplomatic pressure on Argentina. Our naval task force is steadily approaching the area of the Falklands, and we are continuing to strengthen its ability to carry out whatever tasks may be required of it.

I am glad to tell the House that Norway has today joined members of the European Community and certain important Commonwealth countries in banning imports from Argentina.

The 22 marines who were captured in South Georgia and the remaining seven from the Falklands, as well as 13 British scientists evacuated from South Georgia, have arrived safely in Montevideo. I am glad to say that they are now on their way back to Britain. Fifteen British scientists remain in South Georgia and we have their well-being and safety very much in mind. The latest report on 18 April confirmed that all were safe and well.

The three British journalists arrested last week in Argentina are expected to appear before a judge today. The British interests section of the Swiss embassy in Buenos Aires is keeping us informed of developments.

Argentina must have no doubts about our resolve to exercise our rights to the full if this should prove necessary. However, I can assure the House that we are making every possible effort to get a satisfactory solution to this dispute by peaceful means. The Government will continue to keep the House informed.

Mr. Denis Healey (Leeds, East): . . . The Opposition share the Government's objectives, which include securing the withdrawal of all Argentine troops and other persons from the Falkland Islands before Britain engages in direct negotiations with Argentina for a peaceful settlement of the status of the islands.

I agree with the right hon. Gentleman—as I think all Labour Members would—that Mr. Haig's mission provides the best hope of a peaceful settlement. I hope that we shall all do everything that we can to assist him to succeed. If no immediate agreement on sovereignty can be reached after an Argentine withdrawal—that seems to be the stumbling block at the moment, according to Mr. Secretary Haig's statements—will the Government consider asking the Secretary-General of the United Nations to provide a temporary administrator for the islands after the Argentine forces have left, so that the sovereignty issue can be put on one side for direct negotiation between Britain and the Argentine? I think that that is the desire of both sides of the House. . . .

If Mr. Haig should finally decide . . . that he can contribute nothing more as an "honest broker", will the Government consider asking the Secretary-General of the United Nations to undertake that role, thus freeing the United States Administration to express the views of the American people that America should not behave as neutral between the aggressor and his victim or between a democratic ally and a dictatorship whose actions have often been hostile to the United States in recent years? . . .

Mr. Pym: . . . The first vital step is to secure the Argentine withdrawal in accordance with Security Council resolution No. 502. The methods are open to discussion, but that must be the first objective. It would be wrong at the present time to consider what might happen in the very unfortunate event of that mission not proving successful. . . .

At the moment, the hope and the effort must be to do everything possible to make the mission successful.

It has always seemed to me that while Mr. Haig and the United States Administration are trying to achieve the implementation of the resolution by peaceful means it would be inappropriate for them to be in any position other than a reasonably evenhanded one. That is a fair statement of the position. That must continue at the moment. . . .

Mr. Healey: . . . Will the Government consider trying to take the sovereignty issue out of the immediate argument by inviting the United Nations to provide an administrator purely for the period between the withdrawal of the Argentine forces and the agreement of a permanent settlement?

Mr. Pym: We have never disguised from the House that the negotiations are clearly difficult and that there are a number of obstacles. . . .

It must remain our objective to hope, and to do everything that we can to ensure, that the Haig mission is successful. . . .

Mr. J. Enoch Powell (Down, South): In view of the Government's repeated assurance that no agreement affecting the future status of the Falkland Islands will be made without the consent of the House and the Falkland Islanders, it is not clear that the withdrawal of Argentine forces from the islands cannot be conditional either upon such an agreement or upon the possibility of such an agreement?

Mr. Pym: We have made our position about the status of the islands and the importance that we have always attached to the wishes of the islanders clear from the outset. We have described those wishes as being of paramount importance. Of course, the Argentines have a different point of view about these matters and that is why the negotiations are so difficult and protracted. . . .

Sir Angus Maude (Stratford-on-Avon): . . . Will my right hon. Friend confirm that if we are to uphold the vital principle that unprovoked aggression must not be seen to pay, Argentine withdrawal from the Falkland Islands must be total and unconditional, without any Argentine flags or administrators being left behind?

Mr. Pym: . . . The rapid passing of resolution No. 502 in the United Nations was a substantial achievement. . . . This matter is not only of the utmost importance to Britain but of importance to all freedom-loving countries all round the world. They have just as great an interest in ensuring that withdrawal takes place as we have.

Mr. Jack Ashley (Stoke-on-Trent, South): If it is true that the British Government rightly refuse to surrender sovereignty under duress and in the face of unwarranted armed aggression, but that they are prepared to negotiate sovereignty later, are not both countries getting the whole issue out of perspective? Argentina is doing so by its statement that its soldiers will stay, dead or alive, on the Falkland Islands, and Britain by its declaration that it will shoot first when the task force arrives. Is that still our position?

Mr. Pym: I am not sure that the right hon. Gentleman is right about shooting first. The Argentines invaded the Falkland Islands when we—like previous Governments—were negotiating with them about the future of the Falkland Islands. In the course of those negotiations we gave due weight to the wishes of the islanders, which was not always to the satisfaction of the Argentines. However, those negotiations were going on. Without any notice, and without telling us of their intentions, the Argentines invaded these islands, and that position cannot be allowed to stand.
Some people may take the right hon. Gentleman's view that the Argentines and the British are getting the issue out of proportion, but the principle of one large country taking another country by invasion and military force cannot be allowed to stand. . . .

Sir Nigel Fisher (Surbiton): Will my right hon, Friend keep an open mind about the suggestion of a United Nations presence? If that were offered by the United Nations, it might be the very factor to induce the Argentines to withdraw peaceably. With a United Nations presence, a referendum of the Falkland Islanders could take place, and we all know the probable result of that. That would be a good interim measure.

Mr. Pym: I note that suggestion. During the negotiations, I should not wish to close any options beyond the objectives and principles that we have stated. . . .

Mr. Russell Johnston (Inverness): . . . Do the published views of the

British ambassador in the United States of America represent the Government's position on the attitude of the United States of America? . . .

Mr. Pym: I have made clear our position about the attitude of the United States Government. At present they are involving themselves in negotiations. . . .

Mr. Tam Dalyell (West Lothian): . . . Are we not antagonising the entire Hispanic world—*[Interruption]*—even among those who have suffered from Right-wing Governments? Is it not an illusion to think that the Americans will be less than evenhanded when an American President, based in California, is aware of the Hispanic speaking section of the American population in New Mexico, Arizona and California?

Mr. Pym: It is fair to say that the majority of the South American States have expressed their deep concern over the action taken by the Argentine. They may have a certain sympathy with the Argentine's claims, but they do not have any sympathy with the methods used to try to secure them. I remind the hon. Gentleman that the Organisation of American States did not support the Argentine invasion, and Peru, for example, has proposed a 72-hour truce. Other suggestions are being made. . . .

Sir Bernard Braine (Essex, South-East): . . . Did my right hon. Friend make it plain to Secretary Haig that there can be no preconditions about sovereignty or anything else as long as Argentine soldiers remain on British soil?

Mr. Pym: . . . One of the issues is what the Falkland Islanders will want for the future. . . . However, it is impossible to ascertain those views until the Argentines have withdrawn completely.

Mr. Reginald Freeson (Brent, East): Is it not time that the Government informed the House, by way of a report, of the views that have been obtained from the Falkland Islanders? . . .

Mr. Pym: It is impossible at the moment to claim a general view of what their wishes are while they are under duress. . . . The object remains to secure Argentine withdrawal. There is no other first step that can be taken.

Mr. Maurice Macmillan (Farnham): Will my right hon. Friend accept that negotiations . . . should start from the basis that, legally, sovereignty is in British hands and that it cannot, for mere convenience, be put into abeyance, as it were, under the United Nations or any other organisation?

Mr. Pym: . . . We are in no doubt about our sovereignty position. The Argentine challenges that and makes a separate claim of its own. It is entitled to make that claim, and there are various ways of settling it. The only means that we shall not accept as a method of settling it is the use of force.

Mr. Christopher Price (Lewisham, West): Does the right hon. Gentleman agree that it is not reasonable to expect people overseas to continue with sanctions if those in the City of London and members of Lloyd's syndicates rat on sanctions? Is the right hon. Gentleman aware that members of Lloyd's syndicates, who are well represented on the Conservative Benches behind him, today gave further insurance cover to Argentine Airlines and are already making arrangements to renew an Argentine Airlines' insurance contract, which expires on 1 May, through Swiss banks if necessary, so that the premiums will not have to come into Britain? Will the right hon. Gentleman ensure that the City puts Britain before its own commercial interests?

Mr. Pym: I cannot comment on those allegations—[Hon. Members: "Why not?"]—but, as the hon. Gentleman knows, many of our friends have taken economic measures against Argentina. No new loans are being authorised or made to the Argentine by the City of London. I cannot comment on the allegation that the hon. Gentleman has made.

Sir David Price (Eastleigh): Will my right hon. Friend confirm that the Argentine junta is still unwilling to allow the key question of sovereignty over the Falkland Islands to be determined by the International Court at the Hague, which, I understand, would be the correct United Nations solution to this type of problem?

Mr. Pym: That has always been the junta's position. The Argentines see sovereignty as the critical issue and I have no reason to suppose that they have changed their attitude—their objection—to allowing the issue to go to the International Court of Justice. . . .

Mr. Michael English (Nottingham, West): Does the right hon. Gentleman remember the malignant truism uttered by the United States ambassadress to the United Nations, who said that if the territory in question—the Falklands—was Argentine territory, the Argentine had clearly not invaded anyone else's territory? Will the right hon. Gentleman consider stating the opposite case and putting our case to the International Court of Justice? . . .

Mr. Pym: . . . We have never been in any doubt about our title to the Falkland Islands. Without doubt, the Argentines have invaded the islands. The Argentines have a claim that we have been discussing and arguing about for many years. There has been no movement on the issue under previous Governments, but that does not justify the actions that the Argentines have taken. . . .

Mr. Jonathan Aitken (Thanet, East): . . . Will my right hon. Friend communicate to Washington the profound misgivings that are felt on both sides of the House about the ambivalent sound and signals coming from the United States' Administration on this issue? . . . Will he consider making a protest about the statements made by the United States ambassador to the United Nations? If such statements are not checked, they could damage the future of the Anglo-American alliance.

Mr. Pym: It is clear that Britain has a great deal of public support in the United States. It is our view that the best achievement for us all would be for Mr. Haig's mission to succeed and for resolution No. 502 to be implemented. While that process is in hand, it seems inappropriate in the circumstances for the United States Government to align themselves. . . .

Mr. George Cunningham (Islington, South and Finsbury): Are the Falkland Islanders free to leave the islands if they wish to do so? Are they free in practice to do so, as opposed to what the Argentines say about this? If they are, would it not be right for the British Government to say at this stage that if they do leave temporarily they will assist them to do so, so that they can get out of the combat zone?

Mr. Pym: There is no evidence that Falkland Islanders who wish to leave the islands are being prevented from doing so by Argentina. The hon. Gentleman's second point is one that we are considering sympathetically.

Mr. Peter Viggers (Gosport): . . . When calm has been restored we should look again at the shape of the Royal Navy and of the shore support facilities to see whether they are best suited to guard our vital interests, both inside and outside NATO. . . .

Mr. Pym: . . . The impressive way and the speed with which the Royal Navy assembled the Fleet and set sail indicates that it is in pretty good shape. . . .

Mr. Arthur Palmer (Bristol, North-East): In view of the statement made by the American ambassador to the United Nations, is the right hon. Gentleman convinced that in the end President Reagan will be on our side?

Mr. Pym: I cannot go further on that. I am sure that President Reagan would like to be, but the Americans are acting as negotiators. That is a position that should be respected.

Mr. Michael Marshall (Arundel): Does my right hon. Friend agree that the media have a grave responsibility? Are the Government concerned about the fact that some of the information given on television—for example, about Vulcan and Harrier use and training—seems extremely generous in the circumstances. . . ?

Mr. Pym: . . . I should not wish to be critical of the way in which the issue has been presented on television. I sometimes wish that pictures and film extracts of the Argentine forces had a caption indicating their source, rather than a picture merely showing that something was happening. It is also fair to say that the correspondents who are with the carrier task force are reporting in a way that people find acceptable. . . .

Report Nine

20 APRIL 1982

The House returned to the subject at Prime Minister's question time on Tuesday 20 April.

Mr. Geraint Howells: In view of the seriousness of the position in and around the Falkland Islands, has the Prime Minister any plans to invite the leaders of all the political parties in the House to Downing Street for discussions?

The Prime Minister: I have no such plans at present. . . .
Of course, we shall try to seek a diplomatic solution, but we have to be true to our objectives. I cannot disguise from the House that the Argentine proposals at present before us fall short in some important respects of those objectives and of the requirements expressed in the House.

Mr. Foot: Will the right hon. Lady tell us when she will report to the House—in accordance with what she has said about such reports—on those proposals, on what they are officially and what the Government's views are about all of them? Will she tell us whether they are supported by the United States Administration or whether General Haig was merely acting as an intermediary in the matter?

The Prime Minister: The proposals are Argentine proposals. We are grateful to Mr. Haig for the patience and stamina that he has shown over the proposals, both in Buenos Aires and in his visits to this country, but they are Argentine proposals. He has kept us fully informed, when he has been able to do so, about precisely what they are. We now have full details. . . .
We are examining the proposals very closely and will seek to put forward our own proposals to Mr. Haig. With that in mind my right hon. Friend the Foreign Secretary plans to visit Washington on Thursday.

Mr. Foot: When will the right hon. Lady be reporting to the House again? . . . Does the right hon. Lady agree that, apart from the inherent justice of our cause, a major source of strength is that this country is acting in conformity with the United Nations charter and in pursuance of resolution No. 502? If the right hon. Lady and the Government follow up the proposals made by my right hon. Friend the Member for Leeds, East (Mr. Healey), they could provide some alternatives to the specific proposals from the Argentine and also make sure that we continue to act in full conformity with the United Nations charter and our obligations under the charter.

The Prime Minister: I do not believe that there is much point in reporting to the House before my right hon. Friend has seen Mr. Haig in Washington. Among the many problems presented by the Argentine proposals is that they fail to provide that the Falkland Islanders should be able to determine their own destiny. The House has always said that the wishes of the islanders are paramount.

As regards the proposals put forward by the right hon. Member for Leeds, East (Mr. Healey) that referred to United Nations administrators, we are in the process of one negotiation through Mr. Haig, and it would be better not to get our wires crossed but to go steadily forward on that proposal. I accept what the right hon. Gentleman said. We are trying to secure implementation of United Nations resolution No. 502, which is clear but not so easy to implement. We also have rights on self defence under article 51 of the charter.

Mr. Foot: I wish the right hon. Gentleman well on his visit to the United States. However, I am not at all certain that it will not be necessary for further reports to be made to the House in the meantime. Does the right hon. Lady agree that as these matters are fully discussed in other places there should be constant and persistent reports to the House of Commons?

The Prime Minister: There is no intention to hold up information in any way. The right hon. Gentleman, his right hon. Friends and hon. Members have been extremely understanding that while negotiations are in progress it is difficult to give full details of them. I have indicated one important respect in which the Argentine proposals fall short of the objective of almost every hon. Member. I am here every Tuesday and Thursday, but we will make much fuller statements as often as we can. . . .

We remain committed to seeking a diplomatic solution if an acceptable one can possibly be found.

Mr. David Steel: The Prime Minister knows that she has all-party support for her determination to secure the removal of the Argentine from the islands, to secure implementation of the Security Council resolution and re-establish conditions in which the future of the islanders can be determined in the long term. However, will the right hon. Lady refrain from ascribing to the House as a whole her phrase about the paramountcy of the wishes of the islanders? Does she agree that while their wishes and interests are uppermost in our minds, the long-term issue is a paramount one for the House to resolve?

The Prime Minister: But the House, in exercising its duty, has always said, not only in these negotiations but on many previous negotiations, that the wishes of the islanders are paramount. Many previous negotiations have been on the basis that the Argentines wanted what is called de-colonisation—that has a particular meaning in United Nations terms—but they have not been able or willing to grant self-determination to the islanders. . . .

Mr. Stanley Newens: Does the right hon. Lady agree that it would be a great advantage to involve the United Nations more deeply? That would

111

relieve the United States of the necessity to act in what is called an even-handed fashion.

The Prime Minister: There is a clear mandatory resolution on record by the Security Council which should have the force and effect of international law. At present it is not being implemented. Mr. Haig is trying to see that it is implemented. . . .

Sir John Eden: Are the Government still absolutely determined to use whatever means are at their disposal to secure the withdrawal of the Argentine forces from the islands and to re-establish British administration before any question of a longer-term solution is entered into?

The Prime Minister: I confirm that that is our aim. Our strategy is to try to use diplomatic means, backed up by a task force, which continues steadily on its way.

Mr. Roy Jenkins: In view of the strong all-party support that the Government have rightly received during the past two and a half weeks, will the Prime Minister bear in mind that she will be expected to take future, I hope and believe, un-rushed decisions in an equally non-party way? Does she agree that that demands more than merely asking the right hon. Gentleman the Paymaster General, as chairman of the Conservative Party, to a meeting of senior Ministers last night? . . .

The Prime Minister: . . . On the last occasion that this point was raised the Leader of the Opposition said, rightly, that he would not find that the appropriate way to proceed. . . . I am always available to see hon. Members on these important issues. . . .

Mr. John Townend: Is my right hon. Friend aware that, despite the recent proposals, she has widespread support in the country for the stance she is taking to ensure that dictators cannot get by aggression what they fail to get by negotiation? In particular, in view of the Argentine record on human rights, does she agree that the suggestion to bring Argentine police into the islands is not acceptable is because it could lead to the intimidation of the islanders?

The Prime Minister: My hon. Friend has enunciated a very important principle, not only for the people of the Falkland Islands but for the people of many other territories who may be invaded if unprovoked aggression in this case succeeded . . . there are only two police officers on the islands—it was a very law abiding place—and we are very much aware of the record of the present junta in Argentina.

The Foreign Secretary gave written answers:

Mr. Arthur Lewis asked the Secretary of State for Foreign and Commonwealth Affairs whether, as a means of resolving the dispute between the United Kingdom and the Argentine Government, he will request the United Nations to hold a referendum of the Falkland Islanders. . . .

Mr. Pym: It is too soon to consider in detail possible means of consulting the islanders' views on a long-term solution. The first requirement is the withdrawal of Argentine forces.

Mr. Arthur Lewis asked the Secretary of State for Foreign and Commonwealth Affairs if Her Majesty's Government will take all and every action necessary, including if need be an approach to the Government of the Argentine, or the United Nations, to enable a citizen of the Falkland Islands to emigrate if he should express such a desire.

Mr. Pym: The Government's immediate objective is to secure the withdrawal of Argentine forces in order to enable the islanders to resume their former way of life and their freedom to do as they wish. We have no evidence of any islanders now wishing to emigrate being prevented from doing so by the occupying forces, but would of course do all we could to help, were such clear wishes expressed.

Report Ten

21 APRIL 1982

With the World Cup matches in Spain looming, a new series of questions came on Wednesday 21 April. They were followed by another statement from the Foreign Secretary. Mr. Speaker refused an application for an emergency debate.

Mr. Dennis Canavan: . . . Does the Minister agree that a boycott of the World Cup would not help the oppressed people of the Falkland Islands, but could damage international relations if we allowed a Fascist dictator, such as Galtieri, to spoil one of the greatest international sporting competitions in the world?

The Under-Secretary of State for the Environment (Mr. Neil Macfarlane): There is no question of a boycott. . . .

Sir Hector Monro: Does my hon. Friend accept that many of us agree with his advice? We must hope that FIFA will realise that many European and Commonwealth countries would not wish to be involved in a tournament with Argentina. Should not FIFA take the responsibility of removing Argentina from the World Cup if the present position continues?

Mr. Macfarlane: I cannot anticipate what action FIFA may take, but, as matters stand now, we have no objection to British teams taking part in international competitions where Argentina may also be represented. However, our position must be kept under constant review in the light of changing circumstances. I have nothing more to say now.

Mr. Denis Howell: Does the Minister accept that if resolution 502 of the Security Council has not been honoured by the time of the World Cup the Government must consider what principles will govern their advice? The Labour Party would support the proposal by the hon. Member for Dumfries (Sir H. Monro) that, in such circumstances, the right course would be for FIFA to exclude Argentina.

Mr. Macfarlane: Many millions of British people would think it strange if our three teams were not to participate in the World Cup because of the action of an aggressive nation. All those matters are being kept under the closest review. I cannot comment on any events that may take place during the next few weeks. However, I am in close contact with the representatives of the football authorities, both nationally and internationally. . . .

The Secretary of State for Foreign and Commonwealth Affairs (Mr.

114

Francis Pym): . . . My right hon. Friend the Prime Minister told the House yesterday that I would be travelling to Washington tomorrow to discuss with Mr. Haig our reactions to the latest Argentine proposals. I believe I do so with the support of the whole House.

Any negotiation which is concluded satisfactorily must deal with certain critical points: in particular the arrangements for the Argentine withdrawal; the nature of any interim administration of the islands, and the framework for the negotiations on the long-term solution to the dispute for which the United Nations resolution calls. We put to Mr. Haig, when he was in London, ideas which we believed would commend themselves to the House and accord with the wishes of the islanders. He subsequently took them to Buenos Aires. The latest Argentine proposals—despite Mr. Haig's efforts—still fail to satisfy our essential requirements in certain important respects relating to these points. They reflect continuing efforts by Argentina to establish by her aggression and her defiance of the United Nations—a defiance continued and aggravated by her reinforcement of her invasion force—what could not be established by peaceful means. . . .

Since I last reported to the House, messages from the Falklands suggest that the islanders are still able to leave if they wish: a further party of 30 are on their way to Montevideo. Most of those leaving appear not to be permanent residents of the islands.

The most recent contact with the 15 remaining scientists and wildlife photographers on South Georgia through the British Antarctic survey was at 4 pm yesterday our time. I am happy to report that all were safe and well and in good heart.

I shall continue to keep the House informed.

Mr. Denis Healey (Leeds, East): . . . We welcome the right hon. Gentleman's visit to Washington and hope for its success.

I hope that I may be permitted to express our gratitude to Secretary Haig—I am sure that it is the view of the whole House—for the indefatigable efforts that he has made in the negotiations. I cannot recall any representative of any Government who has shown greater stamina—intellectual, physical and moral—than he has shown. If we are to believe reports from Buenos Aires, he has put the views of the British people with great force and vigour in the discussions, as no doubt he has put the views of the Argentine Government to us. . . . Will the right hon. Gentleman give the House an assurance that any resident of the islands who wishes to come to Britain to settle here will be free to do so whatever decisions the Government may have taken earlier in their drafting of the British Nationality Bill?

I welcome the clear desire of the Foreign Secretary to achieve a peaceful settlement of this dispute. I shall not quote what he has been reported as saying to some of his friends yesterday about the Duke of York, but he can be assured that we, too, wish to see the British forces able to leave the area without using force in order to secure our needs. The right hon. Gentleman must recognise that the quite exceptional support that the British Government have had from the British people, all parties in the House, the European Community, the Commonwealth and the United Nations depends critically on the Government demonstrating continuously that they are determined to seek a diplomatic solution of this crisis by peaceful means, and that they will spare no effort to secure such a result if that proves possible.

It seems that the central problem on which the right hon. Gentleman has fixed his attention is the interim arrangements after the Argentine forces leave the islands. I was surprised that he did not mention among the three critical elements the wishes of the islanders themselves, although he referred to them in a later part of his statement. I hope that he will reassure the House that it is still his intention to ensure that any settlement is one which is acceptable not only to the House but to the inhabitants of the Falkland Islands.

As for the interim arrangements, I hope that the right hon. Gentleman will continue to consider, as he promised last week, the possibility of asking the United Nations to provide an administrator for the islands. . . .

I say on behalf of the Opposition that the strength of the Government's case in the world has depended in large part on the extraordinary and impressive support that we received in the Security Council in the beginning. It is immensely important that we put the United Nations charter at the centre of our policy. . . .

Mr. Pym: I am grateful to the right hon. Member for Leeds, East (Mr. Healey) for what he said at the start of his remarks. I endorse all that he said about the efforts that are being made by Mr. Haig. . . .

My right hon. Friend the Home Secretary has been quite clear about the islanders who may wish to settle here. A number of the islanders already have that automatic right. My right hon. Friend made a statement in which he indicated that there would be no difficulties put in the way of anyone on the islands who wished to settle here. . . .

My journey tomorrow and all the efforts that I am making are designed to secure a peaceful settlement. There is no doubt that that is what everybody would like to achieve. I shall spare no effort in seeking to do that. We must hope that success will attend those endeavours, but one cannot be sure. . . . I would not exclude any possibility at this stage, because that would be a silly stance to take. However, there are other issues that are equally important, including the withdrawal of the Argentine forces, the question of sovereignty and the wishes of the islanders, on which we have made our position clear on several occasions. . . .

Mr. David Steel (Roxburgh, Selkirk and Peebles): The United Nations may well have a role in the long-term administration of the Falkland Islands. However, the Foreign Secretary is right in the immediate crisis to continue to use the good offices of the United States Administration in an attempt to achieve the Argentine withdrawal from the islands. For that reason, he carries the good wishes of all parties in the House in his mission.

Mr. Pym: I am grateful for what the right hon. Gentleman has said. The withdrawal of Argentine forces from the islands is, of course, a prerequisite of any further progress. . . .

Mr. Julian Amery (Brighton, Pavilion): Does my right hon. Friend agree that it may not be possible to reconcile the claims of the Argentine with our responsibilities? Therefore, that may lead inevitably to the use of force. But might not this be the moment to try to raise the level of debate while there is still time? Might it not be the time for my right hon. Friend to propose, while maintaining our sovereignty over the Falkland Islands, the creation of a South Atlantic community to which the riparian States might adhere and which might be extended to the southern hemisphere, along with Australia and New Zealand and the signatories of the Antarctic treaty, for the development of the Antarctic continent? . . .

Mr. Pym: I shall certainly consider my right hon. Friend's suggestion. The concept is essentially a long-term one. I doubt that thinking in that direction will contribute a great deal to the immediate problem which we are discussing. . . .

Mr. J. Enoch Powell (Down, South): Is it still the intention of Her Majesty's Government to restore British administration of the islands?

Mr. Pym: That is still Her Majesty's Government's intention.

Mr. Charles Morrison (Devizes): . . . Can my right hon. Friend give an assurance that all reasonable steps will be taken to remove civilian personnel from South Georgia?

Mr. Pym: We are doing all that we can. In the first instance, we have tried to obtain an International Red Cross presence on the islands. So far, that has not been agreed to. The Argentine Government have said that they do not believe that to be necessary. Such evidence as we have on that issue would suggest that they are possibly right. . . .

Dame Judith Hart (Lanark): Given the complexity of the negotiations that the Foreign Secretary is about to undertake, and the need to involve the United Nations if that is possible, as the task force moves steadily nearer the Falklands, are the Foreign Secretary and the Government giving priority to peace?

Mr. Pym: I do not see how anybody could say that we have done anything other than give a priority to peace. All our efforts are designed to achieve that. I have made it clear how difficult that might be. . . .

Dr. David Owen (Plymouth, Devonport): Is the Foreign Secretary aware that he will carry the support of all hon. Members in giving a priority to peace. . . ?

Mr. Pym: . . . If it is not possible to achieve the result by peaceful means, other methods must be used. The House must face that. I assure the right hon. Gentleman that so long as there is any way in which I can, with Mr. Haig's, or anybody else's help, secure a peaceful solution, that is what my endeavour will be.

Mr. Nicholas Winterton (Macclesfield): . . . Will my right hon. Friend explain how there can be any interim arrangement with the Argentine junta? Surely, when the Argentines evacuate the Falklands, we shall immediately restore British administration. Will my right hon. Friend give an assurance to the House that our interests in the South Atlantic will be safeguarded and that the interests of the islanders will always be paramount?

Mr. Pym: . . . Of course, we want to preserve British interests in the South Atlantic. However, the House understands that at this stage I do not want to involve myself with the House in any details of any negotiations, particularly because there are new ideas and proposals coming forward. In a sense, that is an encouraging sign because, while there are new proposals which may be considered or rejected by one side or the other, there is undoubtedly life in the negotiations. . . .

Mr. Ioan Evans (Aberdare): As well as meeting Alexander Haig, will the right hon. Gentleman also call on the United Nations in case the Haig initiative fails so that we can be thinking ahead as to what course the United Nations can take in the future?

Mr. Pym: . . . It is not my intention on this visit to include a visit to the United Nations. It is not inconceivable that that might happen at some stage. I am going to Washington to see Mr. Haig. That is where the negotiations will take place and that is the right place for me to be in the next day or two.

Sir Frederick Burden (Gillingham): Does my right hon. Friend agree that the basis of this whole matter is that British land, occupied by British people who speak only our language, has been annexed by force by a ruthless dictator by naked aggression? As we have seen in the past, if we bow to that, the civilised world as we know it will start to collapse. . . .

Mr. Pym: I repeat that we are dealing with the fundamental question of international order and how countries order their affairs. It is not only in the Falkland Islands that there has been an invasion. The House must not forget that Afghanistan was overrun about two years ago. That country is denied the possibility of self-determination. . . .

Mr. George Foulkes (South Ayrshire): As time is now running out for a peaceful solution, and as we have now agreed to exchange ideas with Argentina, would it not be quicker and more effective for the Foreign Secretary to meet the Foreign Secretary of Argentina directly, if necessary under the auspices of the United Nations?

Mr. Pym: That would not be helpful at present . . . a solution of the problem by the negotiations undertaken by Mr. Haig is the best outcome that can be achieved. A direct visit by me now would not be helpful. It is better to use Mr. Haig's good offices.

Mr. Patrick Cormack (Staffordshire, South-West): Does my right hon. Friend accept that, although we are prepared to be patient in our search for peace, any settlement that involves an armed or active Argentine presence on the Falkland Islands would not be acceptable in Britain?

Mr. Pym: The withdrawal of all the Argentine forces is the starting point from which everything else must flow. As I have said, I have an open mind about the way in which the long-term solution can, in due course, be achieved. I certainly do not rule out the International Court. Until now

118

Argentina has been unwilling to let its case be heard at the International Court.

As we are in no doubt, and as no British Government have been in any doubt for about 150 years, about the status of the islands, it is up to those who think that they have a claim—contrary to the views of the British Government—to challenge the British Government's claim. However, no one has yet done so. . . .

Mr. Frank Hooley (Sheffield, Heeley): Will the Foreign Secretary, while he is in the United States, think again about having some conversations with the Secretary-General of the United Nations? . . .

Mr. Pym: From the United Nations' point of view, it is important to see that resolution 502 is carried out. I intend to spend the time in Washington, and I do not think that there will be time to fit in a visit to New York. However, I do not exclude any possibility, and I should make it clear that I am not in any way reluctant to talk to the Secretary-General. . . .

Mr. Michael Mates (Petersfield): . . . Although it is perfectly under-standable that the United States of America has been reluctant to exert pressure while there was any hope of its continuing to act as a negotiator between the two sides, will my right hon. Friend make it clear to Mr. Haig . . . that at the very moment that the Americans feel that they can do nothing further we shall look to them to take that action quickly and effectively?

Mr. Pym: . . . I am acutely aware of that point. . . .

Mr. David Stoddart (Swindon): . . . Will he warn the United States of America that any Fascist success in the Falkland Islands will give comfort and encouragement to Fascism throughout the world? . . .

Mr. Pym: I have no doubt that the Administration of the United States of America are as keenly aware of the principles of democracy and representation as we are. . . .

Mr. Alan Clark (Plymouth, Sutton): . . . Will my right hon. Friend confirm that there is no question of ceding our rights either to South Georgia or to the mineral and other resources of the Antarctic, and that these are not dependent on the outcome of the negotiations on the Falkland Islands and will not be allowed to go by default?

Mr. Pym: We have never used any language or thought in terms of ceding what is without any question a British possession and a part of this country. We have always made that clear. Argentina is trying to take by force something that it has failed to achieve by peaceful means. . . . However, if anyone wishes to challenge our claim to sovereignty, there are ways in which that can be done. The House and the world would like to see that happen, but it has not happened. Therefore, to enable that to happen, the first thing to do is to get the Argentine forces to withdraw.

Mr. Andrew Faulds (Warley, East): Since sovereignty is bound to be transferred at some stage, and since it has been a matter of discussion for some years, would it not avoid an unnecessary confrontation if the interim administration—once the Argentine forces had withdrawn—were to consist of the three flags—British, United Nations and Argentine?

Mr. Pym: I am afraid that I do not share the hon. Gentleman's view about the ultimate arrangement. He says that that will happen, but I do not say that. I shall not prejudge the final outcome, and I should not do so; it is none of my business. It must be negotiated and all the factors that we have discussed must be taken into account.

Mr. Churchill (Stretford): When my right hon. Friend visits Washington, will he make it clear, not only to the American Government but to the American people, that the nub of the crisis rests in the apparent determination of the Argentine military junta to ride roughshod over the wishes and liberties of the Falkland Islanders and to impose a neo-colonialist rule over those islands, which is unacceptable under the United Nations charter and to this House?

Mr. Pym: Yes, I will, but that is understood already. It is not only for the United States to understand that; it is for every other country to understand it. They have an interest in it, too.

Mr. Dick Douglas (Dunfermline): Will the Foreign Secretary concede that, while the people of Britain are behind all the actions that he has taken so far, they will not wish anyone to be killed on either side unless and until all other means have been exhausted, including pressure by the United States, and by economic sanctions on the Argentine Government and State?

Mr. Pym: I am doing everything that I humanly can to try to achieve a peaceful settlement, but we have to be realistic, because in an endeavour to uphold the freedom of peoples, to defend the liberty of peoples, it has at times, sadly, in history been necessary to resort to military means. Nobody wants that to happen, but we cannot exclude that possibility. But I will exclude it so long as negotiations are in play. We want to do everything we can to achieve a peaceful result. That is as far as I can go.

Mr. Healey: . . . Most hon. Members on both sides of the House will recognise that the first and best hope for the diplomatic solution to which the Government have pledged themselves is the success of the efforts of Secretary Haig. None of us would wish to do anything to prejudice the possibilities of that success. However, I hope that he will consider very seriously, as he has already expressed his view that any interim arrangements should not prejudice the outcome of negotiations for a permanent settlement in the islands, that the best possible interim arrangement would be one in which the United Nations accepted responsibility for administration. Will he discuss that possibility with Secretary Haig?

Mr. Pym: I want arrangements to be made in which the search for and the finding of the ultimate solution shall not be prejudiced in any way.

. . . A factor in achieving a peaceful settlement is the military pressure that we are applying as well as the diplomatic and economic measures that have been taken. . . .

Later—
Mr. Speaker: I understand that the Foreign Secretary wishes to make a brief statement.

Mr. Pym: After the exchanges in the House just now, it was pointed out to me that I might in a supplementary answer have given a misleading reply.

The whole thrust of my answers throughout the exchanges was to demonstrate that I was using every endeavour—which indeed I am—to achieve a peaceful settlement but that, however regrettably, the use of force could not be ruled out.

I understand that in my penultimate answer there may have been some misunderstanding about that and that I may have used words, which have not yet emerged from the *Hansard* typewriters, giving a different impression. If so, I wish to correct it, because I think that I made it clear throughout the exchanges that, however hard I was trying to achieve a peaceful settlement, the use of force could not at any stage be ruled out. If there was any misunderstanding, I want to clear it up.

Mr. Tam Dalyell (West Lothian): I beg to ask leave to move the Adjournment of the House, under Standing Order No. 9, for the purpose of discussing a specific and important matter that should have urgent consideration,

"the decision of the Organisation of American States at their meeting yesterday to invoke the inter-American treaty of mutual assistance against the wishes of the Government of the United States of America."

This shows that Latin American diplomatic support for Argentina, whether we like it or not, is hardening. It is definite that the Argentine Foreign Ministry had not expected such unanimous support. In fact, it got it by 18 votes to nil. The United States tried to prevent this and abstained. . . .

The matter is urgent because Brazil is agreeing to supply the Argentine navy with material support. It is urgent because democratic Peru is leading the campaign for counter sanctions against Europe. It is urgent because, despite formal Peruvian denials—Peru does not want to see reciprocal sanctions applied against it from the EEC—a squadron or more of Peruvian MiG 15 fighters has been sent to Argentina. . . .

The urgency relates to the matter of the task force having air cover, and whether it is true, as has been reported, that these formidable fighting machines, the MiG 15s, have already been sent from a member of the Organisation of American States—the democratic republic of Peru—to the Argentine. That has urgent military and naval consequences for the air cover protection of the task force. . . .

Mr. Speaker: . . . I have listened carefully to the exchanges in the House this afternoon. I want to make it clear that I have no intention of acceding to the request of the hon. Gentleman for an emergency debate at the present time after what I have heard this afternoon about negotiations. . . .

Report Eleven

22 APRIL 1982

There were more questions to the Prime Minister on Thursday 22 April and Mr. Wiggin gave a written answer.

Mr. Marlow: Despite the strong action taken by my right hon. Friend and despite the Government's proper desire for a diplomatic solution, both of which have the full support of the nation, has my right hon. Friend noticed reports that General Galtieri is on his way to the Falkland Islands? Does she agree that that provocative move will not help towards a peaceful settlement?

The Prime Minister: I confirm that we strive for a diplomatic and peaceful solution. Nothing that General Galtieri can do by visiting the islands today alters the fact that the islands are under British sovereignty. Neither invasion nor a visit can alter that. The best thing that can be done is to implement United Nations resolution No. 502 by the withdrawal of Argentine troops. That resolution was passed nearly three weeks ago.

Mr. Higgins: While we must all hope that the Argentine Government will now comply with resolution No. 502 and the wishes of the House, if they fail to do so, will my right hon. Friend consider going back to the Security Council and asking for economic sanctions so that we can see who is prepared to stand up and be counted in the battle against aggressors, and be seen to have exhausted all other possible means of persuasion short of military force?

The Prime Minister: My right hon. Friend knows that at the moment we are concentrating on negotiations through the good offices of Mr. Haig. If those fail, of course we shall consider what other actions should be taken. I can only remind my right hon. Friend that the history of economic sanctions and their effectiveness is not good.

Dr. Owen: Will the Prime Minister confirm that South Georgia is a direct dependency and is only administered by the Falkland Islands governor and that no Government have ever been prepared to countenance any change in that position in discussions with the Argentine? Will she confirm, further, that there are major British interests in relation to the Antarctic and South Georgia?

The Prime Minister: I confirm what the right hon. Gentleman has said. South Georgia was administered as a matter of convenience through the governorship of the Falkland Islands. Our title to it is different from that to the Falkland Islands. It is a separate dependency. It is extremely important—for the reasons that the right hon. Gentleman gave, among others.

Mr. Jim Marshall: . . . Is the Prime Minister prepared to give an undertaking that no force will be used, either against the East or West Falkland Islands, until all avenues of diplomacy, including the United Nations, have been fully explored and exhausted?

The Prime Minister: I confirm what my right hon. Friend the Foreign Secretary said yesterday, that while we are making every effort to secure a peaceful settlement, the use of force cannot be ruled out.

Mr. Aitken: Will my right hon. Friend . . . note the fact that in recent months the junta has dishonoured its international agreement to uphold the authority of the Pope as mediator in the dispute with Chile? Against that background, what possible confidence can Her Majesty's Government have that any agreement that is signed by the Argentine junta is worth the paper that it is written on?

The Prime Minister: I am well aware of what happened in the dispute to which my hon. Friend refers. . . .
It is for the reasons that my hon. Friend adduces that we should watch very carefully the task force and its presence until the withdrawal of those troops is complete. . . .

Mr. Edward Gardner: Is my right hon. Friend aware that those of us, from both sides of the House, who have just returned from the spring meeting of the IPU in Lagos found that delegates from all parts of the Commonwealth recognised the justice of our cause, and expressed firm and unequivocal support for what Her Majesty's Government are now doing to deal with the crisis with the Argentine?

The Prime Minister: I am grateful to my hon. and learned Friend. I think that nations almost everywhere recognise that unprovoked aggression must not be seen to succeed, for if it does not only will it be impossible for the people of the Falkland Islands but for many other peoples across the globe.

Mr. Spearing: As the Argentine Government are still defying United Nations resolution No. 502, does that not put a greater obligation on the Security Council and all those members of the United Nations who have condemned Argentine aggression? Can the Prime Minister now assure the House that the policy and action of Her Majesty's Government will be to retain the support of all those countries which have condemned Argentine aggression, but who may have other views about wider aspects of the matter?

The Prime Minister: It is certainly true that some countries may have their own views about the actual sovereignty of the Falkland Islands, but most of them have condemned the unprovoked aggression, and would support us in securing the withdrawal of the Argentine forces. They would also recognise that we, too, have rights of self-defence under article 51 of the United Nations charter. . . .

Mr. Gordon Wilson: . . . Does the Prime Minister realise that if the Government engage in hostilities before the processes of negotiation have been fully and adequately carried out, a lot of the support that she has received in the House, and at home and abroad, will disappear like snow off the dike on a hot spring day? Will she, therefore, in pursuit of negotiations for a peaceful settlement, consider the transfer of sovereignty to the United Nations—[HON. MEMBERS: "No."]—so that the people living in the Falkland Islands will be able to have their security guaranteed by an international body?

The Prime Minister: I cannot rule out the use of force. The process of negotiations could go on endlessly. There is a maritime exclusion zone. We must also expect that we have a right of self-defence under article 51 of the charter for islands that have been invaded. Of course, we would all prefer and will do everything possible to seek a peaceful settlement, but, as the hon. Gentleman will understand, that it is not easy, particularly when seeking a settlement with a country some of whose people say that they will withdraw only if they succeed in obtaining sovereignty as the price of that withdrawal.

Mrs. Knight: Will the Prime Minister dissociate herself from those who suggest that the British flag is just another piece of cloth, and those who consider that it might be a convenient ploy to have it fluttering side by side with the Argentine flag, even before the people of the Falklands have had an opportunity to make their decision clear? . . .

The Prime Minister: . . . To all of us here, and in particular to the Falklands, the flag is a great symbol of pride and allegiance to the Crown. No one would quarrel for a moment with that statement.

Mr. Parry: Will not the Prime Minister now offer her resignation, in view of the revelation that her Government have recently been supplying arms to the Argentine that may be used against the Falklanders and British forces? Is that not tantamount to treasonable conduct?

The Prime Minister: If the hon. Gentleman looks at the history of the supply of arms to the Argentine he will find that a number of contracts were negotiated during the lifetime of his own Government.

Mr. Hastings: Does my right hon. Friend agree that the truly remarkable achievement of the Royal Navy and the other Services in mounting this task force with such efficiency and speed has been insufficiently recognised to date? Does she further agree that any continuing plea for a restriction of the use of force, or some other kind of compromise, can serve only to bring comfort and strength to the junta, and thus increase the risk of further miscalculation on its part, and loss of life?

The Prime Minister: I agree with my hon. Friend that the speed with which the Royal Navy assembled the task force, and its efficiency throughout, have been a matter of pride for us all. I entirely agree with him that sending the task force, sending it efficiently and well-equipped, has been a factor that is more likely to lead the junta to a peaceful settlement than would have been the case without it.

Dr. Mawhinney: Does my right hon. Friend agree that if a democracy is unwilling to defend its own territory or people against conventional armed attack after, and only after, all peace negotiations have been exhausted, it might find that its credibility is seriously damaged when it comes together with other democracies in an organisation such as NATO?

The Prime Minister: I fully agree with my hon. Friend. One must be prepared to defend those things in which one believes and be prepared to use force if it is the only way to secure a future of liberty and self-determination. . . .

The Under-Secretary of State for the Armed Forces (Mr. Jerry Wiggin): Since the Falkland Islands emergency began there has been some increase in the numbers enquiring about joining the Armed Forces; but we have not recruited any more people into either the regular or reserve forces specifically in response to recent events, and the rate of acceptances remains as previously expected.

Report Twelve

26 APRIL 1982

On Monday 26 April, the Prime Minister made a statement.

The Prime Minister (Mrs. Margaret Thatcher): . . . In our continuing pursuit of a negotiated settlement, my right hon. Friend the Foreign and Commonwealth Secretary visited Washington on 22 and 23 April. He had many hours of intensive detailed discussion with Mr. Haig. Their talks proved constructive and helpful, but there are still considerable difficulties. Mr. Haig now intends to pursue his efforts further with the Argentine Government.

However, the Argentine Foreign Minister is reported to be unwilling to continue negotiations at present. I hope that he will reconsider this. As the British task force approaches closer to the Falklands, the urgent need is to speed up the negotiations, not to slow them down. We remain in close touch with Mr. Haig.

I now turn to events on South Georgia yesterday. The first phase of the operation to repossess the island began at first light when the Argentine submarine "Santa Fe" was detected close to British warships that were preparing to land forces on South Georgia. . . .

The "Santa Fe" posed a significant threat to the successful completion of the operation and to British warships and forces launching the landing. Helicopters therefore engaged and disabled the Argentine submarine.

Just after 4 pm London time yesterday, British troops landed on South Georgia and advanced towards Grytviken. At about 6 pm the commander of the Argentine forces in Grytviken surrendered, having offered only limited resistance.

British forces continued to advance during the night and are now in control of Leith, the other main settlement on South Georgia. At 10 o'clock this morning the officer commanding the Argentine forces on South Georgia formally surrendered.

British forces throughout the operation used the minimum force necessary to achieve a successful outcome. No British casualties have been notified and it is reported that only one Argentine sustained serious injuries. About 180 prisoners were taken, including up to 50 military reinforcements who had been on the Argentine submarine. The prisoners will be returned to Argentina.

British Antarctic survey personnel on the island were reported to be safe when we last heard from them early yesterday afternoon. Our forces are making contact with them and arrangements are in hand to evacuate them, if they so wish.

I am sure that the House will join me in congratulating our forces on carrying out this operation successfully, and recapturing the island. The action that we have taken is fully in accord with our inherent right of self-defence under article 51 of the United Nations Charter. . . .

I should like to emphasise that the repossession of South Georgia, including the attack on the Argentine submarine, in no way alters the Government's determination to do everything possible to achieve a negotiated solution to the present crisis. We seek the implementation of the Security Council resolution, and we seek it by peaceful means if possible.

Mr. Michael Foot (Ebbw Vale): I am sure that the Prime Minister must appreciate that, along with other moods, there is a deepening sense of anxiety throughout the country and I trust that she and the Government will take account of it. I am sure that the whole country will be relieved to know that the South Georgia operation was carried through without loss of life on our side and without serious injury on either side.

We are entitled to stress to all concerned that the recovery of South Georgia was fully within our international rights. It was in no sense a breach of the charter, as some have falsely alleged. Indeed, it may help us in other areas, particularly in view of the extreme skill with which the operation was executed. Of course, the Falkland Islands and South Georgia are two very different propositions and I am sure that the House and the country understand that.

However, the most important and persistent question remains, and is indeed intensified. I put the question in the light of what the Prime Minister has said. How are we to pursue the search for the diplomatic and peaceful settlement to which she has referred? What is to happen next? The right hon. Lady spoke of speeding up the negotiations. What steps are the Government taking to speed up those negotiations?

What stage has Mr. Haig's mediation reached and what will happen if that mediation is not able to be pursued? . . .

When will we return to the Security Council on these matters? In the meantime, how are we to ensure—indeed, to be absolutely sure—that there will be no dangerous escalation of the crisis in any way?

What is the form of political control over military operations? In present circumstances that political control must be absolute and there must be no possibility of any mistakes whatever.

The Opposition remain firmly, unshakably and persistently committed to fresh initiatives in the search for a peaceful settlement. If one initiative fails, another has to be started. Some Conservative Members are laughing, but the approach that I have outlined is the spirit in which the Government should be going about their business. . . .

The Prime Minister: I thank the right hon. Gentleman . . . especially for stressing that we had a right to retake and recapture South Georgia in accordance with the rules of the United Nations charter. I join the right hon. Gentleman in congratulating our forces on the professional skill with which they carried out their task.

The right hon. Gentleman says that people are anxious. We share that anxiety in the search for a diplomatic settlement. More than three weeks have elapsed since the United Nations Security Council resolution was passed calling upon the Argentine forces to withdraw. During that time, far from withdrawing, the Argentine Government have put reinforcements of men, equipment, and materials on the islands. If we have not yet reached a settlement, the blame lies at the feet of the Argentine Government.

We are naturally ready and anxious at any time to continue these negotiations. We have stayed constantly in touch with Mr. Haig. I hope that Mr. Costa Mendez will reconsider his decision not to see Mr. Haig and that he will see him shortly. If not, Mr. Haig can, of course, communicate with the Argentine Government in other ways. . . .

It is, of course, the United Nations Security Council resolution that we want implemented. I do not think that there is any disposition in New York to involve the United Nations further while the negotiations with Mr. Haig are still continuing . . .

I believe that most people there reckon that the best hope for a peaceful settlement is through the negotiations with Mr. Haig. I believe that we must continue those negotiations with all possible speed.

Of course we search for peace. We did not break the peace. We must remember that while we search for that peace our people—British people—are under the occupation of the Argentine invader. We must remember that in the way in which we carry out these negotiations. . . .

Mr. Foot: . . ."We are keeping in touch with Mr. Haig", was all that she said about the way in which we are making efforts to keep the negotiations going. . . .

The Prime Minister: . . . As I think the right hon. Gentleman will understand, I cannot give him details of negotiations while they continue, but we pursue them as vigorously as possible. After all, what we are asking for is the withdrawal of Argentine troops in accordance with the United Nations Security Council resolution.

Sir Derek Walker-Smith (Hertfordshire, East): Will my right hon. Friend clarify the position about the reference of this dispute to the International Court of Justice. . . ? Can she say that, subject to the prior withdrawal of troops by Argentina in conformity with United Nations resolution 502, is the Government's policy to suggest a reference of the dispute to the court in accordance with the United Nations charter and the statute of the court? . . .

The Prime Minister: I believe that we referred the matter of the dependencies of the Falklands to the International Court of Justice in, I think I am right in saying, 1955. My right hon. and learned Friend will know that both parties have to agree to go to the International Court of Justice for it to adjudicate. We took the case to the court, but the Argentines did not agree to the jurisdiction of the court with regard to the dependencies. It is not through any lack of consent on our part that the case has not gone to the International Court of Justice.

Dr. David Owen (Plymouth, Devonport): Is the Prime Minister aware that we on these Benches fully and unequivocally support the decision to repossess South Georgia and congratulate all the Services and Service men, who have taken considerable risks? We are grateful for the fact that there has been no loss of life. . . .

Many of us believe that it is right, with the Organisation of American

States meeting in Washington today, to give Secretary of State Haig a few more days, but that the time is approaching when the United States, if it is unable to achieve movement, will have to make a decision to apply economic sanctions. Can the House be given some assurance that before any major escalation of violence took place the Prime Minister would be ready to go to the United Nations to discuss, under articles 82 and 83 . . . the possibility of using those provisions for any interim administration?

The Prime Minister: . . . It is, after all, the implementation of the United Nations resolution that we seek. . . . the United Nations is not in a position to implement the resolution itself. . . . I believe that it is right at the moment to continue through Mr. Haig to try to seek a peaceful settlement. . . .

Time is getting extremely short as the task force approaches the islands. Three weeks have elapsed since the resolution. One cannot have a wide range of choice and a wide range of military options with the task force in the wild and stormy weathers of that area.

Mr. Mark Carlisle (Runcorn): . . . Is my right hon. Friend aware of the overwhelming support that exists in America for the action that we are taking and the overwhelming understanding among many Members of Congress and others that the principle at stake is as important to America and the Western world as it is to this country?

The Prime Minister: . . . I believe that the American people know that unprovoked aggression must not be allowed to succeed. If it does, there will be no international law and many people will fear for their future.

Mr. Tony Benn (Bristol, South East): Is the Prime Minister aware that, although the House and the country are united in condemning the aggression, public opinion, so far as it can be ascertained, favours a much more serious attempt at negotiation through the United Nations than has occurred, and that a majority of people would not follow the Government into a war with the Argentine, which would threaten the loss of many lives, including Service men and Falkland Islanders, which might spread the conflict and which would isolate this country? If the Prime Minister continues to underrate the importance of negotiation and proceeds with the war, the responsibility for the loss of life will rest upon her shoulders.

The Prime Minister: The Government lack no vigour or will to pursue negotiations. The lack is on the part of the Argentine Government to obey the Security Council resolution. In the meantime, perhaps the right hon. Member for Bristol, South-East (Mr. Benn) will remember that our people are under the heel of the Argentine invader.

Mr. John Peyton (Yeovil): Is the Prime Minister aware that few things could do more to bring support to the action that she and the Government are taking than the thoroughly mischievous question asked by the right hon. Member for Bristol, South-East (Mr. Benn)?

Mr. Arthur Bottomley (Middlesbrough): What is the attitude to the

Government's policy of Commonwealth countries in general and those in the West Indies area in particular?

The Prime Minister: Commonwealth countries have been most helpful in condemning the unprovoked aggression of the Argentine. Many of them have stopped imports from that country. New Zealand has also stopped exports. Mr. Fraser has sent a very strong message of support to the United States Government.

As to the countries in the Caribbean area, Guyana in particular is a member of the Security Council and voted for United Nations resolution 502. There are many territorial disputes in the Caribbean, and many people realise that it is crucial to them that the Argentine should not succeed in its invasion of the Falkland Islands.

Mr. Russell Johnston (Inverness): Will the Prime Minister convey to the British forces who recaptured South Georgia the admiration of Liberal Members for the skill, courage and restraint that they demonstrated in that operation?

Does she realise that it will inevitably be increasingly difficult to give her a blank cheque without far more information? Has she further considered the suggestion of my right hon. Friend the leader of the Liberal Party that there should be all-party discussions on the matter? Can she say more about economic sanctions, especially the supply of arms? Is it true that Israel is supplying ammunition to the Argentine?

The Prime Minister: The whole House admires what our forces have done, and I shall gladly send that message on behalf of the whole House. . . .

Time is indeed short. There is no lack of will on our part to negotiate. The trouble is in getting Argentina to withdraw. It may not be possible to achieve an Argentine withdrawal by negotiation, but that is what we are seeking. Argentina has had more than three weeks in which to comply with the Security Council resolution, but it has shown no inclination to do so. Indeed, it has reinforced its troops.

The hon. Gentleman will be aware of European sanctions and those taken by a number of Commonwealth countries. I am not in a position to say precisely what Israel has or has not supplied to the Argentine.

Mr. Julian Amery (Brighton, Pavilion): . . . I welcome the decision to keep the door for negotiation open, but does my right hon. Friend agree that we cannot keep the task force treading water indefinitely at the mercy of the Atlantic storms or the changing tides of political opinion?

The Prime Minister: . . . Time is short because of the weather conditions, the distance from home and because the task force is now approaching the islands. We must take account of that and do everything to speed up negotiations. I hope that that message will get through to the Argentine Government, because that is where it needs to go.

Mr. Douglas Jay (Battersea, North): Is it not clear that there will be a far better prospect of an acceptable negotiated settlement if, meanwhile, we fully exercise our unchallengeable rights of self-defence?

The Prime Minister: Yes; I am grateful to the right hon. Gentleman for making that point. We shall have greater chances of a peaceful settlement if we bring greater military pressure to bear on the Argentine Government.

Mr. Robert Rhodes James (Cambridge): Will my right hon. Friend emphasise that since the Government came to office they have done almost everything to attempt to negotiate a peaceful settlement between 1979 and the advent of hostilities and have continued with that approach since? Will she also emphasise that it is not us but the Argentine which has infringed not only the principle but also the letter of the United Nations charter and that it is infringing resolution 502? . . .

The Prime Minister: I confirm what my hon. Friend says. We are doing everything in accordance with the United Nations charter. We continue to seek a peaceful solution. If we are not successful, the fault will lie not with us or Mr. Haig, but fairly and squarely with the Argentine Government.

Mr. Eric Ogden (Liverpool, West Derby): Will the Prime Minister find time to give her attention to the problem of British Falkland Island citizens who are in the United Kingdom? . . .

Will the right hon. Lady also consider the suggestion . . . that a Falkland Islands secretariat or Government office should be established so that they would receive some support and not be dependent on the good will of the Foreign Office or the charity of the Falkland Island Office?

The Prime Minister: I shall examine the matter urgently. We are in touch with those people. If they need help, of course we must give it.

With regard to the Falkland Islanders still in the Falkland Islands, I have made it clear that if some of them wish to be evacuated temporarily and have not the means to do so, the Government will ensure that the necessary means are provided.

Sir John Eden (Bournemouth, West): Did not the Government make it clear from the outset that if Argentina would not be talked out of the Falkland Islands it would have to be fought out? Now that there can be no doubt about the determination and ability of Britain to take any necessary military action, will the Prime Minister ensure that in the continuing negotiations to secure observance of resolution 502 she will keep the initiative firmly in her hands?

The Prime Minister: We are trying constantly to take initiatives to ensure that the negotiations continue. We shall continue doing that. Only one thing needs to be done immediately under the Security Council resolution—the withdrawal of Argentine forces. After that, negotiations can continue. They have been going on for many years. As soon as the Argentine forces withdraw, we shall be prepared to start negotiations once again.

Mr. Tam Dalyell (West Lothian): As the runway at Port Stanley has been strengthened and lengthened to take Mirages, MiGs and Skyhawks, what are the consequences for air superiority and what will be the next action of the task force?

The Prime Minister: I do not wholly accept the premises upon which the hon. Gentleman's question is founded.

Mr. George Cunningham (Islington, South and Finsbury): Will the right hon. Lady, both directly and through the United Nations, bring to the attention of the Argentine Government their obligations under the fourth Geneva convention of 1949 with regard to not compelling Falkland Islanders to remain in those parts of the Falkland Islands that are particularly subject to combat danger?

The Prime Minister: I shall, of course, consider doing what the hon. Gentleman says. Many of the Falkland Islanders have left Port Stanley and gone out to camp. There are far fewer in Port Stanley now than there were previously, but we shall certainly consider the hon. Gentleman's suggestion.

Sir Bernard Braine (Essex, South-East): I am sure that in these circumstances it is right and humane to return prisoners of war to the Argentine, but will my right hon. Friend give an assurance that if any difficulty arises about this the names and state of health of such men will be made known to their anxious relatives. . . .

The Prime Minister: I should make one point clear. These are not prisoners of war. A state of war does not exist between ourselves and the Argentine. They are prisoners, and they will be returned as soon as possible. We shall, of course, let their names and state of health be known to their relatives as soon as possible. I understand that the commander of the Argentine forces on the island is already grateful for the prompt medical attention that was given to the one Argentine marine who was badly hurt.

Mr. Jack Ashley (Stoke-on-Trent, South): . . . Does she agree that neither Britain nor the Argentine can benefit from a war? Will she emphasise that we shall seek a negotiated settlement and that, if that requires economic force, we shall use economic force and economic sanctions and, indeed, every sanction short of war, because war would be disastrous?

The Prime Minister: First, a number of countries have joined us in imposing economic sanctions. As the right hon. Gentleman knows, such sanctions are slow to operate and tend not to be wholly successful as there is a good deal of leakage through third countries. Secondly, I agree that resolution is required—resolution to ensure that unprovoked aggression does not succeed.

Sir Nigel Fisher (Surbiton): . . . Mr. Haig's valiant efforts to mediate have now apparently been ended for the time being by the decision of the Argentine Foreign Minister. Will my right hon. Friend reconsider the position and suggest to the United States Government that it might now be appropriate for them to impose economic sanctions against the Argentine, if only to show which side they are on?

The Prime Minister: I understand the feelings of my hon. Friend and of many right hon. and hon. Members on this matter. Such economic sanctions would be of a kind and a degree perhaps greater than any other that could be brought to bear. I understand, however, that Mr. Haig believes that the meeting with Costa Mendez has only been postponed and will take place. Even if it does not, there are means of contacting and negotiating with the Argentine junta direct.

Mr. Eric Deakins (Waltham Forest): Why must the pace of negotiations be dictated by the requirements of military strategy in the South Atlantic, when our priorities should surely be the other way round?

The Prime Minister: The pace of negotiations has been very swift. When one has a task force such as we have in the wild and stormy weathers of the South Atlantic, that is a limiting factor on possible military activities which any sensible Government must take into account.

Mr. Michael Grylls (Surrey, North-West): . . . Does she agree that it is important to continue to follow the policy of the stick and the carrot—the stick to ensure that aggression pays no dividends and the carrot to show that we have no quarrel with the Argentine people, but only with the illegal actions of their Government?

The Prime Minister: I accept that negotiations are more likely to succeed if military pressure is kept up. One must always consider the military options, and in doing so we must look after our soldiers and marines who have to undertake them. . . .

Report Thirteen

27 APRIL 1982

Questions to the Ministry of Defence were put on Tuesday 27 April. They were followed by a statement by the Prime Minister.

The Secretary of State for Defence (Mr. John Nott): . . . There remains a substantial Argentine force on the Falkland Islands. The Royal Navy task force, deploying to the area of the Falkland Islands, is prepared for a wide range of military options. The House will not expect me to discuss these. However, safeguarding of civilian lives will be one of our highest priorities. . . .

Mr. Kenneth Carlisle: Does my right hon. Friend agree that the only certain way to ensure the future security of the Falkland Islands is for the Argentine to understand beyond any shadow of doubt that it cannot gain its wishes by an act of aggression and that a lasting settlement can be reached only when it has withdrawn its forces?

Mr. Nott: I agree with my hon. Friend. That principle applies to many countries and islands throughout the world.

Sir William van Straubenzee: . . . If it should be necessary to take additional action, which might include the neutralisation of hostile air forces, there would be widespread support, particularly if the objective were the limiting of casualties, as has been so brilliantly displayed up to now.

Mr. Nott: . . . If force becomes necessary, I agree that we should use the minimum amount to achieve our objective.

Mr. Allaun: Do the islanders want the attack that was clearly implied by the Prime Minister yesterday, with all the blood and tears that would entail for their families and for British Service men and their wives, children and parents? No one has asked the islanders what they want. . . .
Should not the United Nations be authorised to send a team to ascertain the Falkland Islanders' views?

Mr. Nott: The Falkland Islanders cannot be consulted about such matters at the moment because they are the victims of an act of aggression. Nobody would be happier than I if we could contact the Falkland Islanders to ascertain their wishes. That is our principal purpose. . . .

Mr. Foulkes: Has the Secretary of State made . . . any arrangements to use an air base in Chile in the event of a military engagement with the Argentine over the Falkland Islands?

Mr. Nott: I cannot comment on that. We have had widespread support from countries all round the world, but I cannot comment on such matters.

Mr. Beith: . . . Does the right hon. Gentleman now realise that visible, flexible, naval power is a more important independent deterrent for Britain—and one that Britain may even be obliged to use on its own—than a nuclear deterrent?

Mr. Nott: I am certainly in favour of visible naval power. . . . Among the lessons that we have learnt from this incident is that, in the last resort, Great Britain must be responsible for its own defence. There is no way in which this country can ultimately be protected without a nuclear as well as a conventional deterrent.

Lord James Douglas-Hamilton: Given that South Thule is in the general Falkland Islands area, will my right hon. Friend tell the House how many Argentines are illegally present on the island. . . .

Mr. Nott: . . . I do not know the exact number involved, but it is between 40 and 70. . . .

Mr. John Silkin: . . . Will the right hon. Gentleman assure the House that the Government intend to provide a strong and proper conventional maritime defence and to scrap Trident?

Mr. Nott: The principal threat to Britain comes from the Soviet Union and its allies, not from Argentina. As a member of NATO, we maintain a range of forces, both conventional and nuclear, to deter that threat. . . .

Mr. Silkin: Has not the right hon. Gentleman yet understood that one-third of the task force will be scrapped two years from now under the defence White Paper scheme?

Mr. Nott: Again, that is an inaccurate remark. Of the destroyers and frigates now in the task force, not one is on the sales list and not one was on the sales list before the incident began. The figure of 17 vessels is a figment of the right hon. Gentleman's imagination.

Mr. Robert Atkins: Does my right hon. Friend agree that the Royal Navy's ability to put together in four days a task force of sufficient size to go to the South Atlantic is a tribute to the Royal Navy's present capability? . . .

Mr. Nott: . . . Nothing in our plans for the future will prevent a naval task force of the type now at sea from being sent on a similar task in 1985 or 1990. However, any such task force in 1985 or 1990 will have been further modernised and will have more up-to-date weapons.

Mr. Skinner: Now that the Secretary of State and his colleagues have found out that they are dealing with a Fascist junta in the Argentine, will they give a categoric assurance, so that similar mistakes are not made in future, not to sell any more arms to Fascist regimes?

Mr. Nott: . . . The vast majority of the modern weapons possessed by the Argentines were sold to them during the time of the previous Labour Government.

Mr. Jim Marshall: On the assumption that we manage to evict the Argentines from the Falkland Islands, how much additional expenditure will be necessary in this year and succeeding years to maintain in that area a permanent naval presence of sufficient strength to deter any future aggression by the Argentines?

Mr. Nott: Clearly a large amount of money will be needed to maintain a substantial naval presence in the South Atlantic. We are seeking a negotiated settlement for the future security of the Falkland Islands without the need for a naval presence.

Mr. Trotter asked the Secretary of State for Defence whether he will now retain HMS "Hermes" in service till the end of the decade.

The Minister of State for the Armed Forces (Mr. Peter Blaker): We . . . plan to phase out HMS "Hermes" once HMS "Ark Royal" joins the Fleet.

Mr. Trotter: The departure of HMS "Invincible" and HMS "Hermes" for the South Atlantic at 72 hours' notice was a great achievement for both the Navy and the dockyards, but does my hon. Friend agree that we were fortunate that one of those carriers was not in for a refit at the time? Does he further agree that it is not merely desirable, but essential, that there should be three major ships if two are to be available for service at any time, as is clearly necessary?

Mr. Blaker: . . . Our strategy . . . was designed with the point in mind that the main threat comes from the Soviet Union. . . .

Mr. Jay: In view of the great success of the task force, will the Government cancel the sale of HMS "Invincible" to Australia?

Mr. Blaker: No, we cannot cancel the sale of HMS "Invincible" to Australia, as it has already been agreed. . . .

Mr. Churchill: . . . Will the Government therefore consider the fact that, in terms of cost-effectiveness, increasing the fleet to three carriers will double the number of carriers that can be put to sea? . . .

Mr. Blaker: I am not sure that my hon. Friend is right to say that such an increase will double the number of carriers that can be put to sea. If we have two, two will be available for two-thirds of the time. . . .

Mr. Denzil Davies: Is the Minister aware that if General Galtieri had

136

waited a few months we should not have had a task force to send to the South Atlantic, because HMS "Hermes" would have been in the knacker's yard and HMS "Invincible" would have been on the way to Australia? . . .

Mr. Blaker: . . . HMS "Hermes" will remain in service until 1985. . . .

Mr. Beith: Do Ministers now recognise that the decision to scrap HMS "Endurance" was taken by the Argentine as a signal that Britain would not be ready to defend the Falkland Islands? . . .

Mr. Blaker: I think that the Government have conceded that the planned withdrawal of HMS "Endurance" may have been taken by the Argentines as some kind of signal, but HMS "Endurance" cannot have been taken by them as a deterrent, because the invasion occurred when it was still on station. . . .

Mr. Newens: How on earth does the right hon. Gentleman expect to inspire any confidence in the future defence policy of the country when he is refusing at this stage to admit, even in the light of the Falkland Islands crisis, that he got any of his priorities wrong, when the whole country realises that we would not be in the present mess if he had got them right? . . .

Mr. Nott: . . . No other nation in the world—and in that I include the two super powers—could have put to sea a task force of this size in three days. There is nothing in our plans that would prevent such a force, with two carriers and an equal number of more modern frigates and more modern weapons, from putting to sea in 1985 and 1990. . . .

The Prime Minister (Mrs. Margaret Thatcher): Following my statement yesterday, I must emphasise again today that, while the Government remain determined to do everything possible to achieve a negotiated settlement, time is fast running out. I know that Mr. Haig understands this, and that he has been in touch with the Argentine Government today.

The Foreign Ministers of the Organisation of American States are still meeting. As Mr. Haig told the meeting yesterday, treatment of the dispute within the framework of the Rio Treaty would be neither appropriate nor effective: UN Security Council resolution 502 provides the surest guide to a peaceful settlement.

British forces in South Georgia have contacted all the British Antarctic Survey personnel and the two wildlife photographers. All are reported safe and well, and food and other supplies are being delivered. Arrangements have now been made for them to leave shortly.

Mr. Dalyell: What did the Prime Minister say to the Secretary-General of the United Nations' earnest request not to escalate the problem?

The Prime Minister: I am very well aware of the Secretary-General's request and that the Security Council's resolution must be complied with. It is Argentina that has flagrantly failed to comply, and it is because of that failure that we must now be free to exercise our right to self-defence under article 51.

Mr. St. John-Stevas: . . . Will she, even at this eleventh hour, consider a new step, namely, utilising the mediation services of the Holy See, which has unrivalled experience in such matters, particularly in Latin America?

The Prime Minister: I am grateful to my right hon. Friend. As he knows, His Holiness is already mediating in a dispute between Argentina and Chile. His Holiness sent a telegram yesterday to Her Majesty the Queen urging the Government to make every effort to find a peaceful solution on the basis of justice and international law, and he hopes and wishes to believe that such a peaceful solution is still possible.

Mr. Foot: The right hon. Lady's reply on the subject of the appeal from the Secretary-General of the United Nations was insufficient and unsatisfactory. Does the right hon. Lady not appreciate that this is a new element in the situation? . . .

Will the Prime Minister look at this matter in a much fuller context? Will she undertake to ensure that the Foreign Secretary goes to New York to discuss this matter with the Secretary-General? . . .

The Prime Minister: We have an excellent ambassadorial representative at the United Nations, and he was there to receive this statement. In the second paragraph of that statement the Secretary-General said:

"In this critical situation, the Secretary-General therefore appeals to both parties to comply immediately with the provisions of Security Council resolution 502". . . .

I am perfectly prepared to read both the first paragraph and the next.

This is a mandatory resolution of the Security Council, which has the force of international law. No statement can overcome something that has the force of international law. Also, under the United Nations charter, until that resolution is complied with Great Britain has the right of self-defence under article 51. We have taken, and continue to take, the view that, unless we bring military pressure to bear, the Argentines are unlikely to withdraw from the Falklands.

Mr. Foot: I put it to the right hon. Lady again that her reply is entirely unsatisfactory and does not come anywhere near measuring up to the scale of events. Will she now tell us the answer that was given by our ambassador to the Secretary-General on this matter? Will she respond to my suggestion. . . .

The Prime Minister: I think that our ambassador's reply is likely to have been . . . of the nature that the best way to comply is for the United Nations to bring pressure to bear on the Argentine to withdraw her forces. If she withdrew them there would be no problem whatsoever.

Mr. Foot: It seems from the right hon. Lady's reply that she does not even know what our ambassador said and was making the answer up as she went along. I say to the right hon. Lady, as straight as I can, that if she does not make a proper response to this appeal from the Secretary-General of the United Nations—who is entitled to make such an appeal under the constitution of the United Nations—along the lines that I have suggested, with either the Foreign Secretary or somebody else going to

New York to discuss the matter—and I put it in a hypothetical manner—she will inflict a grievous blow on our country's cause. I hope that she will consider the matter properly.

The Prime Minister: I totally disagree with the right hon. Gentleman. If we were to refuse to take any further military action during this negotiation, we would put many of our soldiers and sailors in jeopardy. . . .

Mr. Foot: . . . I ask the right hon. Lady not to take any further steps in the escalation of military matters and to give the House of Commons the chance of deciding what should be the proper response to the appeal of the Secretary-General. . . .

The Prime Minister: I stand by the terms of the United Nations resolution and of the United Nations charter. Until the terms of that resolution are complied with and the Argentine forces withdraw, we shall continue to exercise our rights under article 51. My reply to the Secretary-General is to urge him, as well as the right hon. Gentleman, to address his remarks to the junta in the Argentine. . . .

Mr. Crouch: . . . In view of Secretary of State Haig's declaration that the United States will do all that it can to resolve the differences between ourselves and Argentina without further conflict, can my right hon. Friend say what differences stand in the way of a peaceful and honourable settlement?

The Prime Minister: . . . Mr. Haig has been in touch with the Argentine Government today. We hope that that will be fruitful. The main stumbling block is that the Argentines have not withdrawn their forces, but have steadily reinforced their garrison. Throughout the whole of the period since the passage of the United Nations resolution they have continued to reinforce their forces on the Falkland Islands with both men and materials.

Mr. Dormand: Is the right hon. Lady aware that the belligerence that she has shown in the past two days misjudges not only the critical situation in the Falkland Islands but the mood of the British people? I do not in any way underrate the many difficulties and problems involved, but does the right hon. Lady agree that at this stage what is required above all else is a rapid intensification and widening of economic sanctions, particularly through the agencies of the United Nations? At the same time, will she make it clear to President Reagan, in straight talking, that his neutralism will not be forgotten in this country?

The Prime Minister: I do not believe that we have misjudged the views of our citizens over the Falkland Islands. I hope that the hon. Gentleman will remember, too, that there are many British citizens living under occupation on the Falkland Islands. He will be as anxious as I am to see that they are not under that occupation for a moment longer than is necessary. The easiest way to achieve that is for the Argentines to withdraw their forces. They broke the peace first.

Mr. Colvin: . . . The British people are resolutely behind my right hon. Friend. . . .

Can my right hon. Friend confirm that the full resources of our propaganda machine are being mobilised so that the Argentines are aware of the real truth of the situation and are not being force-fed lies by their military dictators?

The Prime Minister: We are doing as much as we possibly can, especially through the BBC external services, to put out the facts of the situation. I cannot say how often they are heard in the Argentine.

Mr. Benn: Is it not clear . . . that the Government never had the slightest intention of using the United Nations for the purpose of negotiation, or of negotiating directly under resolution 502, and that it was always the Prime Minister's intention that there should be only a military expedition? . . .

The Prime Minister: The right hon. Gentleman is talking nonsense. I suspect that he knows it. The Government went immediately, the day after the invasion, to the Security Council, gained the support of many other nations and secured the passage of that resolution. It is over three weeks since that resolution was passed. It has not been complied with. On the other hand, Argentina has continued to make the situation worse. . . .

Sir Paul Bryant: As the rights and wrongs of the dispute have already been established by international law and supported by the Security Council, is not three weeks about as long a period of intense negotiation as can be justified if both parties are negotiating in good faith?

The Prime Minister: My hon. Friend is right. Not only have three weeks passed, but during that time the Argentines have put more and more reinforcements on the islands, which shows that they do not intend to comply with the resolution. As we have been saying recently, and as Mr. Haig has been saying, time is running out, because the military options in that part of the world must have regard to the weather and climatic conditions. We still require a peaceful settlement, and we can get one if the Argentines are willing to have it. . . .

Mr. Foot: . . . Will she publish as speedily as possible the timing and exact wording of the reply given by our ambassador to the Secretary-General's statement, so that we can all see what was said on behalf of our country? . . .

If the case is as good as she says, why should not our Foreign Secretary go to New York and state it there? . . .

The Prime Minister: I do not think that there is a formal reply to such a message. Various views are expressed informally, but it is not a formal reply. Formal reports are given by our ambassador to the United Nations, as they must be, about article 51 and the precise action that we have taken. We have full details of that. I stress to the right hon. Gentleman that resolution 502 is mandatory. Unfortunately, the United Nations does not enforce it and has no means of enforcing it. Therefore, we can only bring the best possible pressure to bear on the Argentine to enforce it.

As the right hon. Gentleman may have heard our ambassador say this morning from New York, there is no disposition there at the moment to return to the United Nations so long as Mr. Haig's peace initiative is in play. My right hon. Friend the Foreign Secretary has recently returned from Washington. I do not think that he could achieve anything by going to New York now.

Mr. Foot: Does the right hon. Lady's reply to me mean—I can construe it only in this way—that there is to be no official reply on behalf of Her Majesty's Government to the appeal from the Secretary-General?

The Prime Minister: I can make an official reply if the right hon. Gentleman wishes. It will not be any different from what I have said, because the governing factor in United Nations law—I use the word "law"—and in international law is the resolution of the Security Council. The only possible thing that one can call upon the Secretary-General to do is to implement it. The only thing that I call upon the right hon. Gentleman to do is to use all his powers and influence with the Argentine Government to implement it.

Mr. David Steel: . . . Were the proposals that the Foreign Secretary brought back from Washington commended to the Government by Mr. Haig? Have the Government made a detailed response to those proposals?

The Prime Minister: The proposals do not yet have the status of formal proposals. They are still discussions. We have let Secretary Haig know of our views, but my right hon. Friend did that while he was still in Washington. . . .

Report Fourteen

28 APRIL 1982

On Wednesday 28 April, Mr. Nott gave written answers to questions. One included the announcement of a total exclusion zone.

Mr. Nott: The following statement was issued by the Government earlier today:

"From 1100 GMT on 30th April 1982, a Total Exclusion Zone will be established around the Falkland Islands. The outer limits of this Zone is the same as for the Maritime Exclusion Zone established on Monday 12th April 1982, namely a circle of 200 nautical miles radius from latitude 51 degrees 40 minutes South, 59 degrees 30 minutes West. From the time indicated, the Exclusion Zone will apply not only to Argentine warships and Argentine naval auxiliaries but also to any other ship, whether naval or merchant vessel, which is operating in support of the illegal occupation of the Falkland Islands by Argentine forces. The Exclusion Zone will also apply to any aircraft, whether military or civil, which is operating in support of the illegal occupation. Any ship and any aircraft whether military or civil which is found within this Zone without due authority from the Ministry of Defence in London will be regarded as operating in support of the illegal occupation and will therefore be regarded as hostile and will be liable to be attacked by British Forces.

Also from the time indicated, Port Stanley airport will be closed; and any aircraft on the ground in the Falkland Islands will be regarded as present in support of the illegal occupation and accordingly is liable to attack.

These measures are without prejudice to the right of the UK to take whatever additional measures may be needed in exercise of its right of self-defence, under Article 51 of the UN Charter."

Report Fifteen

29 APRIL 1982

On Thursday 29 April, the Prime Minister answered questions and then opened the fourth debate.

Mr. Race: Will the Prime Minister tell the House how many British and Argentine soldiers, and how many Falklanders, she is prepared to see killed—*[Interruption.]*—to establish the sovereignty that she will later concede in negotiations?

The Prime Minister: To answer the hon. Gentleman indirectly, there is only one thing that is more important than peace, and that is liberty and justice. If someone had not fought to get that for us, the hon. Gentleman could not even have asked me that question.

Mr. Lennox-Boyd: Will my right hon. Friend find time this afternoon to reflect on the significance of the observations of the Secretary-General of the Commonwealth, which indicated that in his opinion the Commonwealth not only fully supported the British diplomatic position, but accepted that there might be a need for further force?

The Prime Minister: Yes, Sir, I saw Sir Shridath Ramphal's observation, and I might have something to say about it later. It was excellent and showed that the British Commonwealth firmly believes in upholding international law and in seeing that unprovoked aggression does not win.

Mr. William Hamilton: Since the United States of America's attempt to play the honest broker seems to be about to fail, will the Prime Minister give an undertaking that if the American Government do not then come off the fence immediately and impose economic sanctions on Argentina— which could mean the quick end of the dispute without bloodshed—she will consider withdrawing the invitation to President Reagan to address both Houses of Parliament next month?

The Prime Minister: I have every reason to believe that the fundamental friendship between the United States of America and Great Britain will continue, and will continue to flourish.

Mr. Wellbeloved: Will the Prime Minister find time today to tell those who supported the despatch of the task force but who now have doubts about its use that they have a clear duty to spell out their view of the terms of an honourable settlement and the time scale that they would countenance for achieving it? Does the right Hon. Lady agree that there is a world of

143

difference between a genuine search for a negotiated peaceful withdrawal of the Argentine invaders and a disgraceful, blatant policy of appeasement of aggression?

The Prime Minister: The hon. Gentleman has made his point very effectively. The task force has no point, even in support of diplomacy, unless it is clear that one is prepared to use it if necessary. I very much agree with the hon. Gentleman about the time scale for negotiations. The longer they are, the longer our people will be under the heel of the Argentine dictator.

Mr. W. Benyon: Will my right hon. Friend accept that many of us strongly deprecate the discussion of the tactical options facing our forces either here or in the media? Will she persuade them to shut up?

The Prime Minister: I very much share my hon. Friend's concern. If such concern is expressed in the House, some of the media may take notice of it. I hope that all concerned will have in mind only one thing, which is that everything that they say may put someone's life in jeopardy. Therefore, we all have a responsibility to those in Her Majesty's Fleet. . . .

Mr. Thorne: Following the Prime Minister's experiences of the Argentine Fascist junta, will she give the House a categoric assurance that her Government will sell no more arms to Fascist and neo-Fascist States, wherever they may be?

The Prime Minister: Governments of both parties have been responsible for contracts for sales of arms to Argentina. As the hon. Gentleman knows, we look at each and every order as it comes. There is not a general rule.

Rev. Ian Paisley: Does the Prime Minister agree that two considerations must be kept in mind: first, the defence of sovereign British territory; and, secondly, the wishes of the Falkland Islanders, and that they must have top priority in any decision that is made?

The Prime Minister: I think that I see the special point in the hon. Gentleman's question. Of course both those things are supremely important, and they are very much in the forefront of my mind.

Mr. David Steel: Will the Prime Minister confirm that even at this late stage Mr. Secretary Haig is actively pursuing a peaceful solution to the dispute? Will she confirm also that he has sent proposals both to London and Buenos Aires on the matter? Have the Government responded to those proposals?

The Prime Minister: I wonder whether the right hon. Gentleman will leave that question until a little later, when I shall have something to say about it. I should prefer to stick to what I have already prepared.

Mr. Alan Clark: If the Prime Minister has any communication with the Secretary-General of the United Nations, as has been so stridently urged by the Leader of the Opposition, should not the first question to which the

Secretary-General should address himself be the speedy and effective implementation of resolution 502 of his Security Council, which has been outstanding for over three weeks?

The Prime Minister: My hon. Friend is right. If that resolution were to be implemented, there would be few problems left in relation to the Falkland Islands, but it has always been one of the fundamental weaknesses of the United Nations that it does not have the means of implementing its resolutions. If it did, Afghanistan would not be occupied, we would not still have the terrible situation in Vietnam and Cambodia and we would have solved the Cyprus situation. . . .

Mr. Flannery: Has the Prime Minister noticed the decline in bellicosity of the public statements by the task force commander, who now views the situation with more realism and has moved from a "walk-over" to a "long and bloody struggle"? Will she take note of that? Will she realise that even at this very late stage there is still time for her to go to the United Nations and discuss a peaceful solution? . . .

The Prime Minister: The comments of the task force commander are always vivid, if various. We have been to the United Nations. We went to the United Nations before the invasion. We have the Security Council resolution. If that resolution could be implemented, there would be no problems now.

Mr. Churchill: Is my right hon. Friend aware that she and the Royal Navy task force have the full and unqualified backing of the British people as a whole in regaining the Falkland Islands and liberating our people from Fascism? Is she further aware that her leadership and resolve at the moment when thousands of our finest young men are embarked on a hazardous and dangerous enterprise stand in marked contrast to those who run for cover at the first whiff of grapeshot?

The Prime Minister: I think that the vast majority of our people, whatever their political views, are firmly behind the action that the Government are taking. Whatever their political views, they are delighted that Britain is firmly standing up once again for the principles in which she believes.

Miss Joan Lestor: If a negotiated settlement is reached between Britain and Argentina on the question of the Falkland Islands, will the Falkland Islanders, whose wishes the Prime Minister says are paramount, have the right to veto such a settlement, or will their choice be between living under any new administration agreed between the two parties and leaving the Falkland Islands for this country?

The Prime Minister: I have noticed the word "veto" creeping into many commentaries on the present situation. The right of self-determination for inhabited territories is fundamental to the United Nations charter. That is what I believe the House will insist upon. That is what we are trying to ensure for the Falkland Islanders. . . .

Mr. Myles: Does my right hon. Friend realise that there is great support in the country for the leadership that she is showing in this crisis? Does she agree that the greatest deterrent of all to any tinpot dictator or other aggressor, or perhaps a greater power, is resolute and decisive government?

The Prime Minister: I am grateful to my hon. Friend. It is important, if we are to deter dictators, to have the capacity to do so and to demonstrate our resolve, both on the part of Government and of the people.

Dr. Edmund Marshall: In view of the reported statements of Rear-Admiral Woodward, which Minister approved the arrangements for press representatives to be on the flagships?

The Prime Minister: My right hon. Friend the Secretary of State for Defence. I was wholly behind the arrangements. It is absolutely right and fully in accordance with tradition that we should carry war correspondents on Her Majesty's ships when they are on such a mission.

Debate

The Prime Minister: From the onset of the Falklands crisis, my right hon. Friends and I have undertaken to keep the House as closely informed as possible about the situation.

Although my last report to hon. Members was only two days ago, such is the seriousness of this matter that my right hon. Friends and I were glad to agree to the suggestion of the right hon. Gentleman the Leader of the Opposition that time should be found for a debate today—the fourth since the Argentine invasion of the Falkland Islands four weeks ago tomorrow.

During that period, the Government have taken every possible step that had a reasonable prospect of helping us to achieve our objectives—the withdrawal of the Argentine forces and the end of their illegal occupation of the islands, the restoration of British administration, and a long-term solution which is acceptable not only to the House but to the inhabitants of the Falkland Islands.

It is the Government's most earnest hope that we can achieve those objectives by a negotiated settlement. We have done everything that we can to encourage Mr. Haig's attempts to find a solution by diplomatic means. . . .

As the House knows, the Government have also taken military measures to strengthen our diplomatic efforts. Mr. Haig's initiative would never have got under way if the British Government had not sent the naval task force to the South Atlantic within four days of Argentina's aggression against the Falkland Islands. . . .

Our military response to the situation has been measured and controlled. On 12 April we declared a maritime exclusion zone. It has been enforced against Argentine warships and naval auxiliaries. It has been completely successful, and the Argentine forces on the Falkland Islands have been isolated by sea.

Eleven days later we warned the Argentine authorities that any approach by their warships or military aircraft which could amount to a threat to interfere with the mission of the British forces in the South Atlantic would encounter the appropriate response. . . .

146

The latest of our military measures is the imposition of the total exclusion zone round the Falkland Islands of which we gave 48 hours' notice yesterday. The new zone has the same geographical boundaries as the maritime exclusion zone which took effect on 12 April. It will apply from noon London time tomorrow to all ships and aircraft, whether military or civil, operating in support of the illegal occupation of the Falkland Islands. A complete blockade will be placed on all traffic supporting the occupation forces of Argentina. Maritime and aviation authorities have been informed of the imposition of the zone, in accordance with our international obligations.

We shall enforce the total exclusion zone as completely as we have done the maritime exclusion zone. The Argentine occupying forces will then be totally isolated—cut off by sea and air. . . .

On the diplomatic side, Mr. Haig has put formal American proposals to the Argentine Government and requested an early response. I stress the status of those proposals. They are official American proposals. Mr. Haig judged it right to ask Argentina to give its decision first, as the country to which Security Council resolution 502 is principally addressed. He saw Mr. Costa Mendez last night, but no conclusion was reached. Mr. Haig has also communicated to us the text of his proposals. . . .

The proposals are complex and difficult and inevitably bear all the hallmarks of compromise in both their substance and language. But they must be measured against the principles and objectives expressed so strongly in our debates in the House. My right hon. Friend the Secretary of State for Foreign and Commonwealth Affairs remains in close touch with Mr. Haig. . . . It was the Argentine invasion which started this crisis, and it is Argentine withdrawal that must put an end to it.

The world community will not condone Argentina's invasion. To do so would be to encourage further aggression. . . .

As the situation has developed, and as the British Government have made every effort to find a solution, the House has broadly supported both the Government's objectives and their actions. But in the past few days it has been argued in some parts of the House, first, that we should not have resorted to the use of force and, secondly, that we should seek greater involvement by the United Nations.

With regard to the first argument, when the House debated the Falkland Islands on 14 April the Leader of the Opposition supported the despatch of the task force. . . .

But it would be totally inconsistent to support the despatch of the task force and yet to be opposed to its use. What is more, it would be highly dangerous to bluff in that way. British Servicemen and ships would be exposed to hostile action. Argentina would doubt our determination and sense of purpose. The diplomatic pressure would be undermined. Is it really suggested that to use our task force in self-defence for the recapture of British territory is not a proper use of force?

As long as the Argentines refuse to comply with the Security Council resolution, we must continue to intensify the pressure on them. And we must not abandon our efforts to re-establish our authority over our own territory and to free our own people from the invader.

Let me turn now to the question of greater United Nations involvement. All our action has been based on a resolution of the United Nations. . . .

Without Argentine withdrawal, we have no choice but to exercise our unquestionable right to self-defence under article 51 of the Charter. Of course, if Argentina withdrew we should immediately cease hostilities and be ready to hold negotiations with a view to solving the underlying dispute. After all, we were negotiating only a few weeks before the invasion.

It is quite wrong to suggest that because the invader is not prepared to implement the resolution the principles of the United Nations require that we, the aggrieved party, should forfeit the right of self-defence. Such an argument has no validity in international law. It would be to condone and encourage aggression and to abandon our people.

The question that we must answer is, what could further recourse to the United Nations achieve at the present stage? We certainly need mediation, but we already have the most powerful and the most suitable mediator available, Mr. Haig, backed by all the authority and all the influence of the United States, working to implement a mandatory resolution of the Security Council. If anyone can succeed in mediation, it is Mr. Haig.

Of course, we support the United Nations and we believe that respect for the United Nations should form the basis of international conduct. But, alas, the United Nations does not have the power to enforce compliance with its resolutions, as a number of aggressors well know. . . .

The recapture of South Georgia has not diminished international support. No country that was previously with us has turned against us. On Tuesday, my right hon. Friend was able to satisfy himself that the support of the European Community remained robust. The world has shown no inclination to condemn Britain's exercise of the right to self-defence.

In the Organisation of American States itself, Argentina was criticised for her use of force. Despite the claims of traditional Latin American solidarity, the only resolution passed clearly referred to Security Council resolution 502, and called on Argentina not to exacerbate the situation.

The truth is that we have been involved in constant activity at the United Nations. Our representative in New York has been in daily touch with the Secretary-General since the crisis began. He has discussed with him repeatedly and at length all possible ways in which the United Nations could play a constructive role in assisting Mr. Haig's mission and, if Mr. Haig fails, in securing implementation of resolution 502.

Sir Anthony Parsons has also discussed with Mr. Perez de Cuellar contingency planning about the part that the United Nations might be able to play in the longer term in negotiating and implementing a diplomatic settlement.

In the light of those discussions, our representative has advised us that, first, the Secretary-General is very conscious of the complexity of the problem and of the need for careful preparation of any intitiative that he might take. Secondly, as the Security Council is already seized of the problem, it would be inappropriate for the Secretary-General to act under article 99 of the charter. Thirdly, the Secretary-General would not wish to take any initiative which he had not established in advance would be acceptable to both the parties. Fourthly, the Secretary-General would also require a clear mandate from the Security Council before taking any action.

Our representative has also reported that the Secretary-General has several times stated in public that he was not prepared to take action while Mr. Haig's mission was continuing. . . .

But if, at any time, either the Secretary-General or my right hon. Friend thought that a meeting between the two of them would be likely to assist in achieving an acceptable solution, then I say to the House that my right hon. Friend would of course go to New York straight away.

Although we have no doubt about our sovereignty over the Falkland Islands, South Georgia, South Sandwich or British Antarctic Territory, some of my right hon. and hon. Friends have suggested that we refer the matter to the International Court of Justice. Since Argentina does not accept the compulsory jurisdiction of the court, the issue cannot be referred for a binding decision without her agreement.

We have never sought a ruling on the Falkland Islands themselves from that court, but we have raised the question of the dependencies on three separate occasions—in 1947, 1949 and 1951. Each time Argentina refused to go to the court.

In 1955, the British Government applied unilaterally to the International Court of Justice against encroachments on British sovereignty in the dependencies by Argentina. Again, the court advised that it could not pursue the matter since it could act only if there was agreement between the parties recognising the court's jurisdiction.

In 1977, Argentina, having accepted the jurisdiction of an international court of arbitration on the Beagle Channel dispute with Chile, then refused to accept its results. It is difficult to believe in Argentina's good faith with that very recent example in mind.

There is no reason, given the history of this question, for Britain, which has sovereignty and is claiming nothing more, to make the first move. It is Argentina that is making a claim. If Argentina wanted to refer it to the International Court, we would consider the possibility very seriously. But in the light of past events it would be hard to have confidence that Argentina would respect a judgment that it did not like.

Until the end of February, we were conducting negotiations with the Argentine Government. Our delegation was accompanied by representatives from the islands councils. The negotiations took place in a constructive atmosphere, and produced an agreed communiqué, though the Argentine Government chose not to publish it.

On 20 March, the South Georgia incident began with the illegal landing of Argentine civilians. We sought to solve that problem by diplomatic means, and proposed that an emissary should travel to Buenos Aires to pursue negotiations over the problem as a matter of urgency.

It was Costa Mendez himself who on 1 April told us that the diplomatic channel was now closed. That same day, President Reagan's appeal was rebuffed by the President of Argentina. On Friday 2 April the Argentines invaded and the Falklands were occupied.

The following day the Security Council called for Argentine withdrawal. Since that mandatory instruction, the Government of Argentina have made no move to comply. On the contrary, they have poured in additional troops and equipment. There can be no doubt where the intransigence lies in this matter.

The key to peace is in the hands of the Argentine Government. The responsibility is theirs.

Mr. Michael Foot (Ebbw Vale): . . . I am sure that it is right that the House should have constant debates on the subject. . . .

I agree that the House must exercise self-control in this situation where many dangers and difficulties for British citizens and others are involved.

But it is also necessary for the House to exercise control over the Executive, over the military machine and over the diplomatic process. It is essential that that control should be sustained from week to week and from day to day in the most detailed manner. I do not believe that the right hon. Lady will dissent from that view. . . .

The origin of the crisis was a flagrant and unprovoked attack. Of course it is necessary that other countries should take a leading part in ensuring that such forms of aggression shall be stopped now and prohibited for the future. No one would dissent from that. It was also right, although some may not agree, that we should have taken the matter *immediately* to the United Nations as we did. That is the proper forum where we have agreed, as a country, that such questions should be decided. That was absolutely right, and I said so on the first morning when we discussed this matter, even before we knew what the verdict of the Security Council was likely to be.

I also agreed, and still agree, that it was right for the Government to make the arrangements for the despatch of the task force. . . .

If such action had not been taken by the British Government, there would not have been any disposition in the junta in the Argentine to negotiate in any way. I believe also that the support that this country could command, or expect to command, throughout the world would have been considerably less if such action had not been taken. Those were the decisions that were made, that I supported, and still support. I believe that they were right. . . .

Partly, we are acting because of the Security Council decision 502 but partly we are acting, as the Prime Minister said, under article 51 of the charter. But for article 51 of the charter, it would have been difficult for us to act in exactly this manner. Article 51 has been invoked on some previous occasions in this way. . . .

There are, however, some other aspects of article 51, as I am sure the right hon. Lady knows. Under the article, we are expected to report to the Security Council and to the United Nations on the measures that we are taking. I had hoped that the right hon. Lady would give us some account of the reports that we are giving and will continue to give the Security Council on these matters. Article 51 does not give this or any other country operating under it an unlimited right to act as it wishes. It gives to those countries the possibility of acting in certain circumstances and also the possibility that they will have to take account of what the Security Council or other countries may say on the subject. . . .

The right hon. Lady mentioned a moment ago the issue of a reference to the International Court of Justice. I am not saying that this would be a solution to the problem. I do say that, in certain circumstances, it could assist the case that this country presents to the world. . . . I hope that she will look at what has been proposed as one possibility for assisting the position.

Proposals for some form of United Nations trusteeship for the Falkland Islands have been discussed in many quarters. I recognise that there are difficulties. There might be difficulties both from our point of view and also from the point of view of the Argentine Government—*[Interruption.]* I do not know why some hon. Members laugh. Some people are discussing these matters perfectly seriously even if those hon. Members are not capable of doing so. . . .

It might form an essential or possible element in getting a solution. . . .

Other possibilities exist under the charter. The possibilities of action are not restricted to those that are involved in article 51. There is article 41, under which economic sanctions are possible. . . .

Sir, Bernard Braine (Essex, South-East): Is the right hon. Gentleman excluding from his thoughts the fact that we are dealing with a Fascist State where thousands of people have disappeared without trace in recent years? Does he think it right and proper that people of British stock who live in a small democracy should be left at the mercy of that State for one moment longer than is necessary?

Mr. Foot: I agree entirely with the hon. Gentleman about the Fascist character of the regime in the Argentine. I have been as bitterly and as strongly—in some respects, more strongly—opposed to such regimes as Conservative Members. . . .

The question of the possible interim administration also enters into any negotiations. The right hon. Lady and the Government have over this period had discussions of that nature. They have not fully considered, as we have done and as the nature of the case requires, the part that the United Nations could play in providing or assisting in providing a form of interim administration which could be acceptable to this country and acceptable eventually, I would hope, to the Argentine Government. . . .

The right hon. Lady may ask what use is such a discussion because it is the Haig proposals that command the centre of the negotiating process. It is true that they have occupied it. I have not complained and do not complain now about the Government, the Secretary-General or anybody else concentrating first upon the success of the Haig proposals. I am interested to hear what the right hon. Lady has to say about them today.

I understand the problems of publishing the proposals, although I would have thought that at some stage they should be presented for discussion in the House. . . .

Certainly before there was any grave escalation of the crisis those matters are fit matters to be discussed in the House and throughout the country. I am not saying that the right hon. Lady takes a view that is different from mine on that subject, but I hope very much that no military action will be taken which might jeopardise the success of those proposals. It may be that I or the right hon. Lady might not like some of the proposals. I presume that is one of the reasons why Mr. Haig went back to Buenos Aires and was able and willing to take up the matter afresh and why he was prepared to call them American proposals, which I gather is different from the previous position.

It may be that those proposals offer some hope of getting a peaceable settlement. In saying that, I am not giving any bland or blanket support to any proposals that we have not seen; nor can this House or anybody else. If people want to stop the bloodshed, they have to treat that matter with the greatest care, as we do. . . .

The right hon. Lady may ask, particularly in the light of what she has revealed to us today about the stage of the Haig proposals, what is the use of anybody thinking, if the Haig proposals do not succeed, that any other kind of proposals, mediation or negotiation would have any prospect. . . .

That sounds a commonsense conclusion. I am not contesting it except that throughout the dispute we have emphasised, as my right hon. Friend has emphasised on many occasions in debates in the House, that there would have to be an eventual possibility of the matter being referred to the United Nations and to the Secretary-General if there were a breakdown in the Haig proposals, and if they were unsatisfactory. One of the reasons why that might offer greater hope is that in such circumstances the United States Government would have to declare themselves much more clearly on our side. That point has been put on many occasions.

If the Haig proposals break down, we must still be prepared to go back to the United Nations for further negotiation. I repeat that I hope we shall be careful to make them succeed if we can. . . .

We have reached a very serious stage in regard to the inter-connection between the military and diplomatic aspects. I do not wish to be discourteous to the right hon. Lady, but she is saying that she has dismissed the idea of returning very soon to the United Nations. She has not ruled it out entirely, I am glad to say. . . .

What I proposed earlier in the week—and I propose it again now—is that the Foreign Secretary should go to New York to discuss the matter with the United Nations. I believe that he should do so because we must use every possibility to escape from armed conflict. If the right hon. Lady and her Government were to proceed, brushing aside the statement and saying that they are not interested in appeals to stop the escalation or in appeals from the Secretary-General not to broaden the conflict, she would, as I said earlier in the week, inflict grievous injury on our national cause.

It so happens that there is considerable support for this view from the admiral in charge of operations. . . .

I suggest, therefore, that the right hon. Lady ought to take proper note both of the warnings from her admiral, of the invitations from the Secretary-General of the United Nations, and of the opinion of growing numbers throughout the country. The paramount interest of our country and of most other countries is that we should have a peaceful settlement of this dispute. I say that we have to try and try and try again to secure that peaceful settlement.

Mr. Norman St. John-Stevas (Chelmsford): Despite some moments of rowdiness in the House, Members meet this afternoon in a sombre mood as the prospects of war loom before this country. There is no one in the House who is either a jingoist or a triumphalist, and I believe that we should congratulate my right hon. Friend the Prime Minister on having, in her opening remarks, so accurately caught the mood of the House. . . .

My right hon. Friend the Prime Minister rightly stressed throughout her speech that we were still looking for a political solution, that we would still prefer a diplomatic solution to the use of force.

We are right to take that attitude, for two reasons. The first is the gravity of the issue. Human lives are at risk—British and Argentine lives. No one has a right to be bellicose when other people's lives are at risk.

Secondly, we should support the political initiative, because it is vital that we should be seen to be doing so if we are to retain the support of world public opinion. That will be crucial in the coming weeks. The Leader of the Opposition has constantly stressed that important factor. There must be no suspicion in the minds of the leaders of other countries that we are not sincerely and committedly working for peace. Let us remember that even if the fighting escalates, in the end we shall have to come to diplomatic discussions; we shall have to come to consultations; we shall have to try once again to substitute the weapons of peace for those of war. . . .

What is desirable is that, as far as possible, the House should speak with a clear and united voice. Of course the decisions are for the Government and the responsibility is for the Government, but they are immensely strengthened in decisions that they are taking on behalf of the nation if they can show that the House is more united than divided. What I have to say is intended as a contribution to that consensus and to set out certain principles that I believe are widely supported in the House and outside.

First, the entire House is agreed on the strength of our moral and legal case. And why not? Our sovereign territory has been invaded. Our citizens have been deprived of their rights, and there has been a brutal and flagrant violation of international law. . . .

Secondly, of course, we continue to seek a political solution. Military force must be the arm of politics and diplomacy, and not the other way round. That has been fully accepted by Admiral Woodward. . . .

Thirdly, we must constantly have in mind that our task force is on the high seas and at risk. Of course the political aims are paramount, but we must face the fact that we could well reach a point where the safety and well-being of the forces have to modify that. That is the point being made with increasing urgency by my right hon. Friend the Prime Minister. She is right to make it, because the nation would never forgive any Government who put our forces in jeopardy and then did not back them up and minimise the risks to them. . . .

We should resolutely dismiss the anti-Americanism which has surfaced from time to time in our discussions and which we saw again at Prime Minister's Question Time today. There is no doubt about the massive support that this country is receiving from the American people. . . .

But situations alter. It is now my opinion that the chances of preserving peace would be enhanced if the United States threw its weight openly and unreservedly behind Britain. There is nothing inconsistent between those two statements. It is merely recognition of the fact that the situation has developed and altered. . . .

We must never forget that our quarrel is not with the Argentine people. It is with the Argentine junta. It is crucial to distinguish between the two—to distinguish between an odious and corrupt regime which has denied human rights, which has sent people to their deaths, which is reigning by terror, and a people with whom this country has had long and historic ties. . . .

Our first priority, of course, must be the well-being of the Falkland Islanders. They constitute a real community and they have rights of self-determination which are guaranteed by article 73 of the United Nations charter. . . . But there are other British interests in South America, and we must protect them. Countries such as Brazil, Mexico and Colombia have no sympathy with the Argentine, but if our views are expressed in a xenophobic fashion, we shall drive them in that direction. . . .

I hope that the message that will go out from the debate is that once again the House of Commons is expressing the resolution and the will of a united nation.

Mr. James Callaghan (Cardiff, South-East): . . . The right hon. Lady the Prime Minister spoke with restraint and put her case in a way that I found unexceptionable. Indeed, I support much of what she said. My right hon. Friend the Leader of the Opposition has made an important case for never using force if we can continue talking to get the right result. It would be wrong for any Conservative Member to try to assume or to say that that is not worthy of an Opposition. That is exactly what an Opposition should say and should be doing, and I congratulate my right hon. Friend on at least sending nearly all of us scurrying back to study the charter of the United Nations in a way that we have not done for years.

There are three considerations that should govern our actions in this dispute. First, we are the aggrieved party in this aggression. We do not want war. We earnestly desire—I believe that the Prime Minister and the Cabinet are working towards this—a negotiated settlement of the dispute.

Secondly, of the handful of direct invasions of one nation's territory by another since the Second World War, this one by Argentina is certainly the most flagrant and clear-cut defiance of the United Nations charter and its authority. For that reason it will weaken the United Nations even more if resolution 502 is not implemented by the withdrawal of Argentine troops in one form or another.

The third consideration that should govern our approach is that when the withdrawal of Argentine troops has taken place, or even if we are satisfied with the bona fides of the withdrawal, and while the process is continuing, Britain should be ready immediately, as the Prime Minister said, to resume negotiations leading to a settlement of the underlying dispute. I think that I quote the words that she used today.

It should be a settlement that will provide permanent security for the islanders as well as having full regard to their wishes and interests. That will cause much difficulty and it is not something for us to spell out this afternoon. However, we shall have to refine and define much more closely what we mean by the islanders' views and interests than we have done so far. . . .

Secretary Haig is in the lead and I do not dissent from that. The United Nations has been willing to let him act, and that is realistic, because the United States is more likely to produce a negotiated result than the United Nations. That may be regrettable, but it is true. Nevertheless, the United Nations—I wish to support my right hon. Friend's hope—is still central to our case, even if we cannot envisage that if the United States is unable to produce a solution the United Nations will be able to secure adherence to its own resolution. . . .

In my view, the proceedings should take the form of a blockade by air and sea and interdicting any attempt to cross the boundaries that we have laid down. We should take all measures to make that blockade effective. Can we do so? The Government have taken the decision and I fervently believe that the Government and the Armed Forces can sustain such a blockade. . . .

I hope that hon. Members will forgive me if I labour this extremely important point. We must be ready to settle into a long blockade, if necessary for months, to undermine the morale of the garrison on the islands, using all possible means of harassment. We should prevent the islands from being reinforced and make the Argentine forces realise that they are beset, beleaguered, that they have no hope of rescue and no hope of return. I believe that that is the approach of a blockade.

A blockade would involve some hardship to the islanders. Nevertheless, one cannot possibly resolve a dispute of this nature without hardship somewhere. However, this is a beginning and it is completely different from launching a frontal assault, which some of the newspapers have put into people's mind as being the next step. I can understand that being in the front of all our minds, but I believe that a frontal assault—I hope that I do not trespass beyond the bounds of what hon. Members think is right—would result in a heavy loss of life. . . .

There is a difference between launching a bloody assault on the islands and imposing a blockade, as we have done time after time in history, and can do again. I have no doubt that, whatever the hardships involved, the sons of those who ran the convoys to Murmansk and Iceland in the last war can do as well as their fathers. If negotiations break down, I believe that they will. . . .

I wish to see unity maintained in the House and in the country as far as possible. It is not, as I heard a BBC announcer say this morning, a bonus to the Government. It is an essential source of strength that the Government must not dissipate. . . .

I reassert that the aim of the House and the country must be to ensure the safety of our forces, the minimum risk to them, and a willingness, when the Argentine troops have been withdrawn, to negotiate on the underlying dispute and the future status of the islands, subject to the wishes and interests of the islanders themselves. . . . An attempt must be made to restore correct relations, if no better, with Argentina. It is not possible to envisage permanent hostility between the islanders and the Argentine Government and the mainland.

I conclude with one thought: how little is needed to deter, but how much to remedy.

Dr. David Owen (Plymouth, Devonport): . . . There is a great onus of responsibility on the Prime Minister. Her speech today greatly helped to move the country forward at a pace that takes the vast majority of people with her.

The right hon. Member for Cardiff, South-East (Mr. Callaghan) was firm in his belief that the decision to introduce a total exclusion zone to operate from tomorrow is correct, and I strongly support him. That is the next and logical escalation of the pressure on the Argentine junta. I believe that the maritime blockade has been well introduced, but it now needs to be reinforced by preventing the Argentines from continuing to reinforce the Falkland Islands. The rest of the world needs to know that over the past few weeks that is exactly what Argentina has been doing. It would be intolerable for the British Government to hold back when they have the capacity to prevent the continued reinforcement of the Falkland Islands which is being carried out in direct contravention of resolution 502. . . .

Let us be under no illusion. The critical moment in these negotiations is coming very close. As the Prime Minister said, the United States has put forward formal American proposals. . . . I hope that President Reagan has made it abundantly clear to the Argentines that if they reject the proposals there will be immediate application of United States sanctions, rapidly and fully, matching the sanctions imposed on the Argentines by the European Community. Nobody should disparage such a move. It would have a very powerful effect on the Argentines. I hope that the American people, who have been extremely loyal to this country in the past few weeks, will make it clear to the President that there must be no equivocation about this. . . .

Therefore, it is absolutely vital that we do not duck the reality of perhaps having to face difficult compromises before making a decision to repossess the Falkland Islands, before the loss of life. . . .

I believe that it would be wrong to undertake a major escalation of our military commitment and to seek to repossess the Falkland Islands on the basis of the Government alone rejecting proposals put forward by the United States and accepted by the Argentines. I suppose that one has to say that there are circumstances in a very changing position in the Southern Atlantic that might force the Government to take military decisions before the recall of Parliament. If they are faced with that decision, I believe that there is an urgent responsibility to consult the parties and the leaders of the parties. . . .

We are all united on the fact that the first phase must be withdrawal of the Argentines from the islands. It would then be reasonable to push the task force, say, to South Georgia, then back to Ascension Island, and only out of the Southern Atlantic area when the last Argentine soldier had left the islands. I believe that that is an agreed first phase, and there is very little difficulty on that. . . .

All the evidence at present is that the Argentines are stipulating that they will not agree to anything that would involve accepting that their claim to sovereignty is negotiable. That is the crunch issue. If they will not accept that, I do not see how we can reach an agreement. . . . The fact remains, however, that the Government were ready to discuss it. I am not asking them to commit themselves on it, but it would be unrealistic for any Conservative Member, or indeed for any Labour Member, given the decisions taken by the Labour Government—[HON. MEMBERS: "And by the right hon. Gentleman"]—yes, and by me, to exclude negotiating and discussing the issue of sovereignty. It is right that that should be said. There are, of course, Members who believe that that issue is non-negotiable, but I believe that there is a cross-party majority that is ready to negotiate. . . .

How could the issue of sovereignty be put in a way that would save the face of the Argentines? In this sense, I believe that article 38.2 of the statute of the International Court of Justice should be considered. . . .

The attraction of this procedure is that the Argentines would not suffer any loss of face by agreeing to submit the issue to the court, as by agreeing to the adjudication they would not be admitting any possibility that their claim to sovereignty was not justified. I believe that we must look to mechanisms that will save face in this context. We should also not exclude the possibility of a strategic trust territory. Under articles 82 and 83, a strategic trust territory has great importance for us in this country because it would not be right for the strategic and military aspects and matters relating to law and order on the islands to be put to a trusteeship council in which we could be outvoted. The advantage of a strategic trust territory is that the Security Council would effectively govern those aspects, which would allow us to exercise the veto. The Argentines would also have some assurance that either the United States, if their relations with that country were good, or the Soviet Union might exercise the veto. As the administering authority, however, we could maintain the status quo and Britain would be the administering authority. Again, this would avoid either side having to reach a conclusion on sovereignty. . . .

156

I recognise that the Government will need to take decisions at very short notice. I merely ask that if they have to take those major decisions they should do their best to talk to the parties in the House so that we may retain as much unanimity as possible.

Perhaps I am being too optimistic, although I am often optimistic, but it is conceivable that the Argentine junta will crack. It is possible that it will, under immense United States pressure, accept. If so, it will be also because the junta believes that the House and the country are ready to use force, ready, if we had to do so at the last resort, even to repossess the islands. . . .

This is very different from Suez. Let us not make it like Suez. Let us not have what happened in 1956, when Service men went into Suez against a background of bitter party political debate. The onus is not only on the opposition parties. The onus and the responsibility are as much on the Government and the Prime Minister. This debate has strengthened the chances of our retaining unity across the party divisions.

Mr. Robert Rhodes James (Cambridge): . . . The House meets at a particularly grave moment. We have at stake our Service men in the South Atlantic. We have at stake the Falkland Islanders, who are innocent victims of blatant, cruel and unprovoked aggression. We have at stake the credibility of the United Nations, which has been treated with cynical contempt by one of the parties to the dispute—the Argentine junta. We have also at stake the whole delicate fabric of international law, and, perhaps even more important than that, the crucial, unwritten conventions of civilised behaviour between nations in an increasingly dangerous world. . . .

The Leader of the Opposition referred, rather vaguely, but at some length, to the role that could be played by the United Nations. As the House knows, I was a volunteer senior official to the United Nations, in the office of the Secretary-General, for four years. I emphasise one point about the role of the Secretary-General in a problem such as this. Under article 99 he has the right, which is rarely used—rightly—to call a special meeting of the Security Council. In the circumstances that we have faced in the past three weeks he could not have done so, for the simple reason that a party to the dispute was in breach not only of the United Nations charter, but of a mandatory resolution of the Security Council. It was impossible for the Secretary-General to take the action for which the Leader of the Opposition seemed to be pressing the other day. . . .

A remarkable feature of the situation today is that we have overwhelming national and international support. We have a feeling, supported by our friends in the Commonwealth and the EEC, and our allies, that on occasions such as this, which blessedly occur so seldom, when a major principle of international justice, law and humanity is involved, the free nations and their friends must speak with one voice, just as this nation must. . . .

We can all be wise with hindsight. Both this and the previous Government negotiated peacefully and in good faith. We are not the aggressors. We are not the offenders against international law. . . . A strong, unambiguous and determined Britain is the best guarantor of the maintenance of peace and security in the world.

Mr. J. Enoch Powell (Down, South): . . . The right of self-defence—to repel aggression and to expel an invader from one's territory and one's people whom he has occupied and taken captive—is, as the Government have said, an inherent right. It is one which existed before the United Nations was dreamt of. True, it has been accommodated and given a definition in the United Nations charter. However, it is not under that authority that we exercise it: we exercise it as a right which is inherent in us. It is as such that both the British Government and, in large measure, the British people have resolved that we ought to place ourselves in a position to exercise that right, namely, by force, if necessary, to repel the aggression and to repossess our territory.

That resolve, which I believe is widespread not only in the House but outside it, carries with it some important implications.

One is that, having willed and approved that action, we must, as a nation, be prepared to take the consequences. . . . When we took the decision which we did two or three weeks ago, and which we are following through now, it ought to be understood that we were accepting and expressing the will, if necessary, to maintain a long and difficult course of action in which there may be reverses and severe losses. We must not allow that to be misunderstood or played down outside the House. . . .

The notion that if, by whatever means, we regain the administration of the Falkland Islands and reassert our sovereignty in practical terms it will be a mere passing phase is demonstrably false.

It is false because if this Argentine adventure ends sooner or later in the fiasco that it deserves, it will be a long time before anyone will think of repeating it. It is wrong also because if we, the third naval power in the world, a country in the North Atlantic uniquely dependent for its existence upon the ability to command the seas and the air which are relevant to its defence, are unable, in defence of an island group hundreds of miles from the nearest continent, to maintain the necessary availability of strength, and the necessary command of the sea, so that our possession of the Falkland Islands is of a precarious character, we had better resign any notion that we might have had of being able to defend ourselves in our island home in the North Atlantic. . . .

The second implication concerns what follows after repossession. The expressions "diplomatic solution", "solution of the problem", "solution by negotiation" have frequently been used in these last weeks. If those phrases mean that preferably diplomatic and other pressures should induce the aggressor to reverse his act, there would be no problem whatever raised by their use. . . .

However, the House has at no time authorised, or been given the opportunity to authorise, any decision to compromise or part with our sovereignty of the Falkland Islands. . . .

If the consequence of exerting our right—in the way in which we are prepared to exert it if necessary—is that the rightful repossession of the Falkland Islands is only a prelude to a course of action that in due course will place the aggressor in more or less the position that he wished to attain by means of his aggression—if we are exercising our inherent right to recover our own, only in order, thereafter, to trade our own away—how can we face the men whom we are asking to take part in that operation? If we support that operation, we owe it to them, as well as to ourselves, to make it clear that that which we regain if necessary by force—although we hope to regain it without force—will not be cast away, negotiated away or given away by this country. . . .

The Government, who have, on the whole, been supported by the House and the country thus far, have the right also to expect that they will be supported when they refuse to allow our ability to exert our right to be taken away from us by stealth and by the passage of time. . . .

I hope that the Government will make it clear that they remain resolved to retain the power to exercise that right. If they make that clear, I believe that the nation will support them.

Sir Derek Walker-Smith (Hertfordshire, East): . . . I shall start with resolution 502, not because it provides the final solution—it certainly does not—but because compliance with it and the withdrawal of the Argentine troops is an absolute and indispensable condition precedent to finding a solution. It is the non-compliance by the Argentine with the clear terms of the resolution—and that alone—that has occasioned and justified Britain's resort to force or the threat of force. . . .

The issues, when once withdrawal of the troops is achieved, can and should be resolved by other more appropriate means. Of course, that approach is inherent in the charter. The authority in international law for the despatch of troops or of a task force is article 51, which covers the inherent right of self-defence in the event of armed attack. However *[that]* is intended only to be temporary and, as the article states,

"until the Security Council has taken measures necessary to maintain international peace and security.". . .

Furthermore, article 51 is not to be taken in isolation. Like all other such instruments, the charter must be read as a whole. Indeed, article 51 states that action under the article

"shall not in any way affect the authority and responsibility of the Security Council."

The appropriate action is clearly specified in the charter. Under article 33 there is a duty to seek a solution by peaceful means, which are negotiation, arbitration and judicial settlement. . . .

Resolution by war is the least acceptable alternative for obvious humanitarian and practical reasons. If, unfortunately, circumstances should require the engagement of our troops, they will carry with them the good wishes of us all in what Admiral Woodward has said would be a long and bloody campaign. . . .

The case for arbitration is clear. Article 33 imposes a clear obligation to seek a solution by peaceful means which specifically include arbitration. Such arbitration is entrusted to the International Court. . . .

In regard to sovereignty we are concerned with two conflicting bases of claim, which are the Argentine claim based on succession and deriving from the old Spanish position, and our claim based on prescription. Both those bases are considered appropriate bases in international law. An adjudication based on those conflicting claims, which are based on different concepts, is a matter for the court. . . .

The purported reason for non-reference is the alleged disinclination of the junta. However, how do we know that if the matter is not put to them? The last time a British Government raised the matter of reference to the court was in May 1955. . . .

There remain the efforts of Secretary Haig. . . . There also remains the possibility of economic sanctions under article 41 which in any case are a necessary prelude to military sanctions under article 42. It is also worth considering the possibility of an international trusteeship system under chapter 12 of the charter.

All those are peaceful approaches that are sanctioned by the charter and accepted under international law. . . . The prospect of war at a distance can have an intoxicating effect on some. However, the euphoria sometimes does not last for long. . . .

Unhappily, Argentina's intransigence about the withdrawal of troops and its continuing breach of international law have made a show of force inevitable. It may also make the use of force inevitable. That would be an unhappy alternative, justified only by necessity, and a last resort. I urge the House to say that, if at all possible, it does not want to have to ask for whom the bell tolls. Let us do all that is within our power to secure a solution under the rule of law which reason can commend and principle support.

Mr. Jack Ashley (Stoke-on-Trent, South): The atmosphere of the debate is in striking contrast to the reality of the British Fleet plunging through the high seas and the threat of armed conflict and talk of landings on the Falkland Islands. . . .

It is right and proper that the House should unite when it is faced with aggression. Of course, we are bound to hold differences of opinion about how to approach the matter. Nevertheless, we are united in opposition to the unprovoked aggression of Argentina. . . .

There is no disagreement about the House wanting a negotiated settlement. The question is what sort of pressure we should exert to achieve that settlement. Will the pressure be the sanction of world opinion and economic pressure from ourselves and our allies, or the pressure of military force? Our objective and prime concern should be to establish stability in the South Atlantic. . . .

The escalation of the use of force is now a euphemism for war. When we speak of escalating force, we speak of war. We may win the war, but we must face the consequences of it. The right hon. Member for Down, South (Mr. Powell) is right to spell out that there will be consequences, although I hold diametrically opposed views of what those consequences will be.

One of the consequences of war—if we go to war—is that we will probably kill or injure islanders, or provoke Argentine troops to do so. It is the islanders whom we are supposed to be saving. It would certainly kill our young men and those of the Argentine. The reality of war is that it is neither the junta nor the politicians who suffer and die. It is the young men of both sides. That is the cruel reality. . . .

If we go to war, far from impressing the world, I believe that there would be a massive swing of world opinion against us. That would be very damaging to Britain and to our cause. We shall also unite all of Latin America against us. We shall make life-long enemies of the people of Latin America and leave a legacy of bitterness which will damage relationships for generations. . . .

It is an unpopular view in the House, but I believe that geography, and the fact that successive Governments have tried to cede sovereignty, mean that we shall inevitably cede the Falkland Islands. If that happens in one, or two years, or in a decade, it means that every islander, or British soldier, sailor or airman who is killed in this possible war will have died in vain.

Sooner or later the House of Commons must recognise that we cannot perpetually defend the lives and the security of the 1,800 Falkland Islanders and simultaneously defend the security of 55 million people in the British Isles. We must recognise our priorities. . . .

Mr. Nicholas Winterton (Macclesfield): . . . I speak as an officer of the all-party parliamentary Falkland Islands group and, in that capacity, inevitably I have been closely and regularly in touch with the inhabitants of the Falkland Islands and members of the council who visit the United Kingdom from time to time. . . .

Right is on our side, but not only right in trying to restore British administration to the Falkland Islands. The United Nations, the European Economic Community and the Commonwealth have all expressed whole-hearted support for us. . . .

We are living in serious times. The action of the British Government and people was a very unpleasant and unforeseeable consequence for the Argentine junta in Buenos Aires. . . .

Moscow, strangely, has condemned Britian, presumably in the hope that the desperate Argentine governing junta will in time ally itself with the Eastern bloc and with Cuba. What an unholy alliance that is. The cheek and the impertinence of the Russians are so enormous that, in pure stunned astonishment, people are inclined to forget easily the Soviet rape of the Balkan States, the subjugation of Hungary, Czechoslovakia and Poland, the vicious slaughter of Afghan resistance fighters and the colonisation by the USSR of Angola, Mozambique and other nations. . . .

I am deeply concerned about the dangers that face the people of the Falkland Islands. I am also concerned about the safety of all those in the task force who are serving our nation so superbly. Perhaps it would not be an inappropriate time now to say what a splendid operation they mounted in South Georgia. . . .

Every Member should support the Government's action because right is on our side. We have a duty to restore to the islands, which have belonged to us for 149 years, British administration, which has been removed by the occupation. All the islanders wish to remain British. I say to the people of the Falkland Islands from this House that our thoughts are with them. We appreciate the dangers, but the Government are determined to do what is best in their interests.

Mr. Stan Thorne (Preston, South): . . . The Prime Minister and the Government are hell-bent on the use of military force, completely contrary to Security Council resolution 502, which calls on the United Kingdom as well as the Argentine to refrain from the use or threat of force. Why? Is it in order to save the Prime Minister's face, irrespective of the lives that may be lost in the process? If so, it is the act of a desperate woman and, as such, she has no place in running our affairs in the United Kingdom. . . .

The Falkland Islands crisis must be realistically examined, not in terms of military adventures but in terms of what is morally justifiable. That the invasion of the Falklands by the Argentine Fascist junta was criminally wrong is obvious. Galtieri is under pressure from several groups in the Argentine and desperately needs, as does our Prime Minister, a diversion that could transfer concern from domestic plight to national pride—a questionable emotion at best. That the claims of Britain to the territory known as the Falkland Islands are of very doubtful substance is also clear. Possession based upon acquisition 149 years ago is a poor basis for claiming unquestioned sovereignty. That the people of the Falklands are entitled to some form of support from Britain is acceptable. But are the interests of Coalite Limited and the prospects of oil prospecting more in the minds of the class that rules in Britain than is the welfare of the people of the Falklands? . . .

In any event, have the occupants of these islands the right to expect British lives to be sacrificed on their behalf? . . . By all means, let us seek to provide the Falkland Islands people with alternatives to life under the Argentine Fascist regime. It would not be difficult to assist those on the islands who wish to leave for Britain to settle here or to go to New Zealand, Australia or other parts of the world.

If there are those who wish to remain on the Falklands, they must be made aware of the possibility that they will be deemed, whether immediately or in the foreseeable future, to be living on an island scheduled to be returned to the Argentine at some future date. This appears to me to be inevitable.

The negotiations between the Argentine and Britain carried on apparently by Haig, Costa Mendez and our own Foreign Secretary have been doomed from the beginning. Both sides in the dispute made it clear that certain basic things, for example, sovereignty, were not negotiable. . . .

The only solution in diplomatic terms—any sensible person today seeks such a form of solution to conflicts of interest between nations—is through the United Nations. The Prime Minister and the Government stand accused of failing to use to the fullest degree the effectiveness of the United Nations offices in this dispute. It is still not too late providing that no more military or naval moves are authorised by the Government. Only the death of many of those we are supposed to be acting to protect on the islands can emerge from an invasion by Britain. The House is entitled to know the Government's precise intentions.

I am convinced that the British people do not want war over the Falkland Islands. . . .

Mr. Julian Amery (Brighton, Pavilion): . . . The United Nations invited us many years ago to negotiate with the Argentine to try to find a settlement of the conflicting claims which it and we had over the Falkland Islands. There were exploratory talks between officials and sometimes junior Ministers from both countries. They discussed the hypothesis of condominium or lease and other attempts to find compromises. But I understand, and I believe that the then Minister of State, my hon. Friend the Member for Shoreham (Mr. Luce), who resigned recently, along with the Foreign Secretary, will confirm this, that in every discussion of this kind it was made clear to their Argentine opposite numbers that the proposals would require the approval of Parliament and that Parliament was unlikely to give its approval unless the islanders had themselves agreed to the proposals.

Several proposals were made under Conservative and Labour Governments. The islanders always insisted on the maintenance of full British sovereignty. Parliament was informed of the view of the islanders and as a result, to my knowledge, no decision was ever taken by any British Cabinet, let alone put to Parliament, so that nobody can say that Britain was in any way committed to a surrender of sovereignty. . . . No one in the House can say what the position will be in the future. But I should be surprised if this House of Commons were prepared to cede to the Argentine aggressor what no previous House of Commons was prepared to cede at the end of peaceful negotiations. . . .

If the Argentines are forced to withdraw, I hope by diplomacy, but if necessary by force, we can be sure that they will not return to the charge again for many years. They will have learnt a pretty severe lesson.

In any case, if we follow the advice of Lord Shackleton and extend the runway and build a proper airport, we could always reinforce at two or three days' notice, given proper intelligence of any threat from the Argentine. . . .

Whatever the outcome of this crisis—I am assuming that it will be favourable, whether by diplomatic means or otherwise—the Argentines will be humiliated and there may be considerable resentment in other parts of Latin America. The Falkland Islands will have to live with the Argentine, if not in friendship, at least in mutual forbearance. We must see how we can best salve the wound to Latin American pride. This will call for imagination on the Government's part. I am not asking them to exercise it today. It may be too soon. But this is perhaps the time when some of us on the Back Benches should put forward ideas on this subject. . . .

Has the time perhaps come when we should consider the creation not necessarily of a military alliance but of a South Atlantic or Southern Hemisphere community? It would have as its objectives the protection of the sea and airways that use the South Atlantic, both round Cape Horn and the Cape of Good Hope.

It could also turn its mind to co-operative work for the development of the resources of the South Atlantic and of the Antarctic itself. . . .

If we could produce a proposal of that kind—and I am not saying that my right hon. Friends should produce it now, but they should have it in their minds—it might appeal to the imagination of the European Community and of the United States and secure not only their moral but their material backing. It might also offer a way out perhaps even to General Galtieri—and if not to him at least to his successors—from the dead end into which the junta has now led Argentine.

Mr. Tony Benn (Bristol, South-East): . . . I was alarmed to hear so many people say that in moments like this Parliament should, in effect, be shut down. The strength of our democracy is that we respond to crises by free discussion. . . .

The reality is that there is unanimity in the House on the question of opposing the aggression of the junta. There is also unanimity on the right of self-defence against aggression. I deplore the odious hypocrisy of Tory Members who never argued for force when Ian Smith seized a British Colony and ran it for 15 years against the Crown and against the interests of the African people there. . . .

The question is: should we now go to war with the Argentine? That may be determined in less than 24 hours. The second question associated with it is: what are our objectives in war and how do we secure them other than by war? . . .

What I am asking the House to do is to face the reality of the situation and strongly support what the Leader of the Opposition said today: that

163

the United Nations should be used; that it has been entirely ignored by the Foreign Secretary ever since resolution 502.

There are many people who are doubting now, and will doubt still further, whether it was wise to ask General Haig to be the man to handle peace negotiations. General Haig has a very powerful interest in the maintenance of American investment in and military links with the Argentine. The Argentine has been sending troops in to help pull America's irons out of the fire in El Salvador. I tell the Cabinet that the Foreign Secretary should have gone to the United Nations and not left it to General Haig. The Foreign Secretary has not gone—and everybody knows why he has not gone—to the General Assembly: the General Assembly would not support Britain on the question of sovereignty. That is also why General Haig will not go back to the General Assembly.

I support my right hon. Friend the Member for Ebbw Vale (Mr. Foot) most strongly, and so unanimously does the Labour Party, in saying that until the United Nations option is opened and discussed there should be no further escalation of military force. Let there be no doubt: any difference of emphasis that there may have been is over in the sense that the right hon. Gentleman speaks for the whole Labour Party in saying that. . . .

In the first instance the Prime Minister was in charge of the operations. She told the military, whether they wanted it or not, to assemble a fleet: 40 warships and 36 requisitioned merchantmen now in the South Atlantic. But by sending them there she lost control of the situation because those men—God knows how many there are, some of them living in the Canberra, some of them living in sleeping bags on the flight decks of the aircraft carriers with 40 feet waves, 70 feet winds and freezing decks—and the Government are now being told that they must go into action because the admiral cannot keep them in those conditions for much longer.

The reality is that the Prime Minister is no longer in charge. She is now a prisoner of her policies, a spectator of the tragedy that she is about to impose on the country. . . .

It does not require much imagination to realise that if the total exclusion zone means anything there will be shooting tomorrow, either against aircraft or against ships. The first thing that will happen is that British forces will be confronted by Argentine forces armed by Britain with British ships and missiles, with seamen trained in Britain. There is almost certain to be some serious loss of life.

I hope and believe, as all of us must, that such a loss will not occur, but even if the House does not consider it, we may be sure that the military is considering it and that the Cabinet is considering it. If there is the loss of a major vessel the pressure will grow, if the loss has been caused by a Mirage or Skyhawk from an Argentine base, to bomb the mainland of the Argentine. . . .

The Cabinet knows, but will not tell us, that no real victory can come out of this enterprise. There can be no permanent victory. That is what the right hon. Member for Down, South (Mr. Powell) senses. Once we return to the Falklands the first thing that will happen will be an attempt to get rid of the controversy by a transfer of sovereignty of some kind. . . .

It would be a gross act of self-deception to pretend to the British people that we have the power, the means or the will to defend outposts of empire that were left after the self-determination of the major colonies. Our interests in those people must now be redefined, associating ourselves with their interests as individuals. That has much more to do with our immigration rules than with the despatch of task forces.

When it comes to it, we shall have to make sovereignty negotiable, either by ceding it to the United Nations or arranging a transfer in some other way. . . .

I believe that the Cabinet has lost control of the timetable. It has, in effect, been told "You must use the fleet or withdraw it", which is what some of us said from the outset. We said "If you are going to have doubts about using it, do not send it." We foresaw the almost inevitable consequence.

The Government are negotiating without 100 per cent. American support and time is running out. The British people would like to hear from this debate that a clear consensus is developing to prevent a war with Argentina, to put the United Nations in, in whatever form it might be, to protect lives and interests and to bring the Fleet home. That is a message of hope that must and should emerge from the debate. . . .

We have no complaint whatever against the Americans. The Anglo-American alliance was designed against Soviet ambition and not against Argentina. The Americans have been right to behave as honest brokers, and at the same time they have given us satellite information which has been of value. If negotiations were to fail and the clock stands at five minutes to midnight, we in this House would have every confidence in the skill, determination and courage of our Armed Forces, and the entire House would wish them well.

When we win there must be no unseemly exultation. Once the dust has settled we must not give a power of veto over British foreign policy to the Falkland Islanders. It must be for the House to decide the shape and detail of the eventual settlement.

Mr. Russell Johnston (Inverness): . . . An important part of our diplomatic pressure should be to tell the Argentine people what is happening. Are our broadcasts getting through effectively without any jamming? . . .

Italy has a notable trade in leather with the Argentine and is putting itself to considerable financial embarrassment by co-operating with us. Hon. Members should reflect on the fact that if we were doing this for Italy many hon. Members would, I suspect, be making a considerable noise about it. We should express our considerable gratitude to the Italian people and Government, and to our other European colleagues for the action that they have taken . . .

I am anxious to ensure that we make every effort to work through the United Nations against the background of resolution 502. One obvious extension is mandatory economic sanctions. Have the Government had any contact with the Soviet Union on that? Have they established what the Soviet Union's response to such a proposal might be? I see no reason why the Government should not ask them. It would be interesting to know what general contacts the Government have had with the Soviet Union during the crisis. . . .

As a layman I cannot understand why, because an island is 400 miles from a country, it should inevitably be regarded as part of that country's territorial integrity. Anyway, few Argentines have ever shown the slightest enthusiasm for living there. . . .

The immediate and unequivocal support which the Social Democratic and Liberal Parties gave to the Government in their effort to free the Falkland Islanders from the unprovoked attack and occupation to which they were subject has been steadfastly maintained. . . .

We now have every right, with a real possibility of hostilities, perhaps hours away, to ask the Government to lay more cards on the table. We well understand the difficulties that the Prime Minister has in setting out Secretary Haig's proposals. Nevertheless, events have surely reached the stage at which the Government, especially if they are on the brink of action, must give some clear indication of their basic position and the ground from which in no circumstances they will shift. . . .

This afternoon the Prime Minister regretted the absence of the cross-play of opinions, which she said was normal in a democracy. That is part of the case for bringing party leaders into confidential talks. I have said that we understand her difficulty in setting out Secretary Haig's proposals. I am not seeking to be divisive in saying that we feel that we are in this situation because of the Government's misjudgment, which led to the Argentine invasion. . . . For that reason we have some difficulty in offering the Government a blank cheque. . . .

Sir John Eden (Bournemouth, West): . . . The central issue of this debate is that four weeks ago Argentine forces seized the land and homes of the islanders. Four weeks ago, the Security Council, by mandatory resolution, called on the Argentine forces to withdraw. Nothing can change those two facts. . . .

I suppose that one of the prices that we must pay for living in a parliamentary democracy is that, on occasions, we have to listen to speeches that we do not like to hear. . . .

There are hon. Members in the House, and they have shown themselves during the course of the debate, who will seize every opportunity to undermine the position of the Government, so long as it is the opposite party to their own. . . .

However, the fact is that the deployment of the task force has been an essential feature in the promotion of the diplomatic initiatives that have taken place. If the task force had not been deployed, there is absolutely no doubt that the Argentines would not be paying any heed to the further approaches that are being made by Secretary Haig. . . .

Some Opposition Members suggest that the Government should turn to sources of mediation other than Secretary Haig. Their suggestions have concentrated on the United Nations. As of now, the Argentines have apparently not shown a very positive response to the efforts of Secretary Haig, although, as the representative of an enormously powerful State, he has behind him immense economic and military strength.

The United Nations has already entered into this through the medium of the Security Council resolution. That gives power to the position of the Secretary-General, but the power of the Secretary-General can have meaning and substance only if the countries called upon to act by a mandatory resolution of the Security Council actually respond. It is absolutely inescapable that in the negotiations and in any diplomatic discussions the British Government should maintain the position of strength given to them by the deployment of the task force so long as it appears that the Argentines adamantly refuse to withdraw their forces from the islands.

Today, four weeks after the start of these events, we face the reality that the Argentines are still in possession of the territories that they have seized, British people are still under alien military occupation and the occupying forces have not been withdrawn in accordance with the Security Council resolution. The British Government's position must be to be ready to move—with force, should the necessity arise—to retrieve British territory and to free British people. . . .

In all the discussions that have taken place so far, and in the Argentines' actions over the past weeks, it seems clear that it is not possible to trust the word of the junta. . . . It is most important that we maintain our guard for as long as necessary. Equally, it is important that if we do not obtain the response that we should obtain, and which we ought by now have received, we should not hesitate to use the immense striking power that we have marshalled and which is now approaching the Falkland Islands.

As I see it, our purpose is absolutely clear. Our cause is just. Let us now not hesitate to use every method and all means at our disposal to finish the job.

Mr. Stanley Newens (Harlow): . . . From the outset of the crisis I have taken the view that the Argentine invasion of the Falklands was completely unjustified. Accordingly, I believe that the Government were right to take the matter to the United Nations, which condemned the invasion, and to despatch the task force to the South Atlantic. I did not arrive at that decision with any sense of exhilaration or glee, as I believe that the use of force is repugnant to all right-thinking people. . . .

I took the view, however, that the right of the people of the Falklands to self-determination was a basic international principle of importance not only for them but for many other peoples, right across the face of the earth, living in territories to which neighbouring countries lay claim. . . .

The position is underlined by the fact that not to have resisted would have been to accept the de facto incorporation of the community in the Falkland Islands, which has enjoyed free institutions, into a realm ruled by a Fascist junta which has imprisoned, tortured, ill-treated and murdered thousands of its political opponents over the past few years. . . .

We should recognise, none the less, that although our cause is right, that does not automatically justify us in using any means that we have to achieve it. Furthermore, if we are taking a stand on the principle of national self-determination, we must equally take a stand in favour of the resolution of international disputes by peaceful means as far as possible and with the minimum use of force. We must seek to demonstrate this to the international community as fully and as openly as we can.

At this juncture, this does not mean that we should forthwith renounce the use of force as such—such a course of action would be mistaken, particularly having sent the task force—but we should make it clear that we shall explore every possible avenue for a peaceful resolution of the dispute in the first place, and we must not suddenly escalate the military action to a full-scale war. That would be the case if we embarked immediately on a full-scale invasion of the Falklands. . . .

The Government should also make it clear at this juncture to the United States that if its present diplomatic venture fails, as it has more or less failed, the United States should come off the fence. The maximum economic pressure will minimise the likelihood that force will have to be used. In these circumstances, if the United States stands genuinely for a peaceful solution, as it claims, it should give full backing at this stage to our economic sanctions or it will stand condemned for not being prepared to come out against a Fascist military junta in the region that it has regarded as its own sphere of influence.

If that should be the state of affairs, hon. Members on both sides of the House should consider carefully what that means in the future on such issues as cruise missiles being stationed in this country and how far we can rely on an ally who is not prepared to support us fully on this issue. . . .

We must recognise that the principle of self-determination is sacrosanct. Unlike some of my hon. Friends, with whom I have agreed in the past on other issues, I believe that the Government and the country must stand firm behind that principle in the case of the Falkland Islands. . . .

Mr. John Page (Harrow, West): . . . The main interest of those taking part in the debate should be to see that nothing is said which might make the lives of our Service men in the task force or the residents of the Falkland Islands more difficult or dangerous.

An emergency debate *[in Strasbourg]* this morning on the Falkland issue, lasting three hours, followed the extremely successful speech and the brilliant answering of questions on the Falkland Islands in the Assembly yesterday by my right hon. Friend the Minister of State, Foreign and Commonwealth Office. Today's debate was on a resolution which was helpful and supportive of the British point of view. It talked about

"solidarity with the aims of the British Government policy."

That was passed at 12.30 this afternoon by 150 votes in favour, two votes against and six abstentions. It was not a wishy-washy resolution. I only wish that the right hon. Member for Bristol, South-East (Mr. Benn) had met some of the representatives of other countries, because he said today that he thought that other countries' support was disappearing.

I am certain that the main reason for the unity and strength of the international support for our position is that all the political parties up to the last few days have had a united approach. However, it seems now as though the Opposition may be trying to back away. . . .

If the parties in the House had not been united, the same unanimity of support would not have been attributed to us overseas. . . . I beg the Opposition Front Bench . . . to stop backing away and to stick to the position that it maintained 10 days ago. The least that the task force can expect is unanimity from the House today. We know that it will do its duty. The Fleet expects us, this day, to do ours.

Mr. Robin F. Cook (Edinburgh, Central): . . . We meet at a time when we appear to be hovering on the brink of a major escalation and possibly on the brink of an opposed landing on the Falkland Islands. No hon. Member would deny that that would be a hazardous undertaking. We face considerable odds. According to the known figures, the other side has superiority in terms of the number of infantrymen. It certainly has superiority in air cover. We have superiority in naval vessels, but the other navy— although inferior in number—is formidably well armed. One reason for that is that we sold them most of their weapons before some hon. Members discovered that we were dealing with an aggressive, unpredictable Fascist dictatorship. I hope that lessons will be learnt for our future arms sales policy. . . .

Therefore, we must ask ourselves whether we are justified in escalating a conflict with such risks. I do not shrink from the fact that in certain circumstances a State may be justified in applying military force. There may also be occasions when such risks must, inevitably, be accepted. However, to justify the use of such force there must be a major national interest at stake. . . .

If there is a consideration that could lead the House to contemplate further military escalation, it relates to the interests of the Falkland Islanders. That brings us to the first major paradox. There is a stark contrast between the passionate commitment shown in the House since 2 April for the interests of the Falkland Islanders and the long history of indifference and neglect that preceded that date. . . .

The Falkland Islanders have one clear, obvious and overwhelming need—to be freed of military occupation. Is a military escalation and a landing on the Falkland Islands the only way in which they can be freed from military occupation? . . .

Yet for the past three weeks it has been evident that it would be possible to achieve a diplomatic settlement that involved the withdrawal of Argentine forces if there was some recognition by the United Kingdom of Argentina's claim for sovereignty over the Falkland Islands. . . .

For the past two decades all British Governments have been willing to negotiate with the Argentines on their claim of sovereignty over the Falkland Islands. Apparently, we are now preparing to go to war to deny the very claim that we have been negotiating for two decades. . . .

We have enjoyed considerable international support over the past month, which has been the strength of our argument. However, if, in defiance of *[the appeal of the Secretary-General]*, we escalate military conflict and launch what would be perceived in many parts of the world as an aggressive attack on the Falkland Islands, we would sacrifice that international support and our strongest card to enforce our claim to the islands. . . .

I fear that if the Prime Minister embarks on a major military escalation in the immediate future, the judgment of history will be that she incurred risks and losses of life out of all proportion to the issues at stake.

Lord James Douglas-Hamilton (Edinburgh, West): . . . If General Galtieri or his successor agreed to remove Argentine soldiers and eventually reached an agreement that was acceptable to the islanders, ourselves and the Argentine, how do we know that he would keep that agreement? How can we be sure that a man who believes in making his political opponents disappear without trace can be trusted? . . .

In those circumstances, if America is fully involved in an agreement and acts as guarantors, it will be much more difficult for the Argentine to double-cross both Britain and the United States simultaneously, because of the enormous economic and military strength of the United States. . . .

There is a second ground for American involvement. The United States has the resources and the capacity to deliver goods, food, materials and medical supplies to prevent starvation and illness. There is a role for the United States in the interim period. The Leader of the Opposition said that there was a role for the United Nations. That may be so. . . .

Once the Argentine troops have left, I hope peacefully under pressure, there will be a period when the islanders will need to be resettled. In view of their appalling experiences, I hope that they will not be hustled too much.

Thirdly, the question of oil also affects the United States deeply. In the past, Britain, Argentina and the United States have been involved in seismic surveys. They have been carried out by British Petroleum, Texaco and the Argentine State Oil Company, YPF. I understand that the surveys have revealed probable oil reserves literally half way between the Falklands and Argentina, the distance between the Falklands and Argentina being 350 miles. Instead of co-operating and sharing the resources along the median line, the Argentine acted greedily and without regard to the interests of the Falkland Islanders. . . .

If oil is exploited in due course, the Falkland Islanders should benefit through licence fees and the servicing of oil platforms. Here again, if the United States is a participant in an agreement between the Argentine and Britain, there is much more chance that the agreement will be kept.

The United States is involved in Antarctica, where mineral rights are protected by the 1956 Antarctic Treaty. American involvement there also can help to ensure that agreements are kept. . . .

I believe that the Americans will eventually come off their neutral stance, if necessary, and support us wholeheartedly. I hope that they will threaten and be prepared to use sanctions against Argentina. . . . I believe that the Americans will come out in our favour because they are aware that hundreds of thousands of their countrymen fought so that, in Lincoln's words,

"Government of the people, by the people, and for the people, shall not perish from the earth."

Mr. Frank Allaun (Salford, East): This afternoon the Prime Minister said that formal proposals were being made by Mr. Haig to the Argentines. If such proposals are now being made, surely it is utterly wrong to launch an attack on the Falkland Islands. It is incredibly wrong that we should attack while negotiations are taking place. . . . If we attack now it will be much harder to reach a settlement. . . .

It is better to compromise than to fight a bloody war. We must compromise. . . .

Therefore, we are engaged on an impossible task. What is proposed is a completely different matter from taking the rocks of South Georgia. We are not going to take rocks; we are going to attack an island with over 10,000 heavily armed men on it. They are armed with Exocets. . . .

They are armed also with homing torpedos. Only one of those is needed to sink the "Invincible". Once a ship is sunk on either side, it will be far harder to reach peace. . . .

The Prime Minister also said that "the islanders' wishes must be paramount". No one has asked them what those wishes are. The United Nations should send a team to ask them. Those who wish to retain their British nationality and be resettled in Scotland, Wales or New Zealand should be encouraged to do so, with financial grants from the Government. . . .

A month ago, the islanders would have wanted to stay. But now if they stay, and their staying results in an assault, their families will be endangered in the cross-fire, the British Service men's lives will be endangered, the 17,000 British people working in the Argentine could be endangered, although I hope that they will not be, and, lastly, the Argentine conscripts, who after all are human beings, will also be endangered. Even if, after all this bloodshed, we won—the admiral says that it will not be a walkover—how long is the Navy to stay there? Is it to stay indefinitely? I see no other way of retaining for ever the sovereignty of those islands. . . .

Mr. John Farr (Harborough): . . . It is sad that, as a result of one pressure or another, *[the Leader of the Opposition]* has found it necessary to fall away from the very firm line that he took on *[3 April]*. . . .

One reason why I feel especially exasperated about the situation in the Falklands is that some of us, over a number of years, have initiated a succession of Adjournment debates warning what would happen if successive Governments did not take action. . . .

What a foolish policy we have followed. It has resulted in the massive expenditure in which we are now engaged in sending a fleet to the South Atlantic to retake the islands. Thereafter, as has been reported by other hon. Members, apparently we are contemplating a permanent garrison of 3,000. . . .

After the Argentines are cleared out—and time is not on our side—let us get the Shackleton report out and do some of the development which is needed. Let us make use of the tremendous fishing potential which Lord Shackleton found there. Let us make use of the valuable mineral resources which exist in Falkland Islands waters.

Let us also take a fresh look at the people in the Falkland Islands' section of the Foreign and Commonwealth Office. It seems that there has been in the Foreign Office and in that section an element, which has persisted through successive Governments, which finds the Falkland Islands to be rather an embarrassment from imperialistic days. Let us clear them out. . . .

It is right that we should negotiate for a just and peaceful solution. The House must remember that it is futile to rely upon negotiations with dictators. We all hope that this incident will be ended by peaceful means and on peaceful terms, but, however it ends, the military junta in the Argentine must not be seen to have advanced its cause internationally one iota. If the junta has its cause advanced one iota internationally by aggression, it is transparent that aggression pays off.

Secondly, if a peaceful solution cannot be reached, it is transparent that in the three weeks that the military junta has not moved our men have been at sea long enough. The depths of winter in the South Atlantic, in very treacherous waters indeed, are approaching. I hope that my right hon. Friend the Prime Minister and her colleagues in the inner Cabinet who are guiding Government policies will bear in mind that it is impossible to maintain men at peak fighting fitness and efficiency in these conditions for too long, and that time is not on our side. . . .

Mr. Ioan Evans (Aberdare): When I entered the Chamber this afternoon I thought that it might well be the last chance to debate the Falkland Islands before we were involved as a nation in a massive military conflict. . . .

There is no doubt that the whole House condemns this invasion by the Argentine Fascist junta. There is no difference between the two sides on that. What we deplore, without reservation, is the naked oppression of these islands. . . .

The talk in the House over the last few months about the Falkland

Islands could well have led Argentina to think that if it invaded it could get away with it. . . .

My right hon. Friend the Leader of the Opposition was right to say that we must seriously consider the possibility of a diplomatic solution before we endanger the lives of the 1,800 people on the Falkland Islands, who could be involved; before we endanger the 19,000 British subjects in Argentina, who could also be involved; the 100,000 others living in Argentina who have some British connection; and the thousands of Service men in the Royal Air Force, the Royal Navy, the Army and the Royal Marines. Of course we are concerned about the 1,800 people—now somewhat fewer—on the Falkland Islands, but there are more human lives on one of the ships. I am told that there are more Service men on the "Hermes" than there are people on the Falkland Islands. . . .

It may well have been a mistake for us to ask Alexander Haig to be the honest broker. While the United States is involved in NATO and is a friendly ally of this country, it is also very much involved in Central America. It is seeking all sorts of allies in South America to deal with the problems of Nicaragua, Guatamala and other areas. The Americans have been sitting on the fence. . . .

When we talk of the Council of Europe and of Europe being with us, we should speak also of world opinion being very much with us. . . . Although world opinion was with us in condemning Fascist aggression, it will be quite another thing for world opinion if we are involved in a war where there will be massive loss of life. . . .

The crisis has been mishandled. The Pope has sent a message to Her Majesty the Queen, presumably as one Head of State to another, calling for a peaceful solution to the problem. I understand that he has not even received a reply. If we are to have any influence with Catholic countries in South America, we should at least make a response. Our present stance will not win us friends or influence people and it is certainly not the way to keep world opinion on our side and win the peace. . . .

We must try to obtain a peaceful solution. What would be the sense of having a war with Argentina? After a massive loss of life, we would have to negotiate a settlement. For the past 20 years we have been trying to arrive at a formula that will allow us to lose control of the Falkland Islands. We believe in self-determination, but we never thought that certain peoples would determine that they did not want to leave the influence of Britain. . . .

The consensus of the House is that we should have a peaceful solution. We should continue through diplomatic efforts to solve the problem of the Falkland Islands for the benefit of the islanders and for the benefit of the world by retaining peace. I hope that the Government will pursue that aim and not enter into a military conflict and a massive loss of life.

Mr. Peter Hordern (Horsham and Crawley): . . . We have so far relied upon our efforts and sanctions, together with the European Community, in providing trading sanctions and forbidding export credits to Argentina. However, there is one much greater sanction that should be brought into play as soon as the United States has concluded the negotiations for which it is now responsible. I hope, trust and believe that the moment the negotiations which the Americans have conducted are over, the United States will come down firmly and unequivocally on our side. The moment that that is done they will be in a position to create greater pressure on Argentina than any of the other groups of countries have done so far.

Argentina owes about $32,000 million and to service its loan it needs about $7,000 million this year. With the help of the United States, the European Community and our banks, which are heavily committed, I am certain that sufficient pressure could be mounted upon Argentina to make it impossible for its economy to continue in anything like its present state, in which inflation is rising at 130 per cent. annually.

Immediately the negotiations are concluded and if, unhappily, they are unsuccessful, I hope that the Americans can be prevailed upon to enforce economic sanctions at once and to refuse to grant any further loans to Argentina.

Mr. Denis Healey (Leeds, East): This has been a useful debate and it may turn out to have been crucial in the history of this crisis.

The House will agree that the Government's most valuable asset through this difficult period since the Argentine aggression has been the exceptionally strong support from the House, the country, Europe, the Commonwealth and the United Nations. That is a priceless advantage. However, there were moments in the last few days when that support seemed to be in danger of crumbling. I hope that the Prime Minister will forgive me when I say that there have been times in the past day or two when she appeared to surrender to the feelings that she naturally enough felt after the brilliant success of our forces in reoccupying South Georgia. I know that the House will want to pay tribute to the professionalism of our forces which won them victory in so difficult an environment without the loss of a single life.

Some of the words used by the Prime Minister in the emotion of the moment, particularly in the House on Tuesday, suggested that she was in some danger of boxing herself in through the careless use of rhetoric. She led some people to believe that she might be tempted to use force not as an instrument of negotiation but as a substitute for negotiation. Her speech this afternoon did much to set those fears at rest. She insisted again and again on the need for a diplomatic settlement, and she made it clear that minimum force must be used with maximum economy, always subject to our political objectives. While she sticks to that position I believe that she will keep the support of the great majority of the House, of the country and of the world.

I hope that the Government will never forget that the keystone of the support that they have had so far was their immediate resort to the United Nations after the Argentine aggression and the success of our mission in New York in getting a mandatory resolution from the Security Council demanding the withdrawal of the Argentine forces and a diplomatic solution. Again and again, as the Foreign Secretary travelled to Europe and other capitals in the past few weeks, it has been those dual objectives laid down by the Security Council on which the support of our friends and allies depended.

I agree, too, . . . that we would not have received this support had we not proved our determination to assert our position by the despatch of the task force and the prudence and skill with which it has been used in protecting the zone of exclusion and in reoccupying South Georgia. As my right hon. Friend said, quite apart from the folly of relying on General Galtieri's good nature we could not have obtained Mr. Haig's good offices unless he had clearly understood that we were determined to take the aggression seriously and to see that the aggressor did not get away with it.

We have, rightly, reserved our right of individual self-defence while the invaders remain in possession of the islands—in fact, until the Argentine Government have fulfilled the first obligation under mandatory resolution 502 to withdraw its forces. That right of individual self-defence under article 51 requires us to use force in ways that are appropriate to the nature of the aggression and proportionate to its scale. . . .

It is notable that, immediately after the reoccupation of South Georgia, the Organisation of American States condemned the Argentine aggression by endorsing resolution 502 but did not call for action against the United Kingdom Government. It may well be necessary to use our armed strength again in the coming weeks, if the total exclusion zone is challenged, but it is vital that if we are required to use our Armed Forces for that purpose we should observe the same restraints that we have observed so far.

What struck me most in my conversations at the United Nations last Friday was that, so far, there has been no falling away of the support that the United Kingdom received at the very first meeting of the Security Council after the invasion. It was equally evident from what many representatives said to me, however, that if we were felt to be responsible for initiating an operation which led to a massive loss of life—still more, if we were responsible for initiating a long and bloody war, as our force commander put it—the support that we have so far enjoyed would melt away like snow in the sun. I believe that it would melt away not only in the world outside but within Britain, too. All the opinion polls so far taken have illustrated that. . . .

But the excessive use of force would also jeopardise what I believe is a major objective of the present Government's policy and has been a central objective of the policy of all . . . British Governments since the Argentines began to press their claim with vigour [—] to reach a settlement of the Falkland Islands problem which would guarantee those living on the islands lasting security, free from the continuing fear of an Argentine invasion.

In our first debate after the invasion, the Prime Minister rightly stressed that no British Government could maintain continuously in the South Atlantic a force of the size required to guarantee the islands against the consequences of a bitter Argentine hostility. . . . There is no doubt that, if we used excessive force and inflicted a humiliating defeat on Argentina as a whole, the present military regime would probably be replaced by a Peronist regime far more nationalist and far more determined to secure revenge than those at present in power. The chances of achieving a lasting settlement, which the Prime Minister made clear today and a few weeks ago is her final objective, would then be far smaller even than they are now. . . .

There is one problem that we now face. That is to get the Argentines out so that we can establish the basis for a lasting settlement through diplomatic negotiation. Those are the objectives that we set ourselves when we drafted resolution 502. As time passes, it becomes more and more difficult to see a solution to that problem that does not involve the United Nations in one way or another, and perhaps in more ways than one. . . .

On the basis of the discussion that I have had in New York, I believe that the United Nations would be glad to offer a temporary administration for the islands during what the Prime Minister called the "transitional period" between the withdrawal of the Argentine troops and the moment at which Britain and Argentine reached an agreement that it is possible to put to the islanders to ascertain their views. The Prime Minister must be aware of this. The Secretary-General would be glad to produce a police force to guarantee the security of the islands during this period and would be glad to offer a permanent or temporary United Nations trusteeship for the islands, but all on condition that Britain and the Argentine agree to ask him to perform this role. . . .

The United Nations Administration might offer the best political way out of this problem. The role of the United Nations as administrator, provider of a police force or trustee for the island for a short or long period would fit into the context of the negotiations now being pursued by Mr. Haig. As I understand it, there would be little difficulty in the United Nations agreeing to those roles, provided that it was at the request of the British and Argentine Governments.

We must face the possibility that Mr. Haig will come to the conclusion, perhaps even in the next few days, that there is no point in continuing his efforts. In that case, the British Government should immediately ask the Secretary-General to establish a good offices commission to take over the intermediary role and to ensure that the process of diplomatic negotiation continues without interruption. . . .

However, if Mr. Haig decides to discontinue his efforts, unless we immediately go to the United Nations Security Council with proposals of our own, it is almost certain that some Government less experienced or less benevolent may take the initiative and demand a meeting with the Security Council to discuss a proposal which is far less agreeable to us and far less likely to achieve our objectives. It would be better for Britain to take the initiative at the start, as we did at the beginning of the crisis. We should prepare the ground for that now. . . .

I do not want to explore the problem now, but there is no doubt that if the British Government had been able to deploy small forces in the South Atlantic before the aggression took place, it might well have deterred it altogether. There is a risk that the United States, by waiting too long before it exerts the full scope of its potential influence on Buenos Aires, may find itself facing a situation in which it is required to exert far more pressure at far more cost to its other diplomatic and economic interests. . . .

However, the fact is that with all its weaknesses the United Nations provides a better framework for world peace and order than previous generations have known. It provides the only framework at this time for world peace and order. It has served this country well in the crisis. We must now do our best to use all the opportunities that it offers to give it a wider role. If the Government can demonstrate their determination to use the United Nations' opportunities to the utmost, they will be able to rely on continuing support not only from the House but from the people of Britain and all their friends in the world.

The Secretary of State for Foreign and Commonwealth Affairs (Mr. Francis Pym): This has been a thoughtful debate reflecting the gravity of the issues involved. It has also been of exceptional importance. I would not disagree . . . that it may turn out to have been crucial.

Many right hon. and hon. Members have spoken of the significance of unity in the House, especially at times of crisis. I warmly agree with those sentiments. . . .

As the debate began, I heard that reports had begun to appear in the press in the Argentine about the divisions of opinion—as it was alleged—in the House of Commons. The Argentines were trying to make good use of that allegation for their advantage. Today's debate has deprived them of any basis for such allegations. That is extremely important at the present juncture. . . .

We have applied and sustained a combination of pressures, all inter-related and growing in their effectiveness.

The first pressure that we applied immediately was diplomatic. Our first act after the invasion was to go to the United Nations, which has been an important element in the debate, where the Security Council responded to the aggression by passing resolution 502, which called, amongst other things, for immediate withdrawal from the Falkland Islands. That was a most important decision. Ever since, we and our friends around the world have lost no opportunity to press for its implementation and, wherever we can, to increase it.

The second type of pressure is economic. Our partners in the European Community and the Commonwealth—Australia, Canada and New Zealand—and also Norway joined us in banning imports from Argentina and taking other measures to show quite clearly that the whole world has an interest in reacting firmly to aggression. The pressure of those decisions is being maintained. The Assembly of the Council of Europe today passed, by an overwhelming majority, a resolution condemning Argentine aggression and expressing solidarity with Britain.

The third type of pressure is military. The task force that we assembled with record speed has advanced steadily towards the area of the Falklands. The scale of it and the competence with which it was assembled was the clearest demonstration of the professionalism of our forces . . . and the resolve of our nation. Ever since, we have continued to strengthen the force in various ways. The military pressure is still being stepped up. As has already been announced, a total exclusion zone will come into effect tomorrow.

I remind the House that the Government have made clear from the beginning that the pressure exercised on Argentina by our military preparations depended directly on our visible determination to be prepared to use force if we had to. Obviously, our whole intention is to obtain a peaceful settlement if we can, and the Argentine must be in no doubt about our resolution.

If Argentina had gained any impression that we were not so determined, any interest that she had in negotiations would evaporate. She cannot possibly have gained such an impression. We have steadily built up that military pressure by successive steps.

Meanwhile, we have exerted ourselves in every way that we can think of to achieve a peaceful settlement. The House is aware of the herculean efforts of Mr. Haig to promote a negotiated settlement. He visited London twice and spent two periods in Buenos Aires. He has made and is continuing to make every possible attempt to bring about the implementation of resolution 502. . . .

My visit to Washington on 22 and 23 April was a part of that process.

In my detailed discussions with Mr. Haig, we covered all the elements that must be embodied in a settlement. We explored every possible angle, but the truth seems to be that although Britain and America have been working flat out for peace, Argentina has so far shown no indication of working seriously for a negotiated settlement. On the contrary, she has sustained a military build-up of reinforcements. In my view, that is a further and flagrant abuse of resolution 502. It is not just that Argentina has shown no sign of withdrawing; she has taken the positive step of increasing and increasing her military build-up. That is a flagrant abuse of the resolution.

Argentina's public statements show an unaltered insistence on intransigent positions and, above all, that the sovereignty of the Falklands belongs to her. Sovereignty does not belong to her. That is the heart of the dispute. The immediate position is that Argentina has not responded to the United States proposal that was put to her by Mr. Haig on 27 April. While there is still some hope that Argentina might be willing to settle the crisis without the further use of force, I must tell the House that her current position is not encouraging.

I was greatly encouraged by the support that I encountered for Britain during my visit to the United States of America. The Americans are well aware that Argentina is the aggressor in this dispute and I imagine that they are greatly influenced by the ties of history and the shared ideals of freedom and democracy that link their country to ours. I have no doubt that those are some reasons why public opinion polls in America have shown such solid support for the United Kingdom. We are very grateful for it. . . .

After our re-taking of South Georgia by the carefully limited use of force—the minimum use of force is the present instruction and rules of engagement—Argentina surely abandoned any lingering doubts that Britain would exercise her right of self-defence. We shall certainly do so again if Argentina was so reckless as to violate the total exclusion zone. We are ready to do so if, unhappily, Argentina cannot be brought to accept a negotiated settlement. . . .

In the circumstances that I have described, it is not merely permissible for us to use our right of self-defence; it would be irresponsible for us not to exercise it and thus give a proper response to aggression. It is in the interests of the whole free world that the rule of law should be upheld and that aggression should not prevail. It is not just a British interest. The focus of attention is here because of the connection between Britain and the Falkland Islands, but it is an international interest. If we do not stand par excellence—which we do—for international law and order, and if other countries with the same interest in parliamentary democracy do not join us in this endeavour, the outlook for the world is bleak. It is precisely for that reason that our friends all round the world have supported us and why we expect that they will continue to do so.

Mr. Frank Allaun: The Foreign Secretary and the Prime Minister have told us today about Mr. Haig's negotiations. Is it right to launch an assault while those negotiations are taking place?

Mr. Pym: I have made it clear throughout that it has been and is our intention, and we have carried it out, to increase the pressure all the time. That is what we have been doing. We have the right of self-defence to which I have just referred. Therefore, I would say to the hon. Member for Salford, East (Mr. Allaun) "Yes, indeed, it is." A total exclusion zone is a completely proper step to take in relation to self-defence because the Falkland Islands are a British possession and we intend to enforce a total exclusion zone. I would have thought that the hon. Gentleman would be in favour of that.

The right hon. Gentleman the Leader of the Opposition devoted some part of his speech to the possibilities of recourse to the United Nations. . . . The Secretary-General is absolutely right to call for the implementation of resolution 502. No one wants to achieve that more than we do. It is indeed central to all our efforts in the crisis, as the right hon. Member for Cardiff, South-East (Mr. Callaghan) said. But there cannot be any suggestion that Britain and Argentina are on the same footing—the victim and the aggressor—that cannot be right.

It is not we who have refused to implement resolution 502—quite obviously it is the Argentines. So long as Argentina refuses to withdraw and holds on to the islands, it is quite wrong for anyone to suggest that we should tie our hands and forgo in any way our inherent right of self-defence. . . .

Mr. Foot: . . . The first part of *[the Secretary-General's]* statement calls for no escalation and a halt to any escalation. The last part of the statement calls for no extension of the range of possibilities of action. What is the Government's view on those two matters? What have they said to the Secretary-General on it, and what do they propose to say? Even at this stage, will he not go to New York and discuss the matter with the Secretary-General? We believe that it is wrong for the right hon. Gentleman and the Government to proceed with action on these matters until they have had these discussions. If they think that they have a good case, why do they not go to New York and put it?

Mr. Pym: I was coming to that point later. I assure the right hon. Gentleman that if I come to the conclusion that at any stage it would be appropriate, advantageous, helpful and useful, of course I am prepared to go. My right hon. Friend the Prime Minister said that.

With regard to the statement to which the right hon. Gentleman refers, rather accusingly and giving the impression, slightly, that in some way the Government are responsible for escalation and build-up, it is the Argentines who have been building up, in aggravation of their already inherent disobedience of resolution 502. In the interests of our self-defence, it is right for us to increase the pressure in the way that I have described. But I do not think that that compares with what the Argentines have been able to achieve in their build-up in the past three weeks. That must be taken into account. The basic point is that the resolution calls for Argentine withdrawal, and they are flouting it. It is in the interests of the whole world that they do the right thing and retire.

Only the fact that we have maintained our right of self-defence unimpaired has brought the Argentine to consider the American proposals at all. If we gave up that right, who could believe that negotiations could continue for a moment longer? How could that possibly advance the cause of peace or strengthen the authority of the United Nations? I do not see how it could.

The Leader of the Opposition asked whether we had fulfilled our obligation under article 51 of the charter to report to the Security Council the measures that we have taken in self-defence. . . . We have done so scrupulously. Our permanent representative in New York has successively notified the President of the Security Council of our proclaiming of the maritime exclusion zone, of our recovery of South Georgia and, most recently, of our announcement of a total exclusion zone to come into force tomorrow. . . .

The Leader of the Opposition also suggested that we should have gone to the United Nations to get the Security Council to impose economic sanctions on Argentina as a means of enforcing Argentine compliance with resolution 502. I can assure him that we have considered that possibility. But we saw at once that the Soviet Union, in its search for ways of strengthening its influence in Argentina, would certainly veto any such resolution. We have it in mind that that shadow is over the events in the South Atlantic. That would have meant that we would not have succeeded in our aim of increasing pressure on Argentina to fulfil its legal obligations. What we would have done would be to provide the occasion for a tightening of links between the Soviet Union and Argentina, which is not only not in our interests or Argentina's but is not, I think, in anyone else's interests.

The Leader of the Opposition and the right hon. Member for Leeds, East (Mr. Healey) also advanced several ideas for involving the United Nations in a settlement of the Falkland Islands question. . . . I think, however, tonight that I shall not pursue this issue further. But it is one possibility that remains open.

There is also the idea of a United Nations role in the administration of the islands and the possibility of a United Nations trusteeship. . . . These options we have also considered, but they are, I think, for the longer term. Trusteeship is a complex business and takes a considerable time to work out. It has far-reaching implications. We for our part would be entirely prepared to look carefully at any ideas that would secure compliance with resolution 502 without doing violence to the principles that have been supported in this House. So far, however, we have had no indication that the idea of trusteeship would do the trick or have any acceptance whatever by the Argentines. So that does not look very hopeful.

In short, we have considered a whole range of possible diplomatic options. We have always come back to the conclusion that it is Mr. Haig who has the best opportunity. I say again, however to the Leader of the Opposition and to the right hon. Member for Leeds, East that my mind is not closed to this possibility. If I could see anything advantageous, fruitful or hopeful arising from such an approach or such a visit, I would, of course, take it.

Mr. Healey: . . . Can he not accept that there is a difference between the concept of involving the United Nations in a trusteeship in the longer term, which is something that would only emerge from negotiations directly between Britain and the Argentine, and the idea of a temporary regime under United Nations administration that might provide the answer to what is known to be one of the most difficult issues, namely, how to put the issue of sovereignty on one side during the transitional period?

Mr. Pym: Yes; I have thought of that. I have discussed it with Mr. Haig

179

in our consultations, along with many other ideas. I am ready and willing to go if that will be helpful. . . .

It goes without saying that there must be an immediate withdrawal of all Argentine forces as required by the basic resolution. Of course, the necessary time for that must be allowed. We for our part would be prepared to move British forces in parallel. At the same time, we have to ensure that there can be no change of heart or mind on the part of the Argentines during the process of withdrawal and, equally important, I suggest, that there should be no attempt or possibility of an attempt at reoccupation of the islands at some future date. We have the immediate problem of the withdrawal of forces now, but we also have to think beyond that to the circumstances that might subsequently arise.

On the interim arrangements, the British administration was illegally displaced from the islands by the Argentine invasion and must be restored. Withdrawal is the first priority and the British Government have to consider the practical arrangements that will follow after that withdrawal. It is not an easy matter. It is quite complicated, and much time in the discussions that have been going on in the last few weeks has been devoted to it. Provided that the principle of British administration is preserved, the Government are prepared to consider reasonable suggestions and ideas in this field. Indeed, I have been exploring them thoroughly with Mr. Haig. . . .

The third area is the discussion about the status of the islands in the future negotiations. Many hon. Members today and previously have rightly emphasised the principle of self-determination. Not only the Government and the House but also Congress and the people of the United States attach the highest importance to it. Our basic position is that Britain is ready to co-operate in any solution which the people of the Falkland Islands could accept and any framework of negotiation which does not predetermine and does not prejudice the eventual outcome. The prejudicing of that outcome is one of the sticking points of the Argentines which we cannot accept.

As my right hon. Friend the Prime Minister said, it is extremely discouraging that the latest statements from the Foreign Minister of Argentina lay even more stress than before on Argentine determination not to yield an inch on the question of sovereignty. It seems that he does not depart one iota from the position that there must be prior agreement that any negotiation must end in sovereignty being transferred to Argentina, regardless of the views of the people of the Falkland Islands on this point. The Argentines know, of course, and Mr. Haig knows and has accepted, that this is a completely unacceptable position for us. That is perhaps the most fundamental issue of all that we face. . . .

It is our present understanding that the majority of the islanders prefer to stay where they are, which is a remarkable testimony to their attachment to their island. I cannot pretend that the total exclusion zone which comes into effect tomorrow has no implications for their well-being. Clearly, it has. But I have every confidence that they will see why we have acted as we have, because it is for the sake of our common purpose and their main interest—to get the invader out.

It is our hope in the meantime that the International Red Cross will be able to establish a presence on the islands, and that with its help, or by other means, we shall be able to arrange for the evacuation of any islanders who may still wish to depart. Transit through the total exclusion zone is possible with our permission. We shall control it, and if someone wanted to leave for any reason whatsoever with International Red Cross assistance, we would do our best to make that possible. . . .

I know that the House does not forget the members of the task force on board our ships. Our thoughts are very much with them. We are at the beginning of an Atlantic winter, and the task force will face increasingly severe weather on the high seas. But our fleet is designed to cope with harsh conditions similar to those in the North Atlantic which they know so well. Our forces are very experienced in cold and harsh conditions. As they go on their way to fulfil their duties, I know that the whole House has their safety and well-being very much in mind. . . .

Many hon. Members have asked what the Government will do if Argentina rejects Mr. Haig's proposals. Let me emphasise in reply that I very much hope that Argentina will take a reasonable view of her own interests and will not reject a negotiated settlement of the present crisis. If she did reject it, we would consider very carefully how to try to continue the negotiating process, but we have always made it clear that our objective is a settlement and the implementation of the mandatory United Nations resolution, and not the avoidance of hostilities at any price. If Argentina will not accept a negotiated solution, then, reluctantly and with the greatest possible restraint, we must use force. But we shall not relax for a moment in our efforts for a peaceful solution. It is encouraging that today the House has supported us so staunchly in all our views.

Report Sixteen

4 MAY 1982

Following week-end reports of naval and air encounters, on Tuesday 4 May the Prime Minister answered questions about the sinking of an Argentine cruiser, "General Belgrano", and Mr. Pym and Mr. Nott made further statements. Later that night Mr. Nott returned to the House with a statement on the loss of H.M.S. "Sheffield".

Mr. Roberts: In view of the terrible loss of life in the South Atlantic, and the rapidly escalating military confrontation, will the Prime Minister make a further effort today to reach a peaceful solution to the situation, involving probably the United Nations?

The Prime Minister: We all regret the loss of human life in the South Atlantic, but our first duty is to protect, and to minimise the danger to, our own forces in the South Atlantic, who are there because we all agreed that we should send a task force . . . because we all agreed that we must stop the invader, and because the vast majority of people in this House recognise that the best way to stop the trouble is to withdraw the forces from the Falkland Islands. . . .

Sir Peter Emery: Will my right hon. Friend say over and over again that until the Argentine Government withdraw their troops from the Falkland Islands, every injury and fatality in the Southern Atlantic is absolutely due to the action of the Argentine junta?

The Prime Minister: Yes, it was the Argentines who broke the peace with unprovoked aggression. They are on British sovereign territory and there are British people under the heel of the junta. We sent the task force to rectify that situation. We hope to do so by all peaceful means and shall continue to try to do so. In the meantime, our first duty must be to protect our boys.

Mr. Foot: May I press the right hon. Lady on the question of the sinking of the cruiser and the tragic loss of life involved. We are all deeply concerned about it, just as we all are deeply aware that the origin of the crisis was the aggression by the Argentine. None the less, the Government have direct responsibilities in this matter, and the right hon. Lady especially so. Can she tell us what political control there was over this development, which was a major development? Can she say what calculations about the minimum use of force entered into those considerations? . . . What are the next steps that will be taken by the Government to try to deal with the situation? . . .

The Prime Minister: . . . I want to make it perfectly clear that after the announcement of the maritime exclusion zone—I referred to the matter in the House last week—there was another announcement on 23 April, which was communicated to the Argentine Government and also to the United Nations. It may help if I read it in full:

"In announcing the establishment of a maritime exclusion zone around the Falkland Islands, Her Majesty's Government made it clear that this measure was without prejudice to the right of the United Kingdom to take whatever additional measures may be needed in the exercise of its right of self-defence under Article 51 of the United Nations Charter. In this connection, Her Majesty's Government now wishes to make clear that any approach on the part of Argentine warships, including submarines, naval auxiliaries, or military aircraft which could amount to a threat to interfere with the mission of the British forces in the South Atlantic will encounter the appropriate response".

The warning was given to the Argentine Government, I repeat, on 23 April. It was reported to the United Nations on 24 April.

Mr. Foot: . . . The right hon. Lady has not fully explained why such a development as this occurred in the circumstances in which it did occur; nor has she explained why the maximum amount—or, at any rate, a considerable amount—of force was used to carry it out. None of these things has been explained. They will need to be explained much more fully to the country and to others. Does the right hon. Lady appreciate that these are important matters for our own Service men, whom we wish to protect as much as anyone? They are also important for the support that this Government may command throughout the world in these matters. If the right hon. Lady and the Government do not appreciate that the sinking of the cruiser raises great questions of this kind, she does not understand the situation.

The Prime Minister: May I make it perfectly clear that the worry that I live with hourly is that attacking Argentine forces, either naval or air, may get through to ours and sink some of our ships. I am sure that that will also be in the right hon. Gentleman's mind. There was clear aggressive intent on the part of the Argentine fleet and Government. It could be seen first in their claims. They previously claimed that they had sunk HMS "Exeter", that they had damaged HMS "Hermes", leaving it inoperative and badly damaged, and that they had brought down 11 Harriers. That was clear evidence of Argentine aggressive intent. The right hon. Gentleman may also remember the persistent attacks throughout the whole of Saturday on our task force, which were repelled only by the supreme skill and courage of our people. He may also know, or will hear from my right hon. Friend, of the very heavy armaments that the cruiser carried, and, of course, the cruiser was accompanied by two destroyers, which were not attacked in any way.

Mr. Mates: Does my right hon. Friend agree that of all the uses to which the word has been put in the last weeks the word "paramount" applies most of all now to the safety and lives of our Service men in the South Atlantic? . . .

The Prime Minister: I wholly agree with my hon. Friend. Our first duty is to our own forces, who are there on our orders and with our support. We must look after their safety. Our second duty is to see that we try to use minimum force. However, that cruiser and the associated destroyers—and, of course, there are other task forces of the Argentine navy also at large in the South Atlantic, not far from the exclusion zone—posed a very obvious threat to the men in our task force. Had we left it any later, it would have been too late, and I might have had to come to the House with the news that some of our ships had been sunk. . .

Mr. Dalyell: When the Prime Minister referred to political control, did she herself, personally and explicitly, authorise the firing of the torpedoes on the "General Belgrano"?

The Prime Minister: I assure the hon. Gentleman that the task force is and was under full political control.

Sir John Biggs-Davison: Would not some of the ignorant and irresponsible questions coming from the Opposition have been avoided if the Leader of the Opposition had done his duty to his party, to the country, and as a Privy Councillor, by availing himself of the invitation from my right hon. Friend the Prime Minister to acquaint him with matters to which we, who are not sworn of the Privy Council, do not wish to have access because we have confidence in her handling of this affair and in Her Majesty's Forces?

The Prime Minister: It is for the right hon. Gentleman to say whether he will avail himself of any offer to talk on Privy Councillor terms. . . .

Mr. Foot: Would the right hon. Lady care to read to the House what she said about the matter of consultations on "Panorama" a few days ago? Will she also repeat to the House what I think she understood well before, the attitude that has been taken by many Opposition leaders in previous times, who thought that they would be failing in their duty to the House of Commons to gag themselves? . . .

The Prime Minister: I do not quarrel with the right hon. Gentleman's decision in any way. I made an offer available to him on the same basis as I did to the right hon. Gentleman the leader of the Liberal Party and to the leader of the SDP in this House. Whether or not he takes it up is a matter for him. I have been in a similar position. There have been times when I have taken the offer up and times when I have not.

Sir Anthony Kershaw: On the subject of the cruiser, how can anyone maintain that such a ship, armed in that way, and accompanied by those destroyers, was not a threat to our forces? . . .

The Prime Minister: . . . The cruiser posed a real threat to our forces then, and would have continued to do so in the coming days. . . .

Mr. Grimond: . . . Has not the time now come for a fresh, direct approach by Her Majesty's Government to the junta proposing that the Argentines evacuate the Falkland Islands, so that negotiations can then be entered into directly between us? After all, we are still not at war with the Argentine.

The Prime Minister: At the moment we prefer to make our approaches through a third party. Mr. Haig did valiant work, and it is clear that he is still interested in trying to bring about a solution, both through his own efforts and, as the right hon. Gentleman may have read, through certain initiatives that are being undertaken by Mr. Haig through the Peruvian Government, and which we are pursuing vigorously. . . .

Mr. Brinton: . . . Is my right hon. Friend also aware that there are two former colonies in the world today with populations of fewer than 8,000 and about 20 countries which have less land area than the Falkland Islands? Will she ensure that Britain does not deviate from its determination to demonstrate that armed, unprovoked aggression must never pay?

The Prime Minister: I believe that what my hon. Friend says about there being small countries in the Commonwealth and countries with smaller areas than the Falkland Islands is correct. I entirely agree that unless Britain manages to stop and undo the Argentine aggression, many other small countries and territories will go in fear that they may suffer the same fate. . . .

The Secretary of State for Foreign and Commonwealth Affairs (Mr. Francis Pym): Since we debated the Falklands crisis last Thursday, there have been some important military developments. My right hon. Friend the Secretary of State for Defence will report on those in a few minutes. Meanwhile, I wish to pay tribute to the efficiency and courage of our forces. Our relief that British lives have not been lost is inevitably tempered by our deep regret at Argentine casualties. I know that the whole House would wish to be associated with these sentiments.

These military achievements have been in support of our overall strategy; they have not been and will not become a substitute for it. As the House knows, we are maintaining the maximum pressure on Argentina in the diplomatic, economic and military fields with the objective of securing Argentine withdrawal at the earliest possible moment and in compliance with the mandatory resolution of the United Nations Security Council.

The military pressure that we have exercised has been challenged despite our clear warnings and our desire to use the minimum force. Our response in the circumstances was as inevitable as it was right. However, I can assure the House that what we are seeking is not the military humiliation of Argentina but a victory for the rule of law in international affairs.

Since the House last met, I have visited Washington and New York to reinforce our diplomatic efforts to achieve a negotiated settlement as soon as possible. I had extensive talks with Secretary Haig. These covered the diplomatic, economic and military dimensions of the crisis.

On the diplomatic side, Mr. Haig made it clear that, just as we have not abandoned our diplomatic endeavours following Argentina's rejection of the earlier American proposals, nor has he. We discussed a range of ideas for a settlement. We are continuing our work with all urgency. As the House will be aware, other Governments have also been active in promoting a settlement. We welcome this and are in close touch with them. Therefore, we are working actively on various ideas, including those put forward by the President of Peru. I can assure the House that we are losing no time in developing our thoughts about them and communicating our constructive views to those concerned. The framework for a settlement remains as I have outlined it to the House.

Proposals are needed which cover the essential elements of resolution 502—withdrawal, and negotiations on the future, unprejudiced in any way. They must also address the interim arrangements and guarantees required.

On the economic front, Mr. Haig described the measures which the United States has recently announced. They are a tangible sign of American support for our cause. I know that the Americans have not closed their mind to additional steps.

On the military front, Mr. Haig and Mr. Weinberger confirmed that they are ready to provide material support for our forces and I welcomed this. We are following it up in detail and urgently.

In New York I discussed diplomatic possibilities with the Secretary-General of the United Nations and with the President of the Security Council. I made it clear to them that our immediate concern is the implementation of resolution 502, and that we are open to any ideas which would achieve this on a satisfactory basis, namely, an Argentine withdrawal followed by negotiations on the long-term solution without prejudice to basic principles.

We were able to consider together the various possible ways of involving the United Nations. We recognised that a solution will require not only the right ideas but the right timing and the right sequence of events. I know that the Secretary-General is in touch with the Argentine Government. The burden of compliance with what has already been decided, of course, rests squarely with them.

It must not be forgotten that we remain the victims of a totally unprovoked act of aggression in defiance of the United Nations charter. We are seeking to ensure that Argentina does not profit from aggression and to uphold the rule of law in international affairs. That is an interest which all members of the United Nations must share.

Our resolve should not be doubted; nor should our readiness to talk and our will for peace.

Mr. Denis Healey (Leeds, East): I shall not be drawn into discussing now the military operations of the weekend as the Secretary of State for Defence is about to make a statement on them, except to join the Foreign Secretary in paying tribute to the courage and efficiency shown by our forces.

I remind the right hon. Gentleman that Mr. Haig, in announcing the shift in American policy on Friday, said that

"a purely military outcome cannot endure over time. There will have to be a negotiated solution. Otherwise we will all face unending hostility and insecurity in the South Atlantic."

I hope that Her Majesty's Government share those views, because they are shared unanimously by Labour Members.

There is deep concern among Labour Members and many of our allies in case certain types of military action—the attack on the cruiser "General Belgrano" may be such an instance—intended, as the Foreign Secretary said, to back up negotiations, may weaken or even destroy the possibility of negotiations for a long-term solution. He must be aware from telegrams that have been received in the Foreign Office this morning that the operations of the last few days have already cost us a great deal of support among our European allies.

On Friday Mr. Haig said that he had reason to hope that the United Kingdom would consider a settlement along the lines of his proposals. We understand from newspaper reports that Mr. Haig's proposals were put again, although perhaps in a modified form, by the Peruvian Government in the past two days.

Has not the time now come when the Foreign Secretary should tell us a little bit about those proposals as it is the Argentine failure to accept them which has led to the military action over the past few days and the shift in American policy? The House has the right to that information at this time because it is now being made available to Governments in many other parts of the world.

Finally, may I ask the Foreign Secretary about his visit to the United Nations? I understand from newspaper reports that the Common Market Commission will put to the Council of Ministers this week the proposal that the continuing support of the Common Market for the British position over the Falkland Islands should depend on our asking the Secretary-General of the United Nations to provide his good offices. The Foreign Secretary will be aware that the Argentine Foreign Minister, at a meeting last Friday, invited the Secretary-General to give his good offices. He will know that the Secretary-General is able to do so if we, as the other party to the dispute, ask him to do so. . . . Has the right hon. Gentleman asked the United Nations Secretary-General to take over the role of intermediary at this time? If he has not, why not?

Over the weekend the Foreign Secretary said that it was Her Majesty's Government's intention to secure the withdrawal of Argentine forces by negotiation. The Government refuse to negotiate directly with the Argentine Government so long as Argentine troops are still on the Falkland Islands. If they are not prepared to negotiate directly, will they ask the United Nations to take over the role of intermediary?

I hope that there is no truth in the newspaper reports of the past two days that the only reason why the right hon. Gentleman visited the United Nations this weekend was to appease opinion in the United Kingdom and elsewhere. We believe that the time has come when the United Nations must play the central role in securing the withdrawal of Argentine troops from the Falkland Islands and that it will have a very important role in implementing the ultimate settlement.

Mr. Pym: The right hon. Gentleman is less than fair when he suggests that what I have done during this weekend and in previous weeks is anything other than to do everything that I conceivably can to bring about "a negotiated settlement as soon as possible", the words that I used in my statement. We do not yet know whether that can be achieved, but I agree with the right hon. Gentleman that in the end, whenever that is, there must be a negotiated settlement. The sooner that it comes, the better it will be. That is what my expedition was intended to try to further.

I assure the right hon. Gentleman that the Secretary-General is in touch with the Argentine Government and is talking with them in the same way as he is talking with me. He did not describe himself as an intermediary, but, as he is in touch with both Governments, I suppose that one could describe that as his position. I have had many talks with him about the various possibilities, but the essential point remains that the Argentines are already under a mandatory obligation to withdraw. One problem that the United Nations faces is how to ensure that that withdrawal is carried out. That must be a precondition for taking matters further. The other essential condition is that the Argentines must come off their hook of saying that the outcome of the negotiations should be predetermined in favour of Argentina. That clearly cannot be acceptable. It may be that the Argentines will move from both those positions, in which case we may make a real advance.

I visited not only the United Nations but Mr. Haig to explore all those matters. Although the United Nations is a possible forum and can help in many ways, there are other possibilities, and I referred in my statement to the work that is going on, based on ideas that originated with Peru. The original American proposals were rejected last week by the Argentines. We are now working on a new series of proposals. I shall make a constructive input to those proposals and I am already doing so. They are different in character, but they cover the same area that I mentioned in last week's debate—withdrawal, what happens in the interim, and the final negotiations. Whatever detail is discussed, it must cover those areas. That is what we are pursuing actively, constructively and positively, as I am sure the House wishes.

That is the present position. It is difficult in the United Nations at the moment for the simple reason that the mandatory resolution has not been fulfilled by the Argentines. The right hon. Gentleman is right in intimating that one member of the European Community raised a matter with the President of the Security Council today. There may be a meeting, but I do not yet know what specific proposal will be put to the Security Council. That is perhaps not as important as the search for the means by which we can achieve a negotiated settlement. . . .

Mr. Healey: The Foreign Secretary has made two important statements. First, he said that he believed that the word "intermediary" might be appropriate to describe the function that is now being carried out by the United Nations Secretary-General. Secondly—I am surprised that he did not tell the House this in his original statement—he said that a member of the European Community was already in touch with the United Nations Secretary-General with a view to calling a meeting of the Security Council. . . .

In the light of the information that the Foreign Secretary gave us about another possible meeting of the Security Council, it is now very urgent, in the interests of the United Kingdom, that, the Argentine Foreign Minister having already asked the Secretary-General to assume that role, we should do the same now so that no time is lost and the future is not prejudiced, as I warned the right hon. Gentleman in our debate last week it might be, by a decision of the Security Council which might be much more hostile to our interests than the present one.

Mr. Pym: The Security Council has already passed resolution 502, which requires the Argentines to withdraw. That is the basic position. British sovereign territory has been invaded and during the past three weeks the Argentine forces have been heavily reinforced. Clearly, the first move must be an Argentine withdrawal from that territory. The Secretary-General is in touch with the Argentine Government, as I made clear in my statement, and one of his objectives is to ensure that resolution 502 is implemented. . . .

I have had no direct communication from any member of the European Community. However, it is on the tapes and it has been made public knowledge that one member has taken certain action. I shall comment upon that and react to it when I hear from the member State what it intends. However, not only the Secretary-General but the President of the Security Council had consultations throughout yesterday—no doubt they continued today—with all the members of the Security Council. Therefore, the United Nations' work on this important crisis is very active. . . .

Sir William Clark (Croydon, South): Is my right hon. Friend aware that the vast majority of the British public are behind the Government in their resolution against the naked aggression of the Argentines? Is it not regrettable that the right hon. Members for Bristol, South-East (Mr. Benn) and for Lanark (Dame Judith Hart) have recently made statements that have been used by the Argentine Government as propaganda to hoodwink the Argentine people? Is it not a disgrace that two Privy Councillors should make statements that can be used by the Argentine Government and that could extend hostilities and jeopardise British lives?

Mr. Pym: A number of right hon. and hon. Members would agree with my hon. Friend's remarks. The propaganda and the information put out by Argentina have been proved to be extremely inaccurate in many important respects—indeed, deliberately misleading, no doubt for its own purposes. During my visit to America I gave an assurance that what we put out from our forces would be accurate and true. . . . However, it will be helpful if we speak with the greatest unity that we can possibly achieve.

Dame Judith Hart (Lanark): In view of the Foreign Secretary's remark that there must be negotiation, does he agree that it would be helpful in that negotiation if there was now a truce on both sides so that the matter could now go to the United Nations without further loss of life?

Mr. Pym: There can be a truce, but Argentina must withdraw and there must be no prejudgment of the ultimate outcome of the negotiations in the longer term.

Dr. David Owen (Plymouth, Devonport): May I associate the SDP with the expressions of regret at the loss of life of the Argentine Service men and also pay tribute to the courage and skill of the British Service men who have been operating in very difficult circumstances? . . . *[Is]* not Peru uniquely well placed to act in that way, as a friend of the Argentine and with close relations with the United States and friendly relations with Britain—quite apart from its association with the Secretary-General of the United Nations? What does the right hon. Gentleman intend to do about taking up that initiative? Is he ready to negotiate without precondition, and would such negotiations include the acceptance of a readiness to talk about the trusteeship council provision?

Mr. Pym: . . . The President of Peru formulated a series of proposals which he communicated to the United States and directly to the Argentines, who turned them down. With Mr. Haig, I am responding positively to the ideas contained in the proposal and I will communicate some ideas of my own which may lead to a possible basis. I should not like to raise undue hopes, but I will do everything that I can.

The right hon. Gentleman spoke of negotiations without preconditions, but there must be the precondition of the withdrawal of Argentine forces, who have no right to be in the Falkland Islands, and no prejudice to the ultimate negotiations. Then we could start talking. . . .

Mr. James Hill (Southampton, Test): . . . Was the safety of the Falkland Islanders raised in any of his discussions? Is there any way that negotiations would provide for the temporary evacuation of the women and children of the Falkland Islands? . . .

Mr. Pym: I have had the islanders very much in my mind all the time and I appreciate the risks that they are incurring and the difficulties that they face. I have sent messages to them when I have had the opportunity to do so, and I have thought about the possibility of an evacuation. It would be difficult to arrange, but if the islanders want it and we could arrange it, we would naturally provide a passage for them. . . .

Mr. John Morris (Aberavon): Did the Secretary-General of the United Nations tell the Foreign Secretary what he had in mind about how resolution 502 could be implemented?

Mr. Pym: No, he did not. There is a very great difficulty for the United Nations over that. The Secretary-General did not put any specific suggestions to me. Naturally, in expressing and explaining the British point of view to him, I was anxious to hear what views and ideas he had. He had a number and we discussed them, but there was nothing specific. Similarly, the President of the Security Council had no specific proposal to put before me immediately, but we explored the area together and that was useful. We are in daily touch and more often than that through our ambassador.

Mr. J. Enoch Powell (Down, South): . . . *[After repossession]* will he tell the House on what subjects it would be proper, in the Government's view, for those negotiations to take place?

Mr. Pym: The basis on which they should take place is the charter of the United Nations. As to the format, there are a number of possible ways in which it could be done; that has not yet been decided. There are a number of options and we have an open mind about them, but the most urgent requirement is to get into a position where those negotiations can take place.

Sir Bernard Braine (Essex, South-East): My right hon. Friend speaks of a readiness to negotiate, but what does he have in mind that is negotiable? Surely if the Falkland Islanders are in his mind he cannot contemplate discussions over sovereignty, which would mean the handing over of the

Falkland Islanders to a State which has almost the worst human rights record in the world. . . .

Mr. Pym: The sovereignty question is the heart of the issue and dispute. For years we have been negotiating about the future status of the islands.

Sir Bernard Braine: That is what is wrong.

Mr. Pym: But that is a matter of history. That is what has been happening. We are not in any doubt about our title to the Falkland Islands, and we never have been. We have been governing, administering and having a British presence on the islands for the people there and we have always taken full account of their views. The Argentines assert that they have sovereignty and they now assert that they are not prepared to negotiate about it. That is not an acceptable position.

As to the long-term future of the islands, successive British Governments have taken the view that if the people there wished to have a different sort of Government or to organise their affairs in another way, the British Government would not stand in their way. . . .

Mr. Frank Hooley (Sheffield, Heeley): If the Security Council is faced with a resolution calling for an immediate ceasefire, will the United Kingdom veto it?

Mr. Pym: In so far as we are engaged in military operations, we are doing so in self-defence under the United Nations charter. The way that we have done it is by declaring—[HON. MEMBERS: "Answer."] Yes, on the conditions that I have just stated—that there is a withdrawal of forces and no prejudice to the ultimate solution. That is quite clear. In the meantime, in preserving British territory and British citizens, we have said that we will secure the total exclusion zone, and that is what we are engaged in doing.

Mr. Patrick Cormack (Staffordshire, South-West): Will my right hon. Friend lose no chance to point out that the responsibility for the tragic deaths in the South Atlantic lies fairly and squarely with President Galtieri and his junta? Will he also point out that any negotiations would become extremely difficult if British lives were lost or British ships sunk?

Mr. Pym: The truth is—and it cannot be said too often—that the Argentines started this trouble. They invaded the islands, which they had no right to do. That was the cause of the whole trouble and that is where the blame lies. The condition for making any progress is that they withdraw. Any casualty suffered in the meantime, on whichever side, is a tragedy. . . .

Mr. Russell Johnston (Inverness): Is it not the case that, despite the right hon. Gentleman's vigorous diplomatic efforts, on which he is to be congratulated, the essence of his statement is "no progress"? Given that fact, why has not the right hon. Gentleman maintained the closest contact possible with our Community partners to prevent, for example, action by one member with the United Nations such as he mentioned. . . .

Mr. Pym: It may seem that the essence of my statement is "no progress".

Perhaps that is a fair description, but, given the data of the problem, the differences between the two sides, the intransigence of the Argentines and their unlawful occupation of British sovereign territory, it is hardly surprising that it would take some time to arrive at a negotiated settlement. . . .

Mr. Tony Benn (Bristol, South-East): Has the Foreign Secretary's attention been drawn to the fact that in *The Sunday Times* a public opinion poll showed that six out of 10 people in Britain were not prepared to see one Service man's life or a Falkland Islander's life put at risk and that such a majority in Britain will not be rejoicing with the Prime Minister at the loss of life when the ship—[HON. MEMBERS: "Withdraw."]—was torpedoed without a declaration of war well outside the exclusion zone? Will the Foreign Secretary take account of the desire for peace in Britain by agreeing to a ceasefire and to the transfer at once to the United Nations of sovereignty of the Falkland Islands and its administration pending a settlement under United Nations auspices?

Mr. Pym: In making those points and others that he makes from time to time, which may be controversial and with which many people disagree, it is disgraceful for the right hon. Gentleman to attribute to my right hon. Friend the Prime Minister the reaction that he has alleged. I believe that it is utterly wrong to impute such motives or thoughts when they are untrue. That spoils the validity of everything else that the right hon. Gentleman says.

Mr. John Peyton (Yeovil): Does my right hon. Friend regard it as indicative that the right hon. Member for Bristol, South-East (Mr. Benn) should base himself and his argument upon one answer to a question in a popular opinion poll? . . .

Mr. Pym: . . . What the right hon. Member for Bristol, South-East (Mr. Benn) has said this afternoon was disgraceful.

Mr. Andrew Faulds (Warley, East): As the transfer of sovereignty of the Falkland Islands has been considered for 20 years or so, and as the Prime Minister has now had her skirmish in this atavistic and unnecessary exercise in the South Atlantic, which she and the chairman of the Conservative Party have launched, will the Government today order a suspension of hostilities before many more young men are unnecessarily killed and transfer the solution of the problem to where it should be, the United Nations, where eventually a negotiated settlement will have to be reached anyway?

Mr. Pym: I dissociate myself from the hon. Gentleman's remarks. Once withdrawal has taken place and there is no prejudice to the outcome of the long-term negotiations, of course there will be a ceasefire. This issue is already before the United Nations. We took it there right away. Opposition Members sometimes seem to forget that. . . .

Mr. Peter Bottomley (Woolwich, West): If, as has been suggested by the right hon. Members for Bristol, South-East (Mr. Benn), and Lanark (Dame Judith Hart) and the hon. Member for Warley, East (Mr. Faulds),

192

negotiations take place while the Argentines are in occupation, will not that be accepting aggression, which will be regretted not only by the Labour Party but by many other countries?

Mr. Pym: I entirely agree with my hon. Friend. To take such a course would be to acknowledge that an act of aggression could pay the invader. That cannot be allowed. Incidentally, it would be in breach of the resolution passed by the United Nations Security Council. This is not just an argument between Britain and the Argentine. Its implications are wider. We are talking about international order and conducting the affairs of the world on the basis of law and in peace. That is what the United Nations is for. If we carry that through—we hope by peaceful settlement, but ultimately by a settlement—and if we right this wrong, I predict that the world, at any rate for a few years ahead, will be a more peaceful place than it was before. The re-establishment of international order on proper rules will bring an enormous amount of relief to an enormous number of countries and millions of individuals.

The Secretary of State for Defence (Mr. John Nott): . . . In the House on 7 April I announced that our first naval action would be to deny the Argentine forces on the Falklands the means of sea reinforcement and resupply from the mainland. British submarines have achieved that objective. With the arrival of our task force on 30 April our next move was to stop reinforcement and resupply from the air, as well as by sea. Since the passing of resolution 502 the Argentines, instead of withdrawing, had continuously reinforced the islands. We gave two days' prior warning to the Argentine Government of the imposition of this total exclusion zone, and our task force is now enforcing it.

The task force was despatched to the South Atlantic with the support of the House and, I believe, of the country. Since its arrival in these waters our overriding duty has been to protect our task force against attack by Argentine forces. . . .

I shall now describe the military sequence of events. Air attacks by Vulcan and Sea Harrier aircraft against Port Stanley airfield were launched early on 1 May. The runway was cratered and rendered unusable by transport aircraft from the Argentine mainland. A further sortie was made today to render the airstrip unusable for light supply, communications and ground attack aircraft operating within the Falkland Islands themselves. The other main airfield on East Falkland at Goose Green has also effectively been put out of action.

On 1 May the Argentines launched attacks on our ships during most of the daylight hours. The attacks by Argentine Mirage and Canberra aircraft operating from the mainland were repulsed by British Sea Harriers. Had our Sea Harriers failed to repulse the attacks on the task force, our ships could have been severely damaged or sunk. In fact, one Argentine Canberra and one Mirage were shot down and others were damaged. We believe that another Mirage was brought down by Argentine anti-aircraft fire. One of our frigates suffered splinter damage as a result of the air attacks and there was one British casualty, whose condition is now satisfactory. All our aircraft returned safely. On the same day our forces located and attacked what was believed to be an Argentine submarine which was clearly in a position to torpedo our ships. It is not known whether the submarine was hit.

The prolonged air attack on our ships, the presence of an Argentine submarine close by, and all other information available to us, left us in no doubt of the dangers to our task force from hostile action.

The next day, 2 May, at 8 pm London time, one of our submarines detected the Argentine cruiser, "General Belgrano", escorted by two destroyers. This heavily armed surface attack group was close to the total exclusion zone and was closing on elements of our task force, which was only hours away. We knew that the cruiser itself has substantial fire power, provided by 15 6in guns, with a range of 13 miles, and Seacat anti-aircraft missiles. Together with its escorting destroyers, which we believe were equipped with Exocet anti-ship missiles with a range of more than 20 miles, the threat to the task force was such that the task force commander could ignore it only at his peril.

The House will know that the attack by our submarine involved the capital ship only and not its escorting destroyers, so that they should have been able to go to the assistance of the damaged cruiser. We do not know whether they did so, but, in so doing, they would not have been engaged.

On 3 May, at about 4 am London time, a Sea King helicopter keeping watch against submarine attack around the task force was fired on by an Argentine ocean-going patrol craft. This vessel was then attacked and sunk by a Lynx helicopter. A second Lynx then came under attack from another Argentine vessel, which was itself attacked and damaged.

It must be a matter of deep concern to the House that there has been loss of life from these engagements including the sinking of the "General Belgrano", but our first duty must be the protection of our own ships and men. There may be further attacks on our forces and they must be allowed to act in self-defence. We cannot deny them that right. Nor must we forget that military action began by an attack on British marines and the forceable seizure of British territory. The way of stopping the fighting forthwith is for the Argentines to withdraw their garrison from the Falkland Islands in compliance with the United Nations resolution 502.

Mr. Denis Healey (Leeds, East): The right hon. Gentleman rightly said . . . that his policy was and would always be to use minimum force under strict political control to achieve a diplomatic solution. I confess that it is not always easy to achieve that in the stress of battle. Nevertheless, on the evidence that he has just given, it seems that he has successfully achieved that objective, first, in the reoccupation of South Georgia; secondly, in the attacks on the airfields and military facilities on the Falkland Islands; and, thirdly, in the actions that he has just described within the total exclusion zone.

I shall address my questions entirely to the action against the Argentine cruiser "General Belgrano". The right hon. Gentleman said that the Government were concerned about the loss of life that had occurred. I understand that the action took place 36 miles outside the total exclusion zone. Although it appears now that there have not been 1,000 lives lost, as we feared earlier, the number must run into many hundreds. . . .

Almost two days after the event it should be possible for the Secretary of State to give the House more details than were in his statement. . . .

First, will the right hon. Gentleman say how far the Argentine ships were from the task force? . . . It makes a big difference whether they were 50, 100 or 300 miles away. Any of those distances could be described as "hours away".

Secondly, what were the two escorting destroyers? Were they by any chance the type 42 frigate that Britain sold to the Argentine?

Thirdly, if the attack was necessary to protect our forces, could not action have been taken to cripple rather than to sink the cruiser? . . . I accept that it is not easy for submarines that were designed for global war against a great power to exercise the use of minimum force in a police action against a minor power. There remains the question whether it was possible to cripple the cruiser rather than to sink it, as was done to the submarine off South Georgia. That question deserves to be answered. . . .

I ask these questions in no carping spirit. If it is indeed the Government's intention at all times to use minimum force to achieve a political solution, they must avoid risking the lives of half of the population of the Falkland Islands in a single engagement.

Mr. Nott: . . . I said at a press conference yesterday that it was our policy to use minimum force. The task force remains under the political control of the Government. It operates within a political framework. Nevertheless, in exercising minimum force it must bear in mind the overriding need not to endanger itself—our own men and our own ships.

We believe that the action took place just outside—about 35 miles—the total exclusion zone. However, as I said in my statement, the cruiser and the escorting destroyers were only hours' steaming time away. [HON. MEMBERS: "How many hours?"] The right hon. Gentleman asked for the precise distance. I cannot give it, as I am not prepared to reveal the position of our task force. Nor can I give full details of the exact composition of the Argentine forces operating against us. The right hon. Gentleman will know, because he, too, has been Secretary of State for Defence, that communications are not necessarily received instantly by a submarine. It sometimes takes time for communications to be made, for reasons that have to do with the natural concealment of the submarine, but the group was hours away from our task force.

Only two torpedoes were fired at the cruiser. It is impossible to say whether that would have crippled the cruiser—that could not be predicted—but, having fired its torpedoes, the submarine clearly could not remain in the area without endangering itself. Therefore, in accordance with normal procedures, it fired the two torpedoes and then left the area. . . . I can tell the House that in this case, due to the serious threat that the group of Argentine naval vessels posed to our task force, our submarine was ordered to fire some torpedoes at the cruiser.

Mr. Healey: With great respect, the right hon. Gentleman's answer about the distance between the task force and the Argentine forces is inadequate. First, the action took place nearly two days ago. No one could assume that our task force would still be in the position in which, according to the right hon. Gentleman, it was identified by the Argentine destroyers at that time. . . .

I did not ask where the submarine was. I asked where the task force was. The task force is a surface force in continuous communication with the

Ministry of Defence in London, as we know from the hourly press reports from correspondents aboard some of the ships.

Mr. Nott: I realise that the right hon. Gentleman asked where our task force was, but that is not information that I think it would be prudent to give to the House. As he will know, the task force is within the region of the Falkland Islands, around the area of the total exclusion zone, but I cannot be asked to give precise nautical miles in a case of this kind. . . .

Mr. David Steel (Roxburgh, Selkirk and Peebles): I join in the congratulations extended to our forces on the success of the operation so far.

Will the Secretary of State confirm that the military policy remains as described by the Prime Minister in the debate last Thursday as being measured and controlled? The right hon. Gentleman presumably accepts that if the scale of loss of life already suffered by the Argentines were repeated against us in retaliation it would quickly equal the total population of the Falkland Islands. Will he therefore tell us whether there is a general directive to the Fleet commander that all action must be taken only if it is totally unavoidable?

Mr. Nott: I am grateful to the right hon. Gentleman for his remarks about the skill of our men with the task force.

The right hon. Gentleman is quite right. The action of our Fleet in the South Atlantic must at all times be measured and controlled. . . .

I am sure that he will accept from me, however, that in the conditions in which our forces find themselves—repeated air attacks had been launched on them the previous day, we have reason to believe that there is a submarine or perhaps two operating in the area, and the Argentines themselves announced that they had sunk HMS "Exeter", brought down 11 of our aircraft and severely damaged HMS "Hermes", all of which is clear evidence that the orders of the Argentine fleet are to sink our ships—we must do nothing that endangers our task force, which went there and is there with, I believe, the consent of the majority of Members of the House.

Sir John Eden (Bournemouth, West): Is it not absolutely clear that, despite all the efforts of British Ministers, there can be no negotiated settlement unless the Argentines agree to withdraw, and that if they do not repossession of the islands by military means is unavoidable? . . .

Mr. Nott: My right hon. Friend is correct. We require a negotiated settlement—a long-term peaceful solution to the problem—but that must come after withdrawal of the Argentine forces in accordance with resolution 502. . . .

The Argentines have so far rejected every opportunity to withdraw. I should not like to go into detail about the military options, such as repossession, that are open to us, but the best way of avoiding any further loss of life is for the Argentines not to challenge the total exclusion zone and not to pose a threat to our ships and men. The right way to ensure that there is no further loss of life is for the Argentines to withdraw their garrison from the Falkland Islands in accordance with resolution 502.

Mr. Jack Ashley (Stoke-on-Trent, South): Will the Secretary of State assure the House that he fully appreciates that the massive support that we have from the United States and Europe is conditional upon avoiding huge losses of life, British or Argentine? Is he aware that there is now a real danger that we shall lose the support of our friends and allies?

Mr. Nott: I fully agree with the right hon. Gentleman that the support that we have so far received is based to a large extent on the belief that we shall not use more force than is necessary to persuade the Argentines to withdraw from the Falkland Islands. We are attempting to use the minimum force to achieve our objectives. I know that the right hon. Gentleman will agree with me, however, that nothing that we do or say to our forces must put them in peril. We have no choice but to take as our overriding duty the protection of our own ships and men.

Mr. Jim Spicer (Dorset, West): Does my right hon. Friend accept that most people in this country and certainly in the House will welcome his last statement? Is he aware that, above all, given the power, range and accuracy of the weaponry possessed by both the Argentine navy and air force, the House and the country would consider it a dereliction of duty if we did not take such action as was necessary to stop any attack?

Mr. Nott: The cruiser, although elderly, with its two destroyer escorts, posed a very considerable threat to our task force. All were heavily armed and the Exocet missile carried by the destroyer escorts is a potent and dangerous weapon for use against our task force. With a submarine in that area, we could not allow the Argentine group to go on threatening our ships and men, as it would have done if we had simply ignored it.

Dr. John Gilbert (Dudley, East): Is the Secretary of State aware that the Seacat missile on the "General Belgrano" would be of no significance in surface-to-surface engagements and that the dangerous armament—the Sea Dart or the Exocet—was with the destroyer escort? How does he propose to refute the suggestion that the attack was not aimed at using the minimum force to achieve the maximum military advantage, but that, on the contrary, it was aimed at producing the maximum casualties and psychological shock to the Argentines?

Mr. Nott: Obviously, I reject that charge utterly. . . . Seacat is not a surface-to-surface missile, and I never suggested that it was, but the "Belgrano" had 15 6in guns, which were a very considerable threat and have a very considerable range. What he said about the destroyers is, of course, correct as well.

Mr. Keith Speed (Ashford): It is correct that the guns are radar-controlled, that the cruiser carried substantial armour and that these ships would have been a significant threat to our task force had they been allowed to get through. Can my right hon. Friend tell us anything about the reports that the cruiser was afloat for some considerable time before it sank?

Mr. Nott: I cannot confirm the latter point. I understand that a report was issued by the Argentines initially that the cruiser was only damaged—that her propeller-shaft was damaged. If the evidence that we have had from Argentine sources is to be believed, the cruiser was crippled in the initial torpedo attack and did not sink immediately. . . .

Mr. A. E. P. Duffy (Sheffield, Attercliffe): The Secretary of State admits that the Exocet missiles on the destroyers represent a potent threat to the task force. Would not he and the Prime Minister have better met their stated objective of preserving the task force with minimum force if the submarine, if it had to be deployed, had confined its attention to the destroyers?

Mr. Nott: Had one of the destroyers been torpedoed instead of the cruiser and men had lost their lives, the House would have been just as deeply concerned about the loss of human life from the destroyer as about the loss of human life from the cruiser.

Mr. John Roper (Farnworth): Will the right hon. Gentleman accept that we share his view that ensuring the safety of our forces is the highest priority? Is he satisfied that the supply vessels and the troop carriers travelling between this country and the South Atlantic have adequate protection from Argentine surprise attacks?

Mr. Nott: I am very conscious of the need to provide adequate protection for the supply vessels and for troop reinforcements. It is, of course, a very important matter.

Mr. Julian Critchley (Aldershot): What will be the effect of the Falkland Islands affair on the future allocation of resources to defence?

Mr. Nott: With respect to my hon. Friend, I do not think that this is quite the moment to discuss that issue.

Mr. George Foulkes (South Ayrshire): Will the Secretary of State correct the statement by the Prime Minister and confirm that not all Members of the House supported the sending of the task force? Will he accept that it is reasonable for us all to believe that it has always been the intention of the Government to achieve a solution to this problem by military means, unless he can tell us, apart from putting forward one unacceptable precondition and a willingness to listen to other people's ideas, what specific proposals for a peaceful solution have been put forward on the initiative of the Government?

Mr. Nott: The Foreign Secretary devoted a large part of his statement to that latter matter. The House generally, I believe, supported the sending of the task force, although I am not for one moment claiming that every Member of the House did so. In the early stages of this affair, after the Argentine invasion of the Falkland Islands, we had great difficulty in protecting HMS "Endurance" from the Argentines. It was only skill and to some extent good luck that prevented our losing a considerable number of the Royal Marines on HMS "Endurance" at the outset of this affair. When the Argentines first attacked Port Stanley, they heavily mortared the marine barracks, believing that the Royal Marines were there. To suggest that we fired the first shot or that we are responsible for the hostilities—I know that the hon. Gentleman did not suggest this, but it is being suggested in some quarters—is a travesty of the truth.

Mr. Robert Atkins (Preston, North): Does my right hon. Friend begin to agree with the remarks attributed to Air Chief Marshal "Bomber" Harris . . . when he suggested that too much publicity was given to the nitty-gritty of strategic and tactical decisions taken by the people on the high seas facing difficulties in protecting our interests and our troops? If he does agree, what steps does he think can be taken to rebut some of the nonsensical remarks by right hon. and hon. Gentlemen opposite?

Mr. Nott: It would be of assistance to us if retired Service officers and others would not speculate so widely on all the military options that are open to us. It would also, naturally, be of help to us if the BBC and other media could have rather fewer programmes of this kind, because we are talking about lives, and the lives of our own Service men, and at the moment some of these programmes go rather too far.

Mr. William Hamilton (Fife, Central): Will the Minister confirm what the Prime Minister said earlier this afternoon, namely, that the decision to launch the torpedoes was a political decision—in other words, it was made by either the Prime Minister or the right hon. Gentleman, or both of them together? Or was it made by the admiral on the spot? It is extremely important that the country should know who is making decisions to kill in the South Atlantic.

Mr. Nott: Throughout this affair we have kept close control of the rules of engagement that go to the task force, and that must be obvious. The overall political control remains with the Government and my right hon. Friend the Prime Minister was, of course, confirming that. That must be the case. We did not fire the first shot, and the day before the "General Belgrano" was sunk there was launched upon our ships a substantial and dangerous air attack. It was only because of the superior skill and the better aircraft that we have available that our ships were not sunk the day before. I hope that the country understands that very clearly. We cannot allow Argentine naval or air assets to be left free to attack and sink our ships.

Mr. Michael Latham (Melton): Did my right hon. Friend note last weekend the difference between the military dictatorship of Argentina telling lies to its people about alleged losses of British personnel and ships and their subsequent jamming of the BBC, and his duty to respond fully and truthfully in the House, as he has been doing this afternoon, in our democracy? Will he assure the world and the country that any figures given by his Ministry of losses will be absolutely true?

Mr. Nott: We will do our utmost, given the distances and the problem of immediate communications, to publish nothing but facts. My right hon. Friend is absolutely right. A great deal of propaganda and misinformation has been put out by Buenos Aires. There was no great sense of outrage when they announced that they had sunk HMS "Exeter", shot down 11 of our aircraft and severely damaged the "Hermes". Indeed, this was put out from Buenos Aires with great pleasure before we were able to deny it. There does not seem to be any predisposition on their part to hide the fact that they have been attempting to sink our ships and shoot down our aircraft.

Mr. Healey: May I ask the right hon. Gentleman once more if he can give us more details about the distance between the opposing forces, because this is critical in establishing the necessity to attack the cruiser in self-defence? The right hon. Gentleman told the House a moment ago that the Argentine ships were closing on elements of our task force, so presumably they knew where it was, and, since two of them survived, presumably the Argentine Government knows. The Soviet Government certainly knows, because it has three spy satellites over the area. Will the right hon. Gentleman tell us where the task force was 40 hours ago?

Mr. Nott: I have noted that the right hon. Gentleman thinks that the Soviets know where our task force is. I rather doubt that that is the case. The "General Belgrano" was sunk about 30 miles south of the exclusion zone. I repeat that I cannot tell the right hon. Gentleman where our task force was then or where it is now. With respect to the right hon. Gentleman's natural wish to know how close the forces were, given the delay in communications that can arise between London and a submarine, the fact that I have told him and the House that this group was only hours of steaming time away surely gives him sufficient information to appreciate that these ships were a threat to our fleet.

Mr. Alex Pollock (Moray and Nairn): Does my right hon. Friend recall that at the start of the crisis the Government were criticised severely in several parts of the House for failing to anticipate the invasion of the Falkland Islands by Argentina? Does he agree that it is ironic that some of those same elements should now be criticising the Government for meeting the threat on the high seas and thereby protecting the lives of our Service men?

Mr. Nott: I have noted my hon. Friend's point, and I rather agree with it.

Mr. Dick Douglas (Dunfermline): Will the right hon. Gentleman concede that no one in the House in his senses wants to see the conflict escalate? Both sides have proved in crude terms that they can inflict substantial damage upon the other. I do not ask him to give the exact position that was under threat by the "General Belgrano" and the two destroyers, but will he say whether our forces were within or outside the 200-mile exclusion zone?

Mr. Nott: It would be so easy for me to give the hon. Gentleman the answer, but I am sure that it would be wrong for me to do so.

Mr. Michael Colvin (Bristol, North-West): Does my right hon. Friend agree that our attacks on the Falkland Islands airports will have caused heavy casualties among Argentine troops? It is these wounded Argentines and the other Argentines who need evacuation from the Falkland Islands, not the Falkland Islanders. Does he therefore agree that it might be worth while offering to the United Nations for its use the hospital ship "Uganda" to carry out this evacuation of wounded Argentines and any other Argentines who wish to leave? This may well provide the breakthrough in the negotiating position, where there is currently a stalemate. It would be an act of magnanimity and it might enable the Argentine people at home to see the real picture of what is happening on the Falkland Islands, rather than the counterfeit picture.

Mr. Nott: I assure my hon. Friend that if, for example, the Red Cross wants safe passage to collect Argentine wounded, we shall make sure that it has it. If we can recover wounded ourselves, we shall do so. We shall provide them with hospital and medical facilities in our ships. That would be part of the Royal Navy's normal conduct of affairs. However, there is sometimes a problem. For instance, in the case of the "General Belgrano", if we had attempted rescue ourselves we would have been within easy range of Argentine land-air attack. If we are to perform this humane function, we must do so without hazarding our own forces.

Later—

Mr. Dennis Skinner (Bolsover): On a point of order, Mr. Deputy Speaker. About an hour ago it was mentioned on television that one of the British ships, HMS "Sheffield", had been destroyed in the South Atlantic. Has the Prime Minister indicated whether she intends coming to the House tonight to explain precisely what happened?

Mr. Deputy Speaker: As soon as there is any such information, it will be given to the House.

Mr. Leo Abse (Pontypool): Further to that point of order, Mr. Deputy Speaker. While it may be that such information will be given in due course, the alarm, concern and distress that exist as a consequence of the massive folly that is occurring demand that there should be an immediate statement in the House. Surely it is necessary that the Prime Minister should come to the House and tell us precisely what has occurred, so that the House can give a firm indication of the need for a cessation of hostilities on the initiative of this Government and the need for far more urgent attempts to negotiate. . . .

Mr. Frank Allaun (Salford, East): Further to that point of order, Mr. Deputy Speaker. . . .
I put it to you that the sinking of HMS "Sheffield" is so serious, is such a dramatic and tragic event, that hon. Members on both sides of the House really want to hear a statement from the Ministry. . . .

Mr. David Winnick (Walsall, North): Further to that point of order, Mr. Deputy Speaker. . . .
We require the Leader of the House to tell us as quickly as possible when the Defence Minister is going to be at the Dispatch Box, and we certainly expect a statement tonight. . . .

Mr. John Stokes (Halesowen and Stourbridge): On a point of order, Mr.

Deputy Speaker. I think that it would be a great mistake if the House were to panic. This great and ancient nation has been through many wars and struggles and it does not need a debate and a statement every five minutes because a ship has been sunk. . . .

The Lord President of the Council and Leader of the House of Commons (Mr. John Biffen): The loss of HMS "Sheffield" and recent events reported from the Falklands very properly excite the deep concern of the House. Throughout the whole of the Falklands episode the Government have sought to keep the House informed in as comprehensive a fashion as possible for the convenience of the House. The situation concerning the loss of the "Sheffield" is still not totally clarified, but, as my right hon. Friend the Secretary of State for Defence has said that he wishes to make a statement first thing after Questions tomorrow, I am certain that he will then be in a position——

Mr. Winnick: We must have it now.

Mr. Biffen: —to give the House the most up-to-date information that is available, which is consistent with the tradition of informing the House as well as having regard to sheer practicalities.

Mr. George Foulkes (South Ayrshire): Further to that point of order, Mr. Deputy Speaker. The House will not adjourn in the near future. . . .

Mr. Abse: . . . What possible condition exists to justify the right hon. Gentleman's statement that tomorrow is the day to make a statement and not tonight when we are all assembled and when the nation expects a statement from a Minister, so that we all know who is responsible, what is to occur and what fresh initiative will take place before further lives are lost? . . .

Mr. Christopher Price (Lewisham, West): Further to that point of order, Mr. Deputy Speaker. This is not a matter of panicking. . . . The business of the House has been arranged tonight to go on for quite a long time. The Leader of the House, on reflection, might agree that to defer a statement until tomorrow morning is unnecessary. I am not asking for an immediate statement now, but it must be possible for a Minister to come to the House before midnight to inform the House, as the Government are pledged to inform it in statement after statement, of the latest situation as the Government know it. . . .

Mr. Home Robertson: . . . At a time when, quite apart from the number of Argentines who lost their lives yesterday, news has now come through that a substantial number of British Service men must have lost their lives, it is quite inappropriate for the House to continue to debate affairs such as recreational, sporting, cultural and social facilities in Scotland or the peculiarities of the composition of certain committees of a local district council in Kirkcaldy. . . .

Mr. Gordon Wilson: . . . As Ministers are in charge, and as the Prime Minister said today that there has been political control over the task force,

202

would it not be appropriate for a Minister of the Crown to come before the House to answer for what has happened and to give us a statement and information? . . .

Mr. Andrew Faulds (Warley, East): . . . It is really not acceptable that the Leader of the House should use his inexperience in his present office not to fulfil his responsibilities to the House of Commons. There has been a disaster in the South Atlantic engineered by him and his party colleagues, and the least he can do in fulfilment of his duties to the House of Commons is to summon his senior colleagues to explain the present position . . . it would also be necessary for the leaders of my party to attend that post mortem since they were originally party to this whole lunatic exercise in the South Atlantic. . . .

Mr. Martin Flannery (Sheffield, Hillsborough): . . It is disgraceful that we should have to learn from outside what is happening when we have been elected to come to the House and learn whatever is happening. . . .

Sir John Eden (Bournemouth, West): . . . May I respectfully appeal to hon. Members on the Opposition Benches for a moment of calm? Is it not absolutely clear that in a military engagement it is inescapable that there will be casualties on both sides?

Mr. Biffen: I very much wish to assist the House in making progress this evening in the way in which it feels most congenial and orderly: I appreciate that in all parts of the House there is deep concern over the recent news. There is great anxiety that the matter should be fully ventilated in the Chamber. Some feel that it must happen this evening. I believe that the majority feel that the most appropriate occasion would be for my right hon. Friend the Secretary of State for Defence to make a comprehensive statement tomorrow afternoon with all the available information that he will then have. I believe that that would be a gesture consistent with the traditions of the House and with the nature of the situation. . . .

If it will help, I shall convey to my right hon. Friend the Secretary of State for Defence the opinions expressed and the hope that he might be able to come to the House for what I am sure will be understood to be a brief holding statement. . . .

The Secretary of State for Defence (Mr. John Nott): On a point of order, Mr. Deputy Speaker, I should like to make a statement.

Mr. Deputy Speaker (Mr. Bernard Weatherill): Order. Has the Secretary of State the leave of the House to make a statement?

Hon. Members: Aye.

Mr. Nott: In my statement earlier today, I said that we must expect further Argentine attacks on our forces. I deeply regret now to have to inform the House of such attacks.

In the course of its duties within the total exclusion zone around the Falkland Islands, HMS "Sheffield", a type 42 destroyer, was attacked and hit late this afternoon by an Argentine missile. The ship caught fire, which spread out of control. The order was then given to abandon ship. There were accompanying vessels in the immediate area which picked up those who had abandoned ship. Nearly all the ship's company and the captain are accounted for. However, I regret to say that initial indications are that 12 men are missing and there are likely to be other casualties.

Communications with the operational area are difficult at present and this information must be treated as provisional until further reports are received. Next of kin will, of course, be informed first as soon as full details are received.

Further air operations were also conducted over the Falkland Islands today. In the course of Sea Harrier attacks, one of our aircraft was shot down. The pilot has been killed. His name will be announced after we have confirmation that his next of kin have been informed. All the other Sea Harriers returned safely.

The task force is continuing with its operations as planned.

Mr. Michael Foot (Ebbw Vale): May I first thank the Leader of the House for having responded to many of the requests from hon. Members that a statement should be made? May I also thank the Secretary of State for Defence for coming to the House to make the statement? As I am sure we all agree, it contains grave and tragic news. All of us deeply deplore the fact that the right hon. Gentleman should have had to come to the House to make it.

When I first heard the news, I thought that it was right that the House should wait for a while because the next of kin had not yet been informed. That is absolutely necessary as the next stage.

For the House to make the right judgment about this matter, it is better that we should have a statement tomorrow. We can consider that, what the Government may say and what we may say. I do not seek in any sense, in this moment of what could be a tragedy for some of our people, to make any political comments, but I hope that tomorrow the Government will be prepared to make a statement on the whole matter. . . .

There are implications that arise and reflect on some of the things that have been said in the debates over the past few days and to which some of us referred in the debate last Thursday. But I suggest that the best course for the House is that the Secretary of State or perhaps the Prime Minister should come to the House tomorrow and make a further statement in the full light of all these matters. . . .

Mr. Nott: . . . It is of course grave and tragic news; I entirely agree with him. I am sure that the Government will wish to make a statement tomorrow.

Mr. Anthony Buck (Colchester): Does my right hon. Friend accept that the whole House is bitterly distressed at what he has had to announce? Does he agree that probably the best thing, in the interests of all of us, is that we should pause on it until we can talk about it tomorrow, having thought about what has happened here? It is always difficult when one is opposing Fascist dictators, but let us think on it. . . .

Mr. Nott: I thank my right hon. and learned Friend. We shall make a further statement tomorrow, and I hope that we shall be in a position to give more details then. . . .

Mr. Michael Mates (Petersfield): Will my right hon. Friend accept that, tragic though the current situation is, it was unrealistic for anyone to expect that we could embark on this particular and very necessary course without suffering casualties? Will my right hon. Friend further accept that, provided that the Government neither over-react to this tragedy nor in any way weaken their resolve on the course they have set out on, they will have, and will deserve, the respect of the House and of the country?

Mr. Nott: It is the case that there has been a naval battle, if I can describe it as that, going on for several days and casualties to both ships and men are very likely to occur in that situation; so I agree with my right hon. Friend in that respect.

Mr. Ian Mikardo (Bethnal Green and Bow): In the midst of the grief which we all share and which has been expressed from both sides of the House, can the right hon. Gentleman tell us whether the Prime Minister is still inviting us all to rejoice, rejoice?

Mr. Nott: I shall not comment on that matter, but I am afraid that I must make one correction to the remarks I made earlier. I said in making my statement that initial indications were that 12 men were missing. I regret to say that the latest news, which I have just had, is rather worse. It is that the number of deaths may be as high as 30. But we really do not have sufficient information at this stage to give firm news to the House, and that is why I think it is better to wait until tomorrow. . . .

Mr. John Stokes (Halesowen and Stourbridge): Is my right hon. Friend aware that the eyes of the nation are upon this House tonight? As someone who has been here for only 12 years but who spent six years fighting in the war, I found tonight some signs of panic on both sides of the House. May I assure my right hon. Friend that those signs are only temporary and I am sure that tomorrow the House will be resolved that we should carry through what the Government are determined to do.

Mr. Nott: I have noted my right hon. Friend's remarks. I would not wish to comment on them tonight. . . .

Mr. Bill Walker (Perth and East Perthshire): Does my right hon. Friend agree that when many thousands of our Service men are on the high seas with the task force we should be showing our united support for them? The last thing that we should be doing is trying to put a series of questions that cannot find answers because the answers are not available.

Mr. Nott: I very much agree with my hon. Friend.

Mr. Abse: We all share similar thoughts in this tragedy and we are profoundly concerned that further tragedies should not take place. Can we have the assurance that in the statement that will be made there will be no attempt on the part of the Government to compound the initial error that brought us to this situation and left the islands without defence? Can we be assured also that in the light of our obvious vulnerability there will be no absurd reiterations of the inviolability of sovereignty without considering other aspects? Will we be told that our men will not be put to further risks by being sent by the thousands in the "QE2" into areas where quite clearly there could be further tragedies and further deaths? We shall be expecting far more resilience and far more elasticity than we have experienced so far from this Government.

Mr. Nott: The operation has been going on for several weeks and there has been only one fatal accident on the way down and one other accident. This has been due very largely to the great skill of the men taking part. The hon. Gentleman's other remarks were of a wider nature and I do not think that it is appropriate for me to comment on them tonight.

Report Seventeen

5 May 1982

On Wednesday 5 May Mr. Nott gave the House his own detailed statement on the loss of HMS "Sheffield". It was followed by a statement from Mr. Pym.

The Secretary of State for Defence (Mr. John Nott): . . . At about 3.30 London time yesterday afternoon HMS "Sheffield" was attacked by Argentine Super Etendard aircraft which launched Exocet missiles. HMS "Sheffield" was some 70 miles off the Falklands enforcing the total exclusion zone, together with other elements of the task force. One missile missed the ship; the other hit her amidships. The resulting explosion caused a major fire. Although attempts were made to extinguish the fire for nearly four hours, with the assistance of fire-fighting teams from other ships in the area, it eventually spread out of control. At about 7 pm London time the order was given to abandon ship. Ships of the task force in the area picked up survivors, and the latest information I have is that about 30 men are still missing. A further number sustained injuries, and they are being well cared for under medical supervision. We have no further details of casualties at the present time. The ships are still engaged on operations and I know that the force commander will provide further information just as soon as he is able to do so. All the next of kin of the ship's company are being informed. The thoughts of the whole House are with them at this sad time.

Mr. Denis Healey (Leeds, East): I associate the Opposition with the Secretary of State's tribute. . . . *[The men]* gave their lives in defence of a principle which is regarded by all right hon. and hon. Members as one of great importance.

Is there any truth in reports in the American press and on American television that a major naval engagement is proceeding in the South Atlantic? . . .

I think that the right hon. Gentleman will concede that the Argentines knew the position of our task force yesterday and that, therefore, its position on Sunday when the attack on the Argentine cruiser took place no longer needs to be concealed from the House or the world. . . .

I hope that the right hon. Gentleman will give us a better idea of the distance between the point where the engagement took place and the task force. If he is unable to do so, right hon. and hon. Members and foreign countries are bound to take his silence as implying that the decision to attack the cruiser was taken by the submarine commander without reference to the commander of the task force—perhaps because, as the Secretary of

State suggested yesterday, the submarine commander was unable to communicate with the task force commander.

If that were the case, it argues that there is a serious handicap in political control of our forces at a time when, as the House agrees with the right hon. Gentleman, we must always use minimum force under political control to achieve the diplomatic objective.

Mr. Nott: I appreciate the right hon. Gentleman's opening comment. Many men are missing and have probably died defending principles that the right hon. Gentleman said that he thought were supported by the House. I much appreciate those words.

We have no knowledge of any naval battle going on in the Atlantic at present. I am aware that there have been reports from American sources that one is taking place. I cannot be sure, but we have no reports . . . it is impossible at a distance of 8,000 miles to require our task force commander to communicate with London repeatedly during the day. . . .

I see no reason why we should not be able to provide that information *[about the distance]* within a few days. There is no reason to conceal it. We think that HMS "Sheffield" may have been detected by an Argentine reconnaissance aircraft. We cannot be sure, but we think that that may have been the case and perhaps that was the reason why the attack with Exocet missiles was successful. That underlines the fact that we must not, on any account, put our ships at hazard by giving information prematurely. . . .

I made it clear yesterday that every action by our forces in the South Atlantic is taken within strict political control and authority. The actual decision to launch a torpedo was clearly one taken by the submarine commander, but that decision was taken within very clear rules of engagement that had been settled in London and discussed by the Government. . . .

Mr. Alan Clark: (Plymouth, Sutton): Does my right hon. Friend agree that the loss of a ship is a dreadful thing for the Royal Navy and that whatever declamations of national purpose and heroism may be made, and with which I fully concur, nothing can make up for the personal, terrible grief and sense of loss of the next of kin? Will he assure the House that wherever it is humanly possible the next of kin will hear of such events before the news is released to the agencies? . . .

Mr. Nott: As my hon. Friend says, it has been a dreadful event. An organisation has been set up to process all casualty information and there are sub-units in naval bases that receive information and inform the next of kin of men of the Royal Navy. Next of kin are normally informed by selected officers from local establishments. . . .

Mr. David Steel (Roxburgh, Selkirk and Peebles): My colleagues on the Liberal Bench would obviously wish to be associated with the expressions of sympathy from the Government and the official Opposition to the relatives of those lost in this terrible disaster.

Will the right hon. Gentleman accept that this incident, together with the sinking of the Argentine cruiser, gives added urgency to the need to seek an effective diplomatic solution to the dispute? Is it the case that consideration had been given to supplying HMS "Sheffield" with a stretched version of Sea Dart with updated tracker radar, and was that one of the casualties of the defence review?

Mr. Nott: . . . We want a diplomatic solution. We shall continue to strive for it. . . .

The "Sheffield" was armed with Sea Dart missiles of the latest type. The missiles are an area air defence weapon. They can be used, but not very successfully, against incoming missiles of a particular type. They are primarily for engaging incoming aircraft on an area basis. That was the principal defence of the "Sheffield". We do not know why the Sea Dart system did not successfully engage the aircraft. It is possible that the aircraft came in very low under radar cover but there was nothing in the equipment of the ship which differed in any way from the normal complement of weapons on our type 42 destroyers.

Mr. Geoffrey Johnson Smith (East Grinstead): As the battle goes on, more and more of us are concerned about the presentation of what happens. Leaving aside whether the statement last night was necessary, what should be of more immediate concern to my right hon. Friend within his total command is the extent to which we should be briefed in future through television by the Ministry of Defence. . . .

Mr. Nott: . . . The Ministry of Defence spokesman briefs the press every day when there is an incident. He gives a purely factual account of what has arisen.

Mr. Martin Flannery (Sheffield, Hillsborough): Is the Secretary of State aware that the disaster to the "Sheffield", a ship which has immense ties with the city of Sheffield, has resulted in a great groundswell of desire, not only in Sheffield but much further afield, for peace negotiations? . . . Does the right hon. Gentleman not agree that the insistence that no negotiations will take place as long as those troops are on the Falklands is now a brake against the struggle for peace? Is it not time for that to be quashed and for Britain to go to the United Nations to discuss the whole question of a peaceful solution through negotiation?

Mr. Nott: Of course there is a desire for peace . . . widespread in the country. . . . We want to obtain, as soon as we possibly can, a diplomatic settlement to the problem. . . . I repeat a very fair and reasonable comment . . . on the BBC "Today" programme.

The right hon. Member for Leeds, East (Mr. Healey) said:

"It would not be to Britain's advantage to agree to a ceasefire unless we were clear that we had a negotiating process which would get the Argentines off the islands." . . .

Mr. Peter Griffiths (Portsmouth, North): . . . The most appropriate memorial to the brave young men who lost their lives in HMS "Sheffield", . . . would be to carry through the enterprise for which they gave their lives as quickly as possible and with as little further loss of life as may be possible. Does he agree that the quickest way in which that could be done would be for the Argentine Government to agree to remove their troops from the Falkland Islands?

Mr. Nott: I entirely agree with my hon. Friend. As I said yesterday, the way in which the conflict can be ended straight away is for the Argentines to agree to implement resolution 502. . . .

Mr. Jack Dormand (Easington): . . . The Secretary of State said that there were difficulties in maintaining communication between the task force and the Government . . . but . . . went on to say that there was full political control of the decisions of the task force. Some hon. Members are extremely concerned about the way in which the decision was taken on the firing of two torpedoes. Is there not some inconsistency there which requires explanation?

Mr. Nott: . . . When our ships are engaged in extremely dangerous operations in which they are subject constantly to attack, they frequently—and rightly—impose on themselves radio silence. Unless the ships are maintaining radio silence, their position can be detected. Therefore, there will be periods when for very good operational reasons we are not in contact with all our ships. . . .

Sir Frederick Burden (Gillingham): . . . Should we . . . no longer talk about using minimum force against an enemy who is prepared to deploy his greatest strength against us but use our strength as cleverly as possible to bring the dispute to an end and bring the Argentines to the diplomatic table?

Mr. Nott: When we say that we wish to pursue minimum force, that does not mean in any way that we are asking our forces to hold back on the pursuit of their objectives; nor in any way does it suggest that they are not totally free to defend themselves against attack and, when they are threatened, to attack the enemy first. . . .

Mr. Allen McKay (Penistone): . . . Will he assure the House and many people outside that political control does not slow down any defensive action that the Fleet may take in its task, taking into consideration the fact that HMS "Sheffield" was a type 42 anti-aircraft destroyer, built purely and simply as any anti-aircraft destroyer and the fact that radar picks up the planes many miles before they come into firing range?

Mr. Nott: I can given the hon. Gentleman that total assurance. There is nothing in any directives that we have given which can in any way hazard our ships, which are confronted with a difficult task.

Sir Patrick Wall (Haltemprice): Is not the loss of HMS "Sheffield" a clear indication that we have now reached the missile age? Is my right hon. Friend aware that the only effective defence against sea-skimming missiles is Sea Wolf? . . .

Mr. Nott: I share my hon. Friend's concern about the development in missiles. As he knows, we have made the radar tracker for the lightweight

Sea Wolf a major priority in our programme. I agree with my hon. Friend. One of the factors that perhaps has led to us not having anti-missile missiles as fully on our ships as I should like is that the Soviet Union and its Warsaw Pact allies until recently were not deploying sea-skimming missiles. That is one of the reasons why, in retrospect, we have not moved forward as fast as we should.

The Secretary of State for Foreign and Commonwealth Affairs (Mr. Francis Pym): My right hon. Friend the Secretary of State for Defence has just spoken about military aspects of the situation. I should like to add my own tribute to the courage of the crew of HMS "Sheffield" and of the Harrier pilot and my deep sympathy to the families.

The military losses which have now occurred on both sides in this unhappy conflict emphasise all the more the urgent need to find a diplomatic solution.

The House will wish to know that since my return from the United States on Monday I have remained in the closest possible touch with Mr. Haig. As I reported to the House yesterday, we are working very actively on ideas put to us by Mr. Haig, including some advanced by the President of Peru. Yesterday afternoon, after my statement, I sent a constructive contribution of our own to Mr. Haig. He is taking this fully into account. I shall be in touch with him again later on today.

I want to tell the House that a vital ingredient of the ideas on which we are working is an early ceasefire and the prompt withdrawal of Argentine forces. I can assure the House that we are sparing no efforts in the search for an acceptable solution in line with the principles which we have stated on several occasions.

The points which were put to me in New York by the Secretary-General of the United Nations are also receiving our very careful attention. I have been in touch with Mr. Perez de Cuellar about this since my return from New York and will continue to keep in close contact with him.

There are many points of similarity between the Secretary-General's thinking and the points we are pursuing with Mr. Haig. Indeed, Mr. Perez de Cuellar's helpful ideas seem certain to be reflected in the basis of any solution which we may be able to achieve.

I can assure the House that any obstructionism there may be will not come from our side. Although it is we who have been the victims of aggression, it is also we who are working tirelessly and constructively for a peaceful solution.

Mr. Denis Healey (Leeds, East): . . . We all feel that if military escalation continues in the way in which it has done over the last few days, more lives—both Argentine and British—than there are inhabitants on the Falkland Islands could be lost. That underlines the paramount necessity of achieving a diplomatic solution. . . .

Will he confirm reports that the American Secretary of State has asked for a two-day ceasefire so that the diplomatic possibilities can be further explored? If so, what response have Her Majesty's Government given?

I particularly welcome what the right hon. Gentleman said about the United Nations Secretary-General. . . .

I see that the United Nations Secretary-General is reported in today's edition of *The Times* as saying that the suspension of the peace initiative by Mr. Haig had created a diplomatic vacuum which only the United Nations could fill.

As the right hon. Gentleman will know, that has been the view of Her Majesty's Opposition for some time. I understand that the Argentine Government have already agreed to accept the good offices of the United Nations. I appeal to Her Majesty's Government to do the same. . . .

I was particularly glad to hear the Secretary of State for Defence endorse my words this morning that the ceasefire must depend on agreement on a negotiating process which will get the Argentine forces off the islands. That is an important distinction from the demand that has been made occasionally, that the ceasefire cannot take place until the Argentine forces have left. . . .

Mr. Pym: . . . The right hon. Gentleman referred to the possible suggestions by Mr. Haig for a two-day ceasefire. A ceasefire must be a part of any negotiated settlement that involves a withdrawal. That is an area that is and always has been part of the discussions. I am sure that it is helpful that I am in close touch with the Secretary-General. He has offered his good offices both to the Argentine and to the United Kingdom. I have responded in that sense. The Secretary-General has not put any definite proposals to me, but we have shared our ideas and I am responding to the ideas that he sent recently.

The right hon. Gentleman referred to reports of the suspension of the diplomatic mission by Mr. Haig. There has been no such suspension. Perhaps the right hon. Gentleman was implying that in some way Mr. Haig's efforts had come to an end. That is not so. It is clear that they began a new phase when the Argentine rejected the proposals that had been put forward earlier. I am certain that it is helpful that Mr. Haig's efforts are continuing.

I do not agree that the vacuum to which the right hon. Gentleman referred can only be filled by the United Nations. I am not worried about how the vacuum is filled so long as it is filled. I have told the House all along that I believe that Mr. Haig's efforts are the most hopeful basis for a settlement, but I do not exclude anything else, and certainly not the efforts of the United Nations. That is why I talked to the Secretary-General personally. He is in touch with both our Government and the Argentine Government. We hope that that will make a contribution. As I said in my statement, the principles and the basis upon which we are all talking have many aspects in common.

Mr. Healey: . . . It has been widely reported that the United Nations Secretary-General has put forward proposals both to the British and to the Argentine Governments not on a substantive solution of the crisis, but on ways in which negotiations might be carried forward. It is also reported that he has asked the British and Argentine Governments to respond to those proposals today. Will the right hon. Gentleman confirm those reports? Will he assure the House that the Government will take the initiative in responding and will not hide behind the possible refusal of the Argentine Government to respond, as was the case with Mr. Haig's earlier proposals?

Mr. Pym: There is no question of our hiding behind anything or waiting for someone else to refuse or reject. There has been no time when I have not been looking constructively for a way forward. I am in close touch with the Secretary-General and I am responding to the outlines about which the right hon. Gentleman spoke. Nevertheless, I still believe that the work that I am doing with Mr. Haig is most likely to produce a result, but no door is closed.

Mr. Healey: In answer to my earlier question, the right hon. Gentleman said that no proposals had been made by the Secretary-General. Now he tells us that proposals have been made. I do not blame him for not disclosing them. The matter requires to be kept under diplomatic privacy, but, if proposals have been made, the Opposition would wish the right hon. Gentleman to make a positive response without delay.

Mr. Pym: No formal proposals have been put to me. They were ideas. I am not sure what words to choose. The Secretary-General is receiving a response from me. I do not know what the Argentine Government are doing. I am in close touch with the Secretary-General and I am responding to him. That is the most helpful reply that I can give. It is the most positive that I can be. . . .

Mr. Dennis Canavan (West Stirlingshire): How many more lives must be lost before the Government fully realise that there cannot be a purely military solution to the crisis? If the Government are seriously intent on a long-term peaceful solution, why do they not comply with the increasing demands from some Opposition Members, and demands being made nationally and internationally, for an immediate ceasefire and for the United Nations, not the United States, to act as a mediator?

Does the right hon. Gentleman agree that if that is not done, the crisis is in danger of escalating into a full-scale blood bath, which no one will win, and that Britain will find itself increasingly isolated?

Mr. Pym: Of course we would like an immediate ceasefire and an immediate withdrawal. The Argentine is under an obligation under resolution 502 to withdraw its forces. At present, however, it shows no sign of doing so. Indeed, the reverse is true. A withdrawal must be established in the first place. That is what we must achieve.

I am working with all the strength that I can muster to find a solution, notwithstanding the fact that we are the victim. We are suffering from the act of aggression. It is the Falkland Islands that have been invaded. . . .

Mr. Michael Neubert (Romford): Is it not clear that although the 8,000 miles between Britain and the Falkland Islands gave time for negotiations, the indivisibility of sovereignty allowed little scope for such negotiations? Just as the worsening weather in the South Atlantic was undoubtedly a factor in the timing of the Argentine invasion, so the prolonging of negotiations indefinitely without the withdrawal of Argentine troops consolidates Argentine aggression. In those circumstances, does my right hon. Friend agree that the most effective negotiating weapon that is available to us is likely to be the legitimate exercise of force?

Mr. Pym: I note carefully what my hon. Friend has said. I should infinitely prefer, as I am sure would the House, that the Argentine troops left the islands under a peaceful umbrella than have to be driven out by force. If we can possibly achieve that, I believe that everyone will be immensely relieved. We do not know whether that can be done, but I shall leave no stone unturned in an attempt to achieve it.

Mr. Bob Cryer (Keighley): Will the right hon. Gentleman confirm that resolution 502 does not give carte blanche to the Government for any military action, but calls for the cessation of hostilities and the negotiation of a peaceful resolution to the dispute? Do not the Government recognise that escalation of military activity could result in the deaths of Falkland Islanders—the very people we claim to be defending? . . .

As military action goes on, the Government seem to look less and less for a diplomatic settlement and more and more for a military one in what seems to many people to be a tragic and misguided escapade.

Mr. Pym: That is not true. The resolution also calls for a withdrawal. That is the part that the hon. Gentleman did not mention. I think constantly of the islanders. They are suffering at the moment under the heel of the invader, whom they did not want and did not invite and who intends to impose upon them a way of life and government that they do not want. It is in their defence that we have taken the steps that we have. Of course they are suffering. Any invaded country suffers. There are too many invaded countries in the world at the moment. . . .

Mr. Jonathan Aitken (Thanet, East): . . . Will my right hon. Friend be exceedingly cautious about negotiating terms for a ceasefire or anything else until the Argentine has shown, by its deeds, that it is withdrawing its troops from the Falklands?

Mr. Pym: Yes, I shall show appropriate caution. I shall also show appropriate enthusiasm. . . . it is exceedingly difficult to negotiate with the Argentine. . . .

Mr. D. A. Trippier (Rossendale): In view of the events of the past few days, is it correct to assume that the former initiatives that were taken by Mr. Haig are now interlinked with those pursued by the Peruvians?

Mr. Pym: The proposals that were produced by the United States a week or 10 days ago but which were turned down by the Argentines are now over. Since then, a number of Governments have produced ideas. The ideas on which we are now working are a combination of United States proposals and proposals from the President of Peru. It is a mixture. . . .

Dr. David Owen (Plymouth, Devonport): Is the Foreign Secretary aware that we strongly support his insistence on linking any early ceasefire with the prompt withdrawal of Argentine forces, no doubt with phased withdrawal of British forces from the Southern Atlantic as well?

Will the right hon. Gentleman give a little more detail about the activities of the Peruvian Government? . . .

Does the right hon. Gentleman recognise that many people in the world now expect some clear indication of the British Government's long-term position? . . .

Mr. Pym: . . . Some proposals that originated entirely in Peru have now been, as it were, absorbed in the other negotiations designed and thought up by the United States. I have made a constructive contribution to the latest suggestions, and I hope that out of them will come a proposition with some chance of success. I cannot say more than that at this stage. . . .

Her Majesty's Government have an open mind about what might be the ultimate solution. The United Nations trusteeship concept is most certainly one of the possibilities and may eventually prove to be a highly suitable one. Whether it will match the needs of the situation later, I do not know, but I would not exclude anything. . . .

Mr. Norman St. John-Stevas (Chelmsford): Will my right hon. Friend reiterate from the Dispatch Box that it was in support of our diplomacy that the overwhelming majority in the House supported the despatch of the task force to the South Atlantic and that that resolution still holds good? . . .

Mr. Pym: . . . The strategy must be seen as a comprehensive goal. The diplomatic activity, the economic pressure, the task force and the military pressure are all part of the same process of bringing pressure to bear on the Argentines to secure, one hopes by peaceful means, the withdrawal that everybody wants.

Mr. Donald Stewart (Western Isles): I should like to associate my hon. Friend the Member for Dundee, East (Mr. Wilson) and myself with the expressions of sympathy for those who lost their lives in the recent action. . . .

Will the right hon. Gentleman confirm that he will continue to press for negotiation and a ceasefire concurrently with the removal of Argentine troops from the Falkland Islands?

Mr. Pym: . . . I shall certainly continue those efforts. As for the long term, that should be negotiated and discussed around the table with the parties involved and others in whatever forum is thought best at the time. . . .

Sir Frederic Bennet (Torbay): In view of all the remarks about principles today, will my right hon. Friend reclarify for the benefit of all of us the principles which, in his view and ours, morally justify our intervention? I understand them to be, first, the self-determination of the people of the Falkland Islands and, secondly, that in this day and age acts of unprovoked aggression shall not succeed. . . .

Mr. Pym: We are in business to prevent a military dictatorship and an undemocratic Government from imposing on a smaller country, by aggression and invasion, a type of government that the people of the smaller country do not want. The principles that moved Members of the House are set out in the United Nations charter in the principles of democratic rights and so forth. I think that people throughout the world understand very well what this is all about. . . .

Mr. A. J. Beith (Berwick-upon-Tweed): Is there now any prospect that, with the help of the United Nations Secretary-General and perhaps the Peruvian Government, the real holders of power in the Argentine junta may be brought into the deliberations, as Mr. Costa Mendez clearly had his authority to negotiate a settlement cut from under his feet at a crucial moment?

Mr. Pym: I am not in a position to answer that question competently, but the signs are that the junta makes up its own mind with the generals and admirals and anyone else it cares to consult. . . .

Mr. Ian Lloyd (Havant and Waterloo): . . . Is it not preferable that we should recognise, sooner rather than later, that, failing a negotiated settlement, the task force will not be able to achieve its objectives unless the Argentines are not capable of operating missile-carrying aircraft from any runway within striking distance of the carrier fleet?

Mr. Pym: Naturally, the military aspects are being considered in great depth, and possible plans are being prepared. . . . But let us at present concentrate our minds on trying to achieve a peaceful settlement, which is what the House wants.

Mr. Frank Dobson (Holborn and St. Pancras, South): Does the Foreign Secretary agree that there have been serious shortcomings in the conduct of Britain's foreign affairs in that, having set out to build up military pressure and at the same time to seek a diplomatic solution to the problem, the Government found themselves building up military pressure at a time when the Haig initiative had collapsed and the Government had failed to make arrangements at the United Nations or anywhere else for another mediator to be on hand?

Mr. Pym: I can only say to the hon. Gentleman that, without military pressure, there would be no chance whatever of an Argentine withdrawal.

Mr. Nicholas Winterton (Macclesfield): Does my right hon. Friend agree that the brave men and women of our Armed Services in the task force are shouldering the burden for the whole world in upholding law and order? Does he realise that the longer negotiations continue, the greater will be the danger to them? . . .

Mr. Pym: . . . I do not see our diplomatic efforts as in any way conflicting with what is happening to our task force. The task force has its operating instructions and is doing its job as best it can. . . .

Mr. Nigel Spearing (Newham, South): Is it not now opportune for the United Nations and its members to act under article 41 of the charter and to impose much greater economic sanctions on the Argentine? Unless that is done—and, I hope, subsequently lifted—why should the Argentines now agree to a negotiated settlement?

Mr. Pym: I suppose if they come to the conclusion that it is in their interest. Of course, it would be helpful if the United Nations passed such a resolution, and if that resolution were then carried out, but I doubt whether that would happen.

Mr. Eldon Griffiths (Bury St. Edmunds): As my right hon. Friend appeared to imply that a temporary cessation of hostilities might form part of the current proposals, will he assure us that the British Government will agree to no ceasefire if its only or main effect were to reduce the military pressure on the Argentine and enable the Argentine to consolidate its illegal occupation of the islands?

Mr. Pym: As I said earlier, arrangements for a ceasefire are part and parcel of a withdrawal. . . .

Mr. Healey: I thank the right hon. Gentleman again for the frank way in which he has answered questions, and I hope that he will not hesitate to come back to the House. I thank him, too, for the increasing emphasis that he is placing on the United Nations. I say, once again, that there is a risk that, unless we take an early initiative within the United Nations, we may find that our action is pre-empted by representatives in the Security Council whose interests are by no means as benign or well-informed as our own. . . .

Mr. Pym: I thank the right hon. Gentleman for his supportive remarks. The fact that the House of Commons has broadly the same desires can do nothing but help the operations, both diplomatic and military, that are in hand at present. I am not convinced that another initiative by us in the United Nations would help. It is a possible option, but at the moment we have resolution 502, which has to be, but has not yet been, carried out. I have to bear in mind carefully how it is to our best advantage and to the advantage of securing a peaceful settlement to take any further initiative in the United Nations. Nevertheless, I am most grateful to the right hon. Gentleman for what he said. . . .

Report Eighteen

6 MAY 1982

Thursday 6 May brought yet more questions for the Prime Minister.

Mr. John Page: . . . *[Will the Prime Minister]* try to find a few moments to listen to the radio and watch television, and judge for herself whether she feels that the British case on the Falkland Islands is being presented in a way that is likely to give due confidence to our friends overseas and support and encouragement to our Service men and their devoted families?

The Prime Minister: Judging by many of the comments that I have heard from those who watch and listen more than I do, many people are very concerned indeed that the case for our British forces is not being put over fully and effectively. I understand that there are times when it seems that we and the Argentines are being treated almost as equals and almost on a neutral basis. I understand that there are occasions when some commentators will say that the Argentines did something and then "the British" did something. I can only say that if this is so it gives offence and causes great emotion among many people.

Mr. Foot: . . . Does the right hon. Lady agree that there appears to be a real chance of a move towards a sensible ceasefire, leading to other developments, and that there is also a chance of moving towards a real peace settlement? Does she agree that everything possible should be done to nurture that chance, and that nothing should be done to injure it? In particular, will she say what is her response and that of the Government to the proposals from the Secretary-General of the United Nations? . . .

The Prime Minister: Of course, we are doing everything possible to pursue the diplomatic path to a negotiated settlement. However, the right hon. Gentleman knows that at the moment there are two sets of proposals. There is the one that is being pursued by the United States through Peru, to which we have made a very constructive response, and we hope to hear more about that today. Whether the Argentines will respond in the same way, we do not know. The other one is being pursued through the Secretary-General, to which the right hon. Gentleman referred. There have been various rather conflicting reports about the Argentine response to that, but it seems clear . . . that they are very interested in a ceasefire. They may not accept withdrawal, and they may do it on a totally different basis, or require undertakings on sovereignty. So there is some doubt about what they have said. I believe that they have probably said that they are prepared to discuss it further with the Secretary-General. . . .
We welcome the ideas that the Secretary-General has put forward and

can accept them as a framework on which more specific proposals could be built. We are sending a message to the Secretary-General today to that effect. . . .

It would not be impossible—indeed, it may well be likely—that the Argentines are concentrating on a ceasefire without withdrawal. That would be a very evident ploy to keep them in possession of their ill-gotten gains, and we are right to be very wary of it. The whole of the mandatory resolution No. 502 has to be accepted, and there can be no ceasefire unless it is accompanied by a withdrawal that is fully and properly supervised.

Mr. Foot: . . . I well understand that there may well be great ambiguity in the reply that has come from the Argentine Government, but can the right hon. Lady tell us whether the Secretary-General's proposals include a linkage between the withdrawal and the ceasefire? If so, presumably that is one of the reasons why she has given, I should have thought, a positive answer. Certainly I welcome the tone in which she spoke about the response to the Secretary-General's suggestions. I very much hope that we shall be able to proceed along those lines. . . .

In view of the considerable improvement that appears in the diplomatic exchanges that are now taking place—I am not referring to the Argentine Government now, but to the right hon. Lady's response—can she give us an absolute assurance—I am sure that the whole country would want that—that there will not be any deliberate escalation of the military action itself, any escalation that could injure the prospects that now appear to be much more hopeful of getting a real peace?

The Prime Minister: . . . The Secretary-General's proposals . . . are very much a framework. There are no specific details attached to them, and no timetable, but they link cessation of hostilities with withdrawal, as one would expect in view of the Security's Council's resolution. Beyond that, I am afraid, there is no timing and no practical arrangements. They really are a basis for discussion.

With regard to what the right hon. Gentleman said about there seeming to be a change in the climate of diplomatic negotiations, I think that it was not a justifiable comment. The Secretary-General's proposals are now the sixth set of proposals that I and my colleagues have pursued in detail over the past month. That is hardly a lack of diplomatic activity.

Mr. Foot: I am much more interested in getting progress in these discussions than in scoring any point off the right hon. Lady. We who have urged all through the crisis that this kind of response should be made to approaches from the Secretary-General have a right to say that. I fully understand that these are procedural proposals, first of all, from the Secretary-General, but we very much hope that over the next 24 hours or two or three days the maximum possible support can be given to those original proposals.

The Prime Minister: These are framework proposals. We are making a positive response to them. We hope to hear more about the Peruvian-United States proposals today, but I stress again that any proposals, if they are to be acceptable, if they are to work and if they are to command confidence, must be precise as to the timing and sequence and verification of events.

Mr. Viggers: Does my right hon. Friend agree . . . that it is incumbent on the United States now to make quite clear its support for our attitude in resisting aggression, and that in this way it will assist the Argentine leaders and people to realise their true position?

The Prime Minister: . . . We have now the total support of the United States, which we would expect, and which I think we always expected to have. I doubt whether its activities as a mediator—which we supported, and we were grateful to Mr. Haig for what he did—would ever have led people to think that there was any justice in the Argentine cause. The condemnation of the Argentine was almost universal, because the Argentine became an aggressor. . . . Two days before that invasion, the same Mr. Costa Mendez . . . called in our ambassador in Buenos Aires and said to him "The diplomatic channels are now closed". That same Government refused the plea of the Security Council not to invade. That same Government refused the plea of President Reagan not to invade. That same Government invaded, and have been piling in soldiers and equipment, against the United Nations Security Council resolution, ever since. That is the kind of Government with whom we are dealing. . . .

Mr. Cox: Is the Prime Minister aware of the growing views now being expressed by the British people that there must be no escalation of military intervention—*[Interruption]*—on the Falkland Islands issue? Against that background, is she prepared in the House today totally to repudiate those Conservative Members and the retired admirals and generals who now appear on television saying that, if need be, attacks must take place against the mainland of the Argentine? . . .

The Prime Minister: . . . The escalation of the situation while negotiations were taking place was by the Argentine, in the invasion. There has been escalation ever since. In the meantime, our own British people remain on those islands under what I believe the Leader of the Opposition called in the first debate "foul and brutal aggression". We must continue with our military activities. . . .

Again, it would be too easy to say "No military activities during negotiations". What would happen? We should be hamstrung. The people would still remain under the heel of the invader, while the Argentines increased their activities on the mainland and increased their supplies and reserves in order to attack us at will.

Mr. Michael Hamilton: If current peace proposals do not succeed, will my right hon. Friend take comfort from the fact that Army wives at Fulford camp have called for no compromise and have stressed only their wish to save the islanders?

The Prime Minister: That is wonderful of them and I should be grateful if my hon. Friend would pass on that message. Everyone realises that the aggressor must not gain from his aggression. One hopes that the United Nations will be able to carry out the mandatory resolution that it passed.

Mandatory resolutions under chapter 7 are comparatively rare in United Nations history. Unfortunately, those provisions have not been carried out. The important thing is that we should get the Argentines off the islands that they still occupy. If the United Nations cannot do that and if negotiations cannot do that, we shall have to.

Report Nineteen

7 MAY 1982

Friday 7 May—and yet another statement, again from Mr. Pym.

The Secretary of State for Foreign and Commonwealth Affairs (Mr. Francis Pym): The House is aware that, while we have mobilised and despatched the task force to the South Atlantic, where it has already been involved in active operations, we have also been pursuing a highly active programme of consultation and negotiation in the search for a diplomatic solution to the present crisis.

The House has shown exemplary patience with my inability to explain the nature of the proposals that we have been examining. I now have to report to the House that Argentine intransigence has again led it to reject proposals for a diplomatic solution. In these circumstances, I think it is right that I should give the House an account of where we stand—and of where we intend to go from here.

The fact that we were able to reach a point where a new set of firm proposals could be put to both sides owes much to the tireless efforts of Mr. Haig. We are also grateful for the constructive contributions of President Belaunde of Peru. We also put forward practical ideas ourselves which take accout of the Argentine position as well as our own.

Yesterday we signified that we were willing to accept and implement immediately an interim agreement which would prepare the way for a definitive settlement. Such an agreement would have demonstrated substantial flexibility on our part. If it had been accepted by the Argentines, the ceasefire, which would have been firmly linked to the beginning of Argentine withdrawal, could have come into effect as early as 5 o'clock this afternoon.

The interim agreement under discussion yesterday included the following elements: first, complete and supervised withdrawal of Argentine forces from the Falkland Islands, matched by corresponding withdrawal of British forces; secondly, an immediate ceasefire as soon as Argentina accepted the agreement and agreed to withdraw; thirdly, appointment of a small group of countries acceptable to both sides which would supervise withdrawal, undertake the interim administration in consultation with the islanders' elected representatives, and perhaps help in negotiations for a definitive agreement on the status of the islands, without prejudice to our principles or to the wishes of the islanders; fourthly, suspension of the existing exclusion zones and the lifting of economic sanctions.

This agreement would not, of course, have prejudged in any way the outcome of the negotiations about the future. As the House knows, that is a sticking point for us. Pending the outcome of the negotiations, the two sides would simply have acknowledged the difference that exists between them over the status of the islands.

We have worked, and will continue to work, positively and constructively for a peaceful solution. Our agreement to these ideas makes this once again abundantly clear.

I wish I could say that the Argentine junta had been working in a similar spirit; clearly it was not. The Argentines have so far insisted that a transfer of sovereignty to them should be a precondition of negotiations on a final settlement. The Argentines talk much of the need for decolonisation of the islands. What they appear to mean by this is colonisation by themselves.

In addition to this, the Argentines seem now to be obstructing progress in another but equally fundamental way. They appear to be asking for a ceasefire without any clear link with a withdrawal of their invasion force. To grant this would be to leave them indefinitely in control of people and territory which they had illegally seized, and to deny ourselves the right of pursuing our own self-defence under article 51 of the charter.

We have not allowed Argentine military activities to halt the measures which our task force is taking. We will not allow their diplomatic obstructionism to do so either. Nor will they be allowed to halt our vigorous endeavours to find a peaceful way out of the conflict into which they have led us. This is why I welcomed and co-operated wholeheartedly with the initiatives of Mr. Haig, and why I now welcome the efforts of the Secretary-General of the United Nations and am working closely with him.

As the House knows, the Secretary-General has put to both us and Argentina some ideas as a framework around which progress might be made. The Argentine Goverment claim to have accepted these ideas. We are bound to be sceptical of this claim. There is no indication that Argentina has accepted either that she must withdraw, as resolution 502 demands, or that negotiations cannot, as Argentina insists, be made conditional on the transfer of sovereignty to her. Indeed, it is difficult to believe that Argentina, having rejected ideas devised by Mr. Haig and the President of Peru, can now accept the Secretary-General's ideas, which have such a similar basis.

For our part, we have accepted the general approach set out by the Secretary-General. I sent him yesterday a positive and substantive reply, making clear that the elements for a solution put forward by him were close to those which had been the basis of our efforts since the beginning of the crisis.

I made clear at the same time that in our view resolution 502 must be implemented without delay; that an unconditional ceasefire could not under any circumstances be regarded by us as a step towards this; and that implementation of a ceasefire must be unambiguously linked to the commencement of Argentine withdrawal which must be completed within a fixed number of days. I then went on to give details, which it would not be right to reveal to the House now, of what we would be prepared to accept to fill out the framework suggested by him.

If one phase of diplomatic effort has been brought to an end by Argentine intransigence, another phase is already under way in New York. The aim remains the same: to secure the early implementation of resolution 502. We are working urgently and constructively with the Secretary-General to this end. I hope the Argentines will henceforth show that readiness and desire to reach a peaceful settlement which so far has been evident only on our side. If they do not, then let them be in no doubt that we shall do whatever may be necessary to end their unlawful occupation. Our resolve is undiminished.

It remains the Government's highest priority to achieve an early negotiated settlement if that is humanly possible.

Mr. Denis Healey (Leeds, East): I think that all of us in the House deeply regret the breakdown of the initiatives taken by Mr. Haig and President Belaunde. I think that the whole House will also share the Foreign Secretary's concern that it is only the intransigence of the Argentine Government which has prevented a ceasefire from taking place today.

I welcome very much what the right hon. Gentleman said about using the United Nations now as the channel for negotiation. . . .

First, in the light of the Argentine Government's refusal to implement resolution 502, will he seek broader support among the United Nations for economic sanctions against the Argentine? In particular, will he ask the United States Administration to go somewhat further than they went in their announcement last week?

Secondly, will the right hon. Gentleman seek to involve the United Nations not only as an intermediary in contacts between the British and Argentine Governments but as an active participant in an ultimate settlement? In particular, now that the Argentines have rejected the American-Peruvian proposals for multinational interim administration, will he seek to persuade the United Nations to provide a transitional administration after the withdrawal of Argentine troops? Will he also explore the possibilities of a United Nations trusteeship over the islands as a long-term solution, as we suggested a fortnight ago?

Finally, will the right hon. Gentleman assure the House that Her Majesty's Government will respect the advice given by the Secretary-General of the United Nations last week that neither side should seek to broaden the conflict? In particular, will he reject firmly and absolutely pressure from his hon. or right hon. Friends to bomb the airfields on the mainland? This would be a far more difficult and hazardous enterprise than even a mass direct assault on the island of the East Falklands. It would be likely to involve loss of civilian life. It would dismay our friends. It could bring other countries in Latin America into active military support of the Argentine Government.

Mr. Pym: . . . We want the broadest possible support from as many countries as possible for further economic measures. I discussed this matter with Mr. Haig last weekend. The United States has not closed its mind to the possibility of taking further economic measures. Our strategy from the outset has been to build the pressures of the three varieties that we have often spoken about. We have undoubtedly increased pressure in all three areas throughout the period, and that still applies today. We want that to continue into the future with the support of our friends in Europe and the Commonwealth which they have so far shown. If others come along too, that can only be helpful in the overall strategy.

Whether or not the Secretary-General and the United Nations become involved in the transitional administration remains to be seen. At the moment the Secretary-General is waiting to hear what kind of response he gets from Argentina. That is by no means certain. As to the longer term, I certainly would not rule out, and I did not do so in the House the other day, the possibility of trusteeship. Indeed, the British Government's long-term position has been not to rule out anything, but always without prejudice to what those living on the islands prefer.

I assure the right hon. Gentleman that the Government have no desire whatever to escalate military action, let alone to broaden the field of military activity. Clearly, our concern is to confine it. At this point, one cannot rule out any option. That must not be taken by the House to mean anything specific. What we are doing is to ensure that our task force has orders appropriate to the circumstances in which it is engaged in the South Atlantic while, at the same time, we put our maximum weight, effort and emphasis on the attempts that we are making to achieve a negotiated settlement.

Mr. Norman St. John-Stevas (Chelmsford): Is my right hon. Friend aware that, despite Argentine obstructiveness and culpability, if he continues resolutely and intrepidly to pursue a peaceful solution, he will have the support of the House? However, will he bear in mind in the negotiations that the one thing that is paramount in this situation is the safety and security of our British task force?

Mr. Pym: . . . The safety and security of our task force are uppermost in our minds. . . .

Dr. David Owen (Plymouth, Devonport): Is the Foreign Secretary aware that we support his firm stand in insisting that there must be a clear link between any ceasefire and a withdrawal of the Argentine forces? It would be incompatible with resolution 502 were any other proposition to be put to the Security Council, and I hope and believe that it never would be done. . . . Does the right hon. Gentleman accept that it would certainly serve to give the lie to those who claim that we are a colonial power or that we have any wish to do anything other than to resist aggression and to protect the interests of the Falkland Islanders if the British Government stated clearly that they would accept the voluntary placement of the Falkland Islands as a strategic trust area with British administration and protect it for our strategic interests with our veto power in the Security Council?

Mr. Pym: I am grateful for what the right hon. Gentleman has said about the linkage between the ceasefire and withdrawal. That has always seemed to us to be critically important. . . .

I am not in the business of ruling out anything even in the short term in relation to possible interim arrangements. . . .

Mr. Julian Amery (Brighton, Pavilion): I fully support my right hon. Friend . . . but will he give an assurance that in no way shall we hold back the military commanders from achieving our objectives by military means if necessary?

Mr. Pym: I can give my right hon. Friend that assurance. . . . The task force is securing the total exclusion zone. . . . There is a range of military options in the future upon which we could well have to take a decision, or a series of decisions, if these efforts fail and circumstances alter. . . .

Mr. Tony Benn (Bristol, South-East): Will the Foreign Secretary clarify Government policy in some important areas? First, does he rule out any United Nations appeal for a ceasefire that falls short of total agreement to the withdrawal of all Argentine forces? Secondly, does he reject General Haig's proposal published a week ago that the Argentines should be involved in the administration of the islands meanwhile? Thirdly, does he still insist upon British sovereignty subject to the islanders' veto? Fourthly, has he had assurances from President Reagan that American support would continue if British forces were used to bomb the airfields on the Argentine mainland?

Mr. Pym: The first point is ruled out. The connection and linkage between ceasefire and withdrawal is included within resolution 502. It is vital that they go together. . . . More than one series of proposals have been put by the United States and latterly by the United States and Peru to the Argentines. These have been rejected by the Argentines and any further consideration of them does not therefore arise. . . .

One can imagine that interim arrangements that put Argentina in a dominant position would be totally unacceptable, but I have kept our options open. . . .

Our position is that this is British sovereign territory. We are totally clear about that. We acknowledge, however, that the Argentines feel that they have a claim to it. We believe that that claim is invalid but acknowledge that they have that claim. Let that be negotiated about in a peaceful way. That is perhaps the crunch point.

The right hon. Gentleman's last point has not arisen at the moment. I can only say that President Reagan and the United States Administration have, as the right hon. Gentleman knows, come down firmly on the British side. They are giving us all the support they can but are not intending to become militarily involved. Mr. Haig announced the basis upon which the United States was supporting us. We are grateful for that. We respect the basis on which the United States supports us.

Sir Anthony Kershaw (Stroud): Does my right hon. Friend agree that the course of the negotiations so far with Peru and Mr. Haig seems to indicate that Argentina backs off as soon as proposals become more specific? . . .

Mr. Pym: . . . What is to be put to the test now is the response of the Argentines to the Secretary-General. We want to see what it is. They have given the impression by statements, many of which, if not most of which, as the House knows, have been very misleading, that they have accepted it. I have already remarked that we are sceptical about that. We want to find out—no doubt we shall find out in the next few days—what has been their response. We shall then see whether or not we are in business.

Mr. David Alton (Liverpool, Edge Hill): Is the right hon. Gentleman aware that the Liberal Party continues to support the Government's initiatives to try to secure a solution and that we join others in the House in lamenting the fact that the Peruvian initiative has failed? Will the right hon. Gentleman give an assurance that members of the task force, who are clearly in some danger, will be left in no doubt that the additional Harriers that are on their way to the South Atlantic in the "Atlantic Conveyor" container vessel will soon be there to give the necessary air cover to ensure the air exclusion zone? . . .

Mr. Pym: . . . I think that I can give him the assurances for which he asks. I can also tell him that the morale of the task force is very high indeed. It is setting about its work with the professionalism that we have come to expect from all our Services. It is, of course, aware of what is going on and what reinforcements are coming up behind. . . .

Mr. Patrick Cormack (Staffordshire, South-West): . . . The Government fully deserve complete support for any measures that they and our task force commanders consider sensible and feasible. Will he please use whatever channels he can to impress on the Argentines that if we have to repossess the islands by force, it will become extremely difficult to contemplate the sort of package that was on offer yesterday?

Mr. Pym: . . . If all endeavours to reach a sensible, reasonable and fair settlement by peaceful means fail, nobody is in doubt about what we shall do. We cannot allow the occupation of the islands to continue.

Mr. Reginald Freeson (Brent, East): Is it not clear that the recent escalation of military activity has contributed nothing to diplomatic success and that while negotiations continue our paramount concern should be to avoid the loss of more lives, from whatever source? . . .

Mr. Pym: I regret to say that I completely disagree with the right hon. Gentleman. I have not the slightest iota of doubt that the sustained build up of military pressure has had, and is having, its effect. Our securing and protecting of the total exclusion zone is an indispensable element in any possibility of achieving a peaceful result.

Mr. Raymond Whitney (Wycombe): . . . Will my right hon. Friend make sure that every means available to the Government is employed to bring home to world opinion, in its understandable anxiety about a potential increase in armed conflict, that it should not overlook the fact that the Argentine aggressors have continued over the past five weeks blatantly to disregard resolution 502, have sabotaged the heroic efforts of Mr. Haig through his peace proposals, and have now sabotaged the proposals of their Latin American ally, President Belaunde of Peru?

Mr. Pym. . . . It has not been possible hitherto to give anything but the most elementary outline of what might be the elements of a settlement to bring about a withdrawal, and we have, in a sense, been handicapped, compared with the propaganda effort of the Argentines. Although much of it has been misleading, they have been able to say whatever they like and some countries and people are apt to believe what they say. . . . I think that it is clear after what I have said in the House that we have gone as far as we reasonably could to try to get a settlement. Proposals of more or less the same type, though they were different, have twice been rejected by the Argentines and we shall have to see what response they give to the Secretary-General. . . .

Mr. Michael English (Nottingham, West): What steps have been taken, possibly with North or South American assistance, to overcome the jamming of the BBC service to Argentina?

Secondly, do the right hon. Gentleman's options include the possibility of using article 96 of the United Nations charter? . . .

Mr. Pym: We are doing what we can with overseas broadcasts. There are many other channels in the Southern American hemisphere and we are using every channel that we can and doing everything we can to get our message through by those means.

On the hon. Gentleman's second point, we have not ruled out that option. My right hon. Friend the Prime Minister made that clear in our debate just over a week ago.

Mr. Nicholas Winterton (Macclesfield): . . . Is not my right hon. Friend aware that the Argentine junta will never agree to a settlement in accordance with the United Nations Security Council resolution 502 and that the longer our forces are in the South Atlantic, the greater will be the danger to them? Is it not time that we answered with what has to be done, which is to take the Falkland Islands back by force?

Mr. Pym: It remains to be seen whether the Argentines will fulfil resolution 502. I think that not only the exertion of the various measures that we have taken but the influence of public opinion in countries all round the world can have an important influence on the Argentines at the present time. It remains to be seen whether they fulfil the resolution. . . .

Report Twenty

10 MAY 1982

Monday 10 May saw a Minister new to the debate answering questions—Mr. Peter Rees.

Mr. Canavan asked the Minister for Trade whether he will make a statement about the efficacy of the operation of trade sanctions against Argentina.

The Minister of State for trade (Mr. Peter Rees): While the efficacy of sanctions can never be precisely measured, it is already clear that the measures adopted by the European Community and others have put considerable pressure on the Argentine economy and undermined international confidence in it.

Mr. Canavan: Will the Minister order an inquiry into how . . . merchant bankers . . . secretly transferred their entire Argentine loan book from London to Zurich on the day before the Argentine invasion of the Falkland Islands? In view of the fact that a complete economic boycott would be far more effective than military action, why are the Government not bringing pressure to bear on unpatriotic, greedy, British bankers who are using their overseas subsidiaries to prop up the Argentine junta, or do the Tory Government prefer to send young men to their deaths than to offend their friends in the City?

Mr. Rees: The hon. Gentleman speaks from a position of invincible prejudice. Even assuming that the facts outlined by him relating to a well-known City merchant bank are true, they obviously occurred before any measures were introduced by the Government.

The Argentine Government have complained, within the terms of the GATT, about the effectiveness of the measures and the damage that they are likely to do to the Argentine economy in the long run. That suggests that the measures have been well designed and are achieving their objective.

Mr. Eggar: Has my hon. and learned Friend any assessment of the value of trade that has taken place between the Soviet Union and Argentina since the commencement of hostilities?

Mr. Rees: No. We would welcome any information that my hon. Friend can give on that matter.

Report Twenty-one

11 MAY 1982

Tuesday 11 May, and the Prime Minister returned to the Dispatch Box to answer questions.

Mr. Neubert: Is my right hon. Friend aware of the growing belief that the Argentine Government are deliberately, to their own advantage, trying to spin out the negotiations over the Falkland Islands that are at present being conducted through the Secretary-General of the United Nations? . . .

The Prime Minister: The negotiations will take a little time. I must make it clear that the fact that we are negotiating does not close any military options at all. The Secretary-General is pursuing the negotiations vigorously. . . .

There are certain fundamental principles that we cannot fudge in any way. The ceasefire must be accompanied by a withdrawal to a specific timetable and in a comparatively short time. We must make it absolutely clear that the Argentines must not enter into those negotiations in the belief, or on the condition, that by the end of them sovereignty is ceded to them.

Mr. Foot: Since these discussions under the auspices of the Secretary-General are obviously of the very greatest importance, and since the outcome may be of the very greatest importance in the dispute, will the right hon. Lady give a clear undertaking that the House of Commons will have the chance to judge those propositions before the Government take any final decision?

The Prime Minister: We frequently have debates on the Falkland Islands issue, but the Government must be free and, I believe, are inherently free, to make the best judgment that they can in the situation and, finally, to be accountable to the House of Commons for that judgment.

Mr. Foot: Of course the right hon. Lady's Government is responsible to the House for what they do. We are asking for something different. These are important discussions. As the right hon. Lady indicated in her reply a moment ago, important principles are involved. The Government have made some very wise departures from previous utterances on many of these matters, but the House of Commons has the right to make a judgment on this matter before any decision is taken by the Government that would enlarge the conflict. I ask the right hon. Lady and her

Government, who have been very leniently treated by the House on this matter, for that assurance. . . .

The Prime Minister: We have to take our decisions on those discussions. I agree that they are very important, but it is an inherent jurisdiction of Government to negotiate and to reach decisions. Afterwards the House of Commons can pass judgment on the Government.

Mr. Foot: I ask the right hon. Lady to consider this matter afresh. It could be that a decision on these matters made by the Government could utterly frustrate and destroy their outcome altogether. Therefore, I again ask the right hon. Lady to give the House of Commons the chance to make a judgment before the Government themselves make the final judgment.

The Prime Minister: No, Sir. The Government have this responsibility, will shoulder that responsibility and will stand before this House and defend their decision. . . .

Mr. Marlow: . . . Unlike the Commonwealth and the United States, our Community partners, despite their public utterances, seem to have been flapping around like decapitated chickens. Does my right hon. Friend agree that, unless we have their robust, continuing and wholehearted support, it will go ill with the Community within this country and we might be forced to move against the Community, which neither she nor I would wish to do?

The Prime Minister: . . .The European Community has give us staunch support from the beginning of the Falklands campaign. It gave us staunch support by imposing an important ban. It extended it. There are no military exports from the European Community to the Argentine. There are no new export credits, and at present an important ban is in force. The Community will make a decision by the end of this week on whether it should extend that import ban and I hope and believe that it will.

Mr. J. Enoch Powell: . . . Will she bear in mind that at no time has this House been informed, or been invited to accept, that there should be any other sequel to the repossession of the Falkland Islands than the immediate and unconditional restoration of sole British administration?

The Prime Minister: . . . Sovereignty cannot be changed by invasion. I am very much aware that the rights of the Falkland Islanders were to be governed through the means of a legislative and executive council, and that is what democracy is all about.

Mrs. Sally Oppenheim: If my right hon. Friend has time today, will she watch a recording of last night's "Panorama" programme? Is she aware that for the most part, but not all, it was an odious, subversive, travesty in which Michael Cockerell and other BBC reporters dishonoured the right to freedom of speech in this country? Is it not time that such people accepted the fact that if they have these rights, they also have responsibilities?

The Prime Minister: I share the deep concern that has been expressed on many sides, particularly about the content of yesterday evening's

231

"Panorama" programme. I know how strongly many people feel that the case for our country is not being put with sufficient vigour on certain—I do not say all—BBC programmes. The chairman of the BBC has assured us, and has said in vigorous terms, that the BBC is not neutral on this point, and I hope that his words will be heeded by the many who have responsibilities for standing up for our task force, our boys, our people and the cause of democracy.

Mr. Winnick: Does not the Prime Minister agree that one of the virtues of a political democracy is that radio and television should be independent from constant Government control and interference? Would it not be useful if some of her right hon. and hon. Friends stopped their constant intimidation of the BBC? Perhaps the Prime Minister would take that hint as well.

The Prime Minister: It is our great pride that the British media are free. We ask them, when the lives of some of our people may be at stake through information or through discussions that can be of use to the enemy . . . to take that into account on their programmes. It is our pride that we have no censorship. That is the essence of a free country. But we expect the case for freedom to be put by those who are responsible for doing so. . . .

Mr. Body: During the day, will my right hon. Friend indicate the extent to which the Government appreciate the way in which Australia and New Zealand have imposed trade sanctions on Argentina and the manner in which those sanctions were imposed, totally, speedily and unconditionally?

The Prime Minister: Gladly. The Governments of Australia and New Zealand have been absolutely magnificent from the day when the Falkland Islands were invaded. From the very outset they have recognised that pressure must be brought to bear and that the Falkland Islanders wish to have the right to live in their own way under a Government of their own choice.

Mr. Dalyell: Who is there, from Mexico City to Cape Horn, who supports what the task force is doing?

The Prime Minister: If the hon. Gentleman looks even at some of the resolutions . . . of the Organisation of American States, he will see that a number of them condemned the use of force. Some of them may well believe in Argentine sovereignty, but they have totally and utterly condemned the use of force. In any case, I am not circumscribed by the views of those countries but by the interests of our people.

Sir Bernard Braine: . . . Has she been made aware of the rising tide of anger among our constituents at the media treatment and presentation of enemy propaganda and the defeatist views of an unrepresentative minority? Is she aware that an increasing number of people are telling us that this amounts to a sort of treachery?

The Prime Minister: Our people are very robust and the heart of Britain is sound. I hope that individually they will make their views directly known to the BBC, by their letters and telephone calls.

Mr. Ashton: Will the Prime Minister comment on the reports in *The Sunday Times* two days ago that last Thursday Fleet Street was promised an announcement by Mr. Ian McDonald at six o'clock that two Harrier jets had gone down but that it was then delayed until nine o'clock because it was polling day and there would have been an effect on the vote?

The Prime Minister: That reason is totally and utterly untrue. Does it not occur to the hon. Gentleman that there are times when we must try to get the names of those who have been killed and inform their relatives before people hear that these things have happened? In addition, there may well be operational reasons why one does not tell the enemy immediately of every loss.

Mr. Montgomery: Will my right hon. Friend try to study, at some time today, the press reports of the demonstration that took place in London on Sunday and which was graced by the chairman of the Labour Party and by the right hon. Member for Bristol, South-East (Mr. Benn)? Will she especially examine press reports to the effect that certain people at the demonstration were shouting "Victory for Argentina"? Will she not agree that this crisis has thrown up some strange bedfellows when the extreme Left wing of politics in this country is supporting the Fascist junta in Argentina?

The Prime Minister: Whatever the demonstrations that took place, I have no doubt that the vast majority of our people support our task force and our boys in the South Atlantic, who are trying to provide that our people who are under the heel of the Argentine dictator shall have the right to self-determination and democracy.

Mr. Foot: Some of us on the Opposition Benches have been opposed to the Argentine junta a good sight longer than most Conservative Members. I return to the replies that the right hon. Lady gave on the question of the BBC and some of the broadcasts. This is, of course, concerned with the important matter of how freedom of discussion is to be conducted in this country. Some of us are determined to defend it.

Before the right hon. Lady pursues further her strictures of the BBC, where I am sure people are seeking to do their duty in difficult circumstances, will she take some steps to reprove the attitude of some newspapers that support her—the hysterical bloodlust of *The Sun* and the *Daily Mail*, which bring such disgrace on the journalism of this country?

The Prime Minister: Taking the view that the right hon. Gentleman does of the Argentine junta, I hope that he will support the Government in their every act——

Mr. William Hamilton: No.

The Prime Minister:—to free the people of the Falkland Islands from what he called this "foul and brutal aggression" on the very first day. The

233

media are totally free to discuss and publish what they wish. Equally, as the right hon. Gentleman has demonstrated, we are free to say what we think about them.

Mr. Foot: When the right hon. Lady asks that we should support every act of her Government, I am sure that she must understand that this cannot be the case. I am sure that, on reflection, she will not wish to press any such claims. . . . Whatever may be the views on the BBC, the newspapers and the rest, this House of Comons is the place where the most important issues of all should be debated. I ask the right hon. Lady once again to give this House the chance of judging what proposals may come from the discussions with the Secretary-General. She owes that to the House of Commons and to the country.

The Prime Minister: The right hon. Gentleman has asked the same question. I give him the same answer. . . .

And Written Answers:

Mr. Arthur Lewis asked the Prime Minister who were the privy councillors to whom she extended an invitation to join her to discuss matters connected with the Falkland Islands difficulties; whether the leaders of all of the political parties were included; and if she will give reasons for her choice.

The Prime Minister: At their request, I have held meetings on privy councillor terms with the right hon. Members for Roxburgh, Selkirk and Peebles (Mr. Steel) and Plymouth, Devonport (Dr. Owen); the right hon. Member for Down, South (Mr. Powell); and the right hon. Member for Western Isles (Mr. Stewart). The right hon. Gentleman the Leader of the Opposition declined my invitation to join the first of these meetings.

Mr. Foulkes asked the Prime Minister if she will make a statement on the current situation in South Georgia.

The Prime Minister: As I reported to the House on 26 April, British authority was re-established in South Georgia on 25 April. The Argentine troops and civilians captured there have now been taken off the island, as have the British Antarctic survey personnel and the two wildlife photographers. A British presence remains on the islands.

Report Twenty-two

13 MAY 1982

On Thursday 13 May there were more questions to the Prime Minister, followed by debate number five, opened by Mr. Pym.

Mr. Gorst: Will my right hon. Friend give a categoric assurance that the objectives with which the task force left for the South Atlantic are exactly the same today as when it left?

The Prime Minister: Yes, Sir. I have seen various reports in the press. May I make it perfectly clear that we are working for a peaceful solution, not a peaceful sellout?

Sir John Eden: . . . Will my right hon. Friend take this opportunity to reassert that, for the British Government, there are two absolute sticking points? The first is that there must be cast-iron assurances that the Argentines will withdraw all their military and civil personnel, pending which the task force will remain on station. The second is that the aggressor shall not benefit from his aggression, so that there can be no commitment expressed or implied, either now or for the future, regarding Argentine's claims to sovereignty over British territory.

The Prime Minister: . . . All Argentine military and civil personnel must be withdrawn from the Falkland Islands on a special time schedule, and that must be verified. Under the arrangements that have continually been discussed—the proposals changed a little—our task force would not be withdrawn until the Argentines had withdrawn. . . . We must insist absolutely that the Argentines do not enter into any settlement at the outset on the understanding that they have sovereignty at the end. We must have an undertaking from them that sovereignty is not committed, but is negotiable.

Mr. Foot: . . . I put to the right hon. Lady that in view of the importance of the matter—I am sure that she will confirm to some of her right hon. and hon. Friends that the Government said that they were prepared to accept the Peruvian terms—she will surely be ready to agree to the proposal that I made earlier this week, that if there is a settlement, and we all hope that there will be, the terms will have to be put to the House. That is obviously right.

However, if there is a non-settlement—if no agreement is reached in the next few days—will not the right hon. Lady undertake to look afresh at the proposition that the House should have the chance of examining the position . . . before there is any further escalation of the military conflict?

The Prime Minister: . . . The terms proposed by this country through Mr. Haig have not been fully published. The right hon. Gentleman should not take those that have been published in Lima as necessarily an accurate account of those that were put forward by this country through Mr. Haig. A description of our terms was given by the Foreign Secretary in the House last week. That description is, of course, the accurate one. . . .

We do work for a peaceful settlement, but the right hon. Gentleman must accept that it may not be possible, for reasons already stated by my hon. Friends, for us to come to a settlement that is acceptable to us and to the Argentines. We shall try to do so, but, as hon. Members say, there are certain things that we cannot and must not forgo. That must be well understood.

If there is a settlement, the Government would come afterwards to report to the House and would be answerable for the settlement that they had agreed. Equally, if there is not a settlement, the power of action resides in the Government. I make it clear that no military option or action has been stopped by virtue of the negotiations up to date.

Mr. Flannery: They should be.

The Prime Minister: No, they should not be—never. That would be too easy a ploy on the part of the Argentines. If there is not a settlement, the Government inherently have the power to act, and we are answerable to the House for our actions.

Mr. Foot: I understand about answerability to the House, but the Secretary of State for Defence made a statement on Sunday in which he elaborated on another option open to the Government—a continued blockade which, he said, was perfectly possible. I say that the House as a whole should have the chance of passing judgment on that position. We want the House as a whole to dictate the situation, not 60 or 70 of the right hon. Lady's backwoodsmen off the leash.

The Prime Minister: We really cannot have a full debate on military options with the House making a decision. Nothing would be more helpful to the enemy or more damaging to our boys.

Mr. Arthur Davidson: . . . The Prime Minister was at pains to point out on the BBC that we are a democracy. If she really believes that, will she call off the dangerous vendetta against the BBC, because one of the tenets of democracy, law and liberty is the right of people to express their views publicly, even if they happen to disagree with those in authority?

The Prime Minister: The BBC does not lack freedom of expression, I do not lack freedom of expression, the House does not lack freedom of expression and the people do not lack freedom of expression. I believe in all four. . . .

Mr. Adley: . . . Will my right hon. Friend accept that most people in the country, and most of her right hon. and hon. Friends, expect the Government to behave like a Government and not as though they are running a debating

236

society? We expect them to make decisions and to come before the House and defend any decisions that they take.

The Prime Minister: My hon. Friend is right. The Government have an inherent power to act and they must use that power and report to the House.

Mr. George Cunningham: In view of the requests made to us by the Governments of Sweden and France about one of the prisoners taken by us on South Georgia, does the Prime Minister understand that the time is overdue for a formal statement to be made by the British Government about their view of the applicability of the laws of war to the present conflict? I regret to say that it looks, on the face of it, as if both parties have breached at least one of the conditions in the laws of war that we have signed.

The Prime Minister: I think that the hon. Gentleman was referring to Commander Astiz, who was the commander of the Argentine garrison in Grytviken. Since we retook South Georgia, both the French and Swedish Governments have requested an opportunity to question him in relation to crimes against nationals of those countries that allegedly took place in Argentina. For the moment, Commander Astiz has been held on Ascension Island. We shall, of course, comply with the Geneva convention.

Mr. Skinner: He is one of your pals.

Sir Victor Goodhew: Will my right hon. Friend remind the Leader of the Opposition, and those who think as he does, of the 30 million lives that were lost in the last world war in Europe alone because the democracies refused to accept, recognise and resist the aggressive intentions of one dictatorship? . . .

The Prime Minister: I accept that the effects of Argentine aggression would go far beyond the effect on the Falklands if it were allowed to continue without us stopping it, reversing it and ensuring that the Argentine forces withdraw from the islands. That is generally realised throughout the House.

Mr. Hooley: Is it the Government's objective to return to the status quo in the Falklands Islands?

Mr. Nicholas Winterton: I hope so.

The Prime Minister: Our objective would be to allow the people of the Falkland Islands their own wishes, to live their own way of life under the Government of their choice.

Mr. Skinner: Paramountcy?

The Prime Minister: That is known as self-determination and it is in the United Nations charter.

Later:

Mr. Eric Ogden (Liverpool, West Derby): . . . After her robust defence of the situation, did the Prime Minister say that sovereignty is negotiable? Will she take the opportunity to correct it now?

The Prime Minister: I heard a murmur and I thought that perhaps one or two people had misunderstood. . . . May I make it clear? The hon. Gentleman will know that the Argentines have been saying that sovereignty must be transferred to them as a precondition of negotiations or at the end of negotiations. We cannot accept that in any way. . . .

The Secretary of State for Foreign and Commonwealth Affairs (Mr. Francis Pym): . . . The Government's position has remained clear and consistent throughout. Our objectives and our stategy are unchanging. We have of course adapted our tactics in the light of the evolving diplomatic and military circumstances. As the House knows, we have moved through different stages of negotiations: the first with Mr. Haig in London and in Washington; then in reacting to the ideas first launched by the President of Peru and subsequently developed in discussion by him with the United States; and now the talks with the Secretary-General of the United Nations. Through all those stages and throughout this procedure we have shown a careful balance of firmness on the essential principles, tempered by the necessary measure of readiness to negotiate on issues where negotiation is possible. However, in all this negotiation our determination has never wavered—our determination and resolve to end Argentina's illegal occupation and to uphold the rights of the Falkland Islanders. . . .

From the beginning of this crisis, the Government have been trying, as the House well knows, to build up the pressures on Argentina steadily, progressively and remorselessly. Our aim has been to make it withdraw, through a negotiated arrangement if that can be achieved. The pressures we have applied have been of three kinds—diplomatic, economic and military.

The diplomatic pressures bring to bear the moral weight of world opinion upon Argentina and its act of aggression. Just as Security Council resolution 502 was clear and firm in its condemnation of aggression and its demands for Argentine withdrawal, so have the statements of our friends and allies in the ensuing weeks continued to demonstrate the world's expectation that Argentina will end its occupation of the islands.

Last weekend I had full talks in private with the Foreign Ministers of the Ten. I was once again heartened by the expressions of solidarity and support I received. Europe remains on our side. Further evidence of that was provided by the European Parliament yesterday. It passed a resolution recognising that the loss of life in the South Atlantic—which we all regret—is due to the failure of the Argentines to comply with resolution 502. It also reaffirmed its previous tough resolution in our support and called on the Foreign Ministers to renew the import embargo on 17 May.

We have found no inclination among the leaders of the free world to blur the distinction between legitimacy and illegality, between self-defence and aggression, between right and wrong, and between truth and falsehood. The world knows that the international rule of law would be dangerously undermined if Argentine aggression were allowed to stand, and that it is on that international rule of law and its upholding that the prospects for stability and prosperity for people depend.

International support for us remains firm. We continue to receive messages of support from Governments all around the world. The Commonwealth remains steadfast and resolute in its backing of our stand. . . .

The diplomatic pressure remains strong and sustained. So also does the economic pressure. That too has been maintained and increased. . . .

The economic measures taken by many of Britain's closest friends are a further demonstration of the international support that we enjoy. I think here in particular of our partners in the Community, and of those who have done likewise—Australia, New Zealand, Canada and Norway, to name but a few. . . .

The suspension of imports, the denial of credit, the bans on arms sales—all those continue to have a real and biting effect on an Argentine economy already in disarray.

It was estimated earlier this year that Argentina would need to raise some $3 billion in net new loans in 1982. World repugnance at its recent actions has meant that—so far as we can tell—not a single new public sector loan has been agreed since 2 April.

The Argentine peso has been under heavy pressure. Besides expectations of increased inflation and general loss of confidence, the markets of the world have indicated clearly what they think of the Argentine currency: while the official rate remains at 14,000 pesos to the American dollar, even across the River Plate in Montevideo the free market is demanding 20,000 pesos for the dollar.

Those who have given us economic support should not doubt that the consequence of this support has been extremely valuable in concentrating pressure on Argentina to comply with resolution 502. It is, in fact, an essential part of the pressure that we are applying in order to achieve an early negotiated solution.

The third element of our strategy is military. As the House knows, we continue to tighten the military screw. British Service men are experiencing danger and hardship 8,000 miles away. Their presence and their activity are making it increasingly hard and costly for Argentina to sustain its occupation of the Falkland Islands.

We all grieve over British losses. We take no satisfaction at the losses inflicted on Argentina. We regret them, too. As the net closes round the islands, military incidents may occur with increasing frequency. That may be inevitable in the circumstances. But we must never forget who is the aggressor, who invaded whom, who embarked on an unlawful and dangerous course, who first took up arms and thus put lives at risk, who fired the first shot. Argentina knows how to avoid further military conflict. It can begin its withdrawal—now.

The whole House and the country know our clear and decided preference for a negotiated settlement. However, military pressure is necessary to bring Argentina to negotiate seriously and at the same time to strengthen our negotiating hand. I do not doubt that it is having this effect. There are signs that the message is beginning to get through.

We have been and remain indefatigable in the search for that negotiated settlement. I shall not recall now the long and strenuous efforts that we made in co-operation with Mr. Haig, ending in failure because of Argentina's intransigence.

But it is interesting that, in spite of Argentina's rejection then, the elements of an agreement about which I first spoke to the House as long ago as 21 April have remained as elements in subsequent negotiations. . . .

Mr. Alexander W. Lyon (York): During question time the Prime Minister indicated that sovereignty is now negotiable. I thought that we had gone to war to secure our sovereignty. Does that mean that a lot of good men have died in vain?

Mr. Pym: I am sure that my right hon. Friend did not say that. I shall come to that point in a moment.

Mr. Julian Amery (Brighton, Pavilion): The Argentine Government turned down the Peruvian proposals that we had apparently accepted. Will my right hon. Friend make it clear that we are no longer committed to that acceptance?

Mr. Pym: Certainly I can give that assurance. Like the previous proposals that were turned down, they were turned down and that is the end of them. I think that is the assurance that my right hon. Friend asks for.

The negotiations are now going on under the auspices of the Secretary-General of the United Nations. Senor Perez de Cuellar has shown great determination and diplomatic ability in his lengthy and frequent talks in recent days with the British representative, Sir Anthony Parsons. . . .

I hope that more progress will be made—and quickly. If it is not, it will not be for lack of effort and readiness on our part to reach a negotiated solution. Nor have our efforts to this end in any way prejudiced or hindered the necessary build up of military pressure. I want to assure the House that they have not closed off any military option, or affected our military options in any way.

It is not, of course, easy to negotiate with the Argentine authorities. While their representative in New York has appeared to be prepared to recognise many of the realities of the situation, there have been—even within the last two days—a number of unhelpful statements by other Argentine public figures, made in public.

On different occasions the Foreign Minister, one of his senior officials, a general and a junior Minister in another department have all referred to the process of negotiation as if this was designed solely to lead up to a handover of sovereignty to Argentina. That attitude is, I repeat, quite unacceptable to us and we must be absolutely sure that Argentina does not adhere to it, privately or publicly, if a negotiated settlement is to be possible. . . .

The first absolutely fundamental requirement is the need for the withdrawal of the whole Argentine invasion force and civil personnel. We insist on this and until Argentina is committed to such a withdrawal, and is willing to commence it, we cannot commit ourselves to a ceasefire. When it demonstrates that that readiness to withdraw is a reality, we shall feel able and willing to match this—in ways yet to be determined—by standing our own forces off from the area of conflict. . . .

The second fundamental requirement, on which we are absolutely firm, is that the outcome of long-term negotiations about the future of the islands must not be prejudged in advance in any way. . . .

That is a reasonable position and one on which we shall not compromise. It has been a fundamental issue throughout all the negotiations and a major problem in the negotiations. From the outset we have made our position entirely and unmistakeably clear. Nevertheless, even at this point in time it is necessary for me to repeat it, because it is our immutable objective.

Mr. Alan Clark: There is a slight discrepancy between what my right hon. Friend said and an answer given by my right hon. Friend the Prime Minister during Question Time a few moments ago. I understood, and I believe the House understood, that she asserted that withdrawal of our task force would not commence until the Argentine withdrawal was itself completed.

Mr. Pym: My right hon. Friend the Prime Minister may have said that, although I did not hear it, I am informing the House that the precise arrangements on each side remain to be settled. It is a difficult and important area, but it is not settled at present and therefore it is an issue in the present negotiations. . . .

Argentine withdrawal from the Falkland Islands, once agreed, should be carried out within a fixed number of days. Negotiations about the long-term future of the islands will, of necessity, take a matter of months. It follows from this—as I said in this House many days ago, on 21 April, and again in more detail on 7 May—that some interim arrangements will be necessary on the islands. . . . I have already made clear on two previous occasions that we do not debar involvement of third parties in these arrangements. It may or may not be the case that the United Nations will have a role to play. But we could not, of course, agree to a structure, however temporary, which ignored the past and disregarded the administrative experience of the British inhabitants of the islands. They know how to run their affairs in a democratic way. . . .

There are officials and administrators who know their jobs; there are democratically elected members of the councils who know the feelings of their fellow islanders. They must be fitted into whatever is agreed if the islands are to be run fairly and efficiently during whatever interim period proves necessary. . . .

If we get an agreement, long-term negotiations may begin quite soon. I want to make clear to the House that we have no doubt whatever about the British title to sovereignty. All British Governments have taken the same view. However, we did not, before the invasion, rule out discussion of sovereignty in negotiations with Argentina. Again, successive Governments of both parties have taken the same position. We still remain willing to discuss it as one of the factors in negotiations about the long-term future. . . .

The islanders will wish to consider, after a period of respite and recuperation, how their prosperity and the economic development of the islands can best be furthered, how their security can best be protected and how their links with the outside world can best be organised. These questions at present are some way ahead and the Government retain an open mind. . . .

Present negotiations in New York are at an important point. Our resolve has not wavered. There have been some indications—actually the first since the crisis began—of genuine Argentine willingness to negotiate on some of the important points. There will have to be more if we are to succeed.

The Government remain determined to see the implementation of the mandatory resolution of the Security Council. As before, we infinitely prefer to achieve this by negotiation, and we are bending our most strenuous efforts to this end. At the same time our military presence in the South Atlantic continues to become stronger. . . .

If, in the end, Argentine intransigence prevents success in negotiation, Argentina will know that the alternative is another kind of ending to the crisis. We do not want that, but we are ready for it. As it has been throughout this crisis, the choice lies with those who rule Argentina.

Mr. Denis Healey (Leeds, East): This the fifth debate that the House has held since the crisis began. . . . Much has happened since the previous debate. I have in mind the failure of the Haig mission, the failure of the Peruvian initiative, the sinking of the "General Belgrano" and HMS "Sheffield", and something which at least the Opposition welcome—the intervention of the United Nations Secretary-General as an intermediary in the negotiations. . . . I think that today the House will want to concentrate on the United Nations' negotiations, which are now at a critical stage. . . .

The foundation of the negotiations now proceeding in New York is resolution 502 of the Security Council, which links the withdrawal of Argentine forces from the Falklands with a diplomatic settlement. Meanwhile, it leaves the United Kingdom free to use military force in self-defence under article 51 of the charter. I think that it is clear to the House that minimum force is required to be used—it must never be disproportionate to the issue at stake—and the Secretary of State for Defence has rightly added two other criteria, namely, that force should be used under political control, and as a back-up to diplomatic negotiation. Force should never be used in such a way as to jeopardise the negotiations, and still less should it be used as a substitute for negotiations.

The Opposition have supported all military actions taken by the task force so far, although I raised a question on the sinking of the "General Belgrano", which was fully justified if it was necessary to defend our forces, even if it did—and indeed it did—have a damaging effect on one arm of our diplomatic approach to the problem. . . . I hope that he will be able to reassure the House by telling us precisely how urgent a threat to the task force the "General Belgrano" represented, and in particular how far away the task force was from the "General Belgrano", so that we can form a judgment on whether it was necessary to sink it, and to do so 35 miles outside the total exclusion zone.

We shall continue to support the use of the task force within the guidelines laid down by the Secretary of State. I believe, and I think that the House believes, that negotiations would not have proceeded at all, still less reached a stage at which an agreement is at least conceivable, if not in sight, had the task force not been sent on its mission. There would have been no point in sending the task force unless we were prepared in some circumstances to use it. To withdraw the task force now, as some have asked, as part of an unconditional ceasefire would nullify all the efforts of the Secretary-General to get the withdrawal of Argentine troops, as required under mandatory resolution 502, and hand the Falklands to General Galtieri on a platter. It would encourage other Governments to use force to create a fait accompli. . . .

The Government clearly intend to limit hostilities with Argentina in this crisis, and they are right to do so. They have made no declaration of war and they have been 100 per cent. right to reject calls from some of their Back Benchers to extend the fighting to the mainland. So to extend it would broaden the conflict in ways in which the Secretary-General specifically asked us not to do a week ago, and it would certainly lose us the support of the United States.

Mr. Haig is reported in today's *New York Times* as saying that to extend the conflict to the mainland would be

"the worst thing that could happen because what was now simmering resentment in South America of most English speaking countries might well become a volatile anti-American and anti-British movement."

That is a risk that the House must not lose sight of.

It would also risk pushing Argentina into the arms of the Soviet Union. . . .

The present junta is bad enough, but we must recognise that the fall of the present regime is more likely to produce a worse regime than a better one. We could very likely be faced with a Peronist dictatorship which sought active cooperation with the Soviet Union and Cuba. Any successor regime would be dedicated to recover the Falkland Islands by force at the earliest opportunity. . . .

[We] cannot afford to divorce the way in which we conduct ourselves in our conflict over the Falkland Islands with the Argentines from our policy towards Latin America as a whole. Nor can we afford to seek a short-term solution by military force if that excludes the chance of an agreement with Argentina that gives long-term security to those living on the islands. . . .

It is clear that the Peruvian proposals, which we have accepted, and some of the suggestions being made by the Secretary-General have involved the Government in making some important concessions, some of which the Opposition are as reluctant to make as the Government. However, in as far as we understand them, we think that the Government were right to make these concessions.

For some of the changes in Government policy the Opposition have 100 per cent. enthusiasm. These include the readiness to accept the United Nations Secretary-General as an intermediary, the readiness to consider a United Nations administration as the interim regime and the readiness to consider United Nations trusteeship in the longer term, all of which the right hon. Gentleman has said, at different times, he does not rule out.

Much less welcome to us and, I know, to Members on the Conservative Benches, are the agreement to negotiate before the withdrawal of Argentine forces, our readiness to accept the ceasefire before the withdrawal is completed and the qualification in the Government's initial position, which appeared to give the Falkland Islanders an unconditional veto on any ultimate settlement. Nevertheless, the Government were right to make these concessions in the interests of agreement. . . .

If the Argentine Government had made concessions that were remotely comparable, we should have had a ceasefire last Friday. Never let us forget that fact.

I believe that there is still a chance that the Argentines will move on the demands that we consider essential if an agreement is to be reached. I gather that there are some signs that the junta has established its authority over other senior officers in the Argentine—or at least more completely than was the case when Mr. Haig was negotiating in Buenos Aires some weeks ago. . . .

I agree with the Foreign Secretary that there are two fundamental conditions which the Argentine Government must meet if there is to be an agreement. First, there can be no ceasefire without agreement on Argentine withdrawal over a defined and limited period, under proper monitoring. Secondly, the Argentine Government cannot be allowed to set preconditions on the outcome of the negotiations. On that we are agreed. . . .

To insist on an unconditional ceasefire now, at the most crucial moment in the negotiations, would not only destroy all hope of achieving those conditions but would undermine the whole basis of United Nations intervention in the crisis, which is resolution 502. It is possible, I gather, that the Secretary-General will make his own proposals at some time and put them to both Governments. . . . In that case, the Government should reconsider their refusal to allow the House to have a chance to consider these proposals before they make their final response. . . .

On the other hand, if the Argentine Government are responsible for the breakdown of the Secretary-General's initiative or for the rejection of his proposals, the task force will be obliged to continue playing its military role, but, I insist, subject to the conditions that the Defence Secretary has set and directed to the same objective, namely, to create conditions for successful negotiations at a later stage.

I repeat what I have said so often in these debates: to attempt to resolve this problem by force alone can produce no permanent solution. I repeat the words of Mr. Haig, which I have quoted before in the House, that a purely military outcome could not endure over time. Moreover, if we attempted to secure a purely military solution of the conflict, we would lose the support of our European partners, as the right hon. Gentleman must know. We would find it difficult to keep the support of the United States Administration, and we would have no chance whatever of a majority in any organ of the United Nations. . . .

If the Government choose options which lead to a more or less prolonged conflict, it is vital that we seek more support for economic sanctions than we have been promised so far even from our friends in Europe, never mind our American ally. If there is any question of this crisis continuing, the economic measures will have a chance to bite, and it is important that they should be maximised so that they bite as hard and as soon as possible.

Even if the Secretary-General finally decides that he has nothing more to contribute at this stage—I think that the overwhelming majority of us hope that that time will not come—that will not be the end of the role and involvement of the United Nations in the dispute. Far from it. . . .

If the Secretary-General were to give up or suspend his efforts, the Security Council itself would be bound to hold a substantive meeting to decide how to carry matters forward. Any hope of Britain maintaining then the support in the Security council which it achieved on 3 April will depend critically on our observing the limitations on the use of force which are implicit in the right of self-defence under article 51 of the charter. . . .

If the Security Council intervenes direct in the conflict, I fear that

Britain's situation will be a good deal more difficult than it is now. Therefore, Her Majesty's Government and the House have every interest in giving the Secretary-General the time that he considers necessary, so long as he feels that he has a chance of success. . . . So long as he believes that there is a reasonable chance of success, it is overwhelmingly in the Government's and the country's interest that he should be allowed by us the time that he feels necessary, and provided that the Government give him that time they will get unanimous support from this side of the House.

Mr. Edward Heath (Sidcup): . . . I want to give wholehearted support to the Prime Minister, to the Foreign Secretary and to the Government for the strategy which they have followed since the occupation of the Falkland Islands. In particular, I want to say how much I agree with what the Foreign Secretary has said today in his account of the negotiations so far, the negotiating position he has taken up and the considerations of which he believes he ought to take account.

I do not propose to devote time to the military problems or to the Services. The response of the Services in this situation has been everything which one would expect of them. Some perhaps may be tempted to take this for granted. That is understandable because the response has been speedy and efficient. Whatever the Forces may be asked to do, in however difficult circumstances in the future, we know that they will perform those responsibilities in every way to the best of their ability. . . .

[The Foreign Secretary] is absolutely right to pay attention to world opinion and those critics in the press or in the House who are urging him to ignore it and treat it with contempt . . . are completely wrong. If anything, that is particularly important in this case because of the question of sovereignty.

The whole of Latin America as an area believes that Argentina has a justifiable claim to sovereignty over the Falkland Islands. The reason those countries are supporting us is that they are opposed to the use of aggression to enforce that right. We must therefore carry public opinion with us, particularly in the whole of Latin America, on the fact that we are acting against aggression. That is why those countries supported the United Nations resolution. . . .

United Nations resolution 502 consists of three parts. It is well that we should always remember that. The first demands an immediate cessation of hostilities; the second demands an immediate withdrawal of all Argentine forces; and the third calls on the Governments of the Argentine and the United Kingdom to seek a diplomatic solution to their differences. . . .

The Government have an equal responsibility to carry on these diplomatic negotiations to settle what is described as "their differences". A diplomatic solution is requested. . . .

The Foreign Secretary has rightly and constantly emphasised, as has the Prime Minister, that the purpose of the task force is to back up diplomacy. Again, that is something that we must always remember. I believe that it has done so. From such information as is available, I do not believe that the junta expected anyone to take action when it took over the Falkland Islands. Therefore, it has had to give considerable thought to the situation and must continually decide how it will react. . . .

When one is dealing with an opponent—I say this having been involved in many negotiations—it is wise to look over the hill and to see what his position is. We must recognise that it is sometimes prudent and wise—quite apart from being magnanimous, as Churchill said—at any rate to offer some way out if the opponent is sensible enough to take it. . . .

Obviously we cannot accept a situation in which the Argentine insists upon an agreement in which it maintains sovereignty. On the other hand, as sovereignty is in dispute, it must remain an open question. That cannot be doubted. . . .

This dispute has thrown into question the whole of our defence policy and, from the point of view of the islanders, has shown them that a threat of occupation can be carried out successfully. Can one imagine an islander settling down in the Falklands in the future and not asking himself, "Will I at any moment again be invaded?"? From that point of view, the situation can never be the same again.

Therefore, in continuing these negotiations, the Foreign Secretary is right to say that the wishes of those in the Falkland Islands must be given full consideration but not to resume our previous position, which was certainly adopted by the Government of 1970 to 1974, that they could veto any solution that was put forward. I have said that publicly before, but I think that it is right.

The implications for this country of accepting that veto are so great in every respect that I do not believe that the Government are any longer justified in taking up that position. . . .

We have all said that the interests of the Falkland Islanders must be taken into account. There is a variety of ways of dealing with those interests. The point is connected with that of world opinion. Britain has immense interests in Latin America as well as in the Falkland Islands. We should not forget that. The responsibility for safeguarding those interests rests on the Government in their negotiations. There was a time when the world thought that we were rather astute at looking after our interests wherever they were. We must do that. They are widespread.

Sir Bernard Braine: . . . There is no need to speculate what the Falkland Islanders will do. . . . It is clear that they will not live under any form of Argentine rule. If that is known in advance, the pass is already sold according to my right hon. Friend.

Mr. Heath: I often wish that I had the certainty and confidence of my hon. Friend the Member for Essex, South East (Sir B. Braine). I should have thought that that is another matter that has to come out of negotiations. If asked, I do not believe that the Falkland Islanders who remain there would say that they should be the determining factor of the whole of British naval strategy in the South Atlantic.

The Prime Minister is quite right to emphasise that the military forces are under political control. They must remain so. From all I know of the chiefs of staff, that is what they want. They do not want any military control. . . .

Their action was fully justified and is justified by the fact that they have sent the task force to back up diplomacy. If diplomacy is successful, the task force has achieved its purpose with, thank God, less loss of life. . . . I ask the Foreign Secretary not to be moved in any way by the frequent cries of "sell-out". He must justify to the House a complete negotiated position. The House will then be able to give its judgment upon it.

Nor are we taking action because the Argentine Government can be described as Fascist or as one that has a disgraceful record of human rights. I sometimes feel that the attitude of some Opposition Members is motivated or coloured by that. We are dealing with this because there has been aggression against the Falkland Islands. If other types of Government had done that, we would have been in exactly the same position.

Fascism or a disgraceful record on human rights should not be allowed to colour the issue. We did not fight Hitler or Mussolini because they were dictators or because of their internal policies. We fought them because they had reached such a state of power that they were a menace to vital British interests. We must always consider vital British interests. . . .

When one takes account of vital British interests, one must also take account of the long-term position with regard to what will happen afterwards, however the matter is resolved. That will be of vital importance to us. Quite apart from our interests in Latin America, the future of Antarctica may prove to be of immense value to the countries that have established rights there.

I ask the Government to continue strenuously with their efforts to reach a negotiated solution. I ask them to recognise that people who are in the wrong often have to be given some way out to enable them to reach an agreement because they also have to pay a price—a considerable one—on the United Nations resolution. I urge the Foreign Secretary to stand firm against all the criticisms that are now being made in the press of him and the Government, that they are taking time carrying on negotiations. They are trying to take the House of Commons with them—which, on the whole, they are doing successfully—and are trying to carry European, Commonwealth and world opinion with them also. I urge them to continue strenuously in this, to resist and ignore the criticisms and to do their utmost to secure a negotiated settlement. If, finally, that becomes impossible, the House, the country and the Government must face the fact that alternative action will have to be taken.

Mr. David Steel (Roxburgh, Selkirk and Peebles): . . . Continued public discussion and parliamentary debate of the issue is vital. I agree with the Prime Minister . . . that the Government must decide on the negotiations and conduct them. It is not acceptable that the Secretary-General of the United Nations or anyone else has running negotiations with the House. That is impossible.

I dissent from the line that the Front Bench of the official Opposition has taken on the matter. Opposition parties must, of course, be free to criticise, to question and to express their views. . . .

That is why I very much welcomed the Prime Minister's response to the suggestion that there should be talks with the party leaders. I believe that that is desirable. . . .

The Prime Minister's discussions with my right hon. Friend the Member for Plymouth, Devonport (Dr. Owen) and myself have in no way compromised our right to speak in the House and to say what we wish about the Government's policy. If the leaders of the official Opposition availed themselves of the same opportunity, they would find themselves free to ask any questions that they wished on the diplomatic initiatives and on the military situation.

In my view it is not right for the right hon. Member for Leeds, East (Mr.

Healey) to come to the House and ask about the position of ships or the exact stage of negotiations. It would be helpful for the conduct of these debates in the future if the official Opposition availed themselves of the opportunity that the Prime Minister has offered. . . .

The Government's attitude is correct. They are right to maintain their insistence that there can be no substantial negotiations on the issues themselves until there is a verified withdrawal of the Argentine troops. . . .

The Government were right to make adjustments in their original stance. . . . They are right to accept that the interim administration that may follow the withdrawal of the Argentines may be an international rather than a British one. That represents some change in the Government's position, but . . . it is a sensible measure of flexibility.

Secondly, when the Prime Minister says that sovereignty may be negotiable, she is not saying anything new. Attempts to discuss the title of sovereignty, to use the phrase reported to the House in December 1980, have always been part of all Governments' policies. . . .

Thirdly, the Government are right to be talking now in terms of the vital importance of the interests and wishes of the islanders. . . . It was a mistake earlier to refer to their views as being somehow paramount over any other consideration.

The importance of external opinion should not be underrated. European opinion, not only European Governments but the European Parliament, which has twice passed resolutions on this—I am glad to say that this was on the initiative of the Liberal group—is in full support of resolution 502 and in full condemnation of the Argentine position. It is important that European Governments support us, particularly on the economic front. When one considers that 40 per cent. of the Argentine population are of Italian descent, one realises the enormous significance of the support that the Italian Government have given us, as have others. The Government are right to stress the solidarity of European opinion. . . .

I hope that we shall always retain the right, both as Members of Parliament and as members of the public, to criticise programmes put out by the BBC or the IBA. I did not see the "Panorama" programme, but many whose views I respect did not like it. It is quite another matter, however, to conduct a hysterical war against the authority of the BBC and the independence of its reporting and to suggest that it is somehow full of traitors. . . .

When Ministers refer to the islanders as being under the heel of the Fascist junta, it should be remembered that we were happily selling arms to that same Fascist junta not long ago. Moreover, the Exocet missile, which has frequently been referred to as a "fire and forget" weapon, might also be referred to as an "export and forget" weapon. There is a need for at least a European initiative to control and register the sale of arms to third countries. . . .

Finally, the House must not forget that the cost of this exercise for this country is extremely heavy both in lives and in financial terms. When it is all over, we shall have to decide whether we should have the kind of commission that was set up by the House in 1916 after the Dardanelles campaign to examine the origins of this conflict and exactly how it arose. We must never lose sight of the fact that what we have been discussing in these repeated debates is the greatest debacle in our foreign and defence policy for 25 years.

Sir Patrick Wall (Haltemprice): . . . *[A long blockade]* without air superiority can be extremely dangerous, especially when there are two submarines still on the loose.

I should like to ask the Opposition what they would do in the event of the refusal of the junta to accept our minimum conditions. Would they then support a landing in the Falkland Islands. . . . That would give our diplomacy much more strength, because both British and Argentine forces would be in place on the Falkland Islands. Pressure could then be exerted with the minimum of force. . . .

We must not have any misappreciation of intelligence of any movement of Soviet forces in Europe, because any attack that they might decide to launch would be done under cover of a major maritime exercise such as Okean and manoeuvres in East Germany or Poland.

The second lesson is that we in this country have managed to mobilise a fleet and transfer it from peace to war conditions in no more than three days. . . .

The lessons to be learnt are that there is a unity in this nation. Indeed, that has been shown to a large extent in the House this afternoon. Above all, there is a political will on the part of my right hon. Friend the Prime Minister, as has been demonstrated so strongly recently. . . .

Now I shall deal briefly with some of the tactical lessons. . . . The first is that we have now entered the missile age. My right hon. Friend the Secretary of State was right when he said in the House last year that he would give priority to weapon systems. We can be proud of the weapons that this country has managed to produce. . . .

We should remember that the Navy of today has been designed for anti-submarine warfare in the North Atlantic. That is a partnership of maritime patrol aircraft, hunter-killer submarines, small ships with anti-submarine helicopters, and Buccaneers with Sea Eagle operating from shore bases. Suddenly, this fleet is transported to the South Atlantic—8,000 miles away. I do not believe that any fleet in history has had to operate with such long lines of communication, and it has done it extremely well.

The problem facing our forces at the moment is, of course, lack of air superiority. Had "Ark Royal" and "Eagle" been in commission today, the situation in the South Atlantic would be very different from what it is. However, we can take great credit for the development of the Harrier and the fact that it has been proved that this vertical take-off aircraft can deal with supersonic aircraft. . . .

We all hope that we can end this disagreement with Argentina by diplomacy. Many of us believe that that is not possible because the junta cannot accept the minimum conditions that we demand. If it does so, the generals will fall from office and such a dictatorship preserves its own power to the utmost extent. Therefore, . . . force may have to be used. It is no good threatening force if we are not prepared to use it, but I believe that force can be used in the Falkland Islands without the blood bath that the press is so keen to talk about. . . .

The real lesson of the Falkland Islands is that we must not allow aggressors to succeed. . . .

Mr. J. Enoch Powell (Down, South): I agree . . . that the prerogative of war and peace and of treaty-making vested in the Executive is exercised

249

by the Government subject only to retaining the subsequent and continuing confidence of the House. . . .

However, there is a counterpart to the Government's rights, an implication of their constitutional position. It is not just that they continuously maintain contact with the House and, as far as possible, take the House into their confidence; it is also that they do not change the major outlines of policy upon which, with the approval of the House, they have acted, without the change being clearly understood and equally approved by the House. It is because, as I believe, such a change, which the House has not approved and the country has not approved through the House, is taking place— perhaps has taken place already—that today's debate is especially timely.

There is no doubt what were the objects with which the despatch of the task force to the South Atlantic was approved at the beginning of April. They were to repossess the Falkland Islands, to restore British administration of the islands and to ensure that the decisive factor in the future of the islands should be the wishes of the inhabitants. . . .

The fact with which I find myself faced is that the Foreign Secretary on behalf of this country has agreed to a series of propositions which differ radically from the basis upon which this whole operation was undertaken and on which it was supported by the country. . . .

The Foreign Secretary says, correctly of course, that since [the interim agreement] did not come into effect—there was no agreement on the other side—therefore it is void and we are not bound by it. I dare say that technically we are not bound by it, any more than in trade union negotiations an offer made without prejudice is binding if the negotiations do not succeed. But the country and the world have been told through the mouth of the Foreign Secretary that the Government are prepared to accept what six weeks ago was unacceptable, and that the purposes for which our Forces are in the South Atlantic and for which they are exposed to loss of life and loss of vessels have been radically altered.

That is contradiction which is entirely unfair to the country and to the Forces. They have a right to understand for what purpose we are prepared to engage in a war, to use our Forces and to risk the lives of the members of those Forces. We cannot turn round afterwards to those men and their relatives and say, "Oh yes, you thought that it was about what we told you at the beginning of April, but it turns out to have been about something different, the basis of which was not approved either by you or your Parliament."

It is now the duty of the Government to restore that unity of Government without which it is unfair to expect the nation or the Forces to support such an operation as that in which we are engaged. . . .

The supreme duty to maintain the unity of the Government rests upon the Prime Minister. She owes it to the country, to the Forces and to the Falkland Islanders to restore the unity of the Government, to restore the clarity of purpose upon the basis of which the whole operation began and in the name of which alone we in the House are entitled to call upon our Forces and our people for sacrifice.

Dame Judith Hart (Lanark): . . . When the Foreign Secretary was talking of certain immovable conditions in negotiation, he said that one of those was Argentine withdrawal matched by our own ceasefire if there was verification of mutual withdrawal. The Peruvian proposals and the Peruvian proposals that were discussed with Mr. Haig both contained two points followed by three others, which present greater difficulties. . . . The two points in common between the Peruvian proposals and those discussed between Peru and Mr. Haig were, first, a period of truce, described in discussions with Mr. Haig as an immediate cessation of hostilities, and, secondly, the mutual withdrawal of military and naval forces. If the Foreign Secretary is saying that a period of truce with the mutual withdrawal of forces is an acceptable condition, and the remaining items, which I recognise present some problems, are negotiable, it is important that the House should be fully aware of that. . . .

Mr. Pym: I explained last Friday as far as I could the basis upon which the arrangement was made which did not come to fruition last week. I cannot go further than that. As far as I recall, the word "truce" does not come into it.

Dame Judith Hart: I am asking the right hon. Gentleman to clarify further what he said this afternoon. I am relating what he said this afternoon to the Peruvian and the Peruvian–Haig proposals. As I understood it, he said this afternoon that if there was a verification of mutual withdrawal, we would accept a ceasefire.

Mr. Pym: I said that there cannot be a withdrawal without a ceasefire, or the other way round. There must be a method of verification for that process. That has not been established in the current case. Under the previous proposals there was an arrangement for such verification, but in this case that has not yet been negotiated.

Dame Judith Hart: I am a little disappointed. I thought that the Foreign Secretary had taken us a little further this afternoon than he has.

I and many of my right hon. Friends believe in a mutual truce. . . . We believe that there must be negotiations through the United Nations. There must be a peaceful solution, not a war.

I recognise the logic that if one is against a military operation and yet opposed to Argentine aggression against the Falkland Islands one must have another answer. That could be economic sanctions. The argument against that has always been that economic sanctions have never worked. However, we have not tried them often. We tried them with Rhodesia but Rhodesia did not have a foreign exchange problem. Rhodesia had plenty of foreign exchange and it had South Africa to call on if any rescue operation were needed.

As the Foreign Secretary said, Argentina needs $3 billion of new loans this year. The Argentine debt varies according to the newspaper one reads, from $32 billion to $34 billion. It has always been recognised as one of five countries with such an outstanding debt ratio problem that any default in its payments to the banks could bring one of the major international banks tumbling down. The financial element in economic sanctions could be of the greatest importance. . . .

Those of us who believe that there should be no war on this issue have argued from the outset that the task force should not have been sent because, once sent, it would create its own momentum. . . .

I hope that the negotiations will succeed. We were told by Mr. Haig last weekend that he feared a new and terrible wave of fighting, another bloody outbreak of fighting. . . .

Resolution 502 includes a clause about the cessation of hostilities. A good deal of international legal argument would support my view that those three points are not interdependent and that we have as great an obligation to observe the clause about the cessation of hostilities as the Argentines have to withdraw from the Falkland Islands. . . .

There are different views about the principle of sovereignty. The Foreign Secretary implied that negotiations could take place about that. There is also the principle of self-determination and the principle, under the Committee of 24 at the United Nations, of independence. A principle is also involved in any consideration of what should be done if an act of aggression is committed against a piece of territory that historically happens to be British.

There is one other principle. Those of us who have reservations and doubts about the Government's judgments and who believe that there should not be a war and that there must be a peaceful negotiation say that if the world, in an age of high technology warfare, is to have a future, the principle of resolving disputes by negotiation must stand supreme. I hope that the Foreign Secretary will give his full attention to that principle in the course of the next few days.

Mr. Maurice Macmillan (Farnham): . . . The decisions that the Government take in the next few days may well affect our future for a long time. Those decisions may bolster our new-found self-confidence, or destroy it. They will confirm or deny our value as sound and reliable allies and partners in the world. They could well affect . . . the attitude of future Governments to our foreign policy and their freedom to act.

The House and the country have been behind the Government in their willingness to bend over backwards to meet the Argentines in negotiations and in their remarkable firmness of intent. It is only recently that some doubts have arisen about that firmness of intent. Those doubts are partly a result of the long delay. Delay tends to weaken resolution and the longer action is put off, the harder it is to take it.

The Government are right to negotiate. Negotiation means compromise but the extent to which such compromise is justifiable depends, at least in part, on how much movement—to use a trade union term—one can get from the other side and to what extent Argentina is willing to meet our points and does not ask us to make three concessions to every one that she is prepared to consider. . . .

We cannot prevent the Argentine claim to sovereignty or deny that in the past we have been willing to negotiate on it. We have responded to the invasion and use of force by Argentina by saying that force must not succeed. The Government must not now virtually guarantee what amounts to a nearly complete Argentine success. We can perhaps compromise on the second point, that of administration, provided that the islanders are adequately protected and are not faced ultimately with no other choice but either accepting an Argentine administration or getting out. Whatever interim arrangements are made—partly perhaps to satisfy world opinion—they must not imply that Argentina will be the ultimate administrator come what may.

Thirdly, originally, it was the islanders' wishes that were paramount. I believe that gave them too powerful a veto, for it is obvious from a practical point of view that wishes cannot be paramount. The United Nations used the phrase that their interests should be paramount. . . . I do not see how we can abandon the principle of self-determination, at least in its negative sense. It is impossible to say that every community throughout the country or world can choose which country to belong to. . . . We must have a British presence on the islands. If the task force is withdrawn I am sure that my right hon. Friend appreciates the difficulties that would be created if the rest of the world is unwilling, and we are unable, to take any action should the Argentines default on a phased withdrawal. . . .

All democracies which negotiate with intransigent tyrants, such as the present Argentine Government, at some stage have to ask the question: when does compromise become concession? At what stage does concession become appeasement? When does legitimate compromise over conflicting interests become the shameful surrender of vital principles? . . .

My right hon. Friend the Foreign Secretary and the Prime Minister have made it clear throughout the proceedings that we are concerned with principle rather than with possessions. I believe that this distinction, together with the task force, has made negotiation possible. They have stated their principles clearly, although not always consistently. I understand why my right hon. Friend the Foreign Secretary can say no more than he has, but in his account today I felt that there was some danger that the interim arrangements involving withdrawal of the task force, no British administration, and no military presence on the islands, could mean that the long-term negotiations would be prejudiced in favour of Argentina.

We must still hope for a peaceful solution, but the time available is not unlimited. We cannot wait indefinitely and still expect to take effective action if force should be required. I hope that, after all the Government have said and all the task force has done, we do not seek what used to be called peace at any price. . . .

World opinion will respond to success and, in the end, view with contempt too great a retreat from principles which, after all, are the principles of the United Nations as well as our own. Such a retreat would have a disastrous effect on our credibility as a NATO ally and as a European partner and on our own self-confidence. . . .

In their anxiety to get the Falkland Islands problem settled as quickly and as peacefully as possible the Government must not lose sight of other British interests in the world and British credibility at home and abroad.

Dr. David Owen (Plymouth, Devonport): If this fifth debate is to have value, it is important that two messages go from this House. The first is that the House broadly accepts the negotiating framework which the Government have developed over the past few weeks. . . . The second is that the House remains resolved that, if Argentina remains intransigent on the central question of the withdrawal of its forces and the occupation of the islands, we are prepared to exert the full range of pressure on the Argentine Government that we have been building up over the past few weeks. . . .

It would be utter folly for the Government not to have flexibility in their negotiating position. The second flexibility that the Government have introduced into their negotiation position is a readiness to accept an interim administration. . . .

Of course the issue of sovereignty can be discussed, but we cannot enter into discussions with the outcome prejudged by the Argentine. . . . Successive Governments have been ready to discuss an accommodation with Argentina. One of those accommodations was a readiness to discuss the Argentine claim to sovereignty of the Falkland Islands. That did not prejudge the negotiations. . . .

Most people have never accepted that there should be an absolute right of veto by the Falkland Islanders. . . .

It is clear that there are some Members who will not be satisfied with a compromise and who do not want negotiations. But what negotiation is ever conducted in which every word said at the opening of the negotiation marries up with the end of the negotiation? . . .

The central question is what degree of compromise will be involved. I believe as strongly as anyone that there are extremely important issues of principle. . . .

If there were to be a belief in Latin America, or anywhere else in the world, that aggression would meet no response, or would lead merely to a paper formula, many territorial disputes would be unlocked, to the grave disadvantage of us all. . . .

At the end of the day the decision will have to be taken by the Government. None of us can guarantee that next week we might not be debating an even graver military situation. I hope that that is not the case. . . .

I hope that we shall be debating a peaceful settlement. I have made my views clear on the escalation of the dispute to involve the Argentine mainland. That would unlock a major escalation in the international climate. To do so would effectively unify the whole of Latin America. In my view no one would ever enter into that escalation unless the entire Fleet was in jeopardy. At any moment while we are debating the issue one of our ships could be hit by another Exocet missile. It could be HMS "Invincible" or HMS "Hermes". . . .

The chiefs of staff would not be happy to sit back while one wave of bombers came over from Argentina and then allow the next wave to come in, and further waves. . . .

However, there are limits to the extent to which military action can be taken. We must have some idea of what is at risk. What are the risks of casualties? In some instances they could be extremely grave. That factor must be part of a balanced judgment of Britain's interests overall. I believe that the Foreign Secretary is well seized of Britain's interests. I wish him success in the delicate negotiations that will take place over the next few days. . . .

Mr. Arthur Palmer (Bristol, North-East): . . . I agree that policies must change and adapt correspondingly as long as we do not lose sight of certain essential principles. To me, these principles are three. First, unprovoked armed aggression must be resisted when it is defined as such by the United Nations. I should think that this is now the accepted law of the nations. Secondly, the rights of self-governing free peoples to their own way of life must be upheld. Thirdly, while precedence must be given always to diplomatic methods in resisting and throwing back aggression, the use of force in full or in part is equally lawful. . . .

The Government were certainly unprepared for the invasion but, as I hope the coming inquiry will show, I believe that the real situation was worse than that. British representatives, both diplomatic and ministerial, had given the Argentine rulers the impression that we were bored with the Falklands. The trigger-happy junta, anxious for its political survival, took this as an invitation to occupy, because it imagined that the door would be left unlocked when it got there. . . .

I agree entirely here with my right hon. Friend the Leader of the Opposition . . . that without the task force there would have been no hope of useful negotiations with the junta in Buenos Aires. He was right about this. General Galtieri and his kind, who have murdered and kidnapped their political opponents at home with impunity for years, were not likely to pay attention abroad to words without deeds. . . .

I want now to say something about my right hon. Friend the Member for Bristol, South-East (Mr. Benn). . . .

"Bring back the task force" my right hon. Friend says, "Some might be killed. Just transfer the sovereignty of the Falklands to the United Nations." It is very easy to say these things—who could disagree with them?—but how difficult to carry them out. . . . Is it seriously suggested that the leader of Argentina, and his even more sinister colleagues, who have placed large forces of well-equipped troops in the islands, and have increased their numbers, to dispossess Britain of the sovereignty by occupation, will now hand it over to the United Nations? I cannot believe that for one moment. Why should they? Possession is nine points of the law and they well understand that. . . . On the fate of the islanders, I am afraid that my right hon. Friend the Member for Bristol, South-East has been notably silent. . . . That is perhaps why his speeches have been so well received and publicised in Argentina by its controlled press and television. . . .

The regime in the Argentine is also an evil regime. We all want peace and hope that we are going to obtain it but a diplomatic settlement which bound a free people to a squalid military dictatorship would not have the support of this House. I am sure of that.

Mr. W. Benyon (Buckingham): . . . It is essential that our soldiers and sailors in the task force know exactly what the objectives are. The two basic objectives are clear and have been made clear from the beginning. They are the withdrawal of the aggressor and the re-establishment of British sovereignty. Without the re-establishment of British sovereignty it is impossible for the Falkland Islanders to exercise their right of self-determination. I cannot believe that a multinational interim regime can achieve that situation for the islanders when they know that the Argentine fleet and forces are just over the horizon.

Anything less means that the aggressor has won. No amount of talk or diplomatic language can disguise that. This is not said in any jingoistic, warmongering posture, but in a clear, cool appreciation of the two vital issues at stake, which are that aggression must not succeed and that self-determination must be upheld. All my life, ever since I can remember anything about politics, self-determination has been an honoured principle within the world community. It governed the founding of the League of Nations and the United Nations after the war. It motivated the relinquishment of our imperial power throughout the world. Where it is denied today we are loud in our condemnation of those situations.

To me there is no more pernicious doctrine than that which says that because there are only 1,800 Falkland Islanders this principle should not apply. . . .

In a democracy it is difficult to conduct the sort of operation that is going on as advice and comment swirl around by right hon. Friends. I have the greatest confidence in and admiration of the way in which the Prime Minister and her Ministers have faced the problem. I do not wish to press them tonight, but I urge them—I beg them—to stick firmly to these principles and to take comfort from the understanding and robustness of the British people.

Mr. David Stoddart (Swindon): . . . There are many lessons to be learnt from this crisis, some of which have already been mentioned. The first is that before we supply arms to Fascist aggressors we had better understand that they will use those arms not necessarily only against ourselves but against their neighbours and other innocent people in their own countries. I therefore trust that if this Government and a future Labour Government—the previous Labour Government's record might be examined as well—decide to sell arms abroad, which is a disgraceful trade anyway, they will ensure that under no circumstances will they sell arms, particularly sophisticated weapons, to Fascist regimes that might turn them against ourselves or other people. . . .

This country has a democracy that is unequalled in the world. The Falkland Islanders think so too. They believe that they will get fairer treatment under the Crown and this Parliament than they will get from a Fascist junta.

Freedom is indivisible, and freedom of speech is exactly that. It cannot be qualified. Conservative Members have done a disservice to themselves, to the House and to democracy by criticising the coverage given to the Falklands crisis by the BBC. They do themselves no good by doing so.

Whether we like what the BBC does or says, we must always uphold its right to do so and we must not put pressure on it to change, because that will merely undermine the democracy and free speech, in which we all believe. . . .

The fact remains that Argentina has taken by force of arms territory over which this country has a sovereign right and which it has not been able to obtain by negotiation and reference to the international community. I should have thought that everyone would condemn that. Unfortunately, some people in our own country, so far as I can tell, without any knowledge, are at present denying the British claim to sovereignty and in their own minds have handed it over to Argentina by upholding Argentina's claims to sovereignty. I simply do not understand how they can assert that, as one person did last night, with so much certainty. . . .

If Argentina is so confident of its claim, why on earth will it not refer it to international arbitration? . . .

Some people say that we should withdraw our task force forthwith. If we were to do that and allow the Argentine to get away with what it has done, there is no question but that we should be giving comfort and encouragement to every potty little dictator throughout the world. . . .

Ordinary people seem to understand that far better than many of those who go to meetings and pass pious resolutions condemning Fascism, whether it be in El Salvador, Chile or Poland. When it comes to confronting Fascism in areas for which we have a responsibility, such people shrink from doing just that. Ordinary people understand that if we do not confront Fascism now there are great dangers for the future. . . .

I strongly support negotiations. I strongly support the line that has been taken by my right hon. and hon. Friends on the Opposition Front Bench. . . . Nevertheless, I warn that if we withdraw our task force from the South Atlantic, leaving the Argentines in possession of the Falkland Islands, the political repercussions in Britain will be immense. They will redound against Parliament and the parties. We must ensure that the task that we set ourselves on 3 April is carried out. The task is to confront Fascist aggression, to remove the invader from the Falkland Islands and to release the people of the Falkland Islands from that Fascist aggression.

Mr. Michael Colvin (Bristol, North-West): . . . I am surprised that more has not been said about the media. Yesterday, hon. Members were critical of the BBC's coverage of the Falklands crisis. I agree with the vast majority of my constituents who have written to me about the matter. They also think that the BBC got it wrong. Nevertheless, let us give credit where credit is due. The sight of 500 Scouses on the BBC last night singing "There'll always be an England" on Merseyside was welcome after weeks of pictures of howling, hysterical Argentines. . . .

There were major miscalculations both in London and in Washington. I simply hope that our intelligence-gathering services are still able to feed us information and that we understand the signals better than we did before the invasion. Receiving intelligence reports is one thing. Interpreting them correctly is quite another.

The greatest miscalculation of all, however, was made by General Galtieri. . . . The junta never believed that Britain would use armed force to regain our possessions and to save 1,800 British subjects whose freedom, future security and wishes we regard as paramount. . . .

There is no doubt that additional economic pressure by the United States would help rather than hinder our diplomatic efforts and those of the United Nations. It has been reported that some American banks may be vulnerable if the United States impose further sanctions on Argentina. Nevertheless, now that the United States is seen to be firmly on the side of the international rule of law in this matter, rather than continuing to play the game in an even-handed, honest-broker role, it must risk the effect of some economic damage to itself. . . .

Argentina is already £22 billion in foreign debt and needs £2.8 billion annually to service interest payments. It desperately requires to borrow a further £5½ billion, but it cannot do so without Britain's agreement. Thirty major banks will not lend the money while the Prime Minister has the support of our EEC partners and the United States. . . .

We now want America to match what our other allies have done, and to do so fast, because the Argentine economic position could be boosted as soon as next month when revenue from grain sales begins to flow in.

The time for talk is rapidly running out. We must go on trying and pray that the crisis will eventually be resolved diplomatically, but diplomacy will not free the Falkland Islands unless we negotiate from a position of ever-increasing strength. That, at least, is agreed on almost all sides. . . .

As what I see as the final days pass, the Argentine dictator will have to come to terms with three facts which should, as for a man going to the gallows, concentrate his mind wonderfully.

First, despite the Latin temperament, the morale of his teenage conscript forces will fall as it dawns on them that the most powerful fleet that Britain has ever put to sea in peacetime is sinking Argentine ships and shooting down their aircraft because of the intransigence of their military dictator leaders.

Secondly, the occupation forces will face increasing logistic problems which will be very difficult to overcome, especially in the face of a full blockade and deteriorating weather. I suggest that those are far greater problems than those facing our own fleet.

Thirdly, there will be mounting political trouble within Argentina as economic pressure from our allies begins to hurt the Argentine economy, which may eventually collapse. . . .

Today, my right hon. Friend the Prime Minister speaks not only for Britain and the British people, including the families of those who have already laid down their lives in defence of the international rule of law, but for every other person in the world, no matter where he or she is, who has lost or faces the loss of personal freedom and democratic rights. . . .

Mr. David Ennals (Norwich, North): . . . I defend the flexibility shown by the Foreign Secretary. . . . At a time when crucial negotiations are taking place in the United Nations, we have to be prepared, in so far as our principles allow, to seek a diplomatic settlement, which is what is required under resolution 502. . . .

I accept that diplomacy cannot have any effect unless there are forces and an indication that they will be used. I thought that it was right for us to occupy South Georgia, and it was certainly right to establish the exclusion zone. I agreed with the attack on the airstrip at Port Stanley. However, I felt that we went too far when we sank the "General Belgrano". That is the point at which I started to divide myself from the Government. We went beyond the concept of force to back diplomacy. It led to retaliation and the sad loss of HMS "Sheffield" and the members of her crew who died. . . .

I say, as one who was a Minister at the Foreign Office with responsibility for the Falkland Islands and relations with Argentina, that this need never have happened if HMS "Endurance" had stayed in the area—although she would not have been enough on her own—and if we had made it perfectly clear that if there were an attack we would resist it with the forces at our disposal. . . . Very soon after Argentina failed to withdraw its forces, as it was called upon to do under that mandatory resolution, we should have returned to the United Nations with a new resolution condemning Argentina for failing to withdraw its troops and used the other facilities of the United Nations, perhaps article 41, to carry out blockades and other operations by air, sea or land forces involving many other countries. That article gives ample power to the United Nations to do that.

Even more important, we should have involved the United Nations in the negotiations—as it now is, three weeks after it could have been. We should have been in a much stronger position if, instead of the independent negotiations genuinely carried out by Mr. Haig—which kept the Americans on the fence and ensured that they did not turn on the economic screws—we had gone to the United Nations earlier. . . .

Of course, it must mean the withdrawal of all Argentine forces from the

Falkland Islands. That is essential. The Argentines are the aggressors and their forces must be withdrawn. They cannot make acceptance of sovereignty a pre-condition of negotiations. . . .

A diplomatic solution along the lines of resolution 502 must also demonstrate some movement from our extreme position. By "extreme position" I mean that, inevitably, negotiations begin with one party at one extreme and the other party at another extreme. . . .

We cannot refuse to discuss sovereignty. After all, we have been discussing it for years. . . . It is not realistic to believe that we could assemble such a task force again or ever maintain HMS "Invincible", for example, to fulfil a defensive role in the Falkland Islands, as though they can be excluded from the rest of Latin America. I have great sympathy for the long-suffering and much battered but loyal Falkland Islanders, but it does not make sense to give them an absolute veto not only over a settlement but over Britain's defence policy. That is not just because there are only 1,800 islanders, but because we must consider the realities of distance, communication and our own inability—or lack of wisdom—to have a massive defence capability. . . .

We must be prepared to accept the establishment of a United Nations temporary executive authority, or whatever it is called, together with such peace-keeping facilities as we believe are necessary both to monitor the mutual withdrawal of all forces and to administer the islands pending a negotiated settlement of the dispute. After the remarkable assembly of the task force and the highly trained troops, it would be a terrible tragedy if we embarked upon a real war to the death while the United Nations was still struggling for a peaceful settlement. . . .

Mr. James Hill (Southampton, Test): . . . Who would have believed that on the third anniversary of the Government the House would be almost completely dominated by the crisis in the South Atlantic? The speed of events and the almost day-by-day television war game has necessitated the Opposition demanding yet another debate. . . .

Matters such as the economy, industrial growth, social welfare, the pound, Britain in Europe and many other world crises have been completely dominated by the Falkland Islands aggression. . . . There is no way that the debate has brought forward any more conclusions than the first, second, third or fourth debate. . . .

It was perhaps a little sad that [*my right hon. Friend the Member for Sidcup (Mr. Heath)*] did not take the opportunity once and for all to confirm that his support is completely with the Government in this matter and that he no longer wishes to sit on the fence. . . .

The South Atlantic sea lanes are beginning to be critically important to the United Kingdom and the Western civilisation. . . .

There is a danger that the negotiations will go on so long that the task force will have no choice but to winter at the Ascension Islands. That would be fatal because the negotiations would have to drag on right through the long Antarctic winter. . . .

The Prime Minister said that the task force was under political control, but when it has to go into action it should not be a task force with leg irons. It should be given complete freedom of movement. Once the political decision is made, there should be no attempt to change details. . . .

The campaign will resolve so much that the 300 Falkland Islanders who have left the islands over several years and now reside in my constituency will at least know that the United Kingdom has done everything to protect the Falkland Islanders and their right of self-determination. My right hon. Friend the Foreign Secretary must make every provision at all stages of the negotiations for a Red Cross safety corridor to enable the women and children living in the Falkland Islands to be brought out if the fighting is so severe that their lives are in danger. . . .

Mr. Michael Meacher (Oldham, West): By far the most desirable outcome of the Falkland Islands war would be an early ceasefire linked to a balanced and phased withdrawal of the Argentines from the Falkland Islands and of the task force from the area so that negotiations could be finalised on the form and structure of a United Nations or other mutually agreed international interim administration in which sovereignty could be temporarily vested. . . .

The so-called military solution does not make political sense. Even if we succeeded in retaking the islands by sheer force of arms, there is the question whether we could consolidate such a position. We would be faced by a virulently angry and bitterly humiliated Argentina. In that situation, could such a tiny population, not itself a nation, 400 miles from a hostile mainland in whose economic ambit it irrevocably lies, be maintained in safety and freedom indefinitely, except at a cost that any Government must surely find prohibitive? . . .

All this underlines the crucial point that in the end there must be a negotiated settlement that meets at least the minimum of agreement in Argentina. That does not mean that there are not constraining political objectives from which we can or should walk away. Our legitimate political objectives are, as they have always been, first, resistance against unprovoked aggression, so that, in the words of my right hon. Friend the Leader of the Opposition "international anarchy shall not pay"; secondly, to secure the reasonable interests of the islanders, without—I echo many hon. Members—ill-advised talk of paramountcy, granting them an automatic veto over the lives and resources of a nation of 55 million people. . . . To reassert the metaphysics of British sovereignty is not a legitimate aspiration. . . .

Given that there are legitimate political objectives, if a ceasefire is not negotiable because of Argentina's intransigence . . . and if a full-scale military assault is effectively ruled out by the pyrrhic consequences that would ensue, is there another option to overcome Argentina's resistance to a diplomatic settlement that would still safeguard the proper and legitimate political objectives that I have stated? I believe that there is.

So far, pressure on Argentina has been concentrated largely on the military dimension. Other pressures, diplomatic to some extent, but above all economic and financial, have been greatly underdeployed. Yet they could be much more effective in bringing about an early and acceptable settlement than military attack, and certainly without the appalling cost in human lives. . . .

If there is a lesson that the Government should urgently consider at this stage in the conflict it is that finance—not military capability—remains Galtieri's Achilles' heel. Of course, there is a price to be paid for such a plan. It has been estimated that the losses of a total default by Argentina might halve a year's profits for the British clearing banks. However, when the alternative is a mounting scale of carnage, and when even a military victory would make the ultimate goal of a negotiated settlement not less difficult but more difficult, that price should be paid.

Mr. W. R. Rees-Davies (Thanet, West): . . . Despotic dictatorships that go bankrupt do not pay. Not one single penny would be paid and the money would be lost. . . .

It is now 40 days since the Argentines first had an opportunity to say what they proposed to do. I would serve them notice that if they do not come to heel within 10 days, our troops will go straight in to recover our property. We cannot afford more time than that if we are not to jeopardise the lives of all the task force. All hon. Members would rather have a diplomatic solution than a military victory. . . .

Therefore, what are our minimum requirements? First, the House has stated over and over again that the condition precedent to any negotiated settlement is the withdrawal of Argentine troops first—and not at the same time as anything else. Secondly, once they have withdrawn, a trusteeship could be properly set up by the United Nations. . . . Thirdly, the task force must not be withdrawn until the beginning of the trusteeship and until the forces responsible and the administration move in. . . .

What face-saving device could be found for the Argentines? I suggest something along the lines of Cyprus. If we are to be responsible for the islands' administration in due course, we must be prepared to offer the Argentines a small base in the islands where they can assert their rights to be there. When settlements are made, it will be necessary to take into account the education of the children on the Falkland Islands as well as other matters. . . .

Sovereignty is not the main issue. The overriding factor is the strategic importance of the Falkland Islands. . . . I trust that in the end the Foreign Office will recognise for the first time how wrong it has been. The naval base is of strategic importance. It is vital for the development of the wealth in that area and for the development of oil and mineral wealth in the Antarctic. . . .

I beg the Prime Minister and the Foreign Secretary to stand firmly by their principles. Not only our party but the nation will suffer unless we make absolutely certain that the Argentine forces are removed before there is any question of trusteeship or other method of settlement. . . . That can and will be achieved but there must be a deadline. There is a maximum of ten days. Our troops must be told that if the matter is not settled they can go in and recapture our legitimate islands.

Mr. Norman Atkinson (Tottenham): . . . The absence of a vote or some other indication of organised opposition does not mean that one can assume that the House unanimously endorses the task force and its job. That is not so. . . .

There have been statements, particularly by the Left of the Socialist movement, indicating that they did not support the sending of the task force, and there were good reasons why that was so. . . .

Many people in the Socialist movement started to confuse the question of the repulsive administration under the junta with what is happening in the Falklands. The idea was that the despatch of the task force would bring an end to the Fascist regime in Argentina. There was a difference of opinion about that. Many of us made it absolutely clear that we believe that the junta could be dealt with by the imposition of economic sanctions. . . .

It is dangerous and ludicrous to suggest that any invasion of the Falklands can somehow bring about a permanent settlement. It is lunacy to talk in that way. . . .

Britain is now to negotiate conditions for lease-back. Sovereignty is already on the way to being transferred. We should now recognise what is happening. . . .

The Falkland Islanders are in no way involved in direct negotiations. It is not possible to concede to them the right of self-determination as they cannot possibly be signatories to any negotiated settlement. That contradiction is ignored by many hon. Members. . . .

A country that backs its diplomatic initiatives with a task force is saying that it wants to negotiate under duress. Military muscle is added to the negotiating table. Many of us said that it would be much more difficult for the United Nations to intervene when military duress was imposed. Bringing back the task force will allow negotiations to proceed without the duress that military pressures bring. . . . Those who adopted the argument that I have advanced when the crisis began have been proved to have a true understanding of the Falklands' future and to have at heart the best interests of the world Socialist movement in defeating Argentine-type juntas.

Mr. Keith Best (Anglesey): . . . The despatch of the task force, which was endorsed by the leaders of both major parties when the force was sent, was necessary to strengthen the Government's negotiating principles. It was intended to be seen as a manifestation of the Government's resolve to achieve a solution to the dispute in the southern Atlantic. . . .

The assessment of strategic importance must be linked to the final disposition of the Falkland Islands. We all hope that there will be a peaceful settlement that will involve the withdrawal of Argentine troops from the Falkland Islands, but we must ask rhetorically "What is the reality?". I do not think that I shall be accused of abject pessimism if I say that the reality is that the Argentine Government have made it abundantly clear hitherto that they have no interest in withdrawing their troops from the Falkland Islands. . . .

Therefore, it is likely that the islands will have to be retaken by force of arms. Having served briefly in commando forces, I have every confidence that that could be done quickly and effectively and with minimum casualties, although that is not necessarily so.

A British task force should never have been despatched. There should have been a United Nations standing force. The lack of enforceability of world law is perhaps the great lacuna in international order. If nothing else comes out of the crisis, I hope that world opinion will be focused on that issue. A remedy is required.

If I am correct in my assessment that the islands will be taken by force of arms, which may sadly involve some loss of life due to the intransigence and obstinacy of the Argentine Government . . . the British public would not be able to understand the Government's policy if they were to trade away the sovereignty of the islands. That must be manifestly right.

Secondly . . . I do not subscribe to the idea that if the Argentine troops are forced to withdraw through force of arms that will teach them their lesson and they will not seek to retake the islands. I believe that their resolve to take them will be strengthened. If the successor Government in the Argentine are Peronist or another Right-wing regime, they will look for succour to anyone who will aid them in their enterprise. Sadly, it is very likely that it will turn to the Soviet Union, which will be only too amenable because it is trying to destabilise the situation in South America. . . .

I hope that at some stage we can return to an amicable relationship with Argentina. That is why all options, such as a United Nations trusteeship, need to be considered. . . .

The world expects a solution in accordance with resolution 502. . . . Yes, world opinion is important, but the world must realise that things can now never be the same, because not only is the world much older but, I hope, it is much wiser.

Mr. David Winnick (Walsall, North): . . . Although in international law the Falklands are a possession of this country . . . I accept, like most people, that we shall not remain in possession of the Falklands for ever and a day. . . .

Let it be said in the House of Commons that one understands the widespread feeling throughout Argentina—certainly it is not confined to the junta—that what they call the Malvinas are theirs. . . . The essence of the whole matter, however, is that territorial disputes should not be decided by force or aggression. That is why, like all my right hon. and hon. Friends, I condemn entirely the invasion and the aggression which was undoubtedly committed by the junta. Let no one misunderstand our views or where we stand. . . .

What has happened in the Falklands could happen elsewhere if force is to be the decisive factor. . . .

The Government must not allow themselves to be swayed by some of the more jingoistic feelings and emotions that have been expressed by some Conservative Members. At the end of the day, the House wants to see a negotiated settlement. We do not want an escalation of the conflict or an invasion in which thousands of lives could be lost. That is why I hope that the efforts now being made by the United Nations Secretary-General will be successful.

That is the way to bring about a solution. We must try to involve the United Nations and at the same time try to reach an agreement that would ensure the removal of Argentina's troops from the islands. We must also recognise that sovereignty must be negotiated. The parties concerned must realise that once the military conflict comes to an end there can be meaningful talks. . . .

Mr. Stephen Hastings (Mid-Bedfordshire): . . . By now, I estimate, the task force is within days of having the capacity to re-establish British rule. If the Argentines agree to withdraw without any precondition on sovereignty, so be it. There is no engagement. The choice . . . is theirs entirely. The Argentine garrison must be increasingly forlorn. Militarily speaking, I am more optimistic than some hon. Members. . . .

The Argentines can scarcely be full of confidence. Why, then, do they continue to be intransigent? We are told that they are intransigent because the junta is incapable of taking a decision as there are so many internal divisions and because there are other military commanders who must also be consulted.

I am sure that there is something in that, but is it the full story? Is it not also to some extent because the junta is encouraged by what it sees as progress of the negotiations? . . .

Nevertheless, the House might be forgiven for entertaining at least the suspicion that the Foreign Office is at it again and, under American pressure, is trotting out all the old, specious arguments about the Falklands being an unnecessary embarrassment to us and so forth. . . .

My conviction is that the Falklands represent an important long-term strategic and economic interest to us and to the West. Whether we choose to exercise that interest alone or in partnership is a matter for us. . . . Nor can I accept that the future defence of these islands, given our resources, is beyond our means. Those who claim that it is have not thought the matter out. . . .

If the Government should be prevailed upon to surrender now on any essential principle, when victory is within our grasp . . . *[they]* would break the confidence and trust of this nation . . . destroy the special relationship with the United States and do perhaps irreparable harm to the Western Alliance . . . it would mean that those who have died have died in vain. . . .

The critical factor is not the Armed Forces. Thank God, they remain as true as steel. It is not the support of the country, because I am sure that the Government enjoy that. The key factor must be the will of Her Majesty's Ministers. I pray and believe that they will not be found wanting. And I know that it is our clear duty in this House to support them.

Mr. Ray Powell (Ogmore): . . . The worst thing that could happen in the Falklands would be the sinking of the British Fleet, but the next worse thing would be for Britain to get the islands back. We do not want to lose, but if the islanders are the only prize of victory, we hardly want to win.

As brave men prepare to fight to the death, it is worth remembering that this will be the first war over territory that one combatant wished and still wishes to donate to the other. . . .

We now see the consequences of a lack of any foresight appropriate to the risk—the product of a stubborn group of blinkered MPs committed to a principle that they had no means of enforcing but whom no Minister had the muscle, time or the will to overcome. That may have been understandable at the time, but the unalterable fact is that they turned out to be tragically and culpably mistaken. As a result we are now setting out to fight, but not for the Falklands, which we do not want and which we would be happy to trade away in any deal. However, to strike a compromise, it is surely important to remember that we do not wish to keep the land. . . .

How can a Government and some of my hon. Friends refer to the Argentine junta as international thugs and an especially brutal dictatorial Government when only recently we made trading agreements to sell them ships, arms and goods of every description which could be used against us? . . .

There are moments when principles of humanity and principles of justice must be more important in our decision-making than any instinct of political advantage. We must all dissociate ourselves from any policy which even threatens further military action, let alone orders it. For once in this harsh cruel world, for once in our nation's history of war, empire and bloodshed, we must resolve this dispute, even though it is one with a Fascist Government, without the use of instruments of war. That is my heartfelt belief and plea.

I therefore call upon the Government to stop being unrealistic about Britain's role in the world, especially after being responsible for allowing the situation in the Falklands to develop. Stop this jingoism that is leading this and other nations to war. Spell out to the nation the fact that the effects of war mean death to British subjects, death to our Service men and women and death to people of other countries. Wives will be made widows and children made orphans. War will mean crippled and mangled limbs and thousands of lives ruined for those who survive. . . .

Request peacemongers and peace-lovers to use all their influence and power in support of peace and seek to ensure genuine statesmanship based on humanitarian principles and not upon the present plight of a Prime Minister who is fighting to preserve her public position. . . .

Mr. Peter Griffiths (Portsmouth, North): . . . In the battle that is going on at the present moment there is a need to win the hearts and minds of people throughout the world. Much has been said about the influence of overseas countries, their attitudes and the need for us to maintain their support. There is also the need for us to ensure that the Ministry of Defence in particular, and the Government in general, give the highest priority to ensuring that the British people, particularly the families of those serving in the South Atlantic, are well informed and given the widest possible information about what is going on.

There has been a failure to recognise the importance of British news material in this crisis. In the need to transport war materials to the South Atlantic it is not possible for less important items to be included in aircraft and ship cargoes. However, on the return journey from the South Atlantic I should have thought that news material should have the highest priority. With modern technology it is not even necessary that pictures and news are physically brought back to Britain. They can be transmitted by cable or radio from countries in South or Central America to British television and the newspapers. We have missed an opportunity to ensure that our people are well informed of the British point of view about what is happening to British Service men in the South Atlantic. The Ministry of Defence should give this higher priority than it has up to now. . . .

In the end, whether or not military activity takes place on a greater scale than it has hitherto, we shall come back to negotiation. That negotiation must take place sooner or later. I believe that I speak for every hon. Member and for every person in Britain when I say that, whatever our political views, whatever our views about the ultimate solution to the crisis in the South Atlantic, we pray that this dispute can be settled without any more loss of life on either side.

There is no reason whatever why this issue, which has divided Britain from a great nation in the southern hemisphere, should not be settled if there is an element of good will on both sides. We know from what has been said repeatedly that there is that element of good will on the part of the British Government. What we require now is proof from Argentina that there is a willingness to negotiate in good faith. I trust that that is so, but if it is not, the military solution is the only alternative.

Mr. John Silkin (Deptford): . . . In 1980—just a year and a half ago—a draft manifesto was produced. I am glad to say that my right hon. Friend the Member for Bristol, South-East (Mr. Benn) played a prominent part in putting it together. The draft manifesto contained the following paragraph:

"We reaffirm our commitment that under no circumstances will the inhabitants of the Falkland Islands be handed over to any Argentine regime which violates human and civil rights."

That remains the common view of the Labour Party today, and I hope that it remains the view of the Government.

In order to achieve that, the Security Council—following the invasion of the Falkland Islands by Argentine forces—was called upon to introduce resolution 502. . . . It contained three distinct parts that must, nevertheless, be read as a totality. . . . The first part calls on

"the Governments of Argentina and the United Kingdom to seek a diplomatic solution to their differences and to respect fully the purposes and principles of the Charter of the United Nations.". . .

The second part was that Argentine troops should withdraw from the islands that they had invaded. The third part of the resolution was that there should be a ceasefire. They have to be read in the context of the date of the original resolution. The original resolution was tabled by Her Majesty's Government representative on 3 April. It was done before the task force had even been assembled, let alone sailed from the United Kingdom. . . .

Of course our duty is to take all diplomatic measures we can and to negotiate as hard as we can. But suppose that those measures proved ineffective. "All right", say some of my hon. Friends, "Let us take economic and financial sanctions." What if those measures are ineffective? I believe we are then still in the position of having to rely on article 51. My view is that it remains a great pity that the United Nations did not proceed with its original idea of having its own peacekeeping force. The fact that one's own might has to be used in one's own defence means that in a sense one is a judge in one's own cause. . . .

If there is no alternative but the use of force, how much force does one actually use? . . . First, the force to be used should not be so large that it prevents one taking part in diplomatic negotiations.

Secondly, the force that is used should be reasonable in the circumstances. That is the common legal form of self-defence whether it is of an individual citizen or a group of people. Subject to those two qualifications, we might be in the position of having to use force. I have referred to a third qualification . . . one must have political control.

I have no doubt that there is political control over the task force. It is a political decision and it is right that that should be Her Majesty's Government's political decision. Her Majesty's Government have a duty to ensure that our forces are protected, even more so in this particular case when the Fleet is 8,000 miles away from home. . . .

It is easy to say that we should be united. We should in so far as we can be. That is true. This is a time of great crisis and we have to cope with a national emergency. At the same time the Opposition have to take into account the fears, worries, questions, thoughts and problems of our citizens. That is our duty. Sometimes we will diverge from the national view because it is essential to push that point of view. To that we intend to stick.

In those circumstances I do not believe that it could possibly be right for my right hon. Friend to take part in discussions in which, incidentally, he alone in the Labour Party would be involved and in which he would find himself prejudiced . . . in making the kind of attack that he should make. . . .

If I understood the Foreign Secretary correctly, he announced two basic immovable positions from which he would not be budged. I hope that he will confirm, if necessary by a nod of the head, that I have them correct. First, he said that there shall be no ceasefire until there has been an agreement to withdraw the entire Argentine force plus the Argentine civil personnel. That appears to be correct. Secondly, the right hon. Gentleman said that the outcome of long-term negotiations about the future of the islands must not be prejudged by the Argentines. He implied that they can have what opinion they like, but they must not prejudge the negotiations. I think that that is correct also.

If those two bases are the Government's immovable objectives and if they are what they will stick on, the Opposition are with them and will support them. The Foreign Secretary has said that other issues are negotiable. . . .

At some time the result of negotiations will be brought to the House. Responsibility for the items that are negotiable will rest with the Prime Minister, the Foreign Secretary and the Government. At that time there will be no obligation on the Opposition to accept the results holus-bolus or in any other way. At that stage we shall examine what has been given and what has been provided. That is when we and the country will make our judgment on what has happened.

The Secretary of State for Defence (Mr. John Nott): . . . It is now nearly six weeks since Argentine forces invaded the Falkland Islands and imposed on British people and British territory an illegal and alien military rule. The invasion was an unprovoked and obnoxious act, which the United Nations Security Council immediately condemned in resolution 502 . . . *[which]* forms the basis of any negotiation, including Argentine withdrawal. . . . *[Negotiations]* were carried out first with the cooperation of Secretary Haig, then on the basis of proposals from the President of Peru. . . . Now there are the negotiations with the Secretary-General of the United Nations.

Our approach to all these negotiations has been urgent, realistic and constructive. . . .

I am advised that we have no knowledge of the *[Argentine]* amendments *[to the Peruvian proposals]*. . . . However, all that we have been informed of is total rejection of the proposals that were made through the Peruvian President. If there is any subsequent information about Argentine amendments, we shall study them. Up to now, we have only been told of rejection. . . .

Regrettably, throughout the negotiations, the Argentine Government have approached the matter differently from ourselves. They have sought to prolong them in the hope that international opposition to the illegal occupation would falter and that time would act against us militarily. They have been consistent only in their inflexibility and intransigence. Meanwhile, Argentine troops are still on the Falklands Islands. They persist in their illegal occupation. They have taken no steps to withdraw in accordance with the mandatory resolution of the Security Council.

We cannot allow the present situation on the Falkland Islands to endure. . . . We should remember the consequences of allowing the Argentines to get away with this aggression. Our diplomatic efforts are intended to bring it to an end peacefully, but these efforts have been and must continue to be accompanied by military actions. I was naturally encouraged *[by the statement]* that so far the official Opposition had supported all our military actions. . . .

Our military effort has been calculated to serve two purposes: first, to put increasing pressure on the Argentine garrison on the Falklands, and on the Argentine Government, to recognise our resolve and to accept a peaceful withdrawal; and, secondly, to put us into a position from which, if all diplomatic efforts fail, we can take the further military action necessary to end the illegal occupation of the Falkland Islands. . . . There would have been no purpose in sending the task force unless we were in some circumstances prepared to use it.

From the first, our military actions have been complementary to our diplomatic efforts and entirely consistent with our inherent right of self-defence under the charter. These actions have comprised a steady progression. The progression has not been dictated wholly by our diplomatic efforts; it has been necessary as a consequence of the time needed for our forces to deploy to the South Atlantic from the United Kingdom, although while this was taking place we have continued to place whatever military and economic pressure we could on the Argentine Government to recognise their misjudgment of our resolve and to withdraw from the islands.

I can therefore give a complete assurance . . . that any period of delay has been caused not by doubts but by the movement of our forces to the area of potential conflict.

Now our forces are deployed to the Falklands area they will take the action necessary to deny reinforcement and resupply of the Argentine garrison, and to protect themselves against attack from Argentine naval and air forces. The consequent engagements have already led to significant loss of life and casualties on both sides. The whole House regrets that this is so, and mourns those British Service men who have died while performing their duty to this country with conspicuous skill and courage.

The right hon. Member for Leeds, East (Mr. Healey) discussed the degree of force which was acceptable in meeting the Government's aims. Our military build-up has been gradual, graduated and closely controlled. Ministers have never been in any doubt, however, that if it became necessary to use force, force would have to be used.

We do not underestimate the threat posed to our forces by Argentina. The whole House agrees, as the right hon. Member for Deptford (Mr. Silkin) has just said, that we cannot put our Service men at risk by requiring them to pull punches in the face of that threat. However, I can assure the House that our task group will not employ unnecessary force. It will use only the force necessary to fulfil its mission and to protect itself.

The right hon. Member for Leeds, East referred again to the sinking of the cruiser "General Belgrano" and to the fact that she was some 30 miles or so outside the total exclusion zone. That zone was not relevant in this case. The "General Belgrano" was attacked under the terms of our warning to the Argentines some 10 days previously that any Argentine naval vessel or military aircraft which could amount to a threat to interfere with the mission of British forces in the South Atlantic would encounter the appropriate response.

The "General Belgrano" was in a heavily armed group of warships. The cruiser and two destroyers had been closing on elements of our task force. At the time that she was engaged, the "General Belgrano" and a group of British warships could have been within striking distance of each other in a matter of some five to six hours, converging from a distance of some 200 nautical miles.

Following attacks on our ships the previous day, and given the possible presence of an Argentine submarine and other information in our possession, there was every reason to believe that the "General Belgrano" group was manoeuvring to a position from which to attack our surface vessels. Therefore, under certain rules of engagement that we had already agreed, our submarine attacked the cruiser for reasons of self-defence of our own fleet.

In this connection, I again emphasise that at all times the task force has been under political control. The clearest evidence of that is the political oversight we give and the regular, almost daily, meetings that my right hon. Friend the Prime Minister holds with those of her Ministers most closely concerned. At these meetings, political and operational decisions are taken and approved. . . .

It is not expected that any large-scale call-out of reserves will be needed, but we need a small number of skilled personnel, mainly in communications. Therefore, it will be a selective call-out of specialists, and the present plans envisage that in due course up to about 300 may be involved.

Our military action so far has inflicted on the Argentine forces a number of serious reversals. South Georgia was retaken with no British casualties. As many as 10 Argentine aircrart have now been lost, whereas our task force has lost only one aircraft, a Harrier, as a direct result of Argentine action.

Argentine losses include one Canberra, two Mirages, three Sky Hawk aircraft and two Puma helicopters. Three further military aircraft, whose presence was in breach of our total exclusion zone, were severely damaged during attacks on airfields on the Falkland Islands. There have also been significant Argentine naval losses, which I shall not outline on this occasion.

I take no pleasure in the loss of life and the waste of resources that these losses represent. Nevertheless, I do take satisfaction from the evidence that they provide that our task force is discharging its mission effectively, and tightening its grip on the Argentine garrison on the Falklands.

There has been agreement in this debate that the net should be tightened. That garrison is now beleagured. Its supply lines are cut. It may be that under cover of darkness or in adverse weather conditions some supplies are still getting through by air or sea, but it is certain that this is quite insignificant compared with both the scale of resupply before we implemented the exclusion zone and the needs of the garrison.

The House should not be misled by Argentine claims that our exclusion zone is not effective. The Argentine troops on the Falkland Islands know better—to their discomfort and cost. . . .

Everyone accepts that operations in the South Atlantic are difficult and dangerous. The task force is 8,000 miles from home. The weather is bad, with the winter season starting. The Argentine forces are on the alert to break into the total exclusion zone. The 27 [press] correspondents aboard the task force are sharing the rigours and dangers of hostilities with the ships' companies. They are, if I may say so, doing a very impressive job, and I pay tribute to them. They get back to the public—not only the public of this country but throughout the world—the realities, and indeed the personal side, of conflict at sea in the conditions of the South Atlantic. They can communicate as only eye witnesses can.

I must make it clear that the commanding officers of the task force must ensure that the copy leaving their ships does not unintentionally disclose any operational information that would be useful to Argentine forces. . . . In the last resort, judgment of what to release from the task force can come only from the commander on the spot, not on a political level here at home. It cannot be done by me. . . .

It is a matter of great regret to us that we have not been able to send back from the task force the volume of photographs and television reports that we would wish. The purpose embarking journalists with the force was to ensure that there would be a flow of material coming home. The transmission of live television from the ships proved to be impossible because the required power is not available. Nor does the military satellite system have sufficient capacity to carry such signals. Even a recorded film could only be transmitted at a rate of about one still picture every 20 minutes. Any transmission on that basis would have placed quite unacceptable demands on a system that is already hard pressed with urgent operational requirements. . . .

Not merely the Royal Navy has behaved absolutely splendidly—the Army and Royal Air Force have, too. Some of the Royal Air Force's achievements have been quite remarkable. Mid-air refuelling and the Vulcan achievement are but two examples. The Merchant Navy and the civilians working in our dockyards and British industry have also done a magnificent job. I am sure that the whole House would agree that we should pay tribute to them now.

The House will of course be informed of events as they unfold. . . . The options open to us embrace a range, from the long blockade of the Falklands to their repossession by force at an early date.

We will not be hurried. Decisions will be taken at the proper time in the light of all the information and advice that is available to us. Nevertheless, we will not be stalled by Argentine procrastination at the United Nations or anywhere else. . . .

It remains our earnest hope that further military action may not be necessary. This depends on Argentina's willingness to withdraw her forces of occupation. . . .

The search for a diplomatic solution continues as relentlessly as before. Equally relentless is the military pressure that we have applied and shall continue to apply until we have a solution that is acceptable to the House.

Report Twenty-three

18 MAY 1982

Tuesday 18 May, and Prime Minister's question time again.

Mr. Chapman: . . . Will my right hon. Friend reflect on the fact that ridding the Falkland Islands of all Argentine troops is not only the main objective of her Government—backed up by the overwhelming support of the British people—but is seen by millions beyond our shores as an objective that is fundamental to the prospects for international law and order and essential to the security and independence of all small sovereign States—the very point recently made by no less a person that the Secretary-General of the Commonwealth?

The Prime Minister: I warmly endorse what my hon. Friend has said. Our objective in the South Atlantic is not only to ensure that the Argentine troops withdraw from the Falklands but to uphold international law and to see that territorial boundaries are not, and cannot be, changed by force.

Mr. Foot: Does not the Prime Minister agree that matters cannot be left quite where they were at the end of last Thursday's debate and that several important questions should be clarified in debate in the House? I refer, for example, to the questions . . . about the nature of the Peruvian terms and some of the possibilities that were put forward. There are also questions about how far the Argentine Government may have moved towards accepting at any rate two of the requirements that the Government have laid down. Will the right hon. Lady make it quite clear that we shall be able to discuss any response from the Argentine Government in the House as well as any comment that the Secretary-General of the United Nations may make on the situation?

The Prime Minister: This will be a critical week for deciding whether a peaceful settlement is attainable. Our ambassador to the United Nations returned, saw Senor Perez de Cuellar and put some proposals to him, to be handed over to the Argentines. I understand that we expect a reply very shortly—within a matter of a day or so. Therefore, it is a critical week and the Government think that it would be timely to hold a debate later this week. I understand that the matter will be considered through the usual channels.

Mr. Foot: I thank the right hon. Lady for her response. It is right that the House should have such a debate, in which—I assume—the House will able to judge the propositions for a peaceful settlement before any major escalation of the situation.

The Prime Minister: No military action can be held up in any way. To do so would be to give notice to the dictator, who is our enemy.

Mr. Foot: Surely the right hon. Lady has a responsibility to give notice to the dictator that the House has the right to judge such matters before there is any escalation of the situation.

The Prime Minister: The right hon. Gentleman is constitutionally and practically wrong, and wrong when it comes to regarding the interests of our people in the task force and in the Falklands. . . .

We cannot go on prevaricating. The Argentines are trying to spin out the negotiations. So far, no military option has been closed or held up, and it will not be. . . .

Mr. Litherland: . . . Does the Prime Minister think that it is about time that she put pressure on the banks and the financial institutions to play their part, or is it far more convenient for them for there to be a loss of life rather than a loss of profit?

The Prime Minister: I cannot associate myself in any way with what the hon. Gentleman has said. We have frozen Argentine assets in the United Kingdom. The bankers are playing their part, just as everyone else in the country is. I can only condemn what the hon. Gentleman has said. . . .

Mr. Craigen: As those of us in this country know what a determined lady the Prime Minister can be, has she considered at any time the possibility of a face-to-face meeting with the Argentine leader—*[Interruption.]*—to maximise the opportunities for this last attempt at peace?

The Prime Minister: I am a very merciful person. The answer is No, Sir. . . .

Our representative at the United Nations has had a further meeting with Senor Perez de Cuellar. The negotiations are continuing and we are doing all that we can to reach a peaceful settlement, although there are principles on which we cannot compromise. There remain substantial difficulties. I believe that we shall know within the next day or two whether an agreement is attainable. We cannot have endless Argentine prevarication. We have been negotiating in good faith for six weeks and there has still been no sign of Argentine willingness to implement the Security Council's mandatory resolution.

Our determination to ensure that all Argentine forces are withdrawn from the islands remains absolute. We have throughout made it clear that we shall take whatever steps are necessary to bring this about. We are meanwhile increasing the military pressures on the Argentine Government.

Mr. Dykes: . . . Does *[the Prime Minister]* agree that the Government have now done all that they can to achieve a peaceful settlement? Before the awful prospect that full-scale hostilities will have to begin, can we reconsider those specific items of Argentine intransigence that have made them resist, adamantly and stubbornly, the demands of the Secretary-General, to which the British Government have already acceded?

The Prime Minister: We have done everything that we can to try to secure a peaceful settlement. The Argentines have shown their intransigence by flouting every single part of the United Nations mandatory resolution. Not only did they flout the resolution, they have gone in the contrary direction by piling extra men and equipment into the islands.

Dr. Strang: Is the Prime Minister aware that the speech that she made in Perth last Friday convinced many people that she was more intent on a military solution than a peaceful settlement, which would be acceptable to the vast majority of the Commons, but not to the Right wing of the Tory Party? Is it the case that the Argentine Government are prepared to withdraw their troops from the Falklands without requiring Britain to concede the principle of sovereignty first?

The Prime Minister: We were negotiating in February—with the islanders—in New York, long before the invasion. It was the Argentines who broke off those negotiations. We were negotiating over the South Georgia incident. It was—

Mr. Cryer: Answer the question.

The Prime Minister: I shall answer the question in my own way and in my own time.

It was the Argentine Foreign Secretary, Senor Costa Mendez, who broke off a diplomatic solution to the South Georgia incident the day before invasion. For six weeks we have been trying to reach a negotiated settlement. If we are not able to do so, most of my right hon. Friends and hon. Friends and most hon. Gentlemen would not flinch from a settlement by force.

Mr. Waller: If, unfortunately, it became unavoidable at some time in the future that the use of force had to be contemplated in the defence of British interests, would it not be highly irresponsible for any actions to be delayed, not for operational reasons and in defence of Service men's lives, but simply to consult Members of the House, however eminent they might be?

The Prime Minister: I believe that any military action or option cannot and must not be delayed by people who are extending negotiations. To say that we have to consult people in the House, apart from being constitutionally wrong, would give notice to the invader of when we intended to take action. That would be stupid as well as totally unjust to those whom we expect to fight for us.

Report Twenty-four

20 MAY 1982

Thursday 20 May and debate number six followed Prime Minister's questions.

Mr. Ray Powell: Is the Prime Minister aware that the call for a ceasefire in the Falkland Islands is gathering strength nationally and internationally? Will she therefore tell us how many more lives . . . will be sacrificed to satisfy the lust for blood by the hawks on the Government Benches behind her? Will she tell us when the nation can expect the faith, hope and harmony that she promised three years ago from the steps of 10 Downing Street?

The Prime Minister: A ceasefire without withdrawal would leave the invader in possession of the Falkland Islands and our people under his subjection. That is far from our objective.

Sir Anthony Kershaw: Will my right hon. Friend bear in mind that the object of this exercise is to restore freedom and the rule of law to the Falkland Islands? Will she ensure that her view of that is not obscured by any Argentine fancy footwork?

The Prime Minister: I entirely agree with my hon. Friend. Our objective is to restore freedom and the rule of law to the Falkland Islands and we will not be put off by Argentine procrastination.

Mr. David Steel: Will the Prime Minister tell the House, in advance of her speech this afternoon, whether she will be able, in the course of that speech, to inform the House of the terms proposed by the Secretary-General of the United Nations? If that is not possible, can the right hon. Lady give us an idea of when she thinks those terms might be made known to the House?

The Prime Minister: Not in detail, but I shall be able to give some indication of aspects that have yet to be resolved. . . .

Mr. Maxwell-Hyslop: Will my right hon. Friend convey to the New Zealand Government this country's widespread appreciation and gratitude for their generous action in support, not only of Britain but of the rule of international law, not least by offering to support us with Her Majesty's New Zealand ship "Canterbury"?

The Prime Minister: Gladly. The New Zealand Government and people have been absolutely magnificent in their support of this country, of the Falkland Islanders and of the rule of liberty and the rule of law. I shall gladly convey that to Mr. Muldoon who, only yesterday, reminded me "Don't forget. In New Zealand, we are still a member of the same family." . . .

Mr. Ian Lloyd: Since this remarkable document . . . *[outlining proposals]* has revealed that Her Majesty's Government, in the interests of peace, have been prepared to carry compromise almost to the point of folly, has not the time now come for the House to turn its back on timidity and compromise and to make clear to the gauleiters of Buenos Aires that when British Forces are committed in a just cause, they have always triumphed and the consequences for their opponents have been devastating?

The Prime Minister: As I shall say in my speech later, I do not believe that we have, in that document, compromised any of the fundamental principles that I set out at the beginning—none of them. We were prepared to make certain practical changes that were reasonable if we were to obtain the prize of no further loss of life. But there has been no compromise on fundamental principles.

Mr. Rippon: . . . Has my right hon. Friend in mind the terms of the draft Labour manifesto of 1980 published under the authority of the national executive of the Labour Party, of which the right hon. Member for Bristol, South-East (Mr. Benn) is the most prominent member? . . .
The draft said that we will in no circumstances hand over the Falkland Islands to a regime like the Argentine regime that has no respect for human and civil rights. Does that not reflect in a fair way what is the view of the British people as a whole?

The Prime Minister: I believe that it does reflect the view of the British people as a whole that we should not hand over the Falkland Islands to the dictatorship of Argentina. I believe that we have the people united behind us in that resolve. . . .

Mr. Viggers: . . . Will my right hon. Friend draw strength from the fact that those most directly concerned in the Falkland Islands crisis—the men of the Armed Forces and their families—fully understand the issues and the risks involved and are resolute in their will to perform the roles expected of them?

The Prime Minister: We are very fortunate in the men and women who make up the Armed Forces. They are resolute and courageous. We are very proud of them. . . .
Seven weeks ago today the Argentine Foreign Minister summoned the British ambassador in Buenos Aires and informed him that the diplomatic channel was now closed. Later on that same day President Reagan appealed to President Galtieri not to invade the Falkland Islands. That appeal was rejected.
Ever since 2 April Argentina has continued to defy the mandatory resolution of the Security Council. During the past 24 hours the crisis over the Falkland Islands has moved into a new and even more serious phase.
On Monday of this week our ambassador to the United Nations handed to the Secretary-General our proposals for a peaceful settlement of the

dispute. These proposals represented the limit to which the Government believe it was right to go. We made it clear to Senor Perez de Cuellar that we expected the Argentine Government to give us a very rapid response to them.

By yesterday morning we had had a first indication of the Argentine reaction. It was not encouraging. By the evening we received their full response in writing. It was in effect a total rejection of the British proposals. Indeed, in many respects the Argentine reply went back to their position when they rejected Mr. Haig's second set of proposals on 29 April. It retracted virtually all the movement that their representative had shown during the Secretary-General's efforts to find a negotiated settlement. I shall have some more to say about his efforts later.

The implications of the Argentine response are of the utmost gravity. This is why the Government decided to publish immediately the proposals that we had put to the Secretary-General and to give the House the earliest opportunity to consider them. These proposals were placed in the Vote Office earlier today. The Government believe that they represented a truly responsible effort to find a peaceful solution which both preserved the fundamental principles of our position and offered the opportunity to stop further loss of life in the South Atlantic.

We have reached this very serious situation because the Argentines clearly decided at the outset of the negotiations that they would cling to the spoils of invasion and occupation by thwarting at every turn all the attempts that have been made to solve the conflict by peaceful means. Ever since 2 April they have responded to the efforts to find a negotiated solution with obduracy and delay, deception and bad faith.

We have now been negotiating for six weeks. The House will recall the strenuous efforts made over an extended period by Secretary of State Haig. During that period my ministerial colleagues and I considered no fewer than four sets of proposals. Although these presented substantial difficulties, we did our best to help Mr. Haig continue his mission, until Argentine rejection of his last proposals left him no alternative but to abandon his efforts.

The next stage of negotiations was based on proposals originally advanced by President Belaunde of Peru and modified in consultations between him and Mr. Haig. As my right hon. Friend the Secretary of State for Foreign and Commonwealth Affairs informed the House on 7 May, Britain was willing to accept these, the fifth set of proposals, for an interim settlement. They could have led to an almost immediate ceasefire. But again it was Argentina that rejected them.

I shall not take up the time of the House with a detailed description of those earlier proposals, partly because they belong to those who devised them, but, more importantly, because they are no longer on the negotiating table. Britain is not now committed to them.

Since 6 May, when it became clear that the United States-Peruvian proposals were not acceptable to Argentina, the United Nations Secretary-General, Senor Perez de Cuellar, has been conducting negotiations with Britain and Argentina.

Following several rounds of discussions, the United Kingdom representative at the United Nations was summoned to London for consultation last Sunday. On Monday Sir Anthony Parsons returned to New York and presented to the Secretary-General a draft interim agreement between

Britain and Argentina which set out the British position in full. He made it clear that the text represented the furthest that Britain could go in the negotiations. He requested that the draft should be transmitted to the Argentine representative and that he should be asked to convey his Government's response within two days.

Yesterday we received the Argentine Government's reply. It amounted to a rejection of our own proposals, and we have so informed the Secretary-General. This morning we have received proposals from the Secretary-General himself.

It will help the House to understand the present position if I now describe briefly these three sets of proposals.

I deal first with our own proposals. These preserve the fundamental principles which are the basis of the Government's position. Aggression must not be allowed to succeed. International law must be upheld. Sovereignty cannot be changed by invasion.

The liberty of the Falkland Islanders must be restored. For years they have been free to express their own wishes about how they want to be governed. They have had institutions of their own choosing. They have enjoyed self-determination. Why should they lose that freedom and exchange it for dictatorship?

Our proposals are contained in two documents. First, and mainly, there is a draft interim agreement between ourselves and Argentina. Secondly, there is a letter to the Secretary-General which makes it clear that the British Government do not regard the draft interim agreement as covering the dependencies of South Georgia and the South Sandwich Islands.

I deal with the dependencies first. South Georgia and the South Sandwich Islands are geographically distant from the Falkland Islands themselves. They have no settled population. British title to them does not derive from the Falkland Islands but is separate. These territories have been treated as dependencies of the Falkland Islands only for reasons of administrative convenience. That is why they are outside the draft agreement.

The House has before it the draft agreement, and I turn now to its main features. Article 2 provides for the cessation of hostilities and the withdrawal of Argentine and British forces from the islands and their surrounding waters within 14 days. At the end of the withdrawal British ships would be at least 150 nautical miles from the islands. Withdrawal much beyond this would not have been reasonable, because the proximity of the Argentine mainland would have given their forces undue advantage.

Withdrawal of the Argentine forces would be the most immediate and explicit sign that their Government's aggression had failed and that they were being made to give up what they had gained by force. It is the essential beginning of a peaceful settlement and the imperative of resolution 502.

Article 6 sets out the interim arrangements under which the islands would be administered in the period between the cessation of hostilities and the conclusion of negotiations on the long-term future of the islands.

In this interim period there would be a United Nations administrator, appointed by the Secretary-General and acceptable to Britain and the Argentine. He would be the officer administering the government. Under clause 3 of this article he would exercise his powers in conformity with the laws and the practices traditionally obtained in the islands. He would consult the islands' representative institutions—that is the Legislative and Executive Councils through which the islanders were governed until 2

April. There would be an addition to each of the two councils of one representative of the 20 or 30 Argentines normally resident in the islands. Their representatives would be nominated by the administrator.

The clause has been carefully drawn so that the interim administration cannot make changes in the law and customs of the islanders that would prejudge the outcome of the negotiations on a long-term settlement.

This provision would not only go a long way to giving back to the Falklanders the way of life that they have always enjoyed, but would prevent an influx of Argentine settlers in the interim period whose residence would change the nature of society there and radically affect the future of the islands. That would not have been a true interim administration. It would have been an instrument of change.

Clause 3 of this article thus fully safeguards the future of the islands. Nothing in this interim administration would compromise the eventual status of the Falklands or the freedom which they have enjoyed for so long.

Clause 4 would require the administrator to verify the withdrawal of all forces from the islands and to prevent their reintroduction. . . .

We have imported into this agreement article 73 of the United Nations charter, which refers to the paramountcy of the interests of the islanders. During the long-term negotiations we shall closely consult the islanders on their wishes and of course we believe in self-determination. That relates to the long-term negotiations. These articles deal with the interim administration, and I have been trying to make it clear that the interim administration must not have provisions within it which, in effect, pre-empt the outcome of the long-term negotiations.

I return to clause 4 of article 6. We think it likely that the administrator will need to call upon the help of three or four countries other than ourselves and the Argentine to provide him with the necessary equipment and a small but effective force. The purpose of that is that if our troops leave the islands we must have some way of guarding against another Argentine invasion. The safest way under these arrangements would be for the United Nations' administrator to have a small United Nations force at his disposal, of the type I have described.

Articles 8 and 9 are also very important. They deal with negotiations between Britain and Argentina on the long-term future of the islands.

The key sentence is the one which reads:

"These negotiations shall be initiated without prejudice to the rights, claims and positions of the parties and without prejudgment of the outcome."

We should thus be free to take fully into account the wishes of the islanders themselves. And Argentina would not be able to claim that the negotiations had to end with a conclusion that suited her. . . .

I have said that we do not prejudge the outcome. If the islanders wished to go to Argentina, I believe that this country would uphold the wishes of the islanders. After their experience, I doubt very much whether that would be the wish of the islanders. Indeed, I believe that they would recoil from it.

I return to article 9. We have to recognise that the negotiations might be lengthy. That is why article 9 provides that until the final agreement had been reached and implemented the interim agreement will remain in force.

Although this interim agreement does not restore things fully to what they were before the Argentine invasion, it is faithful to the fundamental principles that I outlined earlier. Had the Argentines accepted our proposals, we should have achieved the great prize of preventing further loss of life. It was with that in mind that we were prepared to make practical changes that were reasonable. But we were not prepared to compromise on principle.

I turn now to the Argentine response. This revived once again all the points which had been obstacles in earlier negotiations. The Argentine draft interim agreement applied not only to the Falklands but included South Georgia and the South Sandwich Islands as well. The Argentines demanded that all forces should withdraw, including our forces on South Georgia, and return to their normal bases and areas of operation. This was plainly calculated to put us at an enormous disadvantage.

They required that the interim administration should be the exclusive responsibility of the United Nations, which should take over all executive, legislative, judicial and security functions in the islands. They rejected any role for the islands, democratic institutions. . . .

They envisaged that the interim administration would appoint as advisers equal numbers of British and Argentine residents of the islands, despite their huge disparity.

They required freedom of movement and equality of access with regard to residence, work and property for Argentine nationals on an equal basis with the Falkland Islanders. The junta's clear aim was to flood the islands with its own nationals during the interim period, and thereby change the nature of Falklands society and so prejudice the future of the islands.

With regard to negotiations for a long-term settlement, while pretending not to prejudice the outcome, the junta stipulated that the object was to comply not only with the Charter of the United Nations but with the various resolutions of the General Assembly, from some of which the United Kingdom dissented on the grounds that they favoured Argentine sovereignty.

And if the period provided for the completion of the negotiation expired, the junta demanded that the General Assembly should determine the lines to which final agreement should conform. It was manifestly impossible for Britain to accept such demands. [HON. MEMBERS: "Hear, hear."]

Argentina began the crisis. Argentina has rejected proposal after proposal. One is bound to ask whether the junta has ever intended to seek a peaceful settlement or whether is has sought merely to confuse and prolong the negotiations while remaining in illegal possession of the islands. I believe that if we had a dozen more negotiations the tactics and results would be the same. From the course of these negotiations and Argentina's persistent refusal to accept resolution 502 we are bound to conclude that its objective is procrastination and continuing occupation, leading eventually to sovereignty.

Sir John Biggs-Davison (Epping Forest): . . . Are we to understand that the proposed interim agreement, like some earlier proposals, is no longer on the table. . . .

The Prime Minister: The proposals have been rejected. They are no longer on the table.

As I said earlier, the Secretary-General has this morning put to us and to Argentina an aide-memoire describing those issues where, in his opinion, agreement seems to exist and those on which differences remain.

The first group of issues—those where he believes there is a measure of agreement—would require further clarification, for on some points our interpretation would be different. The aide-memoire states, for example, that Argentina would accept long-term negotiations without prejudgment of the outcome. This important phrase was, however, omitted from the Argentine response to our own proposals and is belied by a succession of statements from Buenos Aires.

Those points where, in the Secretary-General's judgment, differences remain include: first, aspects of the interim administration; secondly, the timetable for completion of negotiations and the related duration of the interim administration; thirdly, aspects of the mutual withdrawal of forces; and, fourthly, the geographic area to be covered. Senor Perez de Cuellar has proposed formulations to cover some of those points.

The Secretary-General, to whose efforts I pay tribute, has a duty to continue to seek agreement. But, as our representative is telling him in New York, his paper differs in certain important respects from our position as presented to him on 17 May and which we then described as the furthest that we could go. Moreover, it differs fundamentally from the present Argentine position as communicated to us yesterday.

It is not a draft agreement, but, as the Secretary-General himself puts it, a number of formulations and suggestions. Some of his suggestions are the very ones which have already been rejected by the Argentine response to our own proposals. Even if they were acceptable to both parties as a basis for negotiation, that negotiation would take many days, if not weeks, to reach either success or failure.

We have been through this often before and each time we have been met with Argentine obduracy and procrastination. Argentina rejected our proposals. It is inconceivable that it would now genuinely accept those of the Secretary-General's ideas which closely resemble our own. . . .

This is the seventh set of proposals that we have considered. We have considered them carefully. Each time we have met with tactics the object of which is procrastination leading to continued occupation of the islands. Because of the record on this matter we thought it best to put up our own specific draft interim agreement in writing so that our position was clear for the world to see and so that it was clear that we were not compromising fundamental principles, but that we were prepared to make some reasonable, practical suggestions if we could secure the prize of no further loss of life. Those proposals were rejected. They are no longer on the table. . . .

What is being considered is what is called an aide-memoire, which is not a draft agreement, but a number of formulations and suggestions. The essence of those formulations and suggestions, where they are clear, is that they are those that have already been rejected by the Argentine response to our proposals. . . .

It seems perfectly clear to me that if the proposals have been rejected it is reasonable to withdraw them. They have been rejected. They are no longer on the table. What we are now considering is an aide-memoire put up by the Secretary-General. It seems right that if one makes an offer and it is rejected, that is the end of the matter, particularly bearing in mind that we are discussing the seventh set of proposals in which I have been involved.

Even if we were prepared to negotiate on the basis of the aide-memoire, we should first wish to see substantive Argentine comments on it, going beyond mere acceptance of it as a basis for negotiation. These are the points that we are making in our reply to the Secretary-General. At the same time, we are reminding him—as my right hon. Friends and I have repeatedly said to the House—that negotiations do not close any military options.

The gravity of the situation will be apparent to the House and the nation. Difficult days lie ahead, but Britain will face them in the conviction that our cause is just and in the knowledge that we have been doing everything reasonable to secure a negotiated settlement.

The principles that we are defending are fundamental to everything that this Parliament and this country stand for. They are the principles of democracy and the rule of law. Argentina invaded the Falkland Islands in violation of the rights of peoples to determine by whom and in what way they are governed. Its aggression was committed against a people who are used to enjoying full human rights and freedom. It was executed by a Government with a notorious record in suspending and violating those same rights.

Britain was a responsibility towards the islanders to restore their democratic way of life. She has a duty to the whole world to show that aggression will not succeed and to uphold the cause of freedom.

Mr. Michael Foot (Ebbw Vale): I believe that it has been to the benefit of the House and the country not only to have this debate, but for the House to have before it in preparation for the debate the document that the Government have presented about the last period of negotiations. . . . First, I refer to the debate of 3 April. I know that there are some people who say that the House reacted in a spirit of impetuosity. I believe that there were good grounds for what was done and that it was the expression by the House of its feeling of moral outrage at what had occurred. . . .

Resolution 502 has been the sheet anchor of the British case throughout the world during the whole period. The passage of that resolution was a matter of major importance. The allegiance of the House to that resolution has been of major importance, and it has been our guide throughout all the difficulties.

I do not believe that it would have been possible for us to proceed without some such resolution to which every Member of the House has given his support in one form or another. It is important that that should be reiterated, because it was primarily on the basis of that resolution that we were able to command support for the British case throughout the world. It was important for us to insist upon it. I do not claim any precedence in the matter, but we on the Opposition Benches attach the greatest importance to upholding the United Nations charter and organisation. The crisis has proved that if we did not have the United Nations charter we would have to invent one, if we did not have the United Nations we would have to invent one. . . .

I believe that in the crisis our allegiance to the United Nations charter and organisation has been of enormous importance and it should be continued. It is the bed rock of our policy.

I know that there may be some doubts on this point, but the view that I have held throughout is that I support the action under resolution 502.

It was necessary for the Government to send the task force. In the debate of 14 April I gave my reasons for that view. I still hold that view about the task force, and it is of absolute importance that it should be under political control. The right hon. Lady has constantly reiterated that that is the case, and, of course, it must always remain the case, especially if there is to be an escalation of the military action over the coming days.

If our troops are sent in to further escalating military action—whatever it may be—I am sure that it is the desire of everyone in the House that the action should be as swift and successful as possible. We said that at the time of the recovery of South Georgia. . . .

As time has elapsed it has become evident that it is incomparably better that the dispute should be settled, if possible, by peaceful means. When I use the expression "incomparably better" I mean exactly that. A long list of factors can be cited to illustrate how much greater would be the advantage if we could have a peaceful settlement.

First, there is the obvious factor, that I am sure is agreed by everybody in the House, of the danger of the loss of life of our young men, the Argentines and the Falkland Islanders themselves. All their lives might be involved. . . . If certain actions were taken, which I do not intend to describe now—all of us can understand them—we could lose some of the backing that we have in some other parts of the world. I am sure that the Government would not ignore such a development. . . .

Other factors are the geography of the matter, its diplomatic history, and many of the other developments that were discussed in the debate last Thursday. They cannot all be pushed aside by impatient Government Back Benchers. . . .

The right hon. Lady and the Government have presented the terms of their document to us. Since I received it earlier today, I have read it, and I believe that it presents a clear and formidable case. Anyone who claims differently would not be reading it intelligently. The Government have stated clearly the principles on which they have acted—the principles of democracy and self-determination—and they have indicated some matters on which they have been prepared, I shall not say to compromise, but at any rate to make proposals which they believed would help towards a settlement.

It is important that that should be underlined, too, particularly in view of the accusation made in some quarters that the Government have been solely intransigent on the matter, as is said in Buenos Aires. . . . If the Government could secure a settlement on the basis that they have proposed, we in the Opposition would be gratified as, I am sure, would the country and the world. In my view, they are fair proposals, and it is right that they should have been presented in those terms. . . .

There are many defects in the Argentine proposals, to some of which the Prime Minister very properly drew attention, because many of them are deeply objectionable to the country. . . . However, I do not believe . . . that the Argentine proposals amount to a complete rejection of all proposals. . . .

The Foreign Secretary suggested that there had been some movement towards the acceptance of two essential requirements that the British Government had rightly insisted on from the very beginning: first, the requirement about withdrawal and, secondly, the requirement of no preconditions about the eventual discussions that were to take place. I do not say that what Argentina proposes on those two items is adequate in any sense, but to say that it is a total rejection on those grounds does not seem to be an accurate account of the state of affairs.

However, the right hon. Lady . . . said that someone has to make an assessment. That is quite right, but it is a question not only of this Government making an assessment, or of an assessment being made in this country; it is also a question of an assessment being made others, and among those who are entitled to make an assessment on how we are to get peace or war in this matter is the Secretary-General of the United Nations. . . .

At the beginning of this week I put it to the right hon. Lady that one of the reasons why I requested this debate and why we should have the documents was not merely that the Government and the House of Commons would demand the right to judge the terms, but, as I said in the letter that I sent to her on Monday, the Secretary-General himself might come forward with proposals at the end to be put to both sides. On Monday I said that I thought that it would be intolerable if, when proposals were coming from the Secretary-General, who knows as much about the intricacies of the negotiations as anyone, we were to go ahead with a great escalation of the conflict without having had the chance to judge what the Secretary-General might propose at the end of the discussions. . . .

The right hon. Lady has said many times that there has been no hold up in the military operations because of the discussions. It is a question not of asking for a great deal of time, but of asking for a proper response to what the Secretary-General has to say. . . .

We said that it would be improper for us to proceed without having the fullest possible discussions with the Secretary-General. That has been repaired in the sense that the Foreign Secretary has had discussions with the Secretary-General.

We have now reached the point at which a breakdown has occurred in the other negotiations, but the Secretary-General believes that the matter is of such supreme importance that, in the words of the right hon. Lady, someone must make an assessment. The Secretary-General has as much right to make an assessment as the Prime Minister or anybody else. The Secretary-General may be listened to in many parts of the world on this subject, and we shall need the support of many countries. I believe that it was a great mistake for the right hon. Lady to say—although I do not suppose it will govern her conduct in future negotiations—that all the proposals that she and her Government had made in the past were now withdrawn . . . because we want the Secretary-General to succeed. We want him to be supported. We want to ensure that the Government will give every proper response to the Secretary-General. . . .

The Prime Minister: The right hon. Member for Ebbw Vale (Mr. Foot) cannot have heard what I said. The Secretary-General has put forward an aide-memoire. I described what we were saying to him. I said that what we were saying to him could not foreclose military options any more than it has in the past. There is his aide-memoire. I do not understand the right hon. Gentleman's point.

Mr. Foot: If the right hon. Lady is now telling us that her response to the Secretary-General is one which she is prepared to follow further at the

United Nations, I am in favour of it. . . . I hope that the right hon. Lady and her Government at such a delicate moment as this, when the command of support throughout the world is of paramount importance, will build on the answer the right hon. Lady has just given, that they will build on the response they have already made about the Secretary-General and that they will carry it much further. I hope that, before they take any further action, they will make a much bigger response. I know that the Government have tried on previous occasions to brush aside the Secretary-General, but they have had to come back to him in the end.

The proper course for both the right hon. Lady and the Foreign Secretary is, either tonight or tomorrow, to go to New York and to discuss the matter. . . . If the right hon. Lady wishes to command support in this situation, she must command support through the United Nations. That means sustaining the Secretary-General in the proposition that he has put before the British Government today.

Mr. David Owen (Plymouth, Devonport): The House has listened to a very grave speech from the Prime Minister. I do not believe that anyone who listened to it can be in any doubt that we have witnessed a serious attempt to seek a negotiated settlement. That should be said and heard in the rest of the world.

I am pleased that the Leader of the Official Opposition was prepared to recognise that the negotiating position adopted by the Government and now before the House and the world is a fair and reasonable one. It ought to be said quite clearly that we support that negotiating position. We recognise that many of us as individuals have had to accept a fair degree of compromise in those proposals. They are not the ideal proposals which each and every one of us in the House would wish to accept.

It is also right that this debate should be heard in the rest of the world. If the Government are advised by the chiefs of staff that the task force needs to take further measures to protect itself or further to tighten the military pressure around the invaders on the Falkland Islands, it is reasonable for them to be given the political authorisation to do so. No one is under any illusion that that would be a grave and dangerous step, and nobody wishes to see any loss of life. We would be fools, however, if we thought that we could take such a step without the real possibility of loss of life, Therefore, this is a very sombre moment, and it should be faced in a sombre and steady mood. . . .

The Secretary-General will face a difficult task. The history of the negotiations does not give ground for optimism. If the Secretary-General is ready to pursue his aide-memoire and to try to reach a negotiated position, we ought to be ready to listen. . . .

I hope that when our friends read the negotiating document and the interim proposals, they will recognise the necessity to continue with economic sanctions. . . .

Furthermore, I hope that the United States is prepared to look at its economic sanctions and to take further economic sanctions. . . .

Surely the aim and object is not unconditional surrender. History shows that by holding out for unconditional surrender one loses unnecessary lives. Unconditional surrender is rarely the right position for a strong democratic country to adopt.

Having put down these proposals, which are essentially proposals for a ceasefire, withdrawal and an honourable negotiation, Britain should be strong enough and clear enough in the justice of its cause to keep those propositions on the table. . . .

It is a ceasefire and a phased withdrawal. It is a proposal for an interim administration. . . .

Mr. J. Enoch Powell (Down, South): Is the right hon. Gentleman saying that if we continue with military action, whatever the outcome may be, we should go back to the position of withdrawing our forces, a phased withdrawal of both sides and someone else's administration?

Dr. Owen: The right hon. Gentleman's perception is remarkable: that is exactly what I am saying . . .

The reality of life is that most of us are prepared to negotiate and to have a measure of compromise. . . .

I urge the Prime Minister to look carefully at this issue because it is on this issue that she could lose opinion not just in the House and in the country but in the rest of the world. There must be a readiness to continue the negotiating process.

These proposals are different from the Peruvian proposals. . . . They contained elements that were unpalatable to the British and the Argentines. In the document the right hon. Lady said that she was prepared to accept the final Peruvian argument, but, the Argentines having rejected it, she withdrew that offer. That is different from withdrawing the proposals that have been put forward by the British Government. . . .

The Prime Minister: . . . We gave a full written interim agreement. It was put to the Argentines with two days to reply. They knew what they were doing when they replied within that time limit: they were rejecting the proposals. If we were to enter into negotiations again, they would probably be totally different because they would be on a different basis.

Dr. Owen: . . . If in the next few days and weeks, as a result of economic and military pressures, the Argentines accept the document lock, stock and barrel, the Prime Minister should recognise that that is an honourable offer on which it is honourable to ask our Forces and Service men to fight. The right hon. Lady should not hold out for a proposition that is as yet unheard of or for unconditional surrender. . . .

[If] military action is totally successful—let us hope that that is possible, although most of us are more objective than that—what would we face? Are we prepared to face a situation in which we have a military garrison in the Falkland Islands for the next 10 or 20 years which is within range of Argentine land-based aircraft? . . . We know that at the end of the day there must be negotiations. It must be said now before lives are lost that this country is prepared to negotiate . . . an honourable ceasefire, withdrawal and negotiations can happen on that basis. If the Argentines lose the lives of their soldiers in order to resist this fair document, the rest of the world will judge them hard. If the rest of the world has any doubts as to what we are fighting for, we shall jeopardise our position. . . .

Mr. Julian Amery (Brighton, Pavilion) . . . The paper that we have before us shows that in a determined and laudable effort to avoid bloodshed the Government were prepared to make substantial concessions from original objectives. They would not necessarily have been inconsistent with the original objectives that we had in mind, but they might have put the fulfilment of those objectives at risk. Many Conservative Members would have found them hard to accept. I do not know how many that applies to, but it would certainly apply to me. . . .

We cannot ask our forces to go into battle . . . to hand over the islands when repossessed to a United Nations trusteeship under the kind of interim administration that we were previously discussing.

We are taking back our own property. We shall be liberating our own people. If we accomplish that, there will not be much to negotiate about, except the surrender of the adversary forces and their repatriation under honourable terms to Argentina. . . .

The Government have shown admirable determination in terminating . . . the negotiating process at the United Nations. Had they made any further concessions, the authority and the standing of Britain in the world would have been seriously undermined. So would the credibility of the Government at home. All policies, economic and social, however sound they may be, are ineffective if the Government's credibility is undermined. . . .

Since 3 April there has been a new spirit abroad in Britain. . . . Without national self-confidence there can be no economic, social or moral revival. . . .

What is at stake in the Falkland Islands crisis transcends the immediate issues of the Falkland Islanders and our own stake in the South Atlantic. The crisis is a catalyst of the basic values of our society. . . .

The editors know that the public are getting what they want. What is happening is not jingoism or war hysteria. It is the expression of the deep feeling of a proud and ancient nation and of the most mature democracy in the world. . . .

Irrespective of party allegiances or political opinions, I hope that both sides of the House will act together to ensure that we prevail.

Mr. Tony Benn (Bristol, South-East): . . . It is apparent that . . . an invasion is imminent, and some hon. Members have already called for it. A tragedy is unfolding, the magnitude of which is not apparent from the speeches that have been made. . . .

One of the arguments given for the Government's reaction to the Argentine invasion of the Falkland Islands was that it took place during a period of negotiation between the British and Argentine Governments. I put it to the Prime Minister that if the interim agreement contained in the document had been made available to Argentina by this Government, or any Government in the past 20 years, the invasion would not have occurred.

Therefore, the task force has not played any part, because . . . the proposals involve the abandonment of the substance of sovereignty, which is the right to have troops on one's territory and to control its administration. By publishing this document . . . the Government have published their readiness to abandon, in substance, British sovereignty over the islands. . . .

What effort did the Government make to bring pressure to bear on the Argentine Government through the world bankers? Had they refused to reschedule the debts, they could have brought the Argentine Government to their knees. . . . If the Argentine Government had not had their debts rescheduled we might have seen something approaching the collapse of the world banking system as a result of the financial losses. To rational people it appears that the Prime Minister was prepared to protect the bankers and to send the soldiers in instead. . . .

The Government's document states that Argentina has been playing for time. Of course it has. But who put the clock in its armoury? The task force gave it the clock as a weapon. It is impossible to leave the task force hanging about. Therefore, once the task force was despatched, time was given to Buenos Aires. . . .

The very presence of the task force gave Argentina the right to dictate an ultimatum to us. Its ultimatum was fight, or withdraw. The Government have decided to fight. When they fight, world support will disappear. . . .

Next, the Government conceded that if there were a ceasefire, economic sanctions would be abandoned at once. Thus the junta—which is properly denounced as representing a denial of human rights—would immediately be supported again. As soon as the ceasefire began, the junta would get back its money and trade. . . .

The Government also conceded that a United Nations' administrator would go to the Falkland Islands. . . .

The essence of sovereignty is administration, but that was abandoned. Paramountcy was also abandoned. With the Government insisting on an indefinite agreement, there was no guarantee in the interim agreement offer . . . that British troops or a British administration would ever return to the Falkland Islands. . . .

If such an offer had been made at any time over the past 20 years there would have been no invasion of the Falkland Islands. . . .

The task force was not needed. That offer could have been made at any time. With the whole British case conceded, what is the case for war? Why should people die for a pre-arranged abandonment of the paramountcy of the interests of the islanders to a United Nations administration? . . .

[If] we land troops they will be attacked, and Argentina must have some strategy for attacking our ships. When the ships, if any, are sunk—and Gods knows none of us wants to contemplate such a possibility—Tory Members will be demanding that we bomb the mainland. Some have already said it. Are we to bomb the mainland so that in the end we can give the Falklands to the United Nations and take our troops out? . . .

We should go for an immediate and unconditional ceasefire. We should hand over to the United Nations the Falkland Islands administration in exactly the same way as the Government have conceded in the document. Far from abandoning sanctions at the moment when we unilaterally hand over responsibility for the administration to the United Nations, which the Government contemplate, we should step up the sanctions against Argentina. Financial and economic sanctions, combined with the transfer of the islands to a UN responsibility, will almost certainly bring Galtieri down. . . . Finally, we should bring the Fleet home. . . .

Sir Paul Bryan (Howden): . . . It is fortunate that the Government have had seven weeks to prepare the nation and world opinion for this desperately serious decision. . . . Immediately after the Argentine invasion, the Prime Minister announced that our intention was to repossess the islands, preferably by diplomacy, otherwise by force, and to restore liberty to the islanders. . . .

No one can doubt that the Government have tried very hard to reach a peaceful solution. . . .

I am sure that the Government have seriously considered the problem of how, in the face of mounting loss of life, we can continue to hold the confidence of our people and of world opinion.

The troops that we have sent to the Falkland Islands—marines, parachute battalions, SAS and Ghurkas—are probably the finest and best trained in the world. . . .

So admirable has been the performance of our forces during the past few years, be it in the Iranian embassy, Northern Ireland or South Georgia, that there is a positive danger of the public expecting too much—of expecting an easy ride. But even with the finest troops, losses must mount as the fighting spreads. . . .

Despite the loss of two major warships, the fighting so far can be no more than a preliminary skirmish with neither side committing its main forces. . . .

The terms that we offered were . . . just about right as the price for a peaceful solution at that time and in those circumstances, but they may well seem to be too generous after we have had to suffer the loss of hundreds of lives and after we are in possession of the islands, or a major part of them. That shows the importance of speed in our military action. The more extensive our occupation of the Falkland Islands by the time the next serious peace offer is made, the stronger will be our negotiating position. . . .

Mr. Ken Weetch (Ipswich): . . . Times change, but in essence the aggression that we have seen by the Argentines is the same species of aggression as we saw in Britain in the 1930s. . . .

As events unfolded the detail was complicated but the profile remained simple. The behaviour of Argentina was condemned in the United Nations resolution 502, but the United Nations' call for withdrawal proved to no avail. Far from it: the Argentine response was to reinforce both troops and equipment. It was evident all along that Argentina did not have the slightest intention of negotiating in any meaningful way—quite the reverse. . . .

I believe that the sending of the task force was right. I put it more strongly than that. Not to have done so would have been an act of the most craven appeasement. If anyone believes that the Argentine military dictatorship would have negotiated without such a task force being sent, he will believe anything. . . .

The United States described itself as an honest broker. Bismarck once said at the Congress of Berlin that he was an honest broker, but that all honest brokers act for a large commission. In political terms, that is what has happened. Given the facts of the dispute, an evenhanded approach from the United States was never justified. If America had given a firm commitment and come in right from the start on the side of Britain—a democracy and a North Atlantic Treaty ally—the dispute would never have reached this stage.

I was not disappointed with the response from Europe, because I never expected anything better. . . . In this dispute our European partners have never lifted their eyes above the cash register. . . .

Sir John Eden (Bournemouth, West): . . . But just as the Argentine act of invasion has altered the circumstances from those which existed before that event, so would repossession of our own territory by our own forces change the situation dramatically from what it is today. . . . First, we can accept the invasion and hand over our territory and our people to Argentina. . . .

The second course would be to continue to negotiate while agreeing to withdraw our task force, to encourage the Argentines to leave and to accept a formula for an interim regime. . . . That appears to be a course that commends itself to some Opposition Members. . . .

The third choice is to increase our efforts to repossess the islands by further military means. . . . Churchmen and others who understandably say that they are practising Christians . . . regard the use of force as an immoral act. . . .

If we were to stand back and do nothing, can anyone doubt the consequences? It seems clear to me that the Argentines have ambitions not just over the Falkland Islands and the dependencies. . . .

Inevitably, in the employment of force, there is the risk of casualty. It is right, on what has been described as a solemn occasion, for hon. Members to recognise that this is not a course that is being embarked upon lightly by Her Majesty's Government. . . .

Britain has the duty to ensure that aggression shall not succeed and that we should uphold the cause of freedom. . . .

Mr. James Callaghan (Cardiff, South-East): . . . I do not see how anyone could have reached a conclusion other than that the Government *[have]* negotiated in good faith and made a number of concessions that were not to have been expected when we set out on this enterprise. . . .

I suggest that the Prime Minister should do what is rarely, but sometimes, done by Heads of Government—send this document to all Heads of Government or Heads of State with a covering note, if she has not already done so, inviting them to study it and asking them what more could have been done by Britain consonant with honour and consonant with accepting and carrying out resolution 502 of the United Nations. I have no doubt that the Government have done their job properly and that they should be supported in the efforts that they have made to secure a negotiated settlement. . . .

I do not think that we could sustain a position in which it was allowed to be thought that, once proposals had been put forward and then withdrawn, we would say, in the event that the Argentines later indicated that they were ready to consider them or similar proposals put forward by the United Nations Secretary-General, "No. They are wiped off the sheet.". . .

We must in the end make some . . . arrangements that will ensure the permanent security of the Falkland Islanders. . . .

We must in the end secure correct relations, if no better, with the Argentine for the future of the Falklands. It is hard to say that at the beginning of what may be a battle. . . .

All that we can do at this stage is to wish our men god-speed. Only the Government have the information and advice to decide whether to continue the blockade, whether there should be a blockade plus landings, or whether there should be some form of multi-pronged invasion. . . . I do not envy their decisions. Only the commander on the spot can decide the time to launch any further acceleration. . . . The Opposition have a duty to give a lead. They also have a duty to make a critical appraisal of what the Government are doing. Some Conservative Members catcall during speeches by my right hon. Friend the Member for Ebbw Vale (Mr. Foot), but they do him less than justice. He has a responsibility. It would be beneath the integrity of the House if he did not carry it out by putting probing and searching points to the Prime Minister. . . .

My right hon. Friend the Member for Bristol, South-East (Mr. Benn) bears some resemblance to the right hon. Member for Down, South (Mr. Powell) in that they both attack a proposition with devastating and impeccable logic, but then proceed to utterly false, eccentric and wrong conclusions. . . . He failed to comment on whether he thought that the continuance of negotiations would lead to the Argentine dropping its claim to the South Georgia and South Sandwich dependencies.

He did not say whether he thought that that was a proper Argentine claim. He did not say whether he thought that it would be proper to concede the Argentine claim that the islanders should be excluded from the United Nations administration. . . . Nor did he comment on the Argentine demand for free access for Argentine nationals to settle on the islands to influence any ballot that may be conducted. . . . This is yet another example of what he has consistently done since the general election. . . . He has chosen to challenge the leadership of the party, whoever it may be, to set out his own position. . . . I strongly regret that my right hon. Friend the Member for Bristol, South-East has put the party in that position again. . . .

Sir Frederic Bennett (Torbay): . . . In the Falklands dispute there has already been an appalling breach of faith by Argentina. . . . When the Security Council issued the mandatory resolution 502 which Argentina refused to follow, it was already in direct breach of faith of international undertakings for the third time in recent years.

If we are successful in accomplishing our aims, we must ensure that the incident does not repeat itself in weeks, months or possibly years. . . .

I do not apologise for repeating that because the record shows that Argentine dictators come and go. There are some even more unpleasant characters in the wings. . . .

Why has there been some erosion of the high level of support that we enjoyed in those first days? Paradoxically, the answer is that my right hon. Friends and, in particular, the Prime Minister, have been so endlessly patient and persevering in trying to achieve a peaceful solution. Because the dispute has gone on for so long, human nature being what it is—I recall the old phrase about a nine days' wonder—people now talk about our invading the Falklands.

Some hon. Members have said that today. The fact that it was the Argentines who invaded the Falklands on 2 April is beginning to become clouded to some extent by that old maxim on which many criminals rely—possession is nine points of the law. The longer the dispute goes on, the more it will appear when it is resolved that we, as some hon. Members have said today, were doing the invading. . . .

Even though I, like anyone else, am appalled by the thought of the casualties that might occur through the pursuance of our policies, I am certain that if we go back to the discredited concept that an act of unprovoked aggression can be allowed to succeed we shall open Pandora's box of casualties in the future in comparison with which our casualties in the Falkland Islands will appear to be an infinitesimal minority.

Mr. Andrew Faulds (Warley, East): . . . For an ex-imperial power to embark on a course of negotiations by pounding shot and shell into countries of the Third world is not an advisable policy. That is, tragically, how we have reacted to the totally illegal Argentine invasion of the Falklands. We intend, apparently with the near unanimous agreement of the House of Commons, to pursue that course by launching an assault on the islands and possibly by attacking the South American mainland. I urge my colleagues to see the absolute lunacy and short-sightedness of such misjudged actions. . . .

Do we really think it worth while damaging Britain's interests, Britain's standing in the world and Britain's enormous and extensive trading interests throughout the world to maintain an imperial outpost in the stormy wastes of the South Atlantic? . . .

We should frankly admit that for 20 years we have been trying to withdraw from this outpost of empire, if we could decently cede sovereignty. Every British ambassador over that period will confirm that view.

Mr. James Callaghan: I completely deny that myth. . . . Certainly the Administration with which I was connected between 1974 and 1979 never made any such proposals or had any such intention. We tried to establish relations between the Falklanders and the Argentines that would recognise the Argentine's special interests. The intention certainly was never to hand over the islands to the Argentines. Such a proposal was never made, nor was it thought of as far as I am concerned.

Mr. Faulds: Of course I accept my right hon. Friend's words because I have the greatest regard for him. My own experience—and I have discussed the issue with a particular ambassador of ours and checked with another—is that the ceding of sovereignty was part of the exercise. . . .

Why should we be so terribly sensitive about our friends the Falklanders, who have Scottish and Welsh blood, when in every geographic and historic circumstance they should be thought of as being much more dependent on their relations with Argentina than on their very distant relations with the British Isles? . . .

Stirred by all that type of rubbish *[in the newspapers]*, Britain goes to war over the Falklands. And for what? For the retention of an outcrop of rocks in the waters of the South Atlantic? For a colonial vestige and perhaps for the reinstitution of a company's right to run the islands? . . .

Are we really intent on launching an assault on the islands? It will be a bloody business because by now the Argentines must have the best part of 10,000 troops on those islands. They have been fortifying them defensively with a whole range of armaments, and they may not prove to be such cowards as our expectations make them out. . . .

I beg my colleagues on both sides of the House to see the danger and damage that the present policy will do to Great Britain if we seek a military solution. We have to come eventually to a negotiated resolution of this little problem. . . . we have to give the Argentines room to get out from under their original offence. . . . We must find a way of avoiding a resolution by military means of this completely unnecessary war. . . .

Mr. Neil Thorne (Ilford, South): . . . I should like to pay tribute to the support that we have received from our Commonwealth friends. Canada, Australia, New Zealand and other Commonwealth members have rallied to our support and given us every possible encouragement in trying to uphold international law and order. I was also pleased to see that our European allies were giving us backing, although I am disappointed that they have decided to extend economic sanctions only for a further seven days. . . .

One of the greatest problems facing the task force is the adverse weather conditions in the South Atlantic and the possible effect on both moral and equipment. . . . I hope that it will soon be possible to land some of our men and equipment on one of the main Falkland Islands. That would relieve a lot of the pressure on the ships maintaining the blockade and would give us additional support for air power. . . . If we need facilities such as hospitals closer to the Falkland Islands than the Ascension Islands, I see nothing wrong in purchasing facilities in Chile. The Government do not have to agree with what the Chilean Government stand for, any more than they should agree with what the Argentine Government stand for. . . .

Much criticism has been mounted in the recent past of the news coverage. . . . We have the good fortune to have a free press, and the way in which it has presented its case to the public has generally been extremely fair and reasonable. The way in which it has spoken to its readers has not been unusual. It knows its readers a good deal better than some hon. Members seem to know them, and it should be allowed to express itself in its own way. I deplore any denunciation of the popular press for what it is doing in support of the Falkland Islanders at this time. . . .

The way that the BBC has conducted its broadcasts recently has been much more balanced. . . . Criticism has been justified to some considerable extent, but I think that the matter has been put right and that we now have a good balance. My view is that the press has done and is continuing to do a good job on this issue.

Mr. Jack Ashley (Stoke-on-Trent, South): . . . The public are becoming quite hysterical about the present situation, and so are some hon. Members. In this respect, we are no different from the people of Argentina. . . .

We are supposed to be defending the islanders' interests and proving to the world that aggression does not pay. These objectives conveniently provoke the primitive reaction that Britain should teach the "Argies" a lesson. . . .

The basic question is whether British interests are being served or damaged by invading the Falklands now that negotiations have broken down. Contrary to the views of most Members of Parliament, and contrary to the views of most people outside, I believe that our interests in Britain will be gravely damaged if we go ahead with the invasion of the Falklands. . . .

If ever there were a classic case of the tail wagging the dog, this is it. Unfortunately, we have had a vociferous group of Members of Parliament who have elevated that tail into a holy shrine and a matter of golden principle. Never did any nation lose its sense of proportion so foolishly and never did it dissipate its armed forces and the good will of its friends so wantonly.

Britain at war in defence of its own people against armed aggression from any quarter would win the admiration of the world, but Britain at war for islands that it has neglected and sought to abandon for two decades is an absurdity.

If we win the battle for the repossession of the Falklands it will be the beginning of a long war with Argentina in particular and Latin America in general. The islands and the islanders—assuming that any of them are left alive after the battle—would be isolated from all supplies from the mainland and vulnerable to continuous harassment and missile attack from Argentina. . . .

The Government are right to resist aggression, but let them do it by maintaining the blockade. Let them do it by intensifying economic sanctions and negotiating now what must be negotiated eventually. . . .

Mr. David Atkinson (Bournemouth, East): . . . The decision to liberate the Falkland Islands now will receive the unreserved and wholehearted support of the vast majority of my constituents and of the British people.

It goes without saying that no one wants to see further bloodshed. Already we have seen hundreds of British and Argentine lives lost, both on land and at sea, for which the junta must be held wholly responsible. I have no doubt that the foundations have long been laid by those Forces of ours who have already been on the Falkland Islands in the past few weeks for the most efficient occupation with the minimum of casualties on both sides. . . .

There will be faint hearts and cold feet at home and abroad as we go through with the liberation of the islands. Never let us cease to remind ourselves or the world that our action now is in response to Argentina's absolute and blind refusal to comply with United Nations resolution 502 and that we are acting in self-defence, totally compatible with United Nations article 51. . . .

We shall be told that we are putting Britain's long-term interests in South America and elsewhere in the world at risk. . . . That must be a consideration, but let us also consider why and how we came to establish our world interests and presence in the first place. . . .

Many countries choose to associate and to trade with us still because of other qualities for which we are peculiarly known as a nation—qualities which we are displaying and principles which we are now defending. . . .

Nothing in history is directly comparable, but Britain's long-term interests will be far better served by standing up for ourselves and by liberating those islands now than by pussy footing, delaying and relying instead on economic sanctions and eternal negotiations. . . .

But for the sovereignty issue, industry today would have been exploring and developing the substantial hydrocarbon accumulations that are known to exist, despite the depth and hostility of the waters. We should be foolish now to ignore, abandon or concede that long-term source of oil and gas. For that we shall require Argentine co-operation. That will be a factor in any future negotiations. . . . He who hesitates is lost. He who dares, wins.

Mr. Russell Johnston (Inverness): . . . The Government . . . have unquestionably been prepared to make considerable concessions to achieve a peaceful settlement. . . .

There is no doubt that the sending of the task force was supported by all parties in the House. It was seen as a necessary backing without which, given the nature of the Argentine Government and the fact of their invasion during negotiations, it was unlikely that a peaceful solution would be achieved. . . .

If the Falkland Islands are recaptured by force, we almost certainly commit ourselves to defending them for many years. I do not think that that is necessarily wrong; nor do I say that I do not want to defend them. However, we must appreciate clearly what our action means and what burden it will lay upon us. . . .

If there is a chance of peace, it must be taken unhesitatingly. What do we lose by keeping our proposals on the table? . . . What do we lose by saying clearly that if the Argentines, under pressure, come back with an acceptance of the Peruvian proposals, we would be prepared to reactivate them? We lose nothing. We could gain lives and a stable outcome even at this late hour. . . .

I sense a feeling in the House that a landing is inevitable. It that is to be, the calculation and the responsibility lie with the Government. Our thoughts and prayers will be with our forces who, in the bitter cold of the South Atlantic, will have the job of correcting political misjudgments—some with their lives.

Mr. Ivan Lawrence (Burton): . . . There are only three options at this hour. We could turn, run and quit. . . . We could keep on talking, or we could liberate—that is the word—the islands. From the first moment that the Argentine tyrant invaded the Falkland Islands seven weeks ago . . . we had an inherent right, under article 51 of the United Nations charter, to go in to end the occupation by military means. . . .

It became increasingly obvious as week followed week that the Argentines wanted the sovereignty of the islands and nothing but that sovereignty. . . .

However, we have made no fewer than seven attempts to achieve a negotiated settlement. No responsible country in the world could have done more. It is almost astonishing to relate that there are still more demands for ever increasing delays from the Leader of the Opposition and other right hon. and hon. Members. How many more hours, days, weeks and months must we delay. . . .

It is all very well for perpetual peacemongers to get redder and redder in the face demanding that there should be no military action. Perhaps they do not care whether we betray the Falkland Islanders, the rule of international law, freedom and democracy or whether we betray the memories of those who have unfortunately already died. How long do they want to keep our troops there as sitting targets that are more vulnerable to attack as the days go by? If HMS "Invincible" and HMS "Hermes" are sunk the day after tomorrow and hundreds of British lives are lost, will they still say "Let's talk"? If they will not say that after the ships have been sunk, why say it now? . . .

For the sake of those ships and the men that we have sent into battle, if for no other reason, we can no longer accept delay. . . .

Mr. Geoffrey Robinson (Coventry, North-West): . . . *[The document]* does the country and the Government a great service. . . . It is clear that the Government have shown seriousness of intent and sincerity of purpose in the pursuit of a peaceful settlement. . . .

Where I think that the Prime Minister and the Government have unnecessarily wrong-footed themselves is in the way in which they have abruptly withdrawn the proposals. Having tabled them as a basis for a peaceful settlement, they must have believed that it was an acceptable and honourable settlement—otherwise it would not have been tabled—and one to which they would expect the Falkland Islanders to subscribe, as they did themselves. However, they then withdrew the proposals almost before the Argentines had rejected them. . . .

[Secondly,] that action will tend to foreclose an eventual option if, and every one of us hopes that it will not happen, there is no speedy and successful military solution. . . .

[Thirdly, if] we say that these proposals were all right for a peaceful settlement but not for a military one, it makes the proposals an unworthy settlement for which to fight. . . .

This set of proposals is the only plain, logical and coherent solution for the islands. We must not let the idea of victory or nothing, or that it is a choice between a military victory and a political sell out, get abroad. We must foster the idea that it is not ignoble to fight for a United Nations trusteeship of the Falklands. It is the only sensible and logical conclusion for a long-standing problem in a tiny but troubled part of the world. . . . The fact is that the Government have come forward with a set of proposals that can provide the long-term political solution that we all wish to see. Let us hope that it can still be obtained at this late hour.

Mr. David Crouch (Canterbury): . . . Listening to the Prime Minister this afternoon and reading the document, we realised for the first time how desperately hard the Government have tried over the past seven weeks to obtain a peaceful solution by diplomatic means. . . .

The latest response from the junta has been all too clear and stark. It must know that it and we are on the brink of war, but it seems to be prepared to turn its back on this last chance for peace. . . .

I said *[previously]* that the sending of the task force was right as the strength behind the diplomatic action. I also supported the resolve to use the task force if a peaceful solution could not be found. . . .

I recognised that if the negotiations failed we would have no option but to switch the emphasis to the military solution. I have always had full confidence in the task force. It has my full and loyal support. I have no doubt about its professionalism, courage, modern training and equipment. We wish it god-speed.

I do not believe that I was wrong to speak out for a peaceful solution and to try to avoid the tragedy of war. . . .

I saw it as my duty to speak out. . . . Perhaps it was a dissident voice, but I spoke because I believed that I was right and that I should be heard. That is not disloyalty. It is what we are prepared to fight for today. It is democracy.

Mr. Stuart Holland (Vauxhall): . . . We may all find in an invasion that we face the same disaster as occurred to the "Prince of Wales" and the "Repulse" through superior Japanese air power during the Second World

War. The whole venture of an invasion in these terms may be the most massive misadventure, not only for our troops but for the country. . . . If ever a country was ripe for effective application of sanctions, it is Argentina. It has $32 billion worth of debt. Argentina's total foreign exchange earnings do not cover its debt interest to the international community. We have seen the Bank of England rolling over Argentine debt, and the Government have imposed no sanctions or penalty on British-based merchant banks which have removed to Switzerland to carry on their business during the war. What conclusion can we draw from this? That there is a truce for profits but not for our troops. . . .

So why have our Government not applied sanctions? One is regrettably forced to the conclusion that they could not face the possible collapse of certain banks in the Northern hemisphere if Argentina, with her scale of loans, defaulted. . . . For a Prime Minister who advises us that we need to spend £15,000 million a year on defence because of the Soviet threat in terms of world expansion, she has achieved the almost unparalleled feat of bringing Cuba and Argentina into each other's arms with the sponsorship of the Soviet Union. . . . One thing should be made clear. British occupation of the Falkland Islands was in no sense imperialist. It was not a matter of one State imposing its will over another foreign State. It is Argentina's invasion of the Falkland Islands, where it did not have people settled, which is imperialist. But the moral basis for opposing such action is undermined by precisely the manner in which the Government are pursuing their militarist policies. . . .

Safeguards for the islanders have been neglected and invasion is a risk. With modern missile technology, an invasion now will not be in the style of the raid on Entebbe, not least because we lack the element of surprise. It may be a minor Gallipoli. If so, it will be a disaster not only for those involved but for this country.

Sir Bernard Braine (Essex, South-East): . . . I have stated repeatedly that it has been right for the Government to be patient and to give the Argentine Government a way out, if they were willing to take it. . . . It is not unfair to comment that if more attention had been paid to the Falkland Islands and their inhabitants and if Ministers had been called more frequently to account for their ambivalent attitude over the years, we would not be in this dangerous situation now. . . . The Argentines were given the impression that we did not really care about the islands and that we were not prepared to face any dramatic putsch on their part. If we had paid attention to this matter, as some of us urged repeatedly in the House, we would not now be in this dangerous and worrying situation. . . .

It is ironic in the extreme that the one dependency that . . . *[some say]* should be denied self-determination is one where the population is wholly British, where there is no ethnic minority, no split allegiance and no desire for independence. . . .

But this nation will never forgive a Government who, having expelled the invader from our territory, then submits to pressures which, in the end, give Argentina what it wants. . . . As has been said, in the long term there is plenty of room for a mutually advantageous and functional partnership but it will have to be with a different kind of Argentine. . . . What can one say, however, in defence of those who have been advocating what is effectively a sell-out, either without military action or after it, when it is obvious that we are dealing with a Government who have almost the worst human rights record in the world? . . .

It would be ironic if we were to embark on a course which led the Falkland Islanders to leave and the islands being handed over at some time or other and under some formula or other to Argentina. . . . We would be guilty of a base betrayal and would be regarded both in Britain and throughout the civilised world with contempt, and deservedly so. . . .

Mr. Alfred Dubs (Battersea, South): . . . We have every right to recover the islands—by force if necessary—and to throw the Argentines out. The question is whether we ought to exercise that right. . . .

Are the principles at stake sufficiently important and clear-cut to justify the possible substantial loss of life that would be entailed in the recovery of the islands by force? If our use of force is successful—as I assume it will be—will there be a sufficiently stable and long-term outcome to have made the whole enterprise worth while, bearing in mind the possible loss of life? If the answer to either question is "No"—I suggest that it is—we must ask ourselves whether it is right to recover the islands by force. There would be nothing wrong in our deciding that, having examined the issues at stake, the possible loss of life can not be justified. . . . The Falkland Islands are not and never will be a viable State . . . the only option is for the islands to have closer ties with the South American mainland.

Many of us agree that there is an extremely unpleasant Fascist regime in Argentina. However, it seems an inescapable conclusion that any alternative Government in Argentina—democratic, Socialist, or a combination of the two—would make a territorial claim to the Falkland Islands. I trust that such a Government would not use force to fortify that claim. . . .

We have a responsibility to the islanders to ensure that they are not forced to live under a Fascist regime. Surely, that is different from saying that we have sovereignty over the islands and that it must be re-established by military means. We could, even at this late stage, hand over the islands to the United Nations Trusteeship Council and allow it to exercise administration over the islands, provided that the islanders were involved in their internal self-government under the auspices of the United Nations. . . .

Mr. Ian Lloyd (Havant and Waterloo): . . . If we are right and our consciences are clear, as I believe they are, if the principles of international law have been challenged and gravely breached, as I believe they have, if aggression has taken place, as it has, and if the United Nations has been gravely flouted, as it has, we are entitled to call on the support of the forces of the free world, no less, whenever these principles are attacked on whatever occasion and however embarrassing the geographical circumstances may be. Geography does not determine right and wrong, and it should not be allowed to invalidate alliances. . . .

The Government have leant over backwards. Their generosity has been exceptional. If we are not able to achieve a settlement on that basis, everything that follows will follow, without our feeling that there is a retreat or that we have to requalify and take a different view. . . . When I say that we should carry international opinion with us, I must ask whether it is the opinion of free men whose judgment I value and respect, or the opinion of those for whose judgment I have no respect.

It is sometimes argued that in both the domestic and international spheres we should occupy the middle ground. There is no middle ground in the South Atlantic. There is only a deep, cold and watery grave. Our forces will occupy the high ground. In this Chamber we should be occupying the high ground of opinion, judgment, morale and will, and be seen to be so doing.

Mr. Tam Dalyell (West Lothian): . . . The Government must distinguish between what they want to do and their capacity to do it. Do they have the means to invade the Falkland Islands? An hon. Member's duty is to warn, to warn of loss of lives and—I take no joy whatsoever in saying this—to warn of a possible defeat of the first magnitude. . . . *[I have already said]* that sending the expedition was the most unwise decision since the Duke of Buckingham left for La Rochelle in 1627. . . .

Who said that the military solution would not provide the answer? It was not a member of the Labour Party or one of the dissidents; it was Al Haig's considered judgment. We may be faced with, God help us, something of the order of the 1905 Russo-Japanese war in which we are in the role of the Russians. Because we are in entrenched positions, we could be faced with Dieppe 1942 or worse, Guadalcanal, Iwo Jima or the Solomon Islands. . . .

The Argentine army has 130,000 men, 90,000 of whom are conscripts. . . .

The Foreign Secretary knows that many of the conscripts may fight as if they were fighting a holy war. They are stiffened by the Argentine marine corps, who are professionally well thought of by marines in this country and the United States of America. They are armed with 10 Tiger Cat surface-to-air missiles. . . . It is not a rag-bag force to be despised, and yet it is what we are going in against.

Let us take the Argentine navy, possibly the greatest fear of many of us. There are three Kiel-built diesel electric submarines, capable of 22 knots, so far unlocated in the Atlantic lying doggo. What could they do to the "Canberra" or QE2? The resources of the task force will be locked in self-protection. Faced with airborne surface-skimming launched missiles, what ship can be safe? The tragic sinking of the "Sheffield" was a turning point in naval history because, after "Sheffield", can "Canberra" and other ships loiter around the South Atlantic? . . . Come the next British ship that is crippled, how can we refuse to knock out the land bases from which the attackers come? . . .

It is not a matter of cowardice. The real cowardice of people like myself would be not to tell the truth as we saw it. It does nothing but honour to our forces to say that they are up against highly professional forces, whatever we may think of the Argentine regime. Should we not therefore say, faced with the stark reality of a war with unforeseeable consequences on a continent where we are friendless, that we advocate withdrawal of the task force to home ports? . . .

It is true that some Latin American countries disapproved of Argentina's invasion of the islands as a breach of international law. All of them support its title to the islands, and oppose Britain's use of the task force to recover them. . . .

The only viable policy for Britain in the South Atlantic is based on co-operation with Argentina. . . .

Mr. John Stokes (Halesowen and Stourbridge): . . . I do not believe that these discussions can help our diplomacy very much. I doubt whether they aid morale in our battle fleet. We have pretty conclusive evidence that the public dislike them. . . .

The House of Commons cannot run a battle, and everyone knows it. The suggestion by the Leader of the Opposition that we in the Commons should be in day-to-day charge of operations is not only quite unconstitutional and without precedent in our long history, but is utterly impractical. . . .

If this unprovoked aggression were to succeed, there would be no peace or security anywhere, from West Berlin to the many small countries and islands scattered throughout the world. . . .

I share the view of the vast majority of my constituents and of the people of this country that the invasion of the Falkland Islands must be soon, swift and sure. We want British administration restored. I want to see the Union flag flying there again and the governor returning with plumed hat and carrying his sword. After that victory we can be magnanimous. We might associate Australia, New Zealand and the United States in the administration of the islands and even allow Argentina a place in the development of the assets of the whole of the Antarctic.

What worries me deeply is the attitude of our allies in the EEC. After all, those countries owe their freedom to what we did for them in the last war. France would have been ruined without our nurturing General de Gaulle in these shores. Italy also was helpless when the Germans came in and before we landed to help them. The Benelux countries owe everything to us. At least the Dutch still remember that. Germany would have had a much worse time after the war without the decencies of the British occupation. . . .

Mr. Denis Healey (Leeds, East): The Government's detailed account of their proposals and the Argentine response show beyond any reasonable doubt that the Prime Minister and her colleagues have been prepared to make many concessions, some of them as unwelcome to us as they clearly are to Conservative Members, for the sake of a negotiated settlement. There is no doubt that the Government were right to do so.

Argentina, on its side, has made some concessions. . . . However, the concessions made by Argentina have been nothing like sufficient to guarantee that negotiations on a long-term settlement will not be prejudiced in advance. Inevitably there must be some tightening of the military screw.

The thoughts of the House must first be with the men of the Army, the Navy and the Air Force—some of whom have been at sea for seven weeks in extreme discomfort—who may soon be risking their lives in dangerous operations in appalling weather. They have the right to our unanimous support in the task that the Government now set them. . . .

The House must agree—I hope that the Government agree—that any further increase in the level of military operations must not and cannot lead to a final end of negotiations. The final settlement of the dispute must be a negotiated settlement. As Secretary Haig said, a purely military settlement cannot endure over time. . . .

It is equally clear that any future negotiations are bound, in some way, to build on the proposals put before us in today's document, above all, on the two fundamental conditions described last week by the Foreign Secretary—the withdrawal of Argentine forces and negotiations for a long-term solution without prejudice to their outcome. . . .

However, the House will agree that some flexibility is still possible, for example, on the precise timing and distance of the mutual force withdrawal. We all accept the general point that it would be wrong for the Argentines to withdraw only 200 or 300 miles and for us to send our forces back 8,000 miles. Clearly, there is some scope for negotiation between the two. . . .

Last Thursday, I told the House that Her Majesty's Opposition would support the Government's position, as outlined by the Foreign Secretary, provided that the Government supported the Secretary-General negotiating for as long as he believes there is a reasonable chance of success. The Government are committed by the right hon. Lady's words on the radio on Monday to follow up the proposals that he has made.

I agree with the Prime Minister that this does not, and must not, foreclose any military options. The right hon. Lady has made it clear—and the House and the Foreign Secretary should mark her words—that the long process of negotiation that has now lasted six weeks or so has not in any way inhibited the Government from using the task force as they thought wise. That has been so for the past six or seven weeks and must remain so. . . .

Some increase in the military pressure exerted on Argentina is now justified, and we support it. The task force commander must obviously be able to decide on the options that the Government have given him. I do not seek to inquire, any more than I did last week, what those options are. No doubt, to some extent, his choice would be determined by the weather as well as by his tactical judgment, but the Opposition would insist that any new military action must also be designed to create the possibility of more fruitful negotiations than we have had so far. The connection between military action and negotiation is just as important in the new situation as it was in the old one. . . .

No rational person could believe that the Argentines would already have agreed to withdraw their forces from the islands and to negotiate on the future of the islands without the pressure exerted by the task force. It requires an enviable innocence to believe that of a Fascist military dictator. . . .

However, it is odd to find that those who enjoy this enviable innocence are the same people who asked us to rely not upon military force but upon financial and economic pressure exerted by an American Administration which they lose no opportunity of attacking as hostile to Britain and friendly to Fascism. There seems to be a certain schizophrenia about that approach that many of us noticed earlier in a powerful but somewhat revolving speech by one of my right hon. Friends.

More military pressure is now inevitable, but in this new phase it must be limited and controlled, as it was in earlier phases of the crisis. The Government must observe two basic conditions that I have put before the House. First, the force used must be seen by our friends in the world to be proportionate to the issue at stake. Secondly, the way in which the force is used must not jeopardise the possibility of negotiation. . . .

The Government's duty is to ensure that the military commander is never faced with the position that the only way of achieving the objective that the Government have set him is to use force which destroys the Government's political objective. That is a difficult and unwelcome task for the Secretary of State for Defence and the Government, but in a democracy it is a task that must always be carried out by anyone who is prepared to use force in the pursuit of legitimate political ends.

It is difficult for an Opposition, without full knowledge of the military factors as well as of the diplomatic factors, to judge which operations are possible within those limitations. However, it is clear that in this new phase, in which greater importance may be given to the military arm of our three-pronged diplomacy . . . economic sanctions must be greater rather than less than they have been until now. We are entering a phase in which it is clearly necessary to exert more pressure on the Argentines to produce a successful negotiation.

I hope that the Foreign Secretary can assure us that he is approaching our American ally for help in this area, because it is our American ally on whom the main burden of financial sanctions must inevitably fall, since American banks are much more deeply involved in Argentina than British or European banks. But he will know, as well as I, that if we depend on our friends to increase the economic pressures on Argentina, we must be prepared to take notice of their views on how we should proceed in handling the crisis as a whole. There is no escape from that. . . .

The intransigence of the Argentines . . . has inevitably shifted the balance between diplomacy and military action in the next phase of handling the dispute, but both are still required. . . .

We believe that so far, with one or two minor exceptions, *[the Government's]* military and diplomatic behaviour has deserved the full support of both sides of the House. We recognise that a change in the balance between military and diplomatic action is required because of the failure of negotiation in the latest phase, but a balance must still be maintained. The Government must still see negotiation as the final objective of their actions, both diplomatic and military. So long as they do, they will have the support not only of their allies but of the Labour Opposition.

The Secretary of State for Foreign and Commonwealth Affairs (Mr. Francis Pym): . . . No two debates on the same subject in the House are the same, but tonight's debate has been different in a marked way from the five others that have preceded it on this subject. For the first time since the crisis began the Government have been able to make public a detailed British proposal for a negotiated settlement. . . .

The House has seen the nature of the proposal that was rejected by Argentina. It was rejected in a reply delivered yesterday. That reply makes it clear that Argentina is simply not interested in the peaceful and honourable solution which could have been available and which was, indeed, explicitly offered. Evidently, Argentina is interested only in delay—delay which would allow her to consolidate, if she can, what she has seized by force, to scour the world in search of new weapons and to confuse the issues which were so clearly addressed by the international community in resolution 502. . . .

I agree entirely with what the right hon. Member for Leeds, East (Mr. Healey) said about military and diplomatic pressures going together. Both are required. Neither would be effective without the other. They are part of a comprehensive whole. It has been my responsibility to try to put together, with what patience, persistence and imagination I can command, the elements from which a peaceful solution could be constructed. . . . I had to pursue this goal without being able to feel sure at any time that the goal was a feasible one or that the Argentines were negotiating in a way that made it attainable—indeed, with a mounting suspicion that the reverse was the case. . . .

The reception given by the House today to the document that we have produced and published suggests to me that we have done what we had to do. Indeed, a number of hon. Members were surprised that we went as far as we did. I am convinced that we were right to do so. . . . I assure those hon. Members who raised the point that the document has already been given the widest distribution all around the world. . . .

Our first requirement has been to secure the withdrawal of Argentine forces, which was demanded as a matter of mandatory obligation by Security Council resolution 502. The second has been to establish a ceasefire to avoid further loss of life as soon as withdrawal could be agreed. The third has been to make satisfactory provision for the democratic administration of the islands in any interim arrangements that prove necessary. The fourth has been to ensure that the negotiations with Argentina over the future of the islands should be such as to conform with the principles so strongly supported in the House. We have made it clear in this connection that we remain prepared to negotiate with Argentina about the long-term future of the islands, as we and previous Governments were so prepared before the invasion, that we shall be ready to discuss anything which either side might wish to put forward, and that we insist only that the terms of reference of these negotiations should not be such as to predetermine or prejudge the outcome, whether on sovereignty or on other matters.

The Leader of the Opposition said that he understood that there had been some movement by Argentina towards the position of non-prejudgment. That was right, but the position changed yesterday and on Monday, as it has before, and the Argentines withdrew that position and the reply that we received yesterday did not contain it. . . .

Mr. Healey: The right hon. Gentleman has published a document today in which he made it clear—I presume on the latest information—that the Argentine Government were prepared to initiate negotiations without prejudice to their outcome. The complaint made in the document is that the Argentines are not prepared to accept the Government's formula, which is rather different. As I understand it, the Secretary-General, with knowledge of the Argentine reply as well as of our own document, believes that on this matter at least the Argentines have met us.

Mr. Pym: Last week, the Argentine representative at the United Nations in New York tabled a form of words which certainly went towards, or perhaps actually amounted to, non-prejudgment of the outcome. As I indicated in my speech a week ago, however, the Argentine Foreign Secretary and other Ministers there were making speeches in another sense. In the reply received yesterday, the words about which much play was made by the Argentines in New York last week were omitted, and the words used were not so strong or so clear as before. That is my point.

Mr. Healey: This is very important. Otherwise, I should not press the right hon. Gentleman. Paragraph 11e of the Government's document states:

"Argentina proposed a formula . . . which stated that they should be 'initiated' without prejudice to the rights and claims and positions of the two parties."

I agree that that is different from the formula preferred by the British Government, but it is this formula that the Secretary-General regarded as acceptance that the outcome of the negotiations should not be prejudiced.

Mr. Pym: I stick to my reply, because the words to which I referred last week, which were proposed by the Argentines in New York but rejected or denied in Buenos Aires, were stronger and clearer. Those words were omitted from the reply that we received yesterday. There were some words in that direction, but they were not so convincing. . . . There is certainly no question of our ceding sovereignty in advance, and the right hon. Member for Cardiff, South-East (Mr. Callaghan) said that there was no such intention on the part of the Labour Government in the last Parliament. . . .

We have stood firm where we had to and we have shown flexibility where we could. In the event of withdrawal, we put forward proposals to secure the rapid, complete and verifiable withdrawal of Argentine forces. It could, of course, be argued that Argentina should have fulfilled its international obligations in this respect without any corresponding move on the part of the British forces, whose presence in the area was fully justified. To this day we are exercising only our rights of self-defence under article 51 of the charter. No doubt that is right in principle, but in practice a degree of flexibility on our part was clearly unavoidable if we were to achieve our basic purpose of getting the Argentines out by peaceful means. It seemed to us that our withdrawal was an inevitable part of that. . . . We have never lost sight of the importance of the democratic element in the life of the islanders. . . .

The interim arrangements have been controversial throughout. I explained previously to the House that it quickly became clear during the course of the negotiations that as a practical matter some interim arrangements would have to be made to supervise the withdrawal, to ensure that Argentine forces would not be reintroduced and to provide a degree of international involvement in the administration of the islands until a longer-term solution was achieved.

I think that we have shown flexibility both in agreeing to the need for such arrangements and in the discussion of the precise details. However, we insisted that the details should not be such as to predetermine or prejudge the longer-term settlement. In my view that is just as important in this context as it is in that of the terms of reference for the negotiations in the longer term. We also insisted that there could be no question of ignoring the democratic institutions which had been established by the islanders as the channel for the exercise of their democratic rights.

Responsibility for the present crisis lies entirely with the Argentines. As I have said, they responded to our proposals yesterday through the Secretary-General. Their reply reached us late last night and it was all too clear that it was the equivalent of a total rejection of all that we had proposed. . . . Argentina came back with proposed terms which would have included the following features: entirely unbalanced provisions for withdrawal; nothing less than destruction of the previous democratic structures and arrangements on the islands; the chance to change the character of the islands irreversibly in their favour; terms of reference for long-term negotiations which led in only one direction; and the need to withdraw from South Georgia. . . .

I invite the House to consider the likely sequence of events if the Argentine terms had been accepted. Within a month the armed forces of the two sides would be back in what are called their normal areas: 400 miles away in the Argentine case, 8,000 miles away in our case, with nothing whatsoever to prevent theirs from returning to the Falklands at any time. The islanders, whose fortitude we have so much admired and whose sufferings are, sadly, not yet at an end, would find themselves enjoying the same status as the handful of Argentines who lived there before the crisis, together with such inhabitants of the mainland as might choose to come over, by whatever means and in whatever numbers they wished.

Britain, which has enjoyed peaceful possession and administration of the islands for almost 150 years, and Argentina, the aggressor and the international outcast, would be obliged to sit down and negotiate not only about the Falkland Islands but about South Georgia. Such negotiations would have been conducted against a deadline to be succeeded next year by a vacuum. One can well imagine what would be the nature of that vacuum, what the Argentines had in mind for dealing with the vacuum, and who, in their estimation, would be in a position to fill it. . . .

Any lingering doubts that some may have had about Argentine good faith could hardly survive such a reply. . . . *[The]* House can judge for itself which party has been negotiating in good faith and which has made no genuine attempt to address the issues in any reasonable spirit, which party has made every effort to achieve a peaceful settlement and which has at every turn responded grudgingly and negatively, which party wants peace and the avoidance of further loss of life and which talks so blithely of its readiness to throw away any number of lives in the cause of aggression. . . .

Mr. John Gorst (Hendon, North): . . . Could he say bluntly whether he intends to issue an ultimatum to the Argentines either to get out or be kicked out? When will he do that?

Mr. Pym: We are maintaining and increasing our pressures. That is our strategy. An ultimatum has never been part of it. . . .

[The Secretary-General's suggestions] include formulations covering some of the most important matters of disagreement. They do not touch on some of the other crucial elements of the negotiations. For instance, they contain no specific proposals on the practical details of mutual force withdrawal. . . .

In some respects the Secretary-General has come to the same conclusions as we have. In other respects his ideas differ from proposals in our draft interim agreement. We made it clear on Monday that these were our final positions. Even if the suggestions by the Secretary-General were acceptable to both parties as a basis for further negotiation, there could be no doubt that negotiations on the outstanding points would take many days—if not weeks, or more than a week—to reach either success or failure. . . .

We have been through this so many times. My right hon. Friend the Prime Minister talked about six or seven sets of proposals. Although only three have been specifically put, we have explored all the areas of possible disagreement.

Because of the prolonged Argentine prevarication, we have made it clear to the Secretary-General throughout, and particularly since the beginning of this week, that we simply could not allow the negotiations held under his auspices to be spun out indefinitely. The Secretary-General acknowledged that. We have accordingly made it clear to the Secretary-General that, our final position having been rejected, the existence of his overnight suggestions cannot be allowed—any more than at any other stage in all the negotiations—to affect the military options at our disposal. . . .

On that understanding and basis, we naturally await the Argentine response to the Secretary-General's ideas. We do not yet know what that is. I cannot conceal from the House, however, that, on the basis of the known Argentine position as it was communicated to us as recently as yesterday, I am far from hopeful, to put it no more pessimistically than that, that the Argentine response will be such as to enable an immediate ceasefire to be achieved, followed by the immediate withdrawal of Argentine forces from the islands.

Mr. Healey: . . . Do we understand that the Government are prepared to pursue suggestions put forward by the Secretary-General so long as he thinks that there is a chance of their leading to a settlement, without prejudice to military action in the meantime?

Mr. Pym: I was coming on to the future of negotiations. . . . There is no question of the Government having turned their back on the idea of a negotiated settlement. The diplomatic option and effort continues as vigorously as before . . . but a carefully balanced offer made at a particular stage in complex negotiations cannot just be left on the table.

The Argentines, having rejected our offer, cannot be allowed to think that they can continue their unlawful occupation of the Falkland Islands, continue their attacks on our task force and continue their diplomatic prevarication and public misrepresentation of our position, then hope to come back a few days or weeks later and pick up a position which had been put to them previously. . . . We cannot ignore the realities and the conditions that existed at each stage in the negotiations. . . .

The House will recognise the position that I have described as the one which common sense requires. It does not in any way mean that we are no longer prepared to talk or that we will not follow up with imagination and energy any ideas which may lead to a fair settlement. We shall remain in the closest touch with the Secretary-General, who is doing all that he can to secure the implementation of resolution 502. He deserves the constructive support of all members of the United Nations. He will continue to get it from us. . . .

We remain ready to negotiate, but we shall not do anything to give credit to the cynical Argentine pretence that they are negotiating in good faith when they are not. We have set out today what we have been prepared to do to achieve a peaceful settlement. Throughout the crisis we have been upholding the essential principles of freedom, democracy and international law and order. That is why we have been able to attract such widespread international support for our strategy since the invasion.

The House divided on the closure motion, which was moved by Mr. Dalyell. The motion was defeated by 296 votes to 33.

Report Twenty-five

24 MAY 1982

On Monday 24 May Mr. Nott announced the re-establishment of a firm base on the Falkland Islands.

The Secretary of State for Defence (Mr. John Nott): Seven weeks ago, when Argentine forces invaded the Falkland Islands, my right hon. Friend the Prime Minister stated that the Falkland Islands remained British territory, that no aggression and no invasion could alter that simple fact, and that it was the Government's objective to see that the islanders were freed from occupation.

On the night of Thursday 20 May, Her Majesty's Forces re-established a secure base on the Falkland Islands and the Union flag is today flying over the settlement of San Carlos in East Falkland—where it will remain. The whole House will have been delighted to see the expressions of delight on the faces of the islanders and their children—published widely yesterday.

The amphibious landing was the culmination of a long period of planning by the force commander and of preparation by the Royal Marine commandos, members of the Parachute Regiment and supporting arms during their six weeks' voyage into the South Atlantic. Whilst they sailed south, the Government worked unremittingly to persuade Argentina to withdraw peacefully and honourably from the Falkland Islands. But the Government met only with Argentine intransigence.

Last week it became clear that the only possible course left open to us was the repossession of the Falkland Islands by military means. In this the Government have been encouraged—as I think has the country as a whole—that Her Majesty's Opposition and the other main political parties in the House have supported us. Certainly I believe that our Service men have been greatly encouraged by the support that they have received from right hon. and hon. Members of this House.

I will not go over all the details of the amphibious landing: the approach by the task force under the cover of darkness, widespread raids on Argentine military targets, the entry into Falkland Sound and the disembarkment into landing crafts leading to assault in the San Carlos area, but I think I can say that it was an exploit which captured the imagination of our people.

Argentine forces did not interfere to any significant extent with the landing itself. The amphibious ships involved in the first stages of the operation were able to withdraw without incident to safer waters to the east of the Falkland Islands, and I must here pay tribute to the men and women of the merchant marine for their heroism and skill in these dangerous operations; their role is vital.

The landing itself was complemented by attacks in other parts of the Falklands including the airfield at Goose Green and bombardment of military installations south of Port Stanley. Carrier-based RAF Harriers launched attacks against Argentine defences at Port Stanley airfield. These operations were an essential part of the overall plan. I deeply regret, however, that in the course of these operations three Royal Marines were killed when their Gazelle helicopters were shot down and that one RAF Harrier pilot is missing. And, as we have announced, 21 men were tragically lost when a Royal Navy Sea King ditched in the sea shortly before the operations began.

To protect the landing operation the Royal Navy maintained a gun-line of destroyers and frigates in the Falkland Sound. Other warships provided close protection for our amphibious forces; overhead, Sea Harriers from our carriers provided continuous combat air patrols. The waves of Argentine air attacks had to run the gauntlet of these air defences. The Sea Harriers shot down eight of their aircraft, and total Argentine losses that day are estimated at 14 Mirages and Sky Hawks, two Pucaras and four helicopters. These losses represent more than a third of their combat aircraft taking part that day.

During these continuous air attacks the Royal Navy fought with great skill and bravery. Nevertheless, those Argentine aircraft which had penetrated our air defence screen inflicted damage on five of our ships. Of these, the type 21 frigate HMS "Ardent" was severely damaged but, despite the efforts of her crew to control the damage, she sank in the course of Friday night. Twenty-two of her crew died and 17 were injured. The injured are now receiving full medical attention in hospital ships of the Fleet.

Since that action the task force has been reinforced by the arrival of more, highly capable, warships, more than compensating for those damaged or lost in action so far.

The following day, Saturday, saw a lull in the fighting. Although the weather was good, the Argentine air force launched only one attack by two Skyhawks on our ships, which was not pressed home. Yesterday the Argentine air force resumed its attacks on ships of the task force in San Carlos water. The aircraft were engaged by missiles from ships, by shore-based Rapier batteries and by the combat air patrols of Sea Harriers. Six Mirage aircraft and one Skyhawk are known to have been shot down—one aircraft more than was first announced—and there have been unconfirmed reports of a further one Mirage and two Skyhawks also shot down. Yesterday's events involved the loss of two-thirds of the Argentine aircraft taking part.

In the meantime, action taken to make the blockade effective has continued. Sea Harriers from the task force yesterday destroyed two Argentine helicopters and caused serious damage to another. Task force action also resulted in the beaching of a ship used by the Argentines to ferry troops and ammunition around the islands. With the loss of re-supply ships and six helicopters, the Argentine commander has lost all but a very limited capability to supply his forces and move them around the islands.

I regret to confirm that in yesterday's action the frigate, HMS "Antelope", suffered severe damage. Our latest information—and this based on preliminary reports—is that one of her ship's company was killed and seven others were wounded. I must also inform the House, with great regret, of the loss of one of our Sea Harriers last night. This aircraft met with an accident shortly after launching from one of our carriers and the pilot was killed. This accident was not as a result of Argentine action, and the cause has yet to be established. Next of kin have been informed.

The intensive fighting of the last few days has produced tragic loss of life on our side, and the House will join with me in conveying the deep sympathy of the whole nation to the relatives and friends of those killed and injured.

We all feel deeply too for the constant concern and worry of the families and friends of our Service men. They are showing great patience and understanding in very difficult circumstances.

Names of casualties will not be released until the next of kin have been informed, although to counter the false propaganda coming out of Argentina we have had to give some general information on the progress of military action as soon as it is confirmed.

Our forces are now established on the Falkland Islands with all the necessary supplies, together with their heavy equipment and air defence missiles. They have mobility with a large number of helicopters at their disposal—and their spirits are high. But I must emphasise that our men still face formidable problems in difficult terrain with a hostile climate. We must expect fresh attacks upon them, and there can be no question of pressing the force commander to move forward prematurely—the judgment about the next tactical moves must be his—and his alone.

But one thing is certain: the days of the occupying Argentine garrison are numbered and it will not be long before the Falkland Islanders once again have their democratic rights restored.

Mr. John Silkin (Deptford): The Opposition are very glad that a number of our fellow citizens in the Falkland Islands have now been liberated. We associate ourselves with everything that the Secretary of State for Defence has said about the men of the Services, and we send our sympathy to the relatives and friends of those who have been killed or injured.

I am glad that the right hon. Gentleman mentioned the men and women of the Merchant Navy. They have played a tremendous part in this operation, as we always knew they would. We hope that the Government will send a message to the National Union of Seamen, which has responded so magnificently at this time. . . . Will the right hon. Gentleman reaffirm that the door to negotiations does not remain shut?

Secondly, a disturbing item of news on the tape concerns the possible supply of arms from South Africa to Argentina. . . . I hope that he will at least assure the House that the matter will be investigated. . . .

Mr. Nott: . . . At the moment we must concentrate on the military aim of repossessing the Falkland Islands. Any question of talks about the long-term future of the Falkland Islanders must be left aside for the moment. The crucial thing is that we should find out the wishes of the Falkland Islanders. We can do that properly when we have repossessed the islands.

I confirm what I said the other day, that eventually some long-term accommodation will be needed between the Falkland Islands and other countries in that area. That must be right. I shall check on the supply of arms from South Africa. . . .

Dr. David Owen (Plymouth, Devonport): Will the Secretary of State convey the congratulations of my right hon. and hon. Friends to the Service men and the men of the Merchant Navy on a remarkable operation and wish them every success in the formidable task that still must be done? . . .

Will the Secretary of State confirm that the Government's intentions remain as they have always been, namely, to use force in this context under the United Nations charter and to accept the dual obligation of self-defence and the pursuance, wherever possible, of a negotiated settlement?

Mr. Nott: . . . We have taken our action in the Falkland Islands under article 51 . . . when we put forward our proposals last week we referred to article 73 . . . which recognises the principle that the interests of the inhabitants of territories are paramount. . . . It is wrong to talk in terms of negotiations until we have repossessed the Falkland Islands. We are there and must go forward to achieve our military aim.

Sir Peter Emery (Honiton): Will my right hon. Friend ensure that . . . no pressure will be brought to bear on the military commanders in order to make political decisions override proper military judgments. . . . Everyone in the House was proud of what the British forces did, from the top right through to a NAAFI manager who manned a machine gun. . . .

Mr. Nott: . . . No pressure will be brought to bear on the military commanders in the way that my hon. Friend fears. It is for them to make the tactical decisions about the next move.

Mr. J. Enoch Powell (Down, South): While all this is going on, why is the Foreign Secretary still permitted to continue to use language that is plainly incompatible with our continued possession of the islands in the long term?

Mr. Nott: I do not believe that my right hon. Friend the Foreign Secretary has made any statements that would imply that.

Dr. John Gilbert (Dudley, East): . . . *[Which instruction to the force commander is supreme?]* Is it to move ahead with the maximum speed, or is it to minimise casualties?

Mr Nott: We want the task force commander to move forward as rapidly as is reasonably possible. . . . *[We do not need]* to give any advice to the task force commander about minimising casualties. . . .

Sir Frederick Burden (Gillingham): . . . *[Is not]* the best way to minimise casualties on both sides . . . to ensure that overwhelming force, wherever, we possess it, is brought to bear against the enemy? It is overwhelming force that brings about defeat earlier and ensures that there are fewer casualties.

Mr. Nott: I would confidently leave it to the task force commander to decide the manner in which he fights this battle. I can be sure that he will use as much force as is necessary to achieve his aims.

Mr. Gerard Fitt (Belfast, West): . . . Will he further accept that the bellicose and belligerent statements emanating from the extremely anti-British Government in Dublin are not representative of the Irish people, who do not see Britain as the aggressor in this conflict.

Mr. Nott: . . . I share . . . great admiration for the merchant marine. Several of our merchant ships were brought right into San Carlos water and were in great danger for a period. I am glad to say that most of them are now in greater safety. . . .

Mr. Frank Allaun (Salford, East): To stop the growing casualties, will the Secretary of State now ask the War Cabinet to consider a ceasefire or at least a truce by both sides for 48 hours? Would that not also give a chance for United Nations' negotiations now rather than later, when they are bound to come?

Mr. Nott: The casualties have arisen as a direct result of the illegal aggression by Argentina and her failure to comply with resolution 502—a mandatory resolution—of the United Nations. There is no question of a truce. We are now established firmly on the island. We shall go through with the necessary means of repossessing the islands as a whole.

Mr. Robert Rhodes James (Cambridge): . . . All observers have been astounded by the achievement of the Sea Harrier pilots and their supporting staff and believe that that achievement against overwhelming odds once again represents what can be done by a few against the many?

Mr. Nott: I agree with my hon. Friend. The performance of both Sea and RAF Harriers in the contest has been remarkable. They have been extremely successful. The attrition of the Argentine air force has been huge as set against the small number of Harriers that we have lost. The skill of our pilots has been immense and the Harrier has proved itself to be an exceptional aircraft.

Mr. A. E. P. Duffy (Sheffield, Attercliffe): Is the right hon. Gentleman aware that anyone with an inkling of the operational environment of the South Atlantic will be moved to sorrow at the loss of our Service men who have fallen victim to it and feel deep pride at the achievement of our Service men and members of the National Union of Seamen who have met its severest challenges and gone on to execute a brilliant and humane landing? Will he say something about any further Etendard platform Exocet attacks which may have been mounted against the Fleet since the loss of HMS "Sheffield"?

Mr. Nott: As the hon. Gentleman says, the whole House shares a feeling of great pride for our Service men and the merchant marine. I do not wish to be drawn into saying which Argentine aircraft have been involved in action. . . .

Mr. Russell Johnston (Inverness): Is the right hon. Gentleman aware that the Liberal Party wishes to express its admiration for the courage and skill of our forces and the merchant marine in this enterprise? We also wish to extend our sympathy to the merchant marine. . . .

Mr. Anthony Buck (Colchester): Is my right hon. Friend aware that the vast majority of our constituents are enormously proud of the achievements of our Armed Forces? Is he further aware that they reserve their anger for the Fascist junta and the, fortunately, small number of people throughout the country who make utterances against the junta but refuse to support the actions against it? . . .

Mr. Tam Dalyell (West Lothian): . . . Is it true that the Americans have asked for the shooting to stop?

Mr. Nott: . . . Washington is perfectly clear that the shooting would stop immediately if the Argentines had agreed, during the preceding seven weeks, to obey the mandatory resolution of the Security Council and had withdrawn their forces.

Mr. Alan Clark (Plymouth, Sutton): . . . Will my right hon. Friend confirm that all decorations for gallantry for which the men would be eligible in a state of war will be available? . . . *[Does not the operation deserve a campaign medal?]*

Mr. Nott: I assure my right hon. Friend that awards for gallantry for the present campaign will be made in the normal way. We will almost certainly agree to *[a campaign medal]*.

Mr. Dafydd Wigley (Caernarvon): Is the Secretary of State aware that yesterday I had the unfortunate experience of visiting two families in my constituency . . . who had lost sons in the preceding 48 hours? Is he aware that the reaction in such areas is to question whether the end justifies the bloodshed? In the light of that, will he reconsider his earlier remark that the so-called exploits have caught the imagination of the people?

Mr. Nott: I agree that, for a family, nothing can replace a lost son. In general terms, however, the British people support what the task force achieved and understand why it was necessary to send it.

Sir Frederic Bennett (Torbay): My right hon. Friend said that he will not be deflected by pressures from any source. . . . Will he confirm that that also applies to the considerations of our EEC partners when, with their varying degrees of support, they shortly decide whether to renew sanctions?

Mr. Nott: My hon. Friend will learn shortly that EEC Foreign Ministers have agreed, informally and subject to the decision of the Council, to renew sanctions on the same basis as those which were renewed at Luxembourg last week.

Mr. Allen McKay (Penistone): Does the right hon. Gentleman agree that there are two ways to repossess the islands? Does he agree that the first is a military solution, which leads to unconditional surrender, and the second is a military solution combined with a political solution, which could lead to a ceasefire sooner than the right hon. Gentleman implies? . . .

Mr. Nott: I understand the hon. Gentleman's feelings on the matter.

However, the proposals that we advanced last week in good faith and to avoid further fighting cannot any longer be relevant. We are now firmly established on the islands. The position is new. . . .

Mr. Jim Spicer (Dorset, West): Does my right hon. Friend . . . agree that it seems likely that there will be a vast upsurge of people wanting to contribute to some form of fund? . . .

Mr. Nott: My hon. Friend has made an interesting and important point, which I shall consider, in the form of an appeal that funds should be given to the British Legion and other existing Forces' charities. . . .

Dr. Gavin Strang (Edinburgh, East): . . . Is it now Government policy to recapture the Falklands, regardless of the loss of young British and Argentine life?

Mr. Nott: Yes, it is the Government's intention to repossess the Falkland Islands and to return them to full British administration.

Mr. Christopher Murphy (Welwyn and Hatfield): Will my right hon. Friend take the opportunity to remind the world and, I am sorry to say, some Opposition Members, that the Union Jack flying again on the Falkland Islands is not merely the symbol of our sovereignty, but is the front-line banner for international freedom, justice and democracy.

Mr. Nott: . . . We are doing more than repossessing the Falkland Islands, which are British territory, peopled by British people. We are standing for a principle which is vital for the future peace of the world.

Mr. Sydney Bidwell (Ealing, Southall): As we often hear conflicting stories of the state of morale of the Argentine forces on the islands, particularly the conscript element, has the Minister anything to impart to the House today on that subject, as it will greatly determine the amount of blood that is shed?

Mr. Nott: I do not believe that the morale of the Argentine forces on the island is high. They are clearly suffering from a shortage of supplies and, in some cases, a shortage of food. It would be wrong to assume from that, however, that the Argentine forces will not fight—and fight hard. I emphasise that we may still have a very difficult fight on our hands. . . .

Report Twenty-six

25 MAY 1982

On Tuesday 25 May, after Prime Minister's questions, Mr. Dalyell unsuccessfully attempted to secure an emergency debate on "the operations of the SAS on the South American mainland."

Mr. Proctor: . . . Will my right hon. Friend take time to pay tribute, with the support of the whole House, to the bravery and sacrifice of our Armed Forces and merchant seamen in defence of British interests in the Falkland Islands? In the light of this, will my right hon. Friend give an assurance that there will be no negotiations on sovereignty with the Argentine or anyone else, because this would be unforgivable and unforgettable?

The Prime Minister: I respond gladly to my hon. Friend's invitation to pay tribute to the courage and skill of our Armed Forces and of the merchant marine in the splendid work that they are doing. Our object is to retake the Falkland Islands. They are British sovereign territory. We wish to restore British administration. There will be a good deal of reconstruction to be done and then the future will have to be discussed with the Falkland Islanders. I shall be amazed if the Falkland Islanders are not now more hostile to the Argentines than they were before.

Mr. Foot: I certainly join the right hon. Lady in paying tribute to the courage and skill of the British troops. . . . Can she clarify the attitude of the Government on the state of the possibilities of negotiation now? Does she agree that it is absolutely essential in the interests of saving lives—British lives along with other lives—that the possibilities of negotiation should be kept open, along with the military action?

The Prime Minister: Security Council resolution 502 has yet to be implemented. If it was implemented and the Argentine troops withdrew from the islands, peace would follow.

Mr. Foot: That is not the question I put to the right hon. Lady. The reason I put it—we have every right to put it and the country has the right to put it to her—is that the Secretary of State for Defence appears to us to speak in these matters in somewhat different terms from those used by the Foreign Secretary at the end of the debate on Thursday. I wish therefore to give the right hon. Lady a full opportunity to reply to this question. Does she agree fully with what was stated by the Foreign Secretary at the end of the debate on Thursday, when he said that we remained ready to negotiate, and expanded upon what he meant? Does the right hon. Lady confirm that the Government absolutely adhere to what was stated by the Foreign Secretary on that occasion?

The Prime Minister: Yes, but I do not think that the right hon. Gentleman has quite got the import of what I said. The end of the conflict would occur if there was withdrawal of Argentine forces in accordance with resolution 502. Unless that occurs, I do not think that any negotiation would get very far.

Mr. Foot: The right hon Lady cannot leave these matters here. There are the questions that may be raised by the Secretary-General of the United Nations, as he is entitled to do. I ask the right hon. Lady clearly, does she or does she not agree with what was said by the Foreign Secretary at the end of the debate on Thursday, when the decision to send in British troops had already been made?

The Prime Minister: I do not think that the Foreign Secretary would disagree for one moment with what I have said, or with what I am saying now. I make it perfectly, fully and abundantly clear that there can be no progress without Argentine withdrawal.

Sir Timothy Kitson: Will my right hon. Friend give an assurance to the House that, however difficult it may be, she will encourage those Falkland Islanders who can to leave Port Stanley before a major military confrontation takes place?

The Prime Minister: A number of Falkland Islanders have already left Port Stanley. I do not think that I can do more to encourage them to leave. Many of them have already gone to the camps, and I am sure that they will be the best judges of their interests.

Mr. James Lamond: When the right hon. Lady is repeatedly asked if she adheres to what her Foreign Secretary says in a debate in this House, why does she not simply answer "Yes"?

The Prime Minister: Because, like me, my right hon. Friend has made about five different speeches. I wish to know precisely—*[Interruption.]*—He has made five different speeches, as the circumstances have changed. It would be amazing if circumstances had not changed. I agree with the Foreign Secretary's speeches, and the Foreign Secretary agrees with mine, which is totally unlike the Labour Party. . . .

Mr. Cunliffe: Does the right hon. Lady agree with another view of her Foreign Secretary, that once British rule is back in force on the islands and a period of resettlement follows—between six and 12 months was the period quoted—Britain will then seek, the Foreign Secretary has hinted, the aid of other Governments within the area a means of guaranteeing the long-term security of the islands? Can the right hon. Lady assure the House that these Governments will not be of a Fascist or military character, and especially that the despicable policy of South Africa should not be involved in any participation arrangements?

314

The Prime Minister: I hardly think that Fascists or military Governments would be the appropriate guarantors for any democracy. . . .

Mr. David Steel: I wish to ask the Prime Minister a question on the distressing but necessary subject of compensation for the dependants of those who have been killed. . . .
Will the Government publish a list of existing organisations that already cater very well for those problems? . . .

The Prime Minister: My right hon. Friend the Secretary of State for Defence announced earlier the setting up of a South Atlantic fund, which will have full charitable status, under the Ministry of Defence.

Mr. John Townend: Does my right hon. Friend agree that the reported proposal of the Irish Government to table a resolution calling for a ceasefire at this stage is most unhelpful? Will she reassure the House that we shall not agree to a ceasefire until the Argentines agree to withdraw their troops or when the occupation of the islands is complete? Will my right hon. Friend use the veto if necessary?

The Prime Minister: Yes. There can be no ceasefire without full withdrawal of Argentine troops. That is in resolution 502 and if necessary, if there were an attempt to have a ceasefire without that, we would have to use the veto. . . .

Mr. Flannery: In view of the confident assertion yesterday—some people might think over-confident—that the days of the Argentine garrison are numbered——

Mr. Nicholas Winterton: They are.

Mr. Flannery:—could we now have a cessation of hostilities? . . . I know that the bloodthirsty hooligans on the Tory Benches do not want that, but could we not discuss future sovereignty of the Falklands under the aegis of the United Nations, especially in view of the fact that the Tory British Nationality Act has deprived at least a third of the islanders of British nationality? What shall we do with those islands once we have them? Are we to have a permanent fleet on a vast scale there indefinitely, and are we to have an army down there indefinitely to protect them?

The Prime Minister: . . . Does the hon. Gentleman not want those days to be numbered? We wish them to be numbered. He then called for a ceasefire while the invader was in occupation. We totally reject that. It would leave the whole paraphernalia of tyranny in place. . . .

Miss Fookes: Is my right hon. Friend satisfied with the flow of mail to and from the Falkland force. . . . Mail is important for morale.

The Prime Minister: I am sure that everything possible under the circumstances is being done to get mail both to the Armed Forces and from them. I recognise the importance of mail, and I am confident that everything is being done. . . .

315

Mr. Bidwell: While in no way condoning or wishing to condone the Fascist junta's military aggression against the Falkland Islands, may I ask whether the Government are studying the situation being conveyed to us about the state of the junta in Argentina and the possibility of being able to make overtures to saner voices there? In that context, would it be better if the right hon. Lady dropped the idea of not allowing some Argentine families eventually to settle on the islands?

The Prime Minister: The islanders have enjoyed democratic government for quite a long time. What the hon. Gentleman has spoken of is a matter for the executive and legislative councils under British administration. The present law must continue until it is changed through the proper authority of those councils.

Mr. Fairbairn: Will my right hon. Friend ensure that no order is given restricting military action of the task force in any way that could possibly jeopardise one life of our Forces, whatever the cost to the enemy?

The Prime Minister: We are concerned for the safety of our task force. We are also concerned not to have one more life than is necessary lost. We rightly rely totally on the professional views of those who are in charge. We have every confidence in their judgment and in their care for human life.

Mr. Race: As Argentina is likely to become a nuclear weapon State in the near future, is it not essential to recognise that that would raise the stakes considerably in the South Atlantic? Does not that point to the need for a rational negotiated settlement on a permanent basis for the Falkland Islands?

The Prime Minister: I should not have thought that the second question followed from the first. Argentina has nuclear power stations. I understand that those who have supplied the requisite uranium have done so under the authority of the International Atomic Energy Agency, which supervises its use extremely carefully. Naturally, one hopes that countries such as Argentina that have nuclear power stations will join the nuclear non-proliferation agreement. . . .

Mr. Tam Dalyell (West Lothian): I beg to ask leave to move the Adjournment of the House, under Standing Order No. 9, for the purpose of discussing a specific and important matter that should have urgent consideration, namely,
"the operations by the SAS on the South American mainland". . . .
I believe that it would not be right to argue the case one way or the other for those operations. Many of us understand that in view of Exocet and other subjects discussed at Question Time.
Whatever one's view, surely the matter must be cleared up one way or the other as a matter of importance and urgency. . . . Some of us would argue, whatever our views on the general issue hitherto, that any operation on the mainland of the South American continent raises the matter to an entirely different order of importance and urgency. . . .

316

Mr. Speaker: . . . I am grateful to the hon. Gentleman for confining himself to the question of urgency and importance rather than seeking to make the speech that he would have made had his application been granted. I listened with anxiety to the hon. Gentleman, but I must rule that his submission does not fall within the provisions of the Standing Order. . . .

Report Twenty-seven

26 MAY 1982

On Wednesday 26 May, Mr. Nott made a statement. Mr. Dalyell again unsuccessfully sought an emergency debate.

The Secretary of State for Defence (Mr. John Nott): . . . During the past 24 hours there has been a major increase in operational activity in the South Atlantic.

On the Falkland Islands themselves, three successive raids were made from the task force on the Port Stanley airfield. These raids were successful and all our aircraft returned safely. As a result of the action of the ships and aircraft of the task force, the blockade of the remaining Argentine garrison on the Falklands remains effective.

During last night and during the course of yesterday the loading of heavy supplies into the San Carlos area has continued. Five major supply ships left San Carlos during the night having offloaded their cargoes. The force ashore is full established with sufficient supplies to carry out its tasks for an extended period, but the build-up will continue, and 5 Brigade is on its way.

Two warships, including HMS "Coventry", were based to the north, outside the opening of Falkland Sound, to provide early warning of air attack and to provide an air defence screen for the supply ships unloading in San Carlos water.

At approximately 1.30 pm London time an aircraft, probably on a reconnaissance mission, was detected by HMS "Coventry" and was shot down using her Sea Dart missile system. This was followed later in the afternoon by separate attacks by four Argentine Sky Hawks, which were shot down by HMS "Coventry's" Sea Dart, and by Sea Cat and Rapier missiles. This brings the total number of Argentine fixed-wing aircraft destroyed to over 50.

At approximately 7.30 London time a further raid of Sky Hawks approached HMS "Coventry". She was hit by several bombs and suffered severe damage. She later capsized. Initial casualty figures are that 20 members of her crew died in the attack, about 20 were injured and the remainder of her crew of some 280 are safe on board other ships of the task force.

After this attack on HMS "Coventry", at about 8.30, "Atlantic Conveyor", a Merchant Navy ship protected by escorts and employed in the resupply task, was attacked by two Super Etendard aircraft which fired Exocet missiles. She was hit and set on fire. She was loaded with supplies for British forces on the Falkland Islands. She had no Harriers embarked. In this attack, four of those on board "Atlantic Conveyor" were killed and a small number were injured. The remainder of those 170 who were on board are now safe on other ships.

Yesterday's losses were tragic both for the Royal Navy and the Merchant Marine. The House will join with me in expressing our admiration and gratitude for the bravery and dedication of all concerned. Our thoughts are with the families of the men at this tragic time. . . .

During the past seven weeks the Royal Navy has assembled, organised and despatched over 100 ships, involving over 25,000 men and women, 8,000 miles away to the other end of the world. The task force has recaptured South Georgia and successfully accomplished a hazardous amphibious landing of around 5,000 men without a single fatal land casualty. The morale of our Forces is high. By any historical standard, this will be seen to have been one of the most remarkable logistic and military achievements of recent times.

In planning this operation substantial attrition of our ships, aircraft and equipment was both anticipated and expected. In spite of the loss of four naval warships, the task force has more escort vessels today than a week ago. Ten more destroyers and frigates have joined the force in the past two days. Attrition of our Harrier force has been much less than we had assessed and it has achieved complete dominance in air combat and land attack. Otherwise, in spite of massive movements of merchant ships in and out of hostile waters, the "Atlantic Conveyor" is the first supply ship that we have lost.

When a setback occurs, there is always a danger that it brings in train undue pessimism about the future, just as success sometimes creates needless euphoria. Neither is justified at the present time.

Our forces on the ground are now poised to begin their thrust upon Port Stanley; behind them are another 3,000 men of 5 Brigade, whilst reinforcements and resupply are virtually denied to the Argentine garrison on the island Generally the military objective to repossess the Falkland Islands has gone forward exactly as we planned it We have had losses and there may be more on land and sea, but the people of the Falkland Islands can be assured that our resolve is undiminished. We intend to free them from occupation and to restore their democratic rights.

Mr. John Silkin (Deptford): The loss of HMS "Coventry" and the supply ship "Atlantic Conveyor" comes as grievous and disturbing news, and the Opposition would like to join the Government in sending our deepest condolences to the families of those who have died or been injured in this occurrence. . . . We are very glad that *[the Minister has]* announced, in addition to the existence of the pension rights for the naval personnel, the enhanced levels of compensation for death and injury for those serving in our Merchant Navy. . . .

Will the right hon. Gentlemen and the Government give us their undertaking that every door—military, financial and diplomatic—will remain open to *[conclude the matter at the speediest possible pace?]*.

Mr. Nott: . . . I can give him *[that]* complete assurance.

Mr. David Steel (Roxburgh, Selkirk and Peebles): We in the Liberal Party wish to join the Government and the official Opposition in expressing our distress at the loss of lives and our profound sympathy with the relatives of those killed in the course of their duty on behalf of this country. We also join in the Secretary of State's mood of congratulation to the task force on its remarkable achievement so far. Were any helicopters lost on the "Atlantic Conveyor"?

Mr. Nott: I decided that it would be unwise to give details of what was contained in the "Atlantic Conveyor". It was full of supplies for the task force, and it would not be in its interests to give details of what she contained. I have announced that there were no Harriers on board.

Sir Paul Bryan (Howden): Does my right hon. Friend agree that the courage shown by the Forces' families is an example to hon. Members to keep our nerve and our resolution?

Mr. Nott: I entirely agree. . . .

Mr. J. Enoch Powell (Down, South): Will the Government bear in mind for their encouragement and that of the nation the words of the Duke of Wellington at Waterloo:
    "Hard pounding this, gentlemen; let's see who will pound longest." Will the right hon. Gentlemen bear in mind that no battle worth fighting is won except at the margin? A pushover is meaningless and leads to no result.

Mr. Nott: I have heard what the right hon. Gentleman has said.

Mr. Churchill (Stretford): . . . *[Was not the]* shooting down of no fewer than 30 Argentine aircraft by Sea Harriers of the Royal Navy without loss in air combat . . . without parallel?

Mr. Nott: . . . The performance of the Sea Harriers has been remarkable. There has not been a single Sea Harrier loss in air combat with the Argentine air force and navy. . . . The landing of 5,000 men without a single casualty in a hostile environment . . . has been a major achievement by the Royal Navy, and the whole nation realises what they have achieved. . . .

Mr. Peter Temple-Morris (Leominster): . . . Does my right hon. Friend accept that the only real option that we have now is to press on for the victory that will make their supreme sacrifice worth while?

Mr. Nott: . . . Those who have died in the Falkland Islands and around its shores are fighting for the freedom of other British people. They must feel that it is for their own people that they are defending democratic rights and resisting aggression. . . .

Mr. Peter Griffiths (Portsmouth, North): . . . Will he consider again the wisdom of giving further protection to our Fleet by the destruction of the bases from which the aircraft are making their attacks?

Mr. Nott: I note my hon. Friend's feelings on the subject.

Mr. Tam Dalyell (West Lothian): Note or deny?

Mr. Nott: I understand his strong feelings, but the task that has been suggested is militarily not feasible.

Dr. David Owen (Plymouth, Davenport): . . . Will the Secretary of State reaffirm that the Government are prepared to look at any proposals that firmly link a ceasefire with an immediate withdrawal and eventual negotiated settlement? Nothing that has happened over the past few days excludes them from the obligation to search at all times for a negotiated settlement that can be defended in the House and under the terms of the United Nations charter.

Mr. Nott: I agree with a great deal of what the right hon. Gentleman says, but it needs two to bring about a peaceful solution. . . .

Mr. Robert Parry (Liverpool, Scotland Exchange): . . . The general message from *[merchant seamen's letters to me]* is that we should call an immediate halt to hostilities to prevent further loss of life?

Mr. Nott: The whole House wants to see the earliest possible end to hostilities but not on the basis that the Argentines remain on the islands, on British territory, and deny democratic rights to British people.

Mr. Ian Lloyd (Havant and Waterloo): . . . In the past few weeks the Royal Navy has lost a percentage of its strength equal to that lost in the first year of the Second World War. Has not the time come when an unmistakable signal should be sent to the Argentine Government and people that unlimited attacks on British ships in British territorial waters justify and provoke an unlimited response?

Mr. Nott: I understand my hon. Friend's strong feelings. I do not believe that such a signal would bring a very ready or helpful response from Argentina.

Mr. Eldon Griffiths (Bury St. Edmunds): . . . *[Will the Minister]* give two assurances; first, that there is available to the Fleet the best possible means of dealing with the Etentard-launched Exocets; and, secondly, that there is no way in which the Argentines can succeed by war in getting what they can never get by an election?

Mr. Nott: I assure my hon. Friend that the Argentines will not win and keep the Falkland Islands by war. Only out of a peaceful settlement can the rights of the Falkland Islanders be protected and ensured.
There are defences against modern missiles, but I do not believe that any nation possesses a certain answer to every attack by a missile of this kind. . . .

Mr. Tony Benn (Bristol, South-East): . . . *[Is the Minister]* aware that no one believes that a military solution for either side could be sustained? As everyone believes that negotiations will have to take place in the end, how many more lives do the Government believe it sensible to lose before they go to the United Nations for a ceasefire to permit negotiation, or do they intend, in pursuing an ultimate military victory, that the awful tragedy that is unfolding should be continued to its bitter end?

Mr. Nott: I do not believe that it is sensible, to use the right hon. Gentleman's word, to lose one extra life, but in the defence of freedom our forefathers have been prepared to offer their lives. There are British people on the islands who are entitled to be defended by us. Their democratic rights should be upheld, and I am sure that the right hon. Gentleman agrees. There can be no democratic rights for the people of the Falklands while the Argentines remain in possession. . . . The military aim is to repossess the islands. We may have further losses, but we intend to continue until we achieve that aim. . . .

Mr. Keith Speed (Ashford): Does my right hon. Friend agree that the regrettable but comparatively low loss of life in the Royal Navy ships is a great tribute to discipline and damage control arrangements on the ships? With the loss of "Atlantic Conveyor", what are his views about recommissioning HMS "Bulwark", which could provide much needed deck and carrying capacity for aircraft to the South Atlantic or elsewhere?

Mr. Nott: The tremendous discipline on the ships has meant that the loss of life is as low as it is. . . .
We are very active indeed in seeing whether we can get "Bulwark" out of dock and into service should she be needed, but I very much hope that the conflict will be over long before we are in a position to send her to the South Atlantic. . . .

Mr. George Cunningham (Islington, South and Finsbury): Reports have suggested that the Etendards came from the south-east after having been refuelled in flight. Has the Secretary of State anything to say about the implications of that if it is true?

Mr. Nott: I have seen the report, but we have no evidence of that at all. . . .

Mr. John Morris (Aberavon): . . . *[Are]* the Government continuing to consider the balance between the substantial diplomatic risk of immobilising air attacks earlier and better and the military risk of the continuing and unabated loss of ships and men?

Mr.Nott: Yes, Sir, The right hon. and learned Gentleman seems to imply that we might have a military means to put the mainland airfields out of action. There is no simple military means of doing that. Our task is to protect our ships and men ashore as best we can. The task force commander is giving all his time to that question.

Sir Bernard Braine (Essex, South-East): . . . Bearing in mind that Argentina is an authoritarian State with a controlled press, can my right hon. Friend tell us what steps are being taken, or whether any are feasible, to convey by radio or other means to the Argentine people the truth of the situation in the Falklands?

322

Mr. Nott: Not only are there the normal overseas broadcasts of the BBC, but my hon. Friend will have read that we are broadcasting ourselves, under my direct responsibility, from Ascension. Our broadcasts to the Falkland Islands which take place twice each day, bring accurate information to the Argentine garrison on the islands and accurate information to people living in Argentina about the truth of what is happening.

Mr. Dick Douglas (Dunfermline): Will the Secretary of State give attention to a sensitive and delicate issue involving the means and expedition by which the results of such tragedies are conveyed to the next of kin? There is a feeling that there was a delay over last night's episode. . . .

Mr. Nott: . . . When we hear that a ship is in trouble it is a difficult judgment in every case whether we should give the ship's name straight away when we have no idea whether it is badly damaged—we receive only a brief signal initially—or whether it is better to hold the information back until we have more news about the number of casualties and the scale of the problem. . . . We made the judgment last night that it would be better to learn more about what happened before we gave the name of the ship. In retrospect, it may have been the wrong judgment, but in each case it is difficult to decide the right moment to release the name of the ship.

Sir John Biggs-Davison (Epping Forest): Would it not be for the national comfort and a salutary warning to the aggressor if it were known that, were it to become necessary and feasible, the commander was authorised to engage military targets in Argentina? Might that not shorten hostilities?

Mr. Nott: I have explained that I am not sure that it would shorten hostilities. That is the key issue. . . .

Mr. Tam Dalyell (West Lothian): I gave you notice, Mr. Speaker, before 12 o'clock midday, of a subject that should be raised under Standing Order No. 9 namely,
"operations on the South American mainland."
It would be an abuse to make the speech that I would have made had I been given leave to do so. . . . Whatever one thinks of the merits of the issue, the fact is that a helicopter has landed in the Republic of Chile and we know to-day that the crew of the helicopter are now in Santiago. Whether one likes it or not, there should be some explanation of what has occurred. . . .

Mr. Speaker: . . . I have listened carefully to what the hon. Gentleman has said. It is, I believe, the same application as, or almost identical to, his request yesterday. In any case, I listened with great care to what the hon. Gentleman said, but I must rule that his application does not fall within the provisions of the Standing Order. . . .

Report Twenty-eight

27 MAY 1982

On Thursday 27 May, questions to the Prime Minister still concentrated on the Falkland Islands.

The Prime Minister (Mrs. Margaret Thatcher): . . . My right hon. Friend the Secretary of State for Defence made a full statement yesterday. The House would not expect me to go into details about the operations in progress, but our forces on the ground are now moving from the bridgehead. Yesterday my right hon. Friend gave initial figures for casualties on HMS "Coventry" and the "Atlantic Conveyor". The House will wish to know that the latest information is that one of the crew of HMS "Coventry" is known to have died, 20 are missing and at least 23 of the survivors are injured. Four of those on board the "Atlantic Conveyor" are known to have died, eight are missing, including the master, and five of the survivors are injured. The next of kin have been informed. We all mourn those tragic losses.

Yesterday the United Nations Security Council adopted unanimously a resolution on the Falkland Islands. It reaffirms resolution 502 and requests the Secretary-General to undertake a renewed mission of good offices, to enter into contact with Britain and Argentina with a view to negotiating mutually acceptable conditions for a ceasefire and to report again to the Security Council within seven days. We shall, of course, co-operate fully with the Secretary-General in that.

In voting for the resolution, our representative at the United Nations made it clear that, in view of Argentina's continued refusal to implement resolution 502, the only acceptable condition for a ceasefire is that it should be unequivocally linked with a firm and unconditional Argentine commitment immediately to commence withdrawal of its forces from the islands.

Mr. Michael Brown: . . . Will she take this opportunity to make it clear that the diplomatic proposals that were put forward and that have been continually put forward by the United Kingdom contained proposals for a British withdrawal, but that as the position has now changed, and since those proposals have been rejected consistently by Argentina, there can be no question of a British withdrawal of forces?

The Prime Minister: My hon. Friend is quite right. In the published proposals that we debated last Thursday there was a linked withdrawal of British forces and Argentine forces. Those proposals have been withdrawn and, as our ambassador to the United Nations made clear when he voted for the resolution there can now be no question of a British withdrawal. . . .

Mr. Foot: May I first join the right hon. Lady in the expressions of feeling about our Forces and their families, and our concern that the fighting should be brought to an end as soon as possible with the minimum number of casualties. . . . While it is clearly true that the reaffirmation of resolution 502 involves the withdrawal of the Argentine forces, does the right hon. Lady also agree that it is right and in conformity with resolution 502 that there should be further proposals on the table, if not necessarily the same as offered previously, nevertheless one that will offer the Argentines an alternative to unconditional surrender? Does the right hon. Lady agree that that is a sensible approach, that it will reduce the danger of casualties, and that it should be included in her response to the Secretary-General?

The Prime Minister: The essential feature of resolution 502 is the unconditional demand for immediate withdrawal of all Argentine forces from the Falklands. That was to be followed by negotiations. Negotiations were, of course, in progress when the Argentine invaded. They had been in progress for some considerable time, but the Falkland Islanders did not wish British sovereignty to pass in any way to the Argentine. We should co-operate with the Secretary-General, but in the terms I have stated.

Mr. Foot: What I was asking the right hon. Lady to do was not in any way in conflict with resolution 502, and certainly not in conflict with what was decided at the United Nations yesterday. But the Government will have to make some response to those proposals. My suggestion—I believe it to be a sensible proposal that will reduce the prospect of casualties—is that the British Government should be making some proposals in response to the Secretary-General's approaches, which will offer an alternative to unconditional surrender. If the fighting continues to the bitter end, many more lives will be lost.

The Prime Minister: The objective of sending British forces and to try to retake by force what was taken from us by force is first, repossession, second, restoration of British administration and, third, reconstruction, followed by consultation with the islanders—a true consultation—about their wishes and interests in the future.

Mr. Foot: Is that all the right hon. Lady is going to say . . . in response to the Secretary-General's approaches? The resolution that was passed by the Security Council yesterday was properly supported by the British Government. It envisaged discussions on this matter. I urge the Government to consider more far-reaching proposals than the right hon. Lady has given from the Dispatch Box today.

The Prime Minister: The talks with the Secretary-General will be about unequivocal withdrawal of Argentine forces in accordance with resolution 502 as a condition for a ceasefire. After that, we shall be in repossession of the islands. We then wish to restore British administration. Administration has to continue under existing British law and under existing democratic institutions. There will be a great deal of reconstruction work to do, and also talk about development of further resources. It will take some time for the islanders to crystalise their views, but then we must have discussions with them about the longer-term interests. It will be most unwise for us to give away any of that in advance. . . .

Mr. Latham: Since major military action may even now be taking place, will my right hon. Friend confirm that dictatorships rarely understand the moral strength and courage of a democracy and that democracies themselves understand the need to avoid probing questions on military details and secrets that might unintentionally help the enemy?

The Prime Minister: . . . We enjoy full freedom of speech in a democracy. I know that my hon. Friend and many hon. Members are very much aware that too much discussion about the timing and details of operations can only help the enemy, and hinder and make things more difficult for our Forces. In wartime there used to be a phrase "Careless talk costs lives". It still holds.

Mr. Meacher: . . . In view of the further military pressure that is now being extended by British Forces, will the Prime Minister now undertake to re-table the British proposed draft interim agreement so that, without loss of military momentum in the interim but, equally, to avoid risk of substantial loss of life in retaking Port Stanley, these proposals, acceptable to Britain and requiring withdrawal of Argentine forces from the islands, shall lie on the table unamended, ready for immediate Argentine signature as a condition of ceasefire?

The Prime Minister: No, Sir, I reaffirm what I said to the right hon. Gentleman.

Dr. Owen: Will the Prime Minister accept that many hon. Members understand that, following the repossession of part of the Falkland Islands, it is reasonable for the Government to make it clear that the exact parallelism of the withdrawal procedure that was included in the Government's document put before the House of Thursday now has to be re-thought? However, will the Prime Minister be careful before she abandons the principles embraced in that document? It won Britain many friends in the world as being a reasonable negotiating position on which it might be possible to achieve withdrawal of the Argentine forces, leading to an honourable negotiated settlement that would last.

The Prime Minister: The proposals in that document were for an interim arrangement so that we should not have further conflict. The proposals in that document were rejected. We have now gone into the islands to do what I believe the islanders wish—to repossess them, to restore British administration, to reconstruct the life of the islands and then to consult the islanders on what they want. That will obviously depend in some measure on what other nations are prepared to do, how much they are prepared to invest, how much they are prepared to develop the islands and, of course, on what arrangements can be procured for the long-term security of the islands. I am sure that that is the right way to approach the problem.

Mr. Temple-Morris: Can my right hon. Friend give any information about whether known arms suppliers to Argentina have agreed to British requests to cease supplies pending a cessation of hostilities? . . .

The Prime Minister: There appear to be very active efforts on the part of the Argentines to secure further supplies of missiles and spares and armaments in various parts of the world. We have obviously been in touch with the nations concerned about this, and the political heads, but we are very much aware that supplies may be reaching Argentina, not directly from those countries but through third parties.

Mr. Gordon Wilson: Does the Prime Minister appreciate that the closing quote in her speech yesterday:
    "If England do rest but true",
caused considerable offence in Scotland? If this affair is not a purely English one, would the right hon. Lady kindly repair the discourtesy by paying tribute to the sacrifice and role played by Service men of Scottish, Welsh and Northern Irish origin?

The Prime Minister: I am sorry if by quoting Shakespeare I caused offence. I did consider it for a moment, but thought that I could not really edit Shakespeare. As a matter of fact, I thought that Shakespeare belonged to Scotland almost as much as to the rest of the United Kingdom. I remind the hon. Gentleman that I went to Perth and made a major speech, in which I pointed out that some of the best known characters who are regarded as belonging to the whole of the United Kingdom are distinctly Scottish in character. I gladly pay tribute to them and to the splendid efforts of Scottish Service men, merchant men and people everywhere. . . .

Mr. Dubs: Does the Prime Minister agree that the long-term security of the islanders and peace in the South Atlantic could better be established were the Government to make a clearer statement at this stage of the basis on which the foundations for such a settlement could be achieved?

The Prime Minister: It is part of democracy that one consults the people themselves to find out their wishes and interests. I would have thought that every hon. Member understood that. After the hostilities are over it will take some time for the views of the islanders to crystallise. Those views will depend in some measure on what other people are prepared to do. All this will take time to talk through, and I am sure that we are right to take that time.

Report Twenty-nine

8 JUNE 1982

On Tuesday 8 June, following the Whitsun Recess, the Prime Minister answered questions.

Mr. Foot: . . . Since the House last met, the military forces have conducted considerable operations with great skill and courage, as the House would expect. Unfortunately, British diplomacy cannot say the same thing. The right hon. Lady and the Government have sought to use the veto at the United Nations. Does not the right hon. Lady think that that is a most regrettable development? Can she tell us what steps she is proposing to take to bring another resolution before the United Nations Security Council on which we can obtain the same kind of support that we had two months ago?

The Prime Minister: I totally dissociate myself from the right hon. Gentleman's remarks on our activities in the United Nations. The trouble with those latest resolutions was that there was not an unequivocal link between a ceasefire and a withdrawal, which is absolutely vital. In those circumstances we were right to use the British veto. It is only the 20th British veto, compared with the Soviet Union, which has vetoed 112 times.

Mr. Foot: That is not a good example for the right hon. Lady to choose. Some hon. Members believe that the British Government should not have used the veto in those circumstances. . . . Not only is that our view but it was obviously the view of many other countries that were represented at the Security Council. Nine countries voted that way and several abstained.

What will the right hon. Lady do about it next? This may be the best way of preventing further bloodshed. It may well be that the best way of securing an Argentine withdrawal, which we are all in favour of and which is governed by Security Council resolution 502, would be through the United Nations. . . .

As our excellent ambassador at the United Nations made clear, we were close to an agreement a few days ago. Does the right hon. Lady propose, in the interests of preventing further bloodshed, to present a resolution to the United Nations Security Council with the object of achieving an agreement? That is the way to assist.

The Prime Minister: There is no obstacle in the way of Argentine withdrawal, except the Argentines. . . .

Mr. Adley: Is my right hon. Friend aware of the widespread dismay at the support being shown by the Spanish Government for the Argentines in the current dispute and at their apparent inability to differentiate between the aggressor and the aggrieved, and between a free society and a totalitarian regime? In the light of that, will she at least consider reviewing the Government's support for Spain's application to join the EEC?

The Prime Minister: It is in the interests of Britain, and of Spain's long-term future, that Spain should join the EEC. I believe in the wider and longer view that we must keep the democracies together and keep certain countries, such as Spain, within the democratic sphere of influence. Problems are much more likely to be solved if they fall within—rather than outside—the authority of democratic Governments. We very much hope that the gates to Gibraltar, on the Spanish side, will be open on 25 June.

Report Thirty

On Wednesday 9 June, Mr. Pym answered questions.

Mr. Dubs: Does the Secretary of State agree that many of our EEC partners have expressed concern that a military victory will not solve the problem in the South Atlantic? Will the right hon. Gentleman confirm that they have been urging the British Government to lay the basis for a lasting settlement there and to take that on board as a more important responsibility than they have so far?

Mr. Pym: What will happen after repossession exercises the mind of Her Majesty's Government to a great extent. Naturally, there is international interest in what will occur then. I think that it is an open question at this stage. It depends on the precise circumstances at the time. It is right that we should have discussions with our partners and other friendly nations about what will take place. We have thought about a number of possibilities for the future, but exactly what happens at that point must depend on the circumstances.

Mr. John Townend: Were the Government surprised and disappointed at the failure of the French Government to join Britain and the United States in vetoing the ceasefire resolution? If so, what representations have the Government made to France?

Mr. Pym: We have been grateful throughout for the general support which France has given us. That was expressed in a forthright way by President Mitterrand at the conclusion of the summit conference. I can go no further than to draw my hon. Friend's attention to those words. . . .

Sir Anthony Meyer: Does my right hon. Friend agree that the support that we have received from the French Government has been unfaltering throughout? Is my right hon. Friend aware that he will have wide support for his determination to maintain maximum support from our allies for the policies that he is pursuing?

Mr. Pym: I agree with my hon. Friend. It is part of my daily purpose to maintain maximum support from our partners and from other countries.

Mr. Healey: Is not the right hon. Gentleman disturbed that last week we were in a minority of one to nine in the Security Council, whereas on 3 April we were in a majority of nine to one? Does he agree that one reason for that is that none of our allies in Europe or on the other side of the Atlantic supported the British veto last Thursday?

Furthermore, did not the resolution that the British Government vetoed link a ceasefire with the implementation of resolution 502—a link on which the right hon. Gentleman has always insisted? Did not Mr. Haig, a day or two ago, express a view that it might have created a basis for a peaceful withdrawal of the Argentine forces, and did not the British ambassador, on first reading the resolution on Thursday last week, express the same view? Even at this late hour, will the right hon. Gentleman seek to produce a resolution with a satisfactory timetable so that it may still be possible to secure the withdrawal of Argentine troops without the bloodshed that may otherwise follow?

Mr. Pym: No, Sir. The resolution that was vetoed had a superficial attraction, but, when one went into it carefully, it did not adequately link the ceasefire with withdrawal, which we made clear from the very outset was an absolute precondition for accepting any such resolution. The right hon. Gentleman will recall that the United States voted against the resolution, as did the United Kingdom. Therefore, we had that support, Japan voted the other way—I think on the basis that she hoped that Argentina would withdraw, but, of course, that has not yet occurred. The important reason for our action was that the linkage between the ceasefire and withdrawal was not explicit and clear in the way that we believe that it has to be if an agreement of that kind is to be successful.

Mr. Healey: Is it not true that, in trying to explain the shambles of the American voting at the Security Council, Mr. Haig made it clear this week that he believed the resolution on which America finally wished to abstain contained the seeds of a possible basis on which the Argentines might have withdrawn? Five days have now passed. Why have the Government not used those five days to secure agreement in the Security Council on a resolution which moved the other 5 per cent. towards being something which would be wholly satisfactory to all sides?

Mr. Pym: We have had over two months now of trying to negotiate through other people and intermediaries with the Argentine Government, and we have always landed in the same position, and we certainly should have done so had the resolution to which the right hon. Gentleman referred come to fruition. Frankly, the answer is for the Argentines to withdraw. A ceasefire and withdrawal could be arranged immediately. The Argentines show no sign of doing that at the moment. The issue is as simple as that. To try to cause delay at this time and for us to allow ourselves to get bogged down in further rounds of negotiation, which no doubt would end as the previous efforts did, would not be a satisfactory solution, particularly when the simple act of withdrawal is all that the Argentines need to do to end hostilities. . . .

Mr. Viggers: Will my right hon. Friend take an early opportunity to congratulate Mr. Haig on President Reagan's speech yesterday and to point out that there is no better place for the beginning of a crusade for freedom than in the South Atlantic, where the sovereign territory of a democracy has been attacked by a dictatorship? Does my right hon. Friend agree that at this critical point it is important that none of the discussion with the United States, with our allies, and with the United Nations should be allowed to impose any political inhibition on our Forces?

Mr. Pym: I agree with the first part of my hon. Friend's supplementary question. The Prime Minister and the Government have already thanked the President directly for the speech that he made yesterday. I assure my hon. Friend that no political inhibitions have been put on the military commanders in the field.

Mr. Healey: Will the right hon. Gentleman confirm that Mr. Haig made it clear to him that the United States would not feel able to participate in any international force to guarantee the security of the Falklands after repossession, nor would any Latin American country, except in the context of an agreement by Britain to negotiate on their future with the Argentine Government? As the right hon. Gentleman asserted his intention of supporting such negotiations in a television broadcast on 27 May, will he assure the House that the Government have not closed their minds to such negotiations?

Mr. Pym: Mr. Haig did not close the door on the possibility of what might be arranged in future. The future is, of course, unknown, and we cannot say with any precision what arrangements might be made. However, once the islands have been repossessed, it will be the Government's task to do whatever is appropriate, with as many friends as may be available to help us, to re-establish the islanders, who are going through a terrible time, to re-establish security on the islands and to bring about the greatest degree of stability that is possible in the shortest possible time. It is fair to say that the United States has not closed doors on possibilities that might be explored in future. I cannot go further than that at this stage.

Mr. Healey: Is it right that the United States, like Latin American Governments, has made it clear that it is prepared to support participation in a security force for protecting the islands after repossession only if Her Majesty's Government are prepared to negotiate the future of the islands with the Argentine Government? I put it to the right hon. Gentleman again that it is less than a fortnight since he committed himself to such negotiations. What has made him change his mind?

Mr. Pym: There is no commitment of that sort by the Uniterd States and there is no barring of any possible future actions. We must wait and see. We have discussed the possible circumstances that might arise after repossession had been achieved. Until that event takes place and we can see the precise circumstances in which it happens, I do not think that it is possible to go any further. I have made it clear throughout that, in the long term, there must be a settlement in the region if we are to have peace, which must be the precursor and prerequisite of prosperity. If reports are to be believed, during the past fortnight the Argentine forces on the islands have treated the islanders in a way that will cause a good deal of hostility.

I am sure that they will feel like that. We shall have a more difficult situation to deal with after repossession than we would have had a fortnight ago. It remains true that at the end of the day there must be a settlement, however long and whatever form it may take, if there is to be prosperity in the region and for the islanders.

Report Thirty-one

10 JUNE 1982

On Thursday 10 June, Mr. Whitelaw answered questions on the Prime Miinister's behalf. Mr. Nott made a statement.

Mr. Thorne: Since a long-term settlement of the Falkland Islands problem will demand negotiations with the Argentine, are the Government prepared to start now in order to avoid any further loss of life?

The Secretary of State for the Home Department (Mr. William Whitelaw): . . . No Sir.

Mr. Dickens: As the price of the recovery of the Falkland Islands grows in terms of life, injury and cost, will my right hon. Friend accept that the Argentine is simply not interested in just the Falklands or South Georgia, but also the South Sandwich Islands and British Antarctica? Does my right hon. Friend accept that some of that territory is further from Argentina than London Airport is from Moscow?

Mr. Whitelaw: If I knew the correct answer to that question I would say "Yes, Sir." As I do not, I am not sure.

Mr. Foot: . . . I urged upon the Prime Minister on Tuesday, and in a letter to her yesterday, that the Government should take a fresh initiative in the Security Council to see whether an alternative to unconditional surrender can be offered to the Argentine forces. Many hon. Members and people throughout the world have pressed that upon the Government. Such a Security Council resolution would insist that the Argentine agreed to withdraw from the Falklands but would also offer the possibility of negotiation thereafter.

I must urge the right hon. Gentleman to take back to the Cabinet the proposition that the whole. matter should be looked at, because if the fighting continues to the bitter end, many more lives will be lost on both sides.

Mr. Whitelaw: . . . First, it is important to say that at no time have we demanded unconditional surrender. We have made it clear that if the Argentine forces in Port Stanley announced their wish to withdraw to the mainland, they would be given time to do so with dignity and good order. That is their opportunity. Before their invasion we made it clear to the Argentines that we were prepared to discuss matters affecting the future of the islands with them. Even after their invasion we were prepared to do so if they promptly withdrew. However, their response was to insist on ultimate transfer of sovereignty to them as a pre-condition. That was not acceptable.

Since our landings on the islands and the losses that we have incurred, it is unthinkable to negotiate about the future of the islands as if everything was still as it had been before. As I am sure that the right hon. Gentleman will accept, the situation has moved on and the islanders will need a breathing space before they can express their views about their future. . . .

Mr. Foot: . . . We have never disputed the fact that fair offers have been made to the Argentine junta. I am not asking the Government to come forward with a full plan of what they are prepared to negotiate about later, but I repeat that a number of people and countries are saying that the Government should see whether a fresh proposal could be immediately made to the Security Council to help stop the loss of life. The loss of life in the past 24 or 48 hours and the loss of life that may be occurring now add further weight to that proposition. Once again, I urge the Government to do what many people throughout the world are asking them to do.

Mr. Whitelaw: I think that the right hon. Gentleman will agree that I made a careful and considered response to an important request. I stand by that response and have nothing to add to it. . . .

Mr. George Robertson: Since the whole country owes an unrepayable debt to those of our Forces who have given their lives in the Falkland Islands, will the Government give further consideration to the genuine and deeply felt pleas from relatives that the bodies should be brought home for burial?

Mr. Whitelaw: Yes, Sir. My right hon. Friends the Prime Minister and the Secretary of State for Defence said that the matter will be carefully considered, and it certainly will be. . . .

Mr. Dubs: Will the Home Secretary confirm that as soon as hostilities cease in the Falkland Islands the Government intend to hold a full and fair inquiry into the events leading up to the Argentine invasion? When will such an inquiry begin and how will it be set up?

Mr. Whitelaw: . . . My right hon. Friend the Prime Minister undertook that there would be such an inquiry. She will certainly be in contact with the leaders of the Opposition parties to discuss how that might best be produced.

Mr. Lennox-Boyd: Is my right hon. Friend aware that many people are somewhat bewildered by the proposal to repatriate Captain Astiz since we are not required under the Geneva convention to do so at this stage and bearing in mind that there are still three innocent British citizens, who happen to be journalists, who are being unlawfully detained in Argentina?

Mr. Whitelaw: Captain Astiz has been questioned, as agreed, on behalf of the French and Swedish Governments. He is a prisoner of war. Certain dispositions have to be undertaken in relation to prisoners of war, but there are no positions to be taken against him as far as Britain is concerned. . . .

Mr. W. Benyon: Can my right hon. Friend assure me that the Commander of the task force is not being restrained in his operations to recapture Port Stanley for any political reason?

Mr. Whitelaw: He is not being restrained in any way. The operations are entirely a matter for the commander of the task force. . . .

Mr. Amery: Will my right hon. Friend probe the Leader of the Opposition's views a little further? To many of us, it sounds as if he is prepared to hand over the Falkland Islands to a Fascist dictatorship in the hope of saving some lives.

Mr. Whitelaw: It is not for me to probe the views of the Leader of the Opposition under any circumstances. . . .

Mr. Dalyell: At what point did the Prime Minister reveal to her Deputy Prime Minister that she had brushed aside the professional advice on air superiority given by some of her chiefs of staff? As a former Scots Guards officer, what did the right hon. Gentleman say?

Mr. Whitelaw: She did not do so and so I did not have to say anything. . . .

Mr. Canavan: In view of the Prime Minister's statement yesterday that she is ready, if necessary, to turn the Falkland Islands into a fortress for an indefinite period, are we not at least entitled to know the estimate annual cost of all this and where the money is to come from? . . .

Mr. Whitelaw: When the Prime Minister said that freedom was worth defending, she was surely right. The right of self-determination for the Falkland Islanders is worth defending and that is what we are doing.

Lord James Douglas-Hamilton: Given the generous offer made by the Australian Government, will my right hon. Friend seriously consider the possibility of retaining HMS "Invincible", especially as there is an overwhelming case for having two carriers permanently operational?

Mr. Whitelaw: As my right hon. Friend the Prime Minister and my right hon. Friend the Secretary of State for Defence have made clear, we are grateful to the Australians for their offer and it will be most carefully considered.

Mr. Abse: How many more men from the 1st Welsh Brigade are to be killed or cruelly mutilated, how many Welsh mothers are to mourn their sons, before the Prime Minister desists from her provocative and deliberate insistence on unconditional surrender and from an insistence that for eternity the Argentine must not participate in affairs on those islands? Will the right hon. Gentleman ask the Prime Minister to think as a mother, which she fitfully and publicly did some time ago, and stop the role-playing of a warrior queen?

Mr. Whitelaw: The hon. Gentleman has made some personal remarks. Perhaps it would be in order for me to reply to him in a similarly personal way. There are a good number of us in the House who fought for a long time in defence of freedom in the world. We are entitled to say that we did. We are entitled to be worried about what strains we are putting on our young soldiers today, but we know in our hearts that it is right to do so. . . .

The Secretary of State for Defence (Mr. John Nott): Since I reported to the House on 26 May, British Forces have moved forward to positions surrounding Port Stanley, and are in firm control of high ground on an arc surrounding the town.

Earlier on 29 May, 2nd Battalion the Parachute Regiment, supported by units from the Royal Marines, Royal Artillery and the Royal Engineers, captured Darwin and Goose Green. This action, against a greatly superior force, was a remarkable feat and our Forces displayed great determination, valour and fighting skill. At the same time, units of 3rd Commando Brigade liberated the settlements at Teal and Douglas. While these actions were in progress, 5th Infantry Brigade came ashore without incident and the QE2, which carried them, is due back in Southampton tomorrow.

In order to move forward elements of 5th Infantry Brigade as rapidly as possible to the Port Stanley area, and given the appalling weather which was making the logistic problems difficult for helicopters, the force commander moved some forces with heavy stores and equipment around the coast by landing ships.

When the weather cleared on 8 June all but the last elements had moved forward successfully, but the sea movement coincided with better weather and the Argentines at this time renewed their air attacks on our forces. Our latest assessment is that during these attacks at least seven Argentine aircraft were destroyed and maybe another four, making 11 in all.

One air attack was launched against two landing ships "Sir Galahad" and "Sir Tristram". Both ships were hit. The "Sir Tristram" had virtually completed offloading and she was not severely damaged. The "Sir Galahad" had already started unloading, but still had some men embarked.

Having consulted the military authorities, I am not prepared at this stage to give the total numbers of our casualties, and to do so could be of assistance to the enemy and put our men at greater risk. Meanwhile, next of kin are being informed and I shall give further information as soon as is reasonably possible.

In another incident Argentine aircraft attacked a small landing craft. Four Royal Marines and two naval personnel were killed, and their next of kin are being informed. In this incident all four attacking Mirage aircraft were intercepted by our Sea Harriers and were shot down.

HMS "Plymouth" sustained an attack on the other side of East Falkland, in the Sound. Five Royal Naval personnel were injured and their next of kin have been informed. The ship was damaged but she remains operational.

The losses that we have sustained in these incidents are tragic, and as soon as we can give further information to the families we shall do so. I should like to express my tribute to the bravery and skill of those who were involved in the rescue of our men, particularly the helicopter pilots and crews who, in extremely hazardous conditions, were responsible for saving a great many lives by removing men from the damaged ships.

I must tell the House that the task force commander's plans have not been prejudiced by these attacks and the losses of stores and equipment are already being made good from other stocks held ashore.

Mr. John Silkin (Deptford): Despite the skill and valour of our forces, which is one of the bright spots in this continuing story, it is disturbing news that we have received from the Secretary of State. The Opposition wish to add their tribute to that of the Government and would like to send their sympathy to the relatives and friends of those who died and suffered in these attacks. . . .

We owe the nation the feeling that we are doing everything possible to avoid needless danger to our Forces. I am not probing any further than this, but, in the light of the renewed Argentine attacks, can the Secretary of State assure us and the nation that every possible opportunity is being made to re-assess our defensive equipment? . . .

Without prejudice to the task force commander's plan—I keep saying that this is no business of ours; it is his concern—can the Secretary of State reassure us that Britain will be willing to table a resolution at the United Nations so that diplomatic pressure can continue at the same time as military and economic pressures are being reinforced on Argentina?

Mr. Nott: . . . I agree with the right hon. Gentleman that we must do nothing to put our men in needless danger. Clearly, that is the principal concern of the task force commander. I am satisfied that he made the right decision to send round the final equipment and men in these landing ships. There are Harrier combat air patrols active the whole time and there are ships deployed—I cannot say more than that. I regret that some Argentine aircraft got through on this occasion. That may always be the case, however effective our air defence may be. . . .

Mr. Tam Dalyell (West Lothian): With considerable candour the Secretary of State said that, of course, aircraft will always get through. In those circumstances, are we not slipping into a British Vietnam in the South Atlantic, and before we go any further into the mire should not the task force be withdrawn?

Mr. Nott: With few exceptions, the House believes that the despatch of the task force, the manner in which our Forces were landed on the Falkland Islands and our successes since they arrived have been remarkable. With great respect to the hon. Gentleman, any analogy with Vietnam is entirely false. There has been a series of major victories, with some setbacks. I have told the House about those setbacks when they have occurred, but our Forces have been magnificent and will go forward to another victory soon.

Mr. Edward du Cann (Taunton): Although I recognise that there will always be times when my right hon. Friend cannot give the House the information that he might wish—this is undoubtedly one such occasion—can he reassure the House about a matter that is certainly in the minds of every hon. Member and of people outside, namely, that our ships and the gallant men who serve in them are receiving every protection possible, whether at sea, in the air, or on land, from early warning radar systems?

Mr. Nott: Our two aircraft carriers and every ship in the Fleet have the most modern radar and communications systems. One element that we lack in the task force, because we are operating from 8,000 miles and outside the reach of a land base, is an airborne early warning system. We are giving urgent consideration to how we can create one. Apart from that, the radar and communications systems of the Fleet, together with the Harriers, have worked magnificently. The record of the Harriers in shooting down Argentine aircraft has been outstanding. They would not have intercepted those aircraft had not the radar arrangements been working well.

Mr. Richard Crawshaw (Liverpool Toxteth): . . . Can we not take comfort from the fact that until now in the operation losses have been much less than could have been conceived when the operation was started? At such a time, when losses may be greater than they have been until now, should we not steel ourselves to carry through our resolve in what we believe to be a righteous cause in the full knowledge that, whatever the losses, failure to do so would bring much greater losses to Britain?

Mr. Nott: . . . Every soldier, sailor and airman that we lose is a tragedy, not just to his family, but to everyone. With 25,000 people involved in the task force, and with well over 100 ships there, I agree with the hon. Gentleman that it is remarkable that we have not had more casualties and sustained greater losses. We have been remarkably successful, but of course nothing will bring back lives. . . .

The suggestion has been made that my Department has released information that will damage our Forces on the ground. I have carefully checked every such suggestion and I can find no evidence that any damaging information has been given by the Ministry of Defence. What has sometimes happened is that reports have been based on speculation here at home rather than on actual information.

Mr. Reginald Freeson (Brent, East): Will the Secretary of State explain to the House how he could say in his opening statement that the losses that had been suffered would not alter the plan of campaign and yet go on to say that, for operational reasons, the information to which the House and the country were entitled would not be forthcoming? Some of us will not be satisfied and will be worried about what appears to be an unnecessary retention of information.

Mr. Nott: I am conscious of the fact that day by day we are criticised for giving too much or too little information. The criticism comes from different quarters, and sometimes from the same quarter, but from different directions. However, no one is entitled to information that puts any life at risk. In making that difficult judgment in each case it is right that we should rely largely upon the advice that we receive from the operational commanders on the spot. In the last resort they are the people best able to judge whether information is likely to be damaging to their actions.

Mr. Terence Higgins (Worthing): As the Leader of the Opposition seems to distinguish between unconditional surrender of the Argentine forces, which he is against, and our forcing them to withdraw from the islands, of which apparently he is in favour, can my right hon. Friend confirm that our military objective is to remove the Argentine invader from the Falkland Islands—no more and no less?

Mr. Nott; Yes, I can confirm that.

Mr. Frank Allaun (Salford, East): Can the Minister inform the House of the number of casualties among Falkland Islanders, men, women and children? How many are concentrated in the Port Stanley area? Was not the objective the liberation of the islanders, not their annihilation? To avoid their death or wounding, will the right hon. Gentleman now do what our Front Bench has asked and resume negotiations at the United Nations?

Mr. Nott: With regard to casualties among the islanders, we are doing everything that we can through the force commander on the spot to keep these to an absolute minimum. We are in constant contact with the International Committee of the Red Cross to see whether we can find some means whereby islanders who may be in a difficult situation in the town can, with Red Cross assistance, be brought out. The Red Cross is working with us on this. So far we had not had a satisfactory response from the Argentines. Our concern for the islanders is very great, and we share that concern with the hon. Gentleman.

I have already commented on the United Nations. Our objective in the short term is the removal of the Argentines from the Falkland Islands. There is nothing more that the United Nations can do to bring that about. It can be brought about only by British Forces on the ground. We have given every opportunity to the Argentines to withdraw. They have turned down every chance, and we must now remove them by force.

Sir John Biggs-Davison (Epping Forest): Will the entire Government be mindful of the reported words of a Royal Marine colour sergeant in the task force, that since the Falkland Islands are worth dying for they are worth keeping?

Mr. Kenneth Warren (Hastings): Without casting any reflection on the professional skill and, indeed, bravery of the British press men in the Falklands, may I ask the Secretary of State to examine the way in which their personal dispatches are issued? Can he tell us whether there is any monitoring of these reports before dispatch, bearing in mind that often, inadvertently I am sure, targeting information is given to the Argentines, such as the location of a damaged British Royal Naval vessel today?

Mr. Nott: The reports coming from the journalists in the Falkland Islands have, generally speaking, been magnificent. They have been vivid and have given the country much information, which has been of great value to us. I have nothing but praise for what the journalists there have done.

All the journalists' dispatches are looked at on the ground down there. Of course, the lives of the journalists themselves are involved. We do not seek to censor or change their dispatches here. Sometimes we hold them back if we feel that a dispatch has slipped through inadvertently, perhaps in the heat of the battle when no one has had proper time to look at it. We have held back some for a day or two because we felt that it would be wrong for them to go out. We have done that in co-operation and agreement with the press and the newspaper or television company concerned. Generally speaking, the journalists have done a magnificent job. Of course, we are vigilant to ensure that no information is released through them that would damage our Forces.

Report Thirty-two

14 JUNE 1982

On Monday, 14 June, Mr. Onslow made a statement. Late that evening, the Prime Minister reported talks between the British and Argentine commanders.

The Minister of State, Foreign and Commonwealth Office (Mr. Cranley Onslow): Throughout the course of our military operations to repossess the Falkland Islands our Forces have attached the greatest importance to ensuring the safety of the civilian population on the islands. This has been a major consideration in the planning for, and conduct of, all our operations.

The most effective way of protecting non-combatants is through the establishment of a neutralised zone, as provided for in article 15 of the fourth Geneva convention. Such a zone in Port Stanley has been proposed by the International Committee of the Red Cross, which was able to visit Port Stanley for the first time on 10 and 11 June. The ICRC has been trying for several weeks to establish a presence on the Falkland Islands, but hitherto Argentina had not permitted this.

The British Government agreed forthwith to the neutralised zone which had been proposed by the ICRC. We have since been told by the ICRC that the Argentine Government have also agreed to this. The zone will consist of a rectangular area of roughly five acres around the Anglican cathedral. The cathedral is a large prominent building built of red brick. There are a number of other stone and brick-built buildings within the area of the zone, which is bounded by John Street, Dean Street, Philomel Street and Ross Road. Instructions have been sent to the British commander to respect this zone with immediate effect.

Besides the civilian non-combatant population, the zone may also be used for the protection of wounded and sick civilian and Service personnel. The area which has been designated should be large enough for the temporary accommodation of those expected to need protection.

I should like to express the Government's appreciation of the action of the ICRC in arranging for the establishment of this zone.

Meanwhile, as the House will be aware, Argentine sources have reported that some civilian casualties have occurred in Port Stanley during the fighting. We have no official confirmation of these reports. However, there is some independent evidence to support them, and I regret to say that we must regard it as likely that they are true. This tragic incident only underlines the importance of establishing a neutralised zone to minimise the risk to the islanders. We would hope to obtain further details concerning this incident when the representatives of the Red Cross return to Port Stanley.

Mr. Dalyell: Does not international opinion, considered so important in early April, now view with nausea the slaughter of young British men, young Argentines and Falklanders, and does it not call for an immediate end to the shooting? In the light of what is now happening to the Falklanders, is not the reality the same as it always was—that this war is less about the interests of the people on the Falkland Islands and much more to do with the injured pride of politicians making decisions?

Mr. Onslow: I am tempted to repay the hon. Gentleman in kind with use of the word "nausea", which is inappropriate in the sense in which he has imported it into this discussion. It is a fact that everyone in this House, as well as all international opinion, wants to see an end to the fighting, but it is also true that almost everyone, except the hon. Gentleman, understands the principles for which these lives have been lost——

Mr. Dalyell: Not true.

Mr. Onslow: —and much though we regret them, we believe that it is necessary to go through with the enterprise.

Sir Timothy Kitson (Richmond, Yorks): Would it be possible to arrange for the Red Cross to try to get some of the civilian casualties out? While we may not know officially who has been injured, certain people in Britain have been informed about deaths and serious injuries to their relations and are deeply concerned because they cannot get any further information. Could not we attempt to contact the Red Cross to see whether something could be done at least to remove the civilian casualties?

Mr. Onslow: I share my hon. Friend's concern about the uncertainty, but no direct or reliable source of information is available to us. Even the Red Cross has no resident presence in Port Stanley at the moment, and the information made available by it is based on only a brief visit during which its officials were able to meet only a small number of islanders. As soon as it becomes possible for the Red Cross to make an informed assessment, and if that suggests that evacuation is a practical possibility, we would, of course, do everything we could to co-operate with that suggestion.

Mr. Roland Moyle (Lewisham, East): Is the Minister aware that the Opposition fully approve of the concluding of negotiations through the ICRC with the Argentines with a view to securing the safety of the civilian population of Port Stanley? That almost goes without saying. We only regret that it has taken so long because of foot-dragging by the Argentines. We want no more civilian casualties. We regret those that have been admitted this afternoon and wish to express our sympathy for the relatives.

Can the Minister give an authoritative, even if only approximate, figure of the number of civilians in Port Stanley? Various figures have been suggested in recent weeks. Why has the area around the cathedral been selected? I gather that there are a number of wooden buildings in that area. Are the Government satisfied that the arrangements they have now concluded will provide for the safety of the civilian population of Port Stanley, given the difficult situation that has arisen?

Have the British Forces at any time offered a limited ceasefire to allow the civilians to be evacuated entirely from Port Stanley, and has there been any Argentine response either directly or through the International Red Cross? Do the Government accept that the presence of 600 civilians in Port Stanley, however they are arranged, is bound to place a restriction on our military operations? Have our commanders been informed that the preservation of the lives and well-being of the islanders is of prime importance and are the Government confident that future operations will not put them seriously at risk?

Mr. Onslow: I am grateful to the right hon. Gentleman for his preface. The fact that hitherto there has not been an ICRC presence in Port Stanley is no fault of the Government or the ICRC. . . .

The sources of information available to us are sketchy and sometimes of questionable reliability. We have no independent accurate corroboration of the figure of 600 civilians.

I can put forward no particular reason why that part of the town was selected. It must have recommended itself to the ICRC as being most suitable for a variety of reasons, doubtless including the type of buildings and the ease of definition. The safety of the civilians in Port Stanley depends on the ease and speed with which the Argentine authorities can get them into the neutralised zone. That again is not under our control, but I hope that it will receive all necessary priority.

I have no knowledge of ceasefire proposals initiated locally. It is not our intention from here to dictate to the force commander his operational priorities. Although we must accept the possibility of further civilian casualties as long as fighting continues, we should not expect the force commander to endanger the lives of his men by taking decisions that might in other contexts seem commendable.

Mr. David Steel (Roxburgh, Selkirk and Peebles): As the neutral zone has been created through the mediation of the ICRC, can the Minister confirm that the Government have at no stage, even at this late hour, ruled out the possibility of similar third-party intervention to secure a ceasefire and a peaceful Argentine withdrawal?

Mr. Onslow: The issue of a ceasefire goes wider than the context of the question. Our approach to the question of a ceasefire has always been that it must be linked to immediate Argentine withdrawal. If there is evidence to suggest that the Argentines are now willing to proceed direct from the one to the other, we should consider the matter. . . .

Mr. Eldon Griffiths (Bury St. Edmunds): Although everyone will be glad that the Red Cross has established the refuge for civilians and will note my hon. Friend's agreement that the United Kingdom would assist in evacuating civilian casualties, can he tell us what arrangements there are to supervise the zone under the Red Cross so that there is no question of its being used by the Argentines for military purposes while being presented to the world solely as a neutral refuge for civilians?

Mr. Onslow: I am grateful to my hon. Friend for what he says, but I hope that he will appreciate that it is not in our power to monitor the use of a neutralised zone. That responsibility falls to the International Red Cross.

However, I have no doubt that it is well aware of the rules and I am confident that it will do everything that it can to see that they are enforced.

Mr. Donald Anderson (Swansea, East): What is the state of information about the well-being of the British people on West Falkland? As we have more time available before we begin mopping-up operations on that island, is it not possible now to consider means of obtaining evacuation of those residents?

Mr. Onslow: . . . I am sure that any appropriate action will be taken, but at this point I cannot go beyond that. Apart from anything else, our preoccupation must be with where the danger is greatest, which is undoubtedly in Port Stanley. That is where we want the ICRC to operate effectively as soon as possible.

Mr. Robert Banks (Harrogate): Considering the number of civilians in Port Stanley and the volume of the bombardment, is it not a remarkable feat that the task force aimers have been able to select military targets and, however sad, so far there have been only two civilian casualties?

Mr. Onslow: It is a relief that civilian casualties have so far been so small. Additionally, I have no evidence to suggest that the casualties that have unhappily occurred were the result of British military action. The matter has not been investigated and I am not prepared to pronounce on it.

Mr. Eric Ogden (Liverpool, West Derby): . . . Will he bear in mind—perhaps the hon. Member for West Lothian (Mr. Dalyell) will also note—that no one on the islands will blame the British task force *[for the civilian casualties]*? They share pride and sorrow with other British families whose loved ones have been lost or injured in a common and just cause.

Mr. Onslow: It goes without saying that the sympathies of all hon. Members must be with the relations and friends of all who have been killed or injured. I am sure that what the hon. Gentleman says will be noted with appreciation and gratitude by the Falkland Islands community in particular.

Sir Frederick Burden (Gillingham): Although the setting up of a neutral area is welcome to us all, might there not be problems with food, heating and sanitation with the large number of people in the area? Will my hon. Friend keep in touch with the Red Cross and get the latest reports on the situation and, with the agreement of the Argentines, see what might be done to alleviate what might be considerable suffering by those in the refuge area?

Mr. Onslow: I note what my hon. Friend says, but the problem stems from the presence in Port Stanley of civilians. Their concentration in one area, which can be effectively preserved as neutral, should effectively reduce the problem. Any needs that they may have can better be treated there. The area is big enough to satisfy accommodation problems, but if problems become more intractable, we shall look to the ICRC to report on them without delay.

Mr. Ioan Evans (Aberdare); Is it not a tragedy that we went in to defend the lives of the Falkland Islanders and now the first islanders have lost their lives? Will the Minister ensure that the House is kept informed of casualties, not only among the islanders, but among Service men? . . .

Mr. Onslow: The hon. Gentleman is asking questions which are not for me and which have been dealt with by my right hon. Friend the Secretary of State for Defence in his statements. I am sure that my right hon. Friend will keep the House as fully informed as his judgment tells him that it best can be. As soon as it is possible to produce accurate and reliable information on civilian casualties, I intend that it should be made available to the House. . . .

Later—

The Prime Minister (Mrs. Margaret Thatcher): On a point of order, Mr. Speaker. May I give the House the latest information about the battle of the Falklands? After successful attacks last night, General Moore decided to press forward. The Argentines retreated. Our Forces reached the outskirts of Port Stanley. Large numbers of Argentine soldiers threw down their weapons. They are reported to be flying white flags over Port Stanley. Our troops have been ordered not to fire except in self-defence. Talks are now in progress between General Menendez and our deputy commander, Brigadier Waters, about the surrender of the Argentine forces on East and West Falkland. I shall report further to the House tomorrow.

Hon. Members: Hear, hear!

Mr. Michael Foot (Ebbw Vale): Further to that point of order, Mr. Speaker. First, may I thank the right hon. Lady for coming to the House to give us the news, particularly because the news is so good for all concerned, especially because it appears from what she has been able to tell us that there will be an end to the bloodshed, which is what we have all desired. There will be widespread, genuine rejoicing—to use the word that the right hon. Lady once used—at the prospect of the end of the bloodshed. If the news is confirmed, as I trust it will be, there will be great congratulations from the House tomorrow to the British Forces, who have conducted themselves in such a manner and, if I may say so, to the right hon. Lady. [HON. MEMBERS: "Hear, Hear."] I know that there are many matters on which we shall have to have discussions, and perhaps there will be arguments about the origins of this matter and other questions, but I can well understand the anxieties and pressures that must have been upon the right hon. Lady during these weeks. I can understand that at this moment those pressures and anxieties may have been relieved, and I congratulate her on that.

I believe that we can as a House of Commons transform what has occurred into benefits for our country as a whole. I believe that that is the way in which we on the Opposition Benches will wish to proceed. There are many fruitful lessons in diplomacy and in other matters that we can draw from this occasion, and that will be the Opposition's determination. . . .

Mr. David Steel: Further to the point of order, Mr. Speaker. Will the Prime Minister accept that this is an occasion when the whole House should

346

rejoice and congratulate both the Government and the Forces involved on bringing this sad matter to a satisfactory and peaceful conclusion? . . .

Dr. David Owen (Plymouth, Devonport): Further to the point of order, Mr. Speaker. May I join the Leader of the official Opposition and the leader of the Liberal Party in conveying the congratulations of the whole House to the Royal Navy, the Army, the Royal Air Force and the Royal Marines, and to the Government and all the Ministers who played a crucial role in the achievement of an extremely successful outcome? I wish all well, especially—thinking of those who have lost their lives—those families who are currently grieving tonight for their sacrifice. The sacrifice of their loved ones was a sacrifice which was necessary for all.

Report Thirty-three

15 JUNE 1982

On Tuesday 15 June, the Prime Minister answered her questions and then made a statement formally announcing the surrender of all Argentine forces on the Falkland Islands.

Mr. Kenneth Carlisle: In the light of the most welcome news from the Falklands, does my right hon. Friend agree that we should praise and give thanks for the skill, courage and sacrifice of the members of the task force who succeeded so brilliantly in an exercise that was fraught with hazard? Does she agree that it is a fine moment for our country? Does she further agree that it demonstrates that wherever British power can reach, nobody should embark upon aggression?

The Prime Minister: I thank my hon. Friend for his comments. I entirely agree with him. We cannot say enough about how wonderful our Armed Forces and Merchant Marine have been. We salute them all. I hope, as my hon. Friend said, that we have once again restored Britain's dominance and have let every nation know that British sovereign territory will be well and truly defended and that we shall never again be the victim of aggression.

Mr. Grimond: Does the welcome ceasefire apply only to hostilities in the Falkland Islands or to all hostilities with Argentina?

The Prime Minister: I shall have something to say about that in my statement. We are endeavouring to achieve a complete ceasefire with Argentina. . . .

Mr. Moate: Does my right hon. Friend agree that the liberation of the Falkland Islands has shown that, although we must be grateful for international support and co-operation, which is always essential, this nation must always retain the freedom, resources and resolve to act independently in defence of the principles for which we stand?

The Prime Minister: I entirely agree. We must have the capacity to act independently. I agree with my hon. Friend that we need both the power to act and the will to see it through.

Mr. Foot: We shall have the opportunity to put further questions to the right hon. Lady about the Falkland Islands when she makes a fresh statement on the subject in a few minutes' time. Will she tell us now about the engagement for which I believe she is leaving tonight or tomorrow—the United Nation's special session on disarmament in New York? Does she agree that events both in the South Atlantic and in the Middle East make all the more necessary the effort to ensure that that disarmament conference is successful? Will she use all the strength of the British Government to try to get serious measures passed? Does she agree that the recent war, and particularly the use of certain weapons by the Argentines, make all the more necessary a concerted effort at the United Nations to stop the obscenity of traffic in arms, as a result of which some of our Service men were killed by weapons that we had sold to the Argentines?

The Prime Minister: I am not certain whether I shall be going to New York tomorrow, or possibly later, if it can be arranged. The disarmament conference is in no way a negotiating forum. Negotiations must be carried on elsewhere. I entirely agree that we should like to have security with a lower level of arms, but that lower level must be capable of being verified. The whole world is learning the lesson that unilateral disarmament leads to weakness and liability to attack by the strong, as it always has. Unilateral disarmament of all kinds leads to weakness and liability to be attacked on the part of the nation that undertakes it. Therefore, we need a proper balance of arms, which is what we are trying to obtain.

Mr. Kilfedder: As the victory in the South Atlantic was made possible by the supreme sacrifice made by our courageous Service men and merchant seamen, will the Prime Minister as quickly as possible promote a memorial to those gallant men who epitomise all that is best in our nation?

The Prime Minister: Of course we shall consider that. I think that what they have achieved is their own best memorial. Indeed, none could better it. . . .

Mr. George Gardiner: In the light of today's marvellous news, will my right hon. Friend study the precedent set by Prime Minister and Monarch in May 1940 and consider the designation of a Sunday very soon as a national day of prayer and thanksgiving for our success in freeing the Falkland Islands? . . .

The Prime Minister: Of course we shall consider that, but I believe that throughout our land this day and the coming Sunday everywhere there will be thanksgiving.

Mr. Campbell-Savours: Will the right hon. Lady give an absolute assurance that neither she nor No. 10 will in any way obstruct the promised inquiry into the events leading up to the invasion of the Falkland Islands and that the determination of the truth will be paramount so that the British people may learn what actually happened as against what the House was told happened?

The Prime Minister: Yes, Sir. I shall shortly be writing to the Leader of the Opposition about the proposed form of the inquiry. I am certain that it needs to go back far further than the events leading up to the conflict.

Mr. Faulds: . . . As British military abilities have once again rescued British politicians from their failures, will the right hon. . . . Lady contemplate today whether this is the right time to offer the Argentines a reasonable involvement in the future of the Falkland Islands to prevent a continuing war on our naval and supply communications for the Falkland Islands?

The Prime Minister: No, Sir. . . .

Later—

The Prime Minister: With permission, Mr. Speaker, I should like to make a statement on the Falkland Islands.

Early this morning in Port Stanley, 74 days after the Falkland Islands were invaded, General Moore accepted from General Menendez the surrender of all the Argentine forces in East and West Falkland together with their arms and equipment. In a message to the Commander-in-Chief Fleet, General Moore reported:

"The Falkland Islands are once more under the Government desired by their inhabitants. God Save the Queen."

General Menendez has surrendered some 11,000 men in Port Stanley and some 2,000 in West Falkland. In addition, we had already captured and were holding elsewhere on the islands 1,800 prisoners, making in all some 15,000 prisoners of war now in our hands.

The advance of our Forces in the last few days is the culmination of a determined military effort to compel the Argentine Government to withdraw their forces from the Falkland Islands.

On the night of Friday 11 June, men of 42 and 45 Commandos and the 3rd Battalion the Parachute Regiment, supported by elements of the Royal Artillery and Royal Engineers, mounted an attack on Argentine positions on Mount Harriet, Two Sisters and Mount Longdon. They secured all their objectives, and during the next day consolidated their positions in the face of continuing resistance.

I regret to inform the House that five Royal Marines, 18 Paratroopers and two Royal Engineers lost their lives in those engagements. Their families are being informed. Seventy-two Marines and Paratroopers were wounded. We have no details of Argentine casualties. Hundreds of prisoners and large quantities of equipment were taken in these operations. The land operations were supported by Harrier attacks and naval gunfire from ships of the task force, which made a major contribution to the success of our troops. In the course of the bombardment, however, HMS "Glamorgan" was hit by enemy fire. We now know that 13 of the crew died in this attack or are missing.

Throughout Sunday 13 June, the 3rd Commando Brigade maintained pressure on the enemy from its newly secured forward positions. Meanwhile, men of the 5th Infantry Brigade undertook reconnaissance missions in preparation for the next phase of the operations. HMS "Hermes" flew her one-thousandth Sea Harrier mission since leaving the United Kingdom.

The Argentines mounted two air raids that day. The first was turned back by Harriers of the task force before it could reach the Falklands. In the second raid A4 aircraft made an unsuccessful bombing run and one Mirage aircraft was shot down.

During the night of Sunday 13 June the second phase of the operations commenced. The 2nd Battalion the Parachute Regiment secured Wireless Ridge and the 2nd Battalion the Scots Guards took Tumbledown Mountain by first light on Monday 14 June. The 1st/7th Gurkhas advanced on Mount William, and the Welsh Guards on Sapper Hill. At 2 pm London time large numbers of Argentine troops were reported to be retreating from Mount William, Sapper Hill and Moody Brook in the direction of Port Stanley.

British Forces pressed forward to the outskirts of Port Stanley. Large numbers of Argentines threw down their weapons and surrendered.

At 4 o'clock the Argentine garrison indicated its willingness to talk. Orders were given to our forces to fire only in self-defence. Shortly before 5 o'clock a white flag appeared over Port Stanley.

Initial contact was made with the enemy by radio. By midnight General Moore and General Menendez were talking. The surrender of all the Argentine forces of East and West Falkland was agreed at 1 am today London time. Some of our Forces are proceeding to West Falkland to organise the surrender of the Argentine forces there.

We are now tackling urgently the immense practical problems of dealing with the Argentine prisoners on the islands. The weather conditions are severe, permanent accommodation is very limited, and much of the temporary accommodation which we had hoped to use was lost when the "Atlantic Conveyor" was sunk on 25 May. We have already repatriated to Argentina almost 1,400 prisoners, and the further 15,000 now in our custody are substantially more than we had expected. With the help of the International Red Cross, we are taking urgent steps to safeguard these prisoners and hope to evacuate them as soon as possible from the islands, in accordance with our responsibilities under the Geneva Convention. This is a formidable task.

We have today sent to the Argentine Government, through the Swiss Government, a message seeking confirmation that Argentina, like Britain, considers all hostilities between us in the South Atlantic—and not only on the islands themselves—to be at an end. It is important that this should be established with clarity and without delay.

We must now bring life in the islands back to normal as quickly as possible, despite the difficult conditions and the onset of the Antarctic winter. Mines must be removed; the water supply in Stanley is not working and there will be other urgent tasks of repair and reconstruction.

Mr. Rex Hunt and members of the Islands Council at present in this country will return as soon as possible. Mr. Hunt will concentrate on civilian matters. General Moore will be responsible for military matters. They will in effect act as civil and military commissioners and will, of course, work in the closest co-operation.

After all that has been suffered it is too early to look much beyond the beginning of the return to normal life. In due course the islanders will be able to consider and express their views about the future. When the time is right we can discuss with them ways of giving their elected representatives an expanded role in the government of the islands. . . .

We shall uphold our commitment to the security of the islands. If necessary, we shall do this alone. But I do not exclude the possibility of associating other countries with their security. Our purpose is that the Falkland Islands should never again be a victim of unprovoked aggression.

Recognising the need for economic development, I have asked Lord Shackleton to update his 1976 report on the economic potential of the islands. He has agreed to do this as a matter of urgency. I am most grateful to him.

The House will join me, Mr. Speaker, in expressing our deep sense of loss over those who have died, and our sorrow for their families. The final details will not become clear for a few days yet, but we know that some 250 British Service men and civilians have been killed. They died that others may live in freedom and justice.

The battle of the Falklands was a remarkable military operation, boldly planned, bravely executed, and brilliantly accomplished. We owe an enormous debt to the British Forces and to the Merchant Marine. We honour them all. They have been supported by a people united in defence of our way of life and of our sovereign territory.

Mr. Foot: The Opposition at once wish to join in the thanks and congratulations that the right hon. Lady has given to the Service men and their commanders on the way in which they have discharged their duties throughout these dangerous weeks. We wish that to be emphasised at the outset.

The relief that the House felt and expressed last night when it first heard the news derived partly from the belief that we had been able to avoid not merely the hideousness of a bloody battle at Port Stanley but also the consequences of such a battle. That sense of relief was rightly expressed, and we wish to express it once again.

Even so, as the right hon. Lady emphasised in her final remarks, there have been severe casualties for this country that affect some of our great naval ports such as Plymouth and Portsmouth. There have been severe casualties affecting other places as well. In addition, there have been severe casualties among the Argentine forces. I am sure that we are all concerned about them, too. However, the sense of relief is very great, and we are all grateful for the fact that the bloodshed is now coming to an end.

I hope that we shall have a further statement soon on the casualties when the right hon. Lady has received the further details to which she referred. In the meantime, we extend our deep sympathy to all the families who have suffered the consequences of the casualties and express our determination—I hope the determination of the House of Commons—that proper ways should be found to assist those families and those who have been afflicted by what has happened.

I do not expect the right hon. Lady to deal now with questions about the future, nor do I think that this is the best time to do so. There is bound to be an interval during which we shall deal with the immediate position on the islands, and that interval is bound to mean that normal operations cannot be envisaged. However, it would be right for the right hon. Lady at an early date to express a view about the future. I do not say that she should describe the whole future, but she should give some commitments about it. In our view, it is not possible for the British Government to contemplate that over the years ahead they alone can deal with these matters.

The right hon. Lady said in her statement "I do not exclude the possibility of associating other countries with their security". That is a modest statement of the requirement. I believe that she will have to go considerably further than that, in the interests of the islanders and of the security of the islands. I do not believe that it is possible for the Government to exclude much greater consultations with other countries. Indeed, we are bound to do so under the resolutions that we have signed. I therefore hope that the

Prime Minister will now give an absolute assurance that we shall be prepared to consult other nations according to our commitments under the United Nations charter to ensure that we provide for future arrangements.

I hope that we shall not exclude the possibility of the trusteeship that was discussed earlier. *[Interruption.]* Those hon. Members who wish to exclude that possibility ought to look at some of the changes in the Government's policy that have occurred during this period. The more they examine them, the more I believe that justice will be seen in the case that we have persistently put throughout these discussions.

Even if the Prime Minister will not give a detailed commitment now, I hope that she will say that she intends to carry out to the full, in the spirit and the letter, the resolution that she and her Government proposed at the United Nations in the name of this country. I do not know whether the right hon. Lady is shaking her head, but it would be a breach of faith if she were to abandon that commitment. I therefore hope that she will reiterate our allegiance on these questions.

All these matters will later have to be examined afresh, including the investigation of how the original crisis arose. Much the best course for the Government is to recognise the commitments that they have made in these international obligations and to say that they will uphold them as determinedly as we have upheld the rights of British territory.

The Prime Minister: I am grateful to the right hon. Gentleman for what he said about our Armed Forces. We mourn the loss of those who were killed and we are dedicated to the cause for which they gave their lives.

As to the United Nations resolution, the withdrawal by the Argentines was not honoured and our Forces had to go there because they would not withdraw. Indeed, they had to recover and recapture British territory. I cannot agree with the right hon. Gentleman that those men risked their lives in any way to have a United Nations trusteeship. They risked their lives to defend British sovereign territory, the British way of life and the rights of British people to determine their own future.

Mr. David Steel (Roxburgh, Selkirk and Peebles): Will the Prime Minister consider allowing the House a special opportunity to pay tribute to our Forces after they have returned? I think that that would be appropriate.

Is the right hon. Lady aware that at lunch time the BBC carried allegedly authoritative reports about the form of inquiry in which she would invite the other party leaders to participate? However, she mentioned nothing about that in her statement. Without going into the form of that inquiry, will she give an undertaking that it will be strong enough to include not just the matters leading up to the invasion but such questions as the sale of arms to Argentina and the defence policy decisions that affect the equipment and operation of our Navy?

The Prime Minister: During Question Time, I referred to the form of inquiry and said that I would shortly be writing to Opposition leaders. I do not believe that the form of the inquiry should be anything like as wide as the right hon. Gentleman suggests; otherwise it would never report. I do not believe that it is the general wish to have the inquiry as wide as that. That is a totally different kind of review from the one on which I thought we were agreed. However, I shall be writing shortly to the right hon.

Gentleman about the matter. Surely today is a day for congratulation and celebration and not for post-mortems. . . .

Mr. Edward du Cann (Taunton): Is my right hon. Friend aware that the House and the nation will have noted with particular approval the sentence in her statement that indicated that we shall not again allow the Falkland Islands to be the subject of unprovoked aggression? In the meantime, is it not possible to say something about the local inhabitants of Port Stanley and West Falkland? I am sure that many people would be grateful for information on that subject.

The Prime Minister: I am grateful to my right hon. Friend for what he said about defending the Falkland Islands so that they are never again the victim of aggression. At present information about the civilian population is sketchy because of appalling weather and the fact that there were only a few hours of daylight before I came to the House. Initial indications are that the islanders are thrilled to see our Forces and that in general they are safe and well, but we have no further details.

Mr. J. Enoch Powell (Down, South): Will the Government be careful to ensure that nothing is done or said in the coming days that could be an obstacle to our securing, both in the Falkland Islands and in Britain, compensation and satisfaction for the loss and damage that have been suffered as a result of this unprovoked aggression?

The Prime Minister: I shall try to refrain from saying anything that will prejudice that, but I must point out that we are not seeking compensation. We went to recapture the islands, to restore British sovereignty, which had not been lost because of the invasion, and to restore British administration. That was our objective, and I believe that we have achieved it.

Dr. David Owen (Plymouth, Devonport): I wish to express our congratulations to the right hon. Lady and sympathy to the relatives of those who were killed. Will the Prime Minister confirm that it is not the intention to return all the Argentine military until Argentina has confirmed that all hostilities in the South Atlantic have ended? When considering the association that might be developed with other countries for the long-term development of the Falkland Islands, and before making any final decision—it is too early to reach a firm conclusion about how we should handle the future—will the right hon. Lady consult the United States of America, which has been one of our most loyal allies and which has great interest in the Organisation of American States?

The Prime Minister: It was precisely because we believed that we should not return all the prisoners of war until we were certain that we had achieved a cessation of hostilities with the mainland of Argentina that I said that "we hope" to evacuate the prisoners of war. We must send back a considerable number, but we should withhold some, especially the officers and commanders, until we have achieved a ceasefire with the mainland.

As to the long-term future, as the right hon. Gentleman said, we are talking about British sovereign territory and British people. Many people will be interested in the future of the islands, but we must consult the people and then make the best possible arrangements that we can for them. I recognise that that will need the friendliness of other States in the region. It would not be wise to go beyond that now.

Sir John Eden (Bournemouth, West): Following the successful outcome of the campaign, which would not have been possible without the supreme valour displayed by our Forces nor without the steady and resolute leadership shown from the start by my right hon. Friend the Prime Minister, will she say whether, in attempting to tackle some of the enormous and immediate logistical problems, especially the shortage of water, it would be practicable to turn to Uruguay, Chile or other Latin American countries for help?

The Prime Minister: I am grateful to my right hon. Friend. We wish to have help with the logistical problems from wherever we can get it, but few places are near and therefore we had to prepare for some of those matters in the supplies and provisions that we sent down with the task force. We shall be all right for water. If we cannot return some prisoners, we shall need some help with food and transport, but I believe that the United States of America will be prepared to help with some of those matters.

Mr. Tony Benn: (Bristol, South-East): Apart from the inquiry, will the Prime Minister publish the full text of all the exchanges that took place with the United Nations, Argentina and the Americans so that we may see what happened and a full analysis of the costs in life, equipment and money in this tragic and unnecessary war which the world knows very well will not provide an answer to the problem of the future of the Falkland Islands? Does she agree that in the end there must be negotiations, and will she say with whom and when she will be ready to enter into such negotiations?

The Prime Minister: The texts of all the negotiations are not mine to publish. We entered into the negotiations in confidence and I do not believe in breaking a confidence. I do not intend to negotiate on the sovereignty of the islands in any way, except with those who live there. That is my fervent belief. The right hon. Gentleman called it an unnecessary war. Tragic it may have been, but may I point out to him that he would not enjoy the freedom of speech that he put to such excellent use unless people had been prepared to fight for it.

Mr. Churchill (Stretford): Is my right hon. Friend aware that the nation owes this signal victory not only to the skill and courage of British Forces but to her resolute leadership during the critical weeks? Is she further aware that the entire House will wish to be associated with the tribute that she paid to those who will not return from the South Atlantic? Will she associate us with her condolences to the families of those involved, whose grief the entire nation shares?

The Prime Minister: I am grateful to my hon. Friend. Every hon. Member would wish to pay tribute to those who lost their lives, to those who have been injured and to the families without whose support they could never have done such a wonderful job. . . .

Mr. Jack Ashley (Stoke-on-Trent, South): I appreciate the Prime

Minister's comments and satisfaction today, but does she agree with the view of Secretary Haig that a strictly military outcome cannot endure for all time?

The Prime Minister: I am a little at a loss about the question. We went to recapture what was ours. We had to do it by military means because the Argentines would not leave peacefully. We condemned their military adventurism. We were perfectly right to repossess what was already ours and to look after and defend British subjects. That is not a military solution. That is repossessing what we should never have lost. . . .

Mr. George Robertson (Hamilton): Now that the hostilities are over and we know how many of the British Forces gave their lives in repossessing the Falkland Islands, will the Prime Minister consider the views of their relations about bringing the bodies back to Britain for burial, especially in the light of the distressing sight, for relations, of the inevitable mass burial at Goose Green and Darwin shown on television last night? If the relatives wish the bodies to be returned to the United Kingdom, will she be prepared to arrange for that?

The Prime Minister: I am grateful to the hon. Gentleman for the way in which he has raised this subject, and for his realisation that immediate burial is inevitable. Afterwards, under the normal traditional rules, these people receive a burial, usually locally, and the graves are looked after in perpetuity by the Commonwealth War Graves Commission. Before we decide what should be done in the case of deaths in the Falklands, we shall be considering the views of the relatives.

Mr. John Farr (Harborough): Apart from my expression of admiration for the sacrifices of the three Services, may I ask right hon. Friend whether she can confirm the tremendous price paid by the Royal Fleet Auxiliary? The three Armed Services are frequently mentioned, but the Royal Fleet Auxilliary, through "Sir Tristram" and "Sir Galahad", as two examples, has paid a tremendous price. What it has done for the country should be recognised from the top.

The Prime Minister: The Royal Fleet Auxilliary paid a tremendous price, but neither my hon. Friend the Member for Harborough (Mr. Farr) nor I would wish to single out any particular sacrifice. Each and every one contributed to the successful accomplishment of our objectives. We mourn each and every one in the same way as any other.

Mr. George Foulkes (South Ayrshire): Apart from the appalling loss of life, can the Prime Minister tell us how and when the Government propose to tell the House of the full cost of the operation, the cost of garrisoning and maintaining the islands in perpetuity, and what increases in taxes or cuts in social and other services will be necessary to pay for all these costs?

The Prime Minister: Of course we shall tell the House. Under the ordinary rules of Supply expenditure, we shall have to tell the House. I hope that the hon. Member thinks that the money spent is worth while.

Mr. Keith Speed (Ashford): Can my right hon. friend tell the House whether the arrangements for the Argentine surrender include the surrender of the Argentine mission on Southern Thule, in the South Sandwich group, which has been illegally occupied by Argentine troops since 1976? As I learnt when I was in the Falklands Islands, that is a source of continuing concern to the people who live there.

The Prime Minister: We would wish to arrange for the surrender of not only the Argentines in the Falkland Islands but any Argentines left on the dependencies as well, including Southern Thule.

Mr. Frank Allaun (Salford, East): As the Prime Minister has told an American television audience that she will retain aircraft, Rapiers, submarines and ships in the South Atlantic, will she make some estimate, for our benefit, of how that will be paid for by the British people?

The Prime Minister: If necessary, we have to defend the Falkland Islands alone. We are talking about the lives of British subjects who expect to have the same rights as those that we enjoy. I do not believe that the hon. Member for Salford, East (Mr. Allaun) would wish them to have any less. It will mean allocating some of our defence equipment to that region, but the NATO defences are not wholly exclusive, in the sense that the defence of NATO is affected by what goes on beyond its borders. I should be amazed if the hon. Gentleman, who also makes good use of his freedom, would begrudge the cash necessary and thereby deny it to those people.

Mr. Alan Clark (Plymouth, Sutton): Did the Prime Minister note the comment of a captain in the 2nd Parachute Battalion after the liberation of Goose Green, that we were fighting not for principles but for people? Does my right hon. Friend agree that those who have sacrificed their lives in these battles, besides the brilliant achievements, to which tribute has already been paid, made that sacrifice—this is a source of pride to the whole country—that British families shall be delivered from oppression no matter how far away or how few in number they may be?

The Prime Minister: We do our best to uphold the beliefs spoken of by my hon. Friend. I agree with the person who said in Goose Green that we were fighting for people, but people must have principles by which to live. They have to be governed by fair principles because liberty and justice are the only things that give life its dignity and meaning. We shall try to uphold those on the part of our citizens wherever they look to us for their defence.

Mr. Stanley Cohen (Leeds, South-East): Does the Prime Minister agree about the insensitivity of the statement made—I am not sure who made it—about burial in a mass grave of 21 of those who died in the Falklands? Does she also agree that, even if the bodies are reburied dirty, some assistance should be given to the families of those Service men who died there, bearing in mind that the families have 8,000 miles to travel if they want to pay tribute to their relatives who have died in this conflict?

The Prime Minister: I am grateful to the hon. Gentleman for raising that point. If those Service men find their permanent resting place in the

Falklands in a Commonwealth grave, it is customary to pay for the families to go to see the grave.

Sir Anthony Royle (Richmond, Surrey): Can my right hon. Friend give an assurance that arrangements will be made to look after the families of the Chinese citizens from Hong Kong who were killed in the attack at Bluff Cove?

The Prime Minister: I thank my hon. Friend for raising that point. We recognise that we also have a duty to those people, because they died in serving our cause. We shall make arrangements accordingly.

Mr. Sydney Bidwell (Ealing, Southall): Does the Prime Minister's statement today mean that under her kind of leadership in the future there will be no participatory role for a saner and more civilised Argentine Government in any international system for guaranteeing the peace in that part of the South Atlantic? Is it not unrealistic, in view of the geographical factors, to think that we can carry on as a colonial power on those distant shores?

The Prime Minister: This is British sovereign territory.

Mr. Bidwell: We know that.

The Prime Minister: I know that the hon. Gentleman knows that. I am amazed at how he manages to ignore it in his every question. This is British sovereign territory and they are British people. We need the friendliness of neighbouring States. We do not negotiate sovereignty with them.

Sir David Price (Eastleigh): Does my right hon. Friend agree that resolution 502 of the Security Council was implemented not by the United Nations but by the valour and courage of Her Majesty's Forces and by the determination of my right hon. Friend the Prime Minister? Is there not a lesson there for the whole House to learn?

The Prime Minister: I agree wholly with what my hon. Friend has said. No attempt was made by the Argentines to implement resolution 502.

Mr. Martin Flannery (Sheffield, Hillsborough): Will the Prime Minister not close her mind completely to some discussion, under the auspices of the United Nations, on the ultimate sovereignty of the islands? Is it not a profound anachronism in 1982 for any State to have sovereign territory 8,000 miles away? . . .
Does it not have the seeds of future conflict if we do not act democratically? . . . What would the right hon. Lady say if a powerful Argentina had taken the Shetland Islands? Would we tolerate that?

The Prime Minister: There is one principle—that territorial sovereignty be respected. . . .

Sir Peter Emery (Honiton): Does my right hon. Friend realise that nobody in the House could rise to speak without paying tribute to probably the greatest victory in the history of an army at the end of an 8,000 mile supply line? That achievement is unbelievable. Will my right hon. Friend make it clear that she will resist the siren voices of politicians on both sides of the House or among the media, and that she will make no further statement about the future of the Falkland Islands for at least six months? The dust must be allowed to settle. We must get the people back there. Let us not have the Government permanently being asked what they are doing about the future of the islands. There must be peace there first.

The Prime Minister: I agree with my hon. Friend that this was a great military victory that will go down in the history books. I believe that the brilliance with which it was planned and executed is unequalled. It will take some considerable time for the islanders to settle down, for us to see what development possibilities there are, and to get security for the Falkland Islands, I believe that it will take at least six months. I should not be surprised if it took a good deal longer.

Mr. David Winnick (Walsall, North): Since this country had the support of most international opinion in resisting aggression, is it not equally important to keep the same support on the question of the future of the Falkland Islands? Why is the Prime Minister ruling out completely the possibility of United Nations trusteeship? Can there be no change in the territorial status of the Falkland Islands?

The Prime Minister: The only change in the territorial status of the Falkland Islands that one would consider would be one arranged in conjunction and discussion with the people of the Falkland Islands. That is the way that we have gone about looking after those many territories and colonies that have previously been within our own trusteeship. I believe that that is the way that we should continue to act.

Mr. Robin Maxwell-Hyslop (Tiverton): Will full provision be made from public funds for those who have lost their homes, their stock in trade and their personal possessions in the conflict in a more full and generous manner than the war damage compensation—to which the Falkland Islanders contributed generously in taxation during the war— paid to persons in the United Kingdom who lost their homes or property through enemy action?

The Prime Minister: May I look at that question, Mr. Speaker, before answering? I am not certain what insurance arrangements were made by the Falkland Islanders and how they would operate in conjunction with war damage. It is our intention to be generous in these matters.

Mr. Robert C. Brown (Newcastle upon Tyne, West): I have not heard anything about the Gurkhas. Can the Prime Minister tell us whether any of them lost their lives or were wounded? Will we treat the Gurkhas, who serve for less pay than our men, as generously as we shall treat our own people?

The Prime Minister: I mentioned the Gurkhas. The 1st/7th Gurkhas advanced on Mount William and played a prominent part in the final, crucial stages of the battle. We do not yet have full casualty lists, and that is why I have not been able to give the figures. I gladly pay full tribute to those excellent fighting men, the Gurkhas.

Lord James Douglas-Hamilton (Edinburgh, West): Will my right hon. Friend consider requesting the Government of the United States of America to assist with the return of Argentine prisoners of war to Argentina in view of the enormous numbers involved?

The Prime Minister: We shall have to get help if necessary. First, I want to know whether we can achieve a full cessation of hostilities with the mainland. We have a number of our own ships there. I believe that we could possibly get some of them back faster in our own ships than we could by either chartering ships or securing ships from other nations because of the time that it would take to get there. We might require help with something like Hercules aircraft.

Mr. Alfred Dubs (Battersea, South): Can the Prime Minister say whether, since the Argentine invasion, the British Government requested from the American Government, on a purchase or lease basis, some of the aerial reconnaissance aircraft, the AWACS?

The Prime Minister: I do not give details of help received from the Government of the United States of America. I can say only that it has been splendid. I believe that we have had everything that we have asked for. AWACS aircraft need somewhere to land, and we do not have anywhere.

Mr. Nicholas Winterton (Macclesfield): Does my right hon. Friend accept that the task force, the Services and our maritime marine have proved themselves to be the finest and the most professional in the world as well as being the most compassionate, that her leadership has inspired our nation and that her assurance about the long-term security of the Falkland Islands is much appreciated because of the growing strategic importance of that area to the peace of the world?

The Prime Minister: I agree with my hon. Friend that the Falkland Islands have a strategic importance, not only in shipping terms because of the shipping lanes, but because they are the entrance to the Antarctic, which I believe will become more important. I agree with my hon. Friend about our Armed Forces. Their professionalism has been remarked upon wherever they serve in the world.

Mr. Foot: Will fresh representations now be made about the three British journalists who were detained at the beginning of the incident? They were engaged in carrying out their proper duties. There may also be some British prisoners who will be part of the discussions. In the light of the right hon. Lady's replies about resolution 502 and any participation of the United Nations, is it not a fact that, despite the great military achievement—everybody acknowledges that—we had considerable international support, both from the United States of America and from other countries, at the United Nations and in practical terms?

Were we not glad enough to have that support when we were dealing with some of the problems? Does not the Prime Minister recognise that that international support could be needed in future? Does she accept that we shall have to go to the United Nations and argue our case in the coming months? Is she not, therefore, unwise to resist that approach to the problem? She will have to return to it in the end, and she might as well acknowledge that now.

The Prime Minister: I have no further news about the three journalists. Representations are made through the Swiss embassy, which represents our interests in Argentina. We shall, of course, make fresh inquiries. There are also a few of our British prisoners of war. We hope that they will be returned, as we have returned so many Argentine prisoners of war. The earlier prisoners from the Falklands were repatriated to this country.

I repeat that resolution 502 was not honoured by the Argentines. We have had to secure the withdrawal without resolution 502. Because it was not honoured, we do not need to negotiate in any way with the United Nations or anyone else about British sovereignty of the islands. I make that absolutely clear. For years, under the non-self governing territories article of the United Nations charter, we have reported about the increasing provision for representation of the people in the government of their own territory. That we shall continue to do.

Mr. Foot: The right hon. Lady will have to speak in a different tone if she is to have any successful discussions in New York and elsewhere in the coming months. The right hon. Lady continues to miss the point about resolution 502. Partly because of the passage of that resolution, we received material and other support from the Americans. Partly because of the passage of that resolution we obtained economic support from elsewhere. For the right hon. Lady to suggest that she does not need international support to solve the problem is an absurdity and will be proved to be so in the months ahead.

The Prime Minister: As I did not say that, will the right hon. Gentleman kindly withdraw his remarks?
[The House proceeded to other debates.]

Filmset in Scotland by Her Majesty's Stationery Office at
HMSO Press, Edinburgh

Printed in England by Hobbs the Printers of Southampton
(2122) Dd718603 C30 10/82 203371